The New York Yankees
in Popular Culture

# The New York Yankees in Popular Culture

## Critical Essays

*Edited by* David Krell

McFarland & Company, Inc., Publishers
*Jefferson, North Carolina*

LIBRARY OF CONGRESS CATALOGUING-IN-PUBLICATION DATA

Names: Krell, David, 1967– editor.
Title: The New York Yankees in popular culture : critical essays /
edited by David Krell.
Description: Jefferson, North Carolina : McFarland & Company, Inc.,
Publishers, 2019 | Includes bibliographical references and index.
Identifiers: LCCN 2019012607 | ISBN 9781476674643
(paperback. : acid free paper) ∞
Subjects: LCSH: New York Yankees (Baseball team)—History. |
New York Yankees (Baseball team)—Influence. |
Sports in popular culture—United States—History.
Classification: LCC GV875.N4 N494 2019 | DDC 796.357/64097471—dc23
LC record available at https://lccn.loc.gov/2019012607

BRITISH LIBRARY CATALOGUING DATA ARE AVAILABLE

ISBN (print) 978-1-4766-7464-3
ISBN (ebook) 978-1-4766-3654-2

Front cover: Photograph of a game at Yankee Stadium
on September 18, 2014 (Mark Hecht)

Printed in the United States of America

*McFarland & Company, Inc., Publishers
Box 611, Jefferson, North Carolina 28640
www.mcfarlandpub.com*

For Sheila Krell (née Scherer), the Babe Ruth of moms. She rushed home after school when she was 11 years old to watch the Yankees games on television because she thought the rookie from Oklahoma was cute. Millions of other girls and women thought the same thing about Mickey Mantle.

For David I. Krell (1907–1957), the grandfather for whom I'm named. He got Joe DiMaggio to autograph a copy of *Lucky to Be a Yankee* before a game at Yankee Stadium.

# Table of Contents

# Acknowledgments

To say that this book has an outstanding squad of scribes would be like saying that Reggie Jackson had a little swagger. Mysteries answered, myths debunked, and fresh angles on baseball history are hallmarks of their research.

Kudos are owed to: Jeanine Basinger, Ron Briley, Ron Coleman, Martin S. Lessner, Erin DiCesare, Duke Goldman, Louis Gordon, Paul Hensler, Jeffrey M. Katz, Bill Lamb, Rolando Llanes, Dashiell Moore, Richard Pioreck, and Matt Rothenberg. They did a yeoman's job in penetrating Yankee history, lore, and myth to the granular level. It has been a pleasure working with them and a privilege having my writing alongside theirs.

I take responsibility for fact checking; any oversights and errors are mine.

Tracking down arcane data—page numbers of long-defunct newspapers, for example—during the fact-checking process required the assistance of librarians at the local level. The New York Public Library's Stephen A. Schwarzman Building in midtown Manhattan is a treasure trove of history, literature, and artifacts. The Milstein Microform Reading Room has microfilm of several New York City newspapers that used to be must-read chronicles for Gotham's devourers of sports information—*Brooklyn Eagle*, *New York Journal-American*, and *New York World-Telegram and Sun* and their predecessors (*World-Telegram*, *Sun*). The microfilm archives of the city's presently existing newspapers also reside here (*Post*, *Daily News*, *Times*); microfilm and hard copies of dozens of other publications are elsewhere in the library but accessible from the Milstein staff through the simple process of filling out a slip in pencil. Digital age be damned!

The Milstein staff is to be commended for their patience in fulfilling dozens of requests. Where microfilm was not available, long-distance inquiries to other libraries were answered rapidly: Julie Ensor at Joplin (Missouri) Public Library; Popular Library Department at Detroit Public Library; Mark Quigley at UCLA Film & Television Archive; Diane Parks and Chris Glass at Boston Public Library; Andrew Dauphinee at New Jersey State Library; Daniel Smith at Evansville (Indiana) Vanderburgh Public Library; Kathy Rome at East Baton Rouge Parish Library's Baton Rouge Room Archives; and Terry Metter at Cleveland Public Library's Center for Local & Global History. Independent researcher Virginia Marcellus was instrumental in finding information for the *Watertown Daily Times*.

Also deserving praise is the staff of the Rose Reading Room on the library's third floor. It's a marvelous site with several rows of tables populated by a range of people from college students to retirees. Books in the library's massive collection can be accessed from the librarians in the same manner as the microfilm in the Milstein room.

The National Baseball Hall of Fame and Museum is an American treasure that not only preserves the legacy of the National Pastime, but also provides researchers with arcane information to help fill gaps in baseball history, from wartime major leaguers to WAR statistics (wins above replacement). Besides being a contributor to this volume, Matt Rothenberg served as the Hall of Fame's manager of the A. Bartlett Giamatti Research Center during the writing and editing of this book. He joins Reference Librarian Cassidy Lent and Library Director Jim Gates in forming a triumvirate of archival vigilance in Cooperstown. No question is too obscure for their guidance.

Photographs documenting Yankee history were incredibly important to complement the research. John Horne, the Hall of Fame's Coordinator of Rights and Reproductions, was an invaluable resource. Requests for photographs led to an abundance of possibilities, thanks to John.

Kathy Struss, Audiovisual Archivist at the Dwight D. Eisenhower Presidential Library & Museum, offered terrific photographs of the 34th President of the United States throwing out the first ball at 1950s home openers of the Washington Senators. Valoise Armstrong, Archivist at the Eisenhower library, uncovered information about the president's involvement with this baseball tradition. During his administration, Eisenhower attended every home opener except one. Rumored to have played semipro baseball when he was at West Point, Eisenhower is better known for his passion for golf—he installed a putting green at the White House. But it's possible that this tradition went deeper than ceremony. Perhaps he was one of the thousands of Senators fans who found themselves like Joe Hardy in *The Year the Yankees Lost the Pennant* and *Damn Yankees*—a hopeful devotee of the hapless team in the nation's capital.

Maryrose Grossman of the John F. Kennedy Presidential Library and Museum's AV Archives Reference Department specified information concerning photographs documenting a meeting between home run king Roger Maris and President Kennedy.

Eric McCrory's knowledge of the archives at the George W. Bush Presidential Library helped me track down photographs of the 43rd president with Derek Jeter before Game Three of the 2001 World Series. Bush signaled a moment of national unity after the 9/11 attacks when he walked to the rubber at Yankee Stadium, threw a perfect strike, and ignited the crowd's spontaneous chant of "U-S-A" echoing from the Grand Concourse to Grand Central Terminal.

Andrew Kivette of the Yankees Public Relations Department aided in researching non-baseball events at Yankee Stadium.

Cleveland Indians historian Jeremy Feador provided information on Indians-Yankees games of the 1950s.

Finally, Layla Milholen displayed incredible patience in shepherding this book through the proposal, research, and production phases for McFarland. Gary Mitchem okayed the book proposal before we even had one contributor on board. Every author should be lucky to have editors like Layla and Gary.

# Introduction

The New York Yankees dwell in popular culture like surfers at Malibu on a clear Southern California day—with great numbers, influence, and authority. It is popular culture that embeds stories into our consciousness, though storytellers may sometimes splash fiction into fact. There is no record, for example, of Babe Ruth rushing a dog to the hospital as William Bendix portrayed in *The Babe Ruth Story*.[1]

I first became aware of the Yankees' transcendence of popular culture beyond sports during my Generation X childhood, when I saw *The Pride of the Yankees* starring Gary Cooper as tragic hero Lou Gehrig on WPIX-TV. Growing up in northern New Jersey, I absorbed the Yankees on both local and national levels: Reggie Jackson's image on the Panasonic billboard overlooking the entrance to the Lincoln Tunnel; Joe DiMaggio hawking Mr. Coffee and the Bowery Savings Bank; Bucky Dent as a football player in the TV movie *Dallas Cowboys Cheerleaders*; Phil Rizzuto promoting an alternative to traditional banking on commercials for The Money Store; Michael Douglas as an ex-ballplayer during Old Timers' Day at Yankee Stadium in the film *It's My Turn*; and Billy Martin and George Steinbrenner poking fun at their quarreling on a commercial for Miller Lite.

Fonzie is recognized as "the Mickey Mantle of the grease pit" in a first-season episode of *Happy Days*,[2] a 1950s-based, nostalgia-soaked sitcom that premiered in 1974 and aired for 10 years. Played by Henry Winkler, Arthur "Fonzie" Fonzarelli became an icon known for his toughness, loyalty, and expertise in automotive mechanics. Mantle is an interesting parallel considering the Milwaukee-based show's first two seasons took place in 1956[3]; the Braves lost the National League pennant to the Brooklyn Dodgers by one game that season. In 1957, the Braves won the World Series against the Yankees, but lost the rematch in 1958. Given the team's success, why not dub Fonzie the "Hank Aaron of the grease pit"? Or Eddie Mathews? Or Warren Spahn. They did not have the same resonance as The Mick. Few ballplayers do.

In the 1978 movie *American Hot Wax*, an enjoyable but chronologically incorrect film about the birth of rock and roll in the 1950s, Tim McIntyre portrays radio icon Alan Freed, a disc jockey who became a celebrity during his tenure in Cleveland for popularizing rock and roll, which is why the Rock and Roll Hall of Fame is located there. *American Hot Wax* takes place during Freed's time in New York City with a storyline about the preparation for a rock and roll show at Brooklyn's Paramount Theatre. A moment identifiable to fans rooting against the Bronx Bombers occurs early in the film, when Freed's office is a hubbub filled with acts auditioning for him. Freed breaks into a smile from ear to ear echoed by laughter and clapping when he's told, "Alan! Alan! You're gonna love this! Cleveland took two from the Yankees!"[4]

The moment is rooted in reality. The Indians won three doubleheaders against the fellas in pinstripes during rock and roll's formative years: June 8, 1958; July 27, 1958; and June 21, 1959.[5] Thirty years hence, the fictional Indians in *Major League* defeated the Yankees in a one-game playoff for the American League East championship.[6]

It's a testament to the team's distinction that the presence of pinstripes can be found in a variety of popular-culture categories. This book covers a wide-ranging selection of examples; essays appear in alphabetical order, according to the authors' last names (with the exception of a two-part essay by Ron Coleman and Martin S. Lessner). Through matchless diligence, the contributors have amassed enough research to fill Yankee Stadium in their scrutiny of the Yankees' impact on popular culture. And vice versa.

Jeanine Basinger, one of the world's leading film historians, takes us inside the production of *The Pride of the Yankees*. It was vital that Mrs. Eleanor Gehrig approve of Hollywood's depiction of her husband's life story. Gary Cooper's interpretation of Lou Gehrig underlines the courage that the ballplayer displayed while ALS began to deteriorate his body. A potent hallmark of the 1942 film is a scrapbook of the Iron Horse's baseball achievements. It was a prop donated by producer Samuel Goldwyn to the Baseball Hall of Fame a year after the film's release. The real scrapbook also resides in Cooperstown. Lea Carlson was an invaluable liaison between me and Jeanine.

Ron Briley looks at a dark period for the Yankees—the downturn between CBS purchasing the team in 1964 and selling it to George Steinbrenner's group in 1973. During this period, 1970 proved to be an outlier as the team compiled an impressive 93–69 record.

Ron Coleman and Martin S. Lessner peel back the layers of the Yankees' brand, including the appeal of the Yankees cap. The interlocking "NY" is a world-famous symbol, but merchandising success is just one part of the brand's complex legacy.

Erin DiCesare explores the stories of the "Core Four" players of the 1990s. Her thesis shows that a "Core Four" has existed in other championship generations of the Yankees.

Duke Goldman strikes a new comparative paradigm on the topic of Joe DiMaggio and Mickey Mantle, with particular emphasis on their respective minor-league careers and major-league débuts. Numerous presentations, articles, and books have dissected the careers, personas, and myths about the Yankee Clipper and the Commerce Comet. But Goldman's analysis, over two essays, will make the most erudite fan reconsider the place of these icons in the Yankees' history, lore, and culture.

Louis Gordon puts the Yankees in context with the changes in American society during the 1970s. While disco flourished, the team came out of its doldrums to restore the aura of excellence in the House That Ruth Built.

Paul Hensler homes in on a Yankees hallmark of that era with the rise of Reggie Jackson from All-Star baseball player to iconic celebrity.

Jeffrey M. Katz looks at the history of *Damn Yankees*, a smash Broadway play in the late 1950s. It became a vehicle for anti–Yankees fans dreaming of their teams toppling the austere fellas from the Bronx.

It was my pleasure to write about George Costanza, a *Seinfeld* cornerstone who spoke his mind to George Steinbrenner with disregard for consequences—the opposite of his conniving *schnorrer* persona—and landed a front-office job with the Yankees.[7] A Yankee-hater might think twice about dismissing such a job opportunity—even one who "pahks the cahr in Hahvahd Yad."

Bill Lamb carves new scholarship with a detailed analysis of the team's early years, which had links to two men of questionable character. It's not an unusual circumstance for a sports empire to rest upon a genesis funded by ill-gotten gains. But Bill's contribution highlights New York City in the early 20th century as a highly significant character in the Yankees' beginning.

Rolando Llanes demystifies the architectural hallmarks of Yankee Stadium, one of the most recognizable sports facilities in the world. He wants to acknowledge Bobby Murcer, Thurman Munson, and Abed Mustafa. Without them, he believes the Yankees would be just another team.

Dashiell Moore diagnoses the stadium's cultural impact. Beyond serving as a home for baseball champions, Yankee Stadium has considerable weight as an institution that Dashiell labels the "People's Cathedral."

Richard Pioreck offers a global view of the Yankees in the entertainment world. The team and its players have touched every corner, from vaudeville to video games. Richard's take is a blueprint for the legacy of pinstripes in popular culture.

Matt Rothenberg analyzes the 2001 TV-movie *61\** from a "fact vs. fiction" perspective. It's an invaluable companion piece when watching this HBO offering directed by Billy Crystal about the controversial 1961 home-run race for Babe Ruth's single-season record.

And so, here come the Yankees!

## NOTES

1. "Babe Ruth Carries Dog to Hospital," *The Babe Ruth Story*, directed by Roy Del Ruth (1948; Allied Artists).

2. *Happy Days*, "Fonzie Drops In," ABC, February 26, 1974, Bob Brunner. Richie Cunningham refers to the singular "grease pit" in his analogy to Arthur "Fonzie" Fonzarelli. At the end of the episode, Fonzie uses the plural form.

3. The second-season episode "The Not Making of a President" revolves around the 1956 presidential campaigns of Dwight Eisenhower and Adlai Stevenson. In a nod to the Milwaukee setting, a scene at the Cunninghams' dinner table shows patriarch Howard Cunningham (played by Tom Bosley) remarking, "I heard Aaron and Mathews signed their '57 contract." *Happy Days*, "The Not Making of a President," ABC, January 28, 1975, Lloyd Garver and Ken Hecht.

4. "Alan Freed's Office," *American Hot Wax*, directed by Floyd Mutrux (1978; Paramount Pictures).

5. Jeremy Feador, Cleveland Indians Team Historian, email to editor, August 3, 2018, https://www.baseball-reference.com/boxes/CLE/CLE195807271.shtml; https://www.baseball-reference.com/boxes/CLE/CLE195807272.shtml; https://www.baseball-reference.com/boxes/NYA/NYA195806081.shtml; https://www.baseball-reference.com/boxes/NYA/NYA195906212.shtml; https://www.baseball-reference.com/boxes/NYA/NYA195906211.shtml; Last accessed August 8, 2018.

6. "Yankees-Indians American League East Playoff Game," *Major League*, directed by David S. Ward (1989; Burbank, CA: Warner Brothers).

7. *Seinfeld*, "The Opposite," Castle Rock Entertainment, NBC, May 19, 1994, Andy Cowan and Larry David and Jerry Seinfeld.

# The Pride of the Yankees

## Jeanine Basinger

*The Pride of the Yankees* (1942) is an iconic baseball movie, one of the most famous and successful ever made. It is now ranked #22 on The American Film Institute's list of "most inspiring films," #3 on its list of the top ten best sports movies, and #25 in its category of "greatest movie heroes." It was named to *Film Daily*'s ten best pictures of 1942 and became one of the top ten highest grossing box office hits of the year (based on the records of the *Motion Picture Herald*, *Motion Picture Daily* and *Film Daily*). It was nominated for a total of 11 Oscars by the Motion Picture Academy of Arts and Sciences: Best Picture, Best Overall Screenplay, Best Cinematography, Best Interior Art Direction (in black and white), Best Sound Recording, Best Film Editing, Best Actor (Gary Cooper), and Best Supporting Actress (Teresa Wright). (It won in the category of Film Editing.) By any standards, *Pride* is a prime example of a Hollywood motion picture, setting a high standard of production values in all categories.

When Lou Gehrig (born Henry Louis Gehrig on June 19, 1903) died at the age of 37 on June 2, 1941, Hollywood moguls immediately began competing to film his life story. His exceptional baseball career, coupled with his personal courage in dealing with a rare disease (amyotrophic lateral sclerosis, now known as "Lou Gehrig's disease"), made him an interesting hero for a movie, even though his personality was low-key, modest, and lacking dramatic intensity. On July 15th, producer Samuel Goldwyn announced that he had "won the rights" to a Gehrig film by paying Gehrig's widow, Eleanor.[1] Although various working titles of the movie were considered—*The Lou Gehrig Story*, *The Great American Hero*, *The Life of Lou Gehrig*, and *Lou Gehrig, American Hero*—the resulting movie was entitled *The Pride of the Yankees*.[2] It was officially released by RKO Radio Pictures on July 14, 1942, only a little more than seven months after the United States entered into World War II. *The Pride of the Yankees* was subtly shaped to provide wartime reassurance and uplift for Americans, and to link their need for courage in the face of death to Lou Gehrig's courage in facing his illness. Just prior to the beginning of the story, the screen presented a prologue authored (and signed) by Damon Runyon that read: "This is the story of a young man who in the full flower of great fame, was a lesson in simplicity and modesty to the youth of America. He faced death with the same valor and fortitude that is now being displayed by thousands of young Americans on the far flung fields of battle. He left behind him a memory of courage and devotion that will ever be an inspiration to all men. This is the story of Lou Gehrig."

"The story of Lou Gehrig" was actually already well-known to American movie audiences of the 1940s because he was one of baseball's most legendary players of the era. His record of 2,130 consecutive games played had earned him the nickname of "The Iron Horse," a record that remained unchallenged until it was finally broken in 1995 by Cal Ripken, Jr., of the Baltimore Orioles. Gehrig, like all successful baseball players in the 1920s and 1930s, was often seen in newsreels and newspaper photographs, so audiences for the movie knew what he looked like. Gehrig had also appeared as himself in the 1938 Principal Production of a movie called *Rawhide*, a western with songs. Gehrig's co-stars were Larry Kimball and Evelyn Knapp in a story that began with Gehrig retiring from baseball, announcing that he and his (fictional) sister had bought a ranch near a town called Rawhide. Released by 20th Century–Fox and produced by Sol Lesser, the film utilized Gehrig's fame as a slugger by having him hit a well-aimed baseball into the office of the villain just in time to stop his sister from signing a dishonest contract.[3]

*Rawhide* was supposed to be the first in a series of Lou Gehrig westerns that were never made. According to *The Hollywood Reporter*, Lesser had originally signed Gehrig to play Tarzan, but when it was discovered that Gehrig's iron-man legs were "functional rather than decorative," the idea was dropped.[4] It's almost impossible for a modern audience to imagine the shy Gehrig as a western hero, much less as Tarzan. In 1938, Gehrig's on-screen credit line announced that he appeared by arrangement with Christy Walsh, his business manager, with the *Reporter* pointing out it was undoubtedly the first time in movie history that a baseball manager had received screen credit.

The man who won the right to film Gehrig's biography was Samuel Goldwyn (1884–1974), one of Hollywood's most legendary producers. A Polish immigrant, he arrived in the United States as a child and began work as an apprentice glove maker, ultimately going to night school and becoming a salesman. By 1912, he began his career in the film business and by 1922 had changed his name from Gelbfisz to Goldfish to Goldwyn and formed Samuel Goldwyn Productions. Prior to the creation of *Pride*, his company had presented a diverse line-up of films. In 1937 alone, he had three prestigious movies: *Dead End* (directed by William Wyler), *Stella Dallas* (directed by King Vidor), and *The Hurricane* (directed by John Ford). He had produced *Wuthering Heights* (1939) and *The Little Foxes* (1941) and would later produce the Oscar-winning *The Best Years of Our Lives* (1946). Goldwyn was a master showman, capable of promoting films into hits and publicizing them at a high level. His approach to producing was basically simple: get the best of everything. He spent money to acquire successful plays and novels, and to hire the top personnel in all areas, including writing, cinematography, and directing. He was unique in largely financing his movies himself, but still sparing no expense to get quality on the screen. Inside the business he was famous for his eccentric wording. Goldwyn is the man who said "include me out" as well as what was possibly the definitive word on the Hollywood business environment he fought his way up through: "A verbal contract isn't worth the paper it's written on." He was the Yogi Berra of Hollywood.

As an independent producer not under contract to a studio, Goldwyn could make decisions about the cast he wanted for his baseball film, and he "hit it out of the park" with his three leads: Gary Cooper, Teresa Wright, and Walter Brennan. Both Cooper and Wright were under contract to Goldwyn in 1942, and Cooper was a highly established star who had just won 1941's Oscar as Best Actor for *Sergeant York*, in which he played the famous World War I hero. Goldwyn had produced earlier Cooper films, beginning in 1926 with *The Winning of Barbara Worth*, and including *The Wedding Night* (1935), *The Adventures of Marco Polo* and *The Cowboy and the Lady* (both in 1938), *The Real*

*Glory* (1939), and *The Westerner* (1940). *The Pride of the Yankees* would be their final film together. Goldwyn told interviewers that Cooper was always his first and only choice to play Lou Gehrig; however, *The Hollywood Reporter* magazines of the era indicate that Spencer Tracy was a contender, and that other actors either considered or tested included Eddie Albert, Brian Donlevy, and Cary Grant. Two professional athletes were also mentioned: former middleweight champion boxer Billy Soose and former New York Yankee pitcher Waite Hoyt.

In 1942, Cooper was at the height of his box office powers, having been ranked in the top 10 in 1936, 1937, and 1941. (He would go on to make that mark every year from 1942 to 1949, and 1951 to 1957. He would die of cancer in 1961.) Cooper was an actor who seemed to audiences to be inherently heroic, yet he had a simple, direct quality that could allow him to play a shy and unsophisticated man without losing stature. Popular with both men and women, Cooper was tall and slim, handsome without being pretty, and an actor with a distinct personal style. He had glamour, but kept it tamped down. He had sex appeal, but used it to convey true love, not lechery. He was graceful but in an athletic and wholly masculine way. He was laconic, but one word of dialogue from him—his "yep" or "nope"—could equal pages of speech from other, less natural, actors. No matter what crazy part he was assigned—the role of Marco Polo, for instance—he seemed real. He was as relaxed and natural in front of a camera as any actor could possibly be. Gary Cooper was the perfect choice to play Gehrig.

One thing Cooper was not, however, was a baseball player. He was born in Montana, and had spent his life horseback riding. He was confident that he had the physicality he would need for the role of Gehrig, but as filming got underway he realized he had a problem. "I discovered to my private horror that I couldn't throw a ball. The countless falls I had taken as a trick rider had so ruined my right shoulder that I couldn't raise my arm above my head. Lefty O'Doul, later manager of the Oakland ball club, came down to help me out. 'You throw a ball,' he told me after studying my unique style, 'like an old woman tossing a hot biscuit.'"[5] Although many complained in late 1941 when Cooper was cast as Gehrig because of his lack of baseball skills, no one has seriously complained since. Cooper absorbed the character of Lou Gehrig into himself and masterfully cre-

Legendary film producer Samuel Goldwyn brought Lou Gehrig's life to the silver screen in *The Pride of the Yankees*, which hit movie theaters in 1942, three years after Gehrig's death at 37 from amyotrophic lateral sclerosis. ALS is commonly referred to as Lou Gehrig's Disease (National Baseball Hall of Fame and Museum, Cooperstown, NY).

ated on screen the decency, work ethic, and gratitude of the man known as The Iron Horse.

The calendar year of 1942 would perhaps be the greatest in Teresa Wright's career. Wright was relatively new; she had appeared to great reviews in the prestigious Goldwyn picture, *The Little Foxes*, but in 1942 she was both the leading actress in *Pride* and a prominent supporting actress in the highly successful *Mrs. Miniver* (which would win Best Picture of the Year.) Wright accomplished an unusual feat in the 1942 Oscar race: she was nominated both as Best Actress (for *Pride*) and Best Supporting Actress for *Miniver*. (She won the latter.) Wright is not a well-known name today, but in the early 1940s she was the epitome of a lovely young American girl. Wright was pretty, believably real, and an excellent actress. Her portrayal of the key figure of Eleanor Gehrig in *Pride* was one of its main successes with audiences.

Walter Brennan and Cooper had already appeared together in films such as Frank Capra's *Meet John Doe* (1941) and *The Westerner*. *Pride* was their sixth as co-stars, and their mutual American naturalism made them an excellent duo. Brennan was one of Hollywood's most enduring character actors. At the time *Pride* was being cast, he had won an astonishing three Academy Awards for Best Supporting Actor in the short space of only five years. The Supporting Actor/Actress category was introduced to the ceremonies in 1936, and Brennan won the first award for his work in *Come and Get It* (1936), directed by Howard Hawks and William Wyler and produced by Goldwyn. His second and third Oscars, respectively, were for *Kentucky* (1938) and *The Westerner* in which he played Judge Roy Bean opposite Cooper.

The most successful piece of casting in the movie was that of Gary Cooper as Lou Gehrig, although he was right-handed. It was not a secret to the American movie-going public that Lou Gehrig was left-handed. The film itself makes a joking allusion to the off-screen fact by showing a cake honoring Gehrig that's decorated with a right-handed batter, an error pointed out in the dialogue by Gehrig's father. Today there is much folklore about Cooper's right-handedness and how the problem was solved and who solved it. For many years the credit was given to the film editor, Daniel Mandell (who won the only Oscar the film received). Allegedly, he suggested that Cooper bat right, and then run to third base, not first, so that if the costumer reversed the letters and numbers on the players' uniforms, Mandell could flip the film to look as if a lefty were running to first base.

Film historian James Curtis gives credit to production designer William Cameron Menzies, saying: "Lou Gehrig hit and did most other things from his port side, but he wrote with his right hand. Cooper could indeed act him if his playing could be faked, but Menzies wouldn't abide the old fraud of a double, shot from the rear and matched with shots of the lead actor.... Menzies' solution was absurdly simple: Cooper would swing and catch right-handed then they would flip the film in the lab. For shots such as these Cooper and the other players would be dressed in uniforms on which the names and numbers would be reversed, as in a mirror image."[6]

Tom Sheiber, a curator at the National Baseball Hall of Fame and Museum, provides a different perspective. He says that Cooper actually did learn to bat left-handed and never wore a backwards Yankees uniform nor ran to third base after swinging. Film footage, says Sheiber, was flopped *once* so Cooper could appear to be *throwing* left-handed, a far bigger challenge than batting.[7] (The movie shows Cooper at close range throwing a ball to Babe Ruth during warm-ups on his first awe-struck day with the Yankees.)

Menzies is famous for being known as Hollywood's first ever "production designer"—that is, the first man so recognized with that title. In addition to the overall look of the film, Menzies contributed major solutions regarding baseball. He found the perfect stand-in for Yankee Stadium in Los Angeles: Wrigley Field, home of the Los Angeles Angels of the old Pacific Coast League, which was used for outdoor locations. Menzies used stills of Comiskey Park and Wrigley Field in Chicago and stock shots from Yankee Stadium to fill out his needs regarding baseball montages. When the production faced a problem of the wartime shortage of male extras for the shots of crowds in the bleachers, Menzies solved the problem by persuading the Screen Actors Guild to grant a waiver that allowed nonunion hires.

Menzies was a consummate professional, a man with great visual imagination and a record of cinematic innovation in the movies. His contribution to *Pride* was considered so significant that for the first time ever, a designer shared a credit title card with a film's director. Sam Wood generously allowed his own card to read: "Directed by Sam Wood. Production Designed by William Cameron Menzies."

The cinematographer, Rudolph Maté, is one of film history's greatest. He had been hired by Goldwyn to replace the legendary Gregg Toland while Toland served in the war. Maté had shot such famous movies as *The Passion of Joan of Arc* (1927) and *Vampyr* (1932). For *Pride of the Yankees*, he consistently shot Cooper from below, which helped to erase lines and circles underneath his eyes and make him look more youthful. (Cooper was, in fact, born two years ahead of Gehrig.) Maté created lighting patterns that stressed realism for family scenes, and soft shadows for romantic scenes. For the finale, in which Gehrig walks through the long tunnel to the field, leaving his wife behind, alone in a harsh light surrounded by deepening shadows, Maté's work makes a major contribution to the emotional feeling of the scene. When Gehrig is outside, delivering his farewell address (called "baseball's Gettysburg Address" by his biographer Ray Robinson), he is in a natural light, but when he says goodbye and walks away, he enters a hole of darkness, slowly disappearing out of the light as the sound of the umpire's call to "Play Ball!" is heard on the soundtrack. The sight of Gehrig's disappearing, leaving the light and the sound and action of the game behind him, outside his range, is an eloquent visual finale to *Pride of The Yankees*.

The man who directed *Pride* was Sam Wood (1884–1949). Although his name is not well-known today, he was one of Hollywood's busiest and most prominent directors in the 1930s and 1940s. Among other films credited to him are such successes as the Marx Brothers hit, *A Night at the Opera* (1935), *Goodbye, Mr. Chips* (1939), and *For Whom the Bell Tolls* (1943). Wood also worked on *Gone with the Wind* (1939), filming final scenes, although the directorial credit for that movie belonged to Victor Fleming. Wood began working as a movie director in 1916, and he worked continuously until his death in 1949, averaging nearly three movies per year. (His final two releases in 1949 were *The Stratton Story*, with Jimmy Stewart, also a baseball movie, and *Ambush*.) Wood's career has been somewhat neglected by scholars and critics, possibly due to his role in the organization of a strongly anti–Communist organization (the Motion Picture Alliance for the Preservation of American Ideals). Wood is not known for a dynamic personal style or a particular point-of-view regarding cinema.

Goldwyn was not at first attracted to the idea of a baseball movie. "If people want baseball, they go to the ballpark," he said.[8] Goldwyn's opinion reflected the Hollywood folklore of his era that baseball movies were box office poison. However, the story of Lou

Gehrig was more than a story about baseball, and *Pride* became an example of Goldwyn's business acumen. Not only did the movie-makers find a way to connect the facts of Gehrig's life to the emotional lives of wartime Americans, it cleverly expanded a baseball story into an additional set of genres: the love story, the immigrant family story, the biopic, the romantic comedy, and even the woman's picture. The film includes romance and courtship, mother-in-law/daughter-in-law conflict, married love, comedy, and glamour, including a nightclub with Ray Noble and His Orchestra and a dance number featuring Veloz and Yolanda. The character of Gehrig's wife, Eleanor (Wright), is a central (and noble) figure. The story is about Eleanor's courage and grace as well as Lou's, and since Mrs. Gehrig was alive during production and involved in approving certain details, her influence is heavily felt in the storytelling process.

In later years, Goldwyn said that the most difficult aspect of creating the screenplay for *Pride of the Yankees* was "to watch my baseball so that it didn't get the better of the personal story."[9] A modern viewer can easily see that this is the idea behind *Pride*, but for the original screenwriting team, this was not an obvious way to go, and the screenwriting team must be given credit for finding a structure that could present two movies, only one of which was about baseball.

The first writer assigned to the script was Paul Gallico, the former sports editor of the (New York) *Daily News* who put together the details of Gehrig's life in chronological order. Later, two highly successful writers—Jo Swerling and Herman Mankiewicz—would complete the final screenplay that was shot. Swerling had worked on *Gone with the Wind* (1939) and successfully helped the script for Goldwyn's 1940 hit with Cooper, *The Westerner*. Mankiewicz was the author of *Citizen Kane* (1941). Both men were experienced in visual storytelling and masters of movie narrative structures. They brought their considerable understanding of how to tell a movie story to *Pride*, and Gallico added his awareness of the rules and challenges of baseball itself.

The filmed story of *Pride of the Yankees* moves forward by using baseball as a setting for the story of Lou Gehrig, a brave American hero who just happens to be a player. The movie progresses from baseball montage to baseball montage, stopping to present meaningful episodes in Gehrig's life, and seamlessly flowing through and across the games into plot. This format is a smart way of creating a movie that would not only have the widest possible audience in its own time, but that would have the chance of standing the test of time. The baseball montages show Gehrig's time in Hartford with a farm team; the games in which he sat in the dugout waiting for a chance to play; all the many headlines about his successes and about his "slump" when he becomes ill; etc. After Eleanor and Lou meet and are married, she enters the montage system. There are montages of romantic letters, telegrams, and phone calls; of her pasting clippings and mementos in scrapbooks; of the two of them sitting together while it snows outside; of her hand adding trophy after trophy to his collection; and of her watching him play baseball during his successful as well as his difficult days. The pace of the movie is set by the alternating "montage/plot" system of screenwriting, which creates a rhythm of life.

The Oscar-nominated screenplay was masterful in its ability to tell a true baseball story, putting a satisfying amount of the game on the screen, while still managing to embrace the Gehrigs' love story and ultimately unite the two. The adaptation of Gehrig's life is an excellent example of how to tell a sports story. Movie writers dealing with sports always had to think about a movie-goer who was not familiar with the rules of the game. There needed to be a way to explain easily what was going on. In the case of *Pride of the*

*Yankees,* many of Gehrig's games were still vivid in the audience's minds but the movie did not rely on movie-goer memory. The screenwriters created a fake character, "Sam Blake" (Walter Brennan) who was loosely based on Christy Walsh, Gehrig's manager. Brennan's role in the story was to play someone who discovers Gehrig before he becomes famous, and who stays close to him as his career moves forward, game by game. Each evaluation of skill, success, or change in Gehrig's life can thus be logically and clearly explained through Brennan's dialogue.

In setting out to tell Lou Gehrig's story, the screenwriters faced a dramatic problem: Gehrig's life was straightforward. He worked hard and made a great success. He married only once and happily, and conducted himself with dignity, creating no scandals. The drama that existed in his story was already clearly known to potential audiences—his diagnosis with a mysterious and barely known disease. (Gehrig had died only months before the film's release.) Faced with writing about a lifetime of success with no obvious problems along the way, the screenwriters had to invent obstacles for Gehrig to overcome. There were no true villains in his life, but four useful human adversaries were defined to fill in until the final one, the inhuman one that could not be defeated, appeared. These "adversaries" are: *Gehrig's own mother,* who resists his baseball career and his choice of a marriage partner; *snobbish fraternity boys* who make fun of him; *a sportswriter* who does not believe in him (Dan Duryea); *Babe Ruth,* the greatest ball player of his era, and the competition he is measured by; and, finally, the *mysterious disease* that destroys his baseball career. Each of these is briefly sketched and overcome, as *Pride* is a movie designed to reaffirm positives, not endorse negatives.

## Invented Obstacles and "Adversaries"

The movie story begins by setting up American immigrant life. Just off a crowded city street, in a vacant sand lot, a group of raggedy boys are playing baseball. (As a little in-joke, they are also trading baseball cards, with value going to names such as Christy Mathewson, but none to Babe Ruth. "A rookie!" one scornfully explains.) When finally allowed into the game, a young outsider immediately hits a long run that soars off the lot over the fence and right through a plate glass window. When the police grab the boy and ask his name, he looks up from where he's fallen and says, "Lou Gehrig." It's the perfect introduction to the character the film will feature. It sets Gehrig up at once as an outsider, a poor, but honest boy and a naturally gifted baseball player. Equally importantly, it locates an adversary to his baseball career. His father (Ludwig Stossel) tells the store owner and a policeman that he "can't do anything without my wife," establishing the dominance of Gehrig's mother in the family. When Gehrig's mother (Elsa Janssen) handles the situation, she is stern with her boy about baseball as a poor choice in life. However a police man admiringly tells young Lou: "It was a mighty wallop!"

This opening scene demonstrates clearly the economy and skill of the film's writing team. All necessary elements of plot and character are clearly set up, including the admiration for Gehrig's batting skill that will ultimately make him famous (…"a mighty wallop"…) and Gehrig's dominant mother who adores her son, but who insists he should become an engineer and keep away from baseball. This opening is the only "childhood" sequence in *Pride* and it is built around baseball, Mrs. Gehrig's opposition to it, and her importance in his life. (She's his "best girl.")

Gehrig's mother continues with her dream for him, but he goes behind her back with his father's help to accept an offer to go to Hartford with the New York Yankees farm team. She misunderstands his destination, thinking he's going to "Harvard" to become an engineer. With his father's help in rerouting letters, Gehrig deceives his mother during the time frame necessary; however his fame cannot be contained. When Gehrig is called up by the Yankees, the neighbors excitedly pour into the Gehrig home to share in the joy, and Lou's mother takes it very hard. ("All baseballers are bums.") She laments the loss of "all my plans" (the key word being "my"), but Gehrig, in the guise of Gary Cooper, takes "his best girl" onto his lap and appeases her, reminding her that she's never actually been to a ball game. She might like it.

Using the mother, the movie thus sets up the American audience with an adversary, but also with a reliable movie religion: the love of baseball, and if not baseball, the love of fame and success. Movie-goers had no trouble accepting that "best-girl" mom was going to fall in love with at least one of America's favorite goals—baseball, fame, and success—if not all three.

Lou's mother is seen most negatively after Eleanor enters his life, when his parents and friends are preparing a surprise party in his honor. (This is the scene in which his father points out that the batter on top of his cake is wrong: "They made Louie a right-handed batter.") The surprise turns out to be one for Lou's mom, as Lou arrives with Eleanor. "Mrs. Gehrig, meet Mrs. Gehrig … as soon as we get married!" Lou doesn't notice how upset and unhappy his mom is, but Eleanor does. Mom is cold to her, and Eleanor is disappointed and worried—all simply expressed by facial expressions and action within the frame, not dialogue.

The conflict between the two women—benignly represented by disagreements over wall paper and a chifforobe—finally comes to a head, but Gehrig steps in and settles things. The extended domestic sequence regarding the conflict between Gehrig's two "best girls" is cleverly written to place it dominantly in the story, broadening the appeal of the film, providing some comedy, and connecting the Gehrig story to female viewers of the day. The love story is also linked to baseball: the surprise party (and its cake) are after a World Series win; the Gehrig wedding is topped in drama by a dash to the stadium right after the ceremony so Lou won't miss a game; the conflict between the women is represented by furniture and easily settled by the man who steps up to the plate, etc. The smooth weaving together of a baseball story and a romantic story is beautifully illustrated by these scenes.

During Gehrig's college years at Columbia, he works as a waiter in a fraternity, but is also a four-letter man in sports. He's well-liked by the majority of the frat boys and his sports success has brought him under consideration for membership. However there is opposition from snobs ("…but his mom's a cook! …"). He is nevertheless admitted, but the snobs decide to make a fool of Gehrig at a dance by having a jazzy young lady lead him on. Gehrig falls for her false charms, believing her to be sincere, but when he finds out he's the butt of a joke, he attacks the perpetrators across the dinner table. Gehrig is thus solidified as a common man's hero. Going to college and joining a fraternity do not change him. This college sequence accomplishes several other goals, also with economy. It explains how Gehrig managed to afford college through his baseball success and its ability to open doors for him; his innocence with women; his fundamental decency and naiveté; but the inner fight and strength he possesses if treated badly.

*Pride* puts into place two screenwriting inventions: Brennan's "Sam Blake" and "Hank

Hanneman," a character played by Dan Duryea, who represents "the voice of the other," that is, a skeptical sportswriter who doesn't believe Lou Gehrig is all that great. These fictitious sportswriters conduct arguments about Gehrig's baseball prowess that help to explain two things to the audience: what is going on in any game (in case they aren't fans and don't understand) and how Gehrig's professional career is progressing. Dan Duryea, the observer, says Gehrig is "the chump of all time, a boob, a rube" while Brennan says "he's the best of 'em, a guy who does his job and nothing else."

The two sportswriters are well used in the most fully extended baseball scene of the movie: a game between the Yankees and the St. Louis Cardinals that was part of the 1926 World Series. At the time the movie was made, baseball fans who were in the audience most likely remembered the series, and those who were not baseball fans didn't care anyway. The script takes advantage of three true events: the 1926 game itself; a dramatic hitting competition between Gehrig and Ruth that existed in the 1927 season; and a visit made by Babe Ruth to a children's hospital in 1926. These three elements are woven together as a "story" of the one game, with an added implication that the Yankees afterwards became the World Series champions. (They were, but not in 1926. They lost that World Series to the Cardinals, but won in 1927 with their powerful Murderers' Row lineup, sweeping the Pittsburgh Pirates.)

The scriptwriters—and certainly Gallico—knew that the 1926 series was the time frame in which The Babe made a much publicized promise to an 11-year-old boy named Johnny Sylvester to hit a home run for him. Sylvester had been injured in a fall off his horse, and a friend of his family had presented him with two autographed baseballs signed by the Yankees and the Cardinals. The friend allegedly told Sylvester that Ruth was going to hit a home run for him. After the series was over, Ruth visited Sylvester in the hospital, and the incident was blown out of proportion and legendized into a visit in which the promise was made directly to the boy, saving his life, etc.

The movie uses the story, and weaves Gehrig into it. A scene was written in which Ruth, famous for his love of the limelight and his braggadocio, visits a young boy's hospital bed, posing for photos and handing out autographs, and promising the home run. After Ruth leaves (surrounded by photographers and sycophants), Gehrig stays behind and shyly, modestly agrees to the boy's request for "two" home runs from him. Gehrig says he'll do so only if the boy promises to get well and go home. ("Sam Blake" observes this exchange.)

Instead of depicting a direct rivalry or competition between Ruth and Gehrig, who were teammates and respectful of each other, the movie script sets up a fight between "Blake" and "Hanneman" over whether or not Gehrig can hit the two home runs. As tension escalates, with Gehrig hitting one, but striking out twice until he finally comes up for his last bat in the eighth, the two writers increase the amount of their bet. When Gehrig hits and the game is won, the film slides into a scene of wild celebration on the "World Series Champions" train. There it seems to suggest that the Yankees became champions after the game, even though the Cardinals ultimately beat them in the 1926 series' seventh game.

The boy and the game are used to contrast Ruth and Gehrig indirectly. (And, of course, to provide some baseball in the movie.) During the 1927 season, Gehrig was serious batting competition for Ruth, although in the end Gehrig had hit 47 runs and the Babe got his record-setting 60. Throughout the season both men were in the limelight for their batting statistics, as Gehrig proved capable of challenging Ruth for home runs.

The writers cleverly took light liberty with facts without seriously damaging the truth in order to show how good a hitter Gehrig was, how modest a man he was, how different from Babe Ruth he was, but without alienating Ruth or his fans. The Babe and Lou Gehrig were never close friends. Their lifestyles were just too different. Ruth as a personality was the opposite of Gehrig. Ruth was well-known as a man with big appetites—for booze, for food, and for women and fame. He was the reckless embodiment of his era.

A great coup for the film was the agreement of Babe Ruth (George Herman Ruth, 1895–1948) to participate. Many people went to watch *Pride* simply because The Babe was in it. He was paid $25,000 for his participation and guaranteed third billing. Ruth was like Coca-Cola and Ford automobiles—a symbol of America. Having him agree to appear in the movie was a huge asset. He not only agreed to play himself, but also, being left-handed, to take Gary Cooper's place in long-shot for a scene which required a batting stance by a left-hander. Ruth's enormous popularity gave him plenty of room to act the "villain" if necessary, and feel he could get away with it. He deserves credit for appearing in *Pride*, because the contrast between Ruth's flamboyance and Gehrig's modesty, while not damning Ruth for his ego, helps clarify for an audience who Gehrig was.

*Pride* was not The Babe's first movie—it was his last. Ruth was a veteran of ten motion pictures, one of which, *Headin' Home*, was released as early as 1920, in the days of silent film. Ruth portrayed a small-town guy with an elderly mom, a little sister (called "Pigtails"), a girlfriend (the banker's daughter) and a rival (who's secretly embezzling from the bank). Naturally there's a baseball game in which The Babe hits a winning homer and solves all the problems and in the end not only gets his girl but also becomes a Yankees star in real footage from the Polo Grounds. After making a short in 1927 (*Babe Comes Home*), Ruth also appeared as himself in Harold Lloyd's successful 1928 comedy, *Speedy*. However, The Babe's real claim to movie dominance came when he was signed by Universal Pictures in 1932 for a series of one-reelers perfectly timed to coincide with baseball season: *Slide, Babe, Slide*; *Perfect Control*; *Over the Fence*; *Just Pals* and *Fancy Curves*. These movies were essentially aimed at young boys and were designed to capitalize on Ruth's popularity with that demographic. A story line would set up a situation in which Ruth would play a little baseball and provide instructions for the audience on how to improve their own version of the game. Film historian Leonard Maltin described one of the films: "Franklin Pangborn appears as a stuffy schoolteacher making his class recite the multiplication tables. One youngster dozes off and dreams that Babe Ruth comes by and disrupts the class, calling the boys onto the field for a baseball game.... Babe shows the kids how to pitch, demonstrating the proper technique for throwing a curve ball, fast ball, and so forth."[10] Babe Ruth was a big success in these movies. He was calm and confident in front of a camera, and had real personality on film. Later, in 1937, Warner Brothers also starred him in an oddity, a baseball musical entitled *Home Run on the Keys*.[11]

The relationship of Babe Ruth and Lou Gehrig is developed in *Pride*, but the film is overtly designed to favor Gehrig. The Babe is treated carefully but still used to make Gehrig look good. He's a lovable legend, larger than life, but by contrast, a useful device to show that *some* baseballers didn't live like Lou Gehrig did.

The screenwriters, following their established pattern of meshing a baseball story with a love story, introduce Gehrig's illness through Eleanor. In his 2000th game, Gehrig strikes out three times and looks worried. Eleanor is happily waiting at home, and when Lou arrives, a "love" scene between them consists of a playful, childlike wrestling on the floor which ends with him suddenly, unexpectedly, feeling a sharp pain. This is the screen-play's "AHA!" moment for the audience, who know what the characters don't know: he will die from the disease causing his agony.

The film then moves rapidly to its conclusion. It has introduced the element that will not be pleasant for the viewer—the non-human obstacle that cannot be overcome—and needs to fulfill the promise of the well-known final speech for an audience reward. Eleanor is seen watching Lou play, aware that he's not doing his best, and witnessing that he attempts to cope with his diminishment by working harder and harder. When Gehrig comes into the locker room after a game, he falls off his stool while trying to untie his shoes. (His fellow Yankees pretend they don't see and do not move to help him.)

When Gehrig cannot play up to his standards, the movie presents a resigned looking Cooper walking to the manager during a game and saying, "You'd better send someone in for me. I can't make it anymore." He walks to the dugout and the announcer's voice is heard: "2,130 games. 14 years." A close-up of Cooper's face eloquently says what this means to him.

At the Scripps Clinic, Gehrig learns from doctors that "it's three strikes." (A baseball metaphor.) He doesn't want Eleanor to know, but she, of course, guesses and keeps her knowledge secret.

The final scene of the film takes place at Yankee Stadium for Lou Gehrig Appreciation Day, with the crowd of "over 62,000" present. It begins with a sentimental moment in which the young boy who had requested and received two Gehrig home runs is waiting, to show Gehrig that he kept *his* promise: the boy can now walk. As the ceremony begins, the audience is reminded that Gehrig played a total of sixteen years, and was known as The Iron Horse. When he walks out onto the field for the last time, the tribute ceremony is reproduced, "presenting" "Manager Joe McCarthy, Mayor LaGuardia, the Postmaster General," plus members of Murderers' Row and Babe Ruth. Gehrig comes to the mike to give his final speech, and then disappears into the blackness of the tunnel as the audi-ence hears "Play Ball!" The game goes on, and for wartime audiences, the implication was "and so will America."

## Real-Life Strengths

Working rapidly to complete what was viewed as a timely script, the screenwriters mastered the basic story of Gehrig's life, created "villains" or obstacles, and solved the issues regarding the presentation of baseball. They further enhanced the quality of their work when they found four real-life strengths to be used in turning the film into a classic: the cooperation of Mrs. Gehrig, which allowed them to make her into a heroine to match her husband's heroism; the opportunity to use artifacts from the Gehrig's lives in the visual presentation; the chance to include real life baseball players; and the clearance to rewrite and shape, but nevertheless feature as the climax, Gehrig's famous farewell speech at Yankee Stadium.

Eleanor Gehrig, called "a tower of strength" by her husband in his famous farewell speech, would later in life write a successful book called *My Luke and I*, in which she said "I would not have traded two minutes of the joy and the grief with that man for two decades of anything with another."[12] Theirs was a happy marriage and a true love story. (A 1978 TV movie starring Ed Herrmann as Gehrig was entitled *A Love Affair: The*

*Eleanor and Lou Gehrig Story.*) Having sold the rights to her husband's story, she was naturally concerned that he would be treated with the proper respect, but also that his story would not be turned into an unrecognizable mishmash of false events as was sometimes the case in Hollywood biopics. She made her presence known regarding casting, details, and the proper telling of events. Goldwyn and his film-making team took her seriously, and the resulting movie is unique for its accuracy and sensitivity to mood and nuance. Mrs. Gehrig was given no screen writing credit for her involvement. However, she was awarded a unique tribute. Prior to the title cards for the producer, director and art director, a special credit card says: "Appreciation is expressed for the gracious assistance of Mrs. Lou Gehrig and for the cooperation of Mr. Ed Barrow and the New York Yankees." It was generally believed that had not Mrs. Gehrig cooperated, the Yankees would have followed her lead.

The love story of the Gehrigs, no doubt also due to the participation of Mrs. Gehrig (and her careful scrutiny), is beautifully written and accounts for much of the film's enduring appeal. Their meeting takes place at a baseball game. When Gehrig is finally sent in to sub for a player who is "seeing double," he trips over a row of bats on the ground and his future wife, Eleanor Twitchell calls out "Tanglefoot!," laughing hard at him. The crowd picks it up. He bats, gets on first, and is then beaned with the ball running to second base. Later that night, in a restaurant where the club is eating, he is told that Eleanor is "the hot dog king's daughter" when she walks in with her father. As she walks by him, Gehrig trips her gently, and as she slides to the floor he calls out "Tanglefoot!" But when he laughs good-naturedly, so does she (proving she's a good sport). "Okay," she says, "we're even." They are introduced: he's the Yankees' new first baseman and she's Eleanor Twitchell.

Lou and Eleanor go on their first date to an amusement park (where he shows off for her) and then to a night club. This "date" sequence is important in the overall presentation of the movie, and represents how the movie's designed to appeal to both men and women viewers, as well as both baseball and non-baseball fans. Their love story is turned into a highly democratic romance. There is no emphasis placed on the fact that Eleanor Twitchell came from a wealthy family. It is left up to the audience to "read" the images: she's in a box seat, right down at eye level with the team, when she's at the game in which she first sees Gehrig; she's at the restaurant with her well-heeled father, where she's introduced as the "hot dog king's daughter"; and later, when Gehrig goes to her home, it is a mansion with servants. However, the romance between a poor boy and a rich girl is effectively bridged by two different settings for their "first date": the amusement park (representing who he is) and a very ritzy night club (representing her): two contrasting backgrounds that are united into one love story.

The amusement park sequence is played for comedy about Gehrig's athletic skill in winning armloads of prizes for her. The night club is played for glamour, beauty, romance, and the dream world that success can bring in America. As Lou and Eleanor are waited on and catered to in the softly lit world of luxury, the Ray Noble Orchestra plays while Veloz and Yolanda, a successful ballroom dance team of the era, perform one of their ritzy numbers. (Veloz and Yolanda often turned up in movies, to flash out onto the floor and swirl around in expensive clothes. They were considered to be the epitome of night club sophistication.) Following their art, Noble's vocalist sings the very popular Irving Berlin song, "Always," which was the Gehrigs' real-life favorite song and used at Eleanor's personal request.[13] It was one of the greatest hits of the World War II era, with its heartfelt promise, "I'll be loving you always" in an era in which many couples knew the war might make that an impossibility. As Lou and Eleanor dance, the beauty of the image is paramount, and the song takes on the touchingly tragic quality it was meant to have. An audience sees the lovely Wright and the handsome Cooper in their prime, falling in love at the height of Gehrig's youthful success. "Not for just a year..." says the song, "but always." And yet, as the audience knew, the "always" for the Gehrigs would be cut tragically short by his early death. The use of the song, which has a full credit of its own at the beginning of the movie ("The Song 'Always' by Irving Berlin") was an exquisite and subtly meaningful choice.

The Goldwyn Company—and Menzies, the production designer—were happy to be able to use real Gehrig family objects in the film. Teresa Wright is observed pasting items into large scrapbooks and lovingly looking at the entries. Mrs. Gehrig had carefully made and kept scrapbooks of Gehrig's baseball triumphs, and the movie-makers were allowed to reproduce them. Gehrig had also presented his wife with a special bracelet made of his medals, and Cooper gives this to Wright on the day of his final speech. The scrapbooks and the bracelet were not items invented for the movie. (They are available for viewing in Cooperstown.[14]) Using real objects such as the books and the bracelet helps to give actors a sense of the characters they are playing, and even if the viewing audience at the time didn't necessarily know the items were real, they felt the truth in performance and story. (Publicity, of course, helped sell the usage to audiences.)

*Pride of the Yankees* presents a very important scene in which the audience sees Eleanor Gehrig making her famous scrapbooks that exist in the Hall of Fame. A rose Gehrig sent her with a card signed "Tanglefoot" is included in the oversized album that has "Lou Gehrig" stamped on the cover. There's also a diploma, a photo of him as a football player, a photo of him falling down in the moment she first called him "tanglefoot" and a headline saying that LOU GEHRIG WEDS. The audience watches Eleanor paste things into the scrapbook and turn the pages, having her memories of their life together. It is for the viewer of the movie a touching review of the story they've just watched, so that they, like Eleanor, will remember what they are about to lose. For viewers it will be the end of a good film; for her it was the end of her life with Gehrig.

The final scene between the Gehrigs begins with the scrapbook and the headline: TRIBUTE TO LOU GEHRIG TODAY. When Eleanor peeks in on him, she sees that he cannot tie his own tie, and she covers with a little comedy routine, so she can tie it for him without giving anything away. In this scene, he gives her the bracelet made out of his medals. For the wartime audience, this "goodbye" scene between the couple, in which they both must pretend things are going to be all right and must cover their fear of death, was deeply felt and very emotional.

*Pride of the Yankees* is a modern viewer's delight, baseball fan or not, because the story of the game is enhanced by the presence of real-life players who were teammates of Gehrig's, chief among them, Babe Ruth. The notorious Yankees powerful batting lineup of 1927—Murderers' Row—is represented by the "locker room" appearance of Bill Dickey, Bob Meusel and Mark Koenig, in addition to Ruth, and also by the appearance of the famous sportscaster Bill Stern, playing himself. These well-known names and faces make *Pride* not only more realistic, but visually memorable and believable for baseball lovers. For those who are not fans, they nevertheless provide a sense of accuracy and authority, and the sense that an audience member is looking at the true story of Lou Gehrig.

One of the highlights of the film for baseball fans is the scene depicting Gehrig's first arrival at the locker room in Yankee Stadium. As he reverently walks around, looking at the name plates on the lockers (Babe Ruth's taking pride of place), the players arrive and among them are the real former Yankees. The highlight is the arrival of The Babe, looking healthy and slim and younger than his years. (Ruth reportedly lost 47 pounds to play his role.)

The script builds to the final drama of an event that has become a part of movie history as much as of baseball history: Gehrig's farewell address on Lou Gehrig Appreciation Day at Yankee Stadium on July 4, 1939. Newsreels, as well as radio, covered the tribute, but there is no known complete film of the occasion that exists today. Unlike similar modern events, there was no television that stayed with every moment and "interviewed" everyone attending. A small part of the newsreel coverage survives, and it includes the first and last parts of Gehrig's famous speech. For most people today, Lou Gehrig's farewell speech is the sight of Gary Cooper talking into the microphone in medium close-up, his voice echoing on the sound system.

*The Pride of the Yankees* is an early example of a real time and place in history being replaced by a manufactured movie image. Gehrig's speech was heartfelt, haltingly rendered, and longer than that of Cooper's in the film. In fact, Gehrig's speech was not reproduced in its entirety in the film. It was shortened and reorganized to put the legendary "I am the luckiest man" portion dramatically at the end instead of the beginning. (That's called screenwriting.) The final line in the movie version ("Today, I consider myself the luckiest man on the face of the Earth") is ranked #38 on the AFI's list of 100 great movie quotes. The tone, the true meaning, and the emotional depth of the speech are accurate to what Gehrig said and no doubt felt. Comparing the two speeches reveals how the movie shaped the remarks for a perfect final ending to the story of Lou Gehrig:

### Original Speech

Fans, for the past two weeks you have been reading about a bad break. Yet today I consider myself the luckiest man on the face of the Earth. I have been in ballparks for seventeen years and have never received anything but kindness and encouragement from you fans.

Look at these grand men. Which of you wouldn't consider it the highlight of his career just to associate with them for even one day? Sure, I'm lucky. Who wouldn't consider it an honor to have known Jacob Ruppert? Also, the builder of baseball's greatest empire, Ed Barrow? To have spent six years with that wonderful little fellow, Miller Huggins? Then to have spent the next nine years with that outstanding leader, that smart student of psychology, the best manager in baseball today, Joe McCarthy? Sure, I'm lucky.

When the New York Giants, a team you would give your right arm to beat, and vice versa, sends you a gift—that's something. When everybody down to the groundskeepers and those boys in white coats remember you with trophies—that's something. When you have a wonderful mother-in-law who takes sides with you in squabbles with her own daughter—that's something. When you have a father and a mother work all their lives so you can have an education and build your body—it's a blessing. When you have a wife who has been a tower of strength and shown more courage than you dreamed existed—that's the finest I know.

So I close in saying that I might have been given a bad break, but I've got an awful lot to live for.

### Rewritten Speech

I have been walking onto ballfields for sixteen years, and I've never received anything but kindness and encouragement from you fans. I have had the great honor to have played with these great veteran ballplayers on my left—Murderers' Row, our Championship team of 1927. I have had the further honor of living with and playing with these men on my right—The Bronx Bombers, the Yankees of today.

I have been given fame and undeserved praise by the boys up there behind the wire in the press box, my friends, the sportswriters. I have worked under the two greatest manages of all time, Miller Huggins and Joe McCarthy.

I have a mother and father who fought to give me health and solid background in my youth. I have a wife, a companion for life, who has shown me more courage than I ever knew.

People all say that I've had a bad break … today, I consider myself the luckiest man on the face of the Earth.

*Pride of the Yankees* opened to great reviews. In the *New York Post*, Archer Winston wrote that Cooper's "interpretation of the mental and spiritual side of the character is brilliant." *The New York World-Telegram* felt that "Cooper has seldom been better than he is as Gehrig. His performance grows as the character grows, from the shy gawky undergraduate to the modest, unassuming hero to millions." *Variety*, the trade paper that assessed box office success, called *Pride* "a stirring epitaph … well worth seeing"[15] and the *New York Times* gave it credit for being "tender, meticulous" but also criticized it as "inclines to monotony" because of its length and too many "genial details."[16] (The author of the criticism was the infamous Bosley Crowther, a man who is today thought of as the man who most often got it wrong about the movies in the past.) The excitement over the prerelease responses to *Pride* inspired Goldwyn's advisors to suggest he charge more than regular admission prices and "admit no one for less than fifty-five cents general admission."[17] Goldwyn ultimately made more money from *Pride* than from any film he had yet produced.

*Pride* was adapted into an hour-long radio play for Lux Radio Theatre on October 4, 1943, with Cooper as Gehrig and actress Virginia Bruce replacing Wright. It was also broadcast on September 30, 1949, for the Screen Directors Playhouse, this time pairing Cooper with Lurene Tuttle. Cooper, who was born in 1901, wasn't eligible for the World War II draft. To serve his country, he went on a five-week tour to entertain the troops in 1943, travelling to American bases in New Guinea. He was neither singer nor dancer, so he recited Gehrig's farewell speech from *Pride*. According to those who witnessed his efforts, the soldiers were deeply moved, often to tears, and Cooper's performance inevitably brought heartfelt and resounding applause.

The film story of *Pride of the Yankees* is one of the most effective baseball movies ever made. It elevates the "national pastime" into a metaphor for American life and for why Americans could and would win World War II. What is remarkable is that the film continues to work emotionally years after the war has ended, and for people who are not baseball fans. An examination of the script shows how masterfully the story was constructed to smoothly incorporate different types of meanings and levels of emotion from joy to tragedy. *Pride* stands as exemplary filmmaking, with a very high level of craftsmanship in all areas of production.

Seen in retrospect, *Pride of the Yankees* can perhaps be thought of as the baseball movie that isn't really about baseball, but about what it takes to be a great baseball player and/or a modern American hero. Though modern viewers sometimes call the movie overly long or too sentimental, the basic story has managed to stand in any era as a dramatic and touching one. In its own day—the early years of World War II—it became representative of what America was just beginning to face: untimely death, the importance of love and family in difficult days, and the need to accept courageously whatever fate would bring. Goldwyn, always a showman, had fully understood its significance, and he was pleased with the film's final shape. Perhaps the best opinion of all is that of Mrs.

Eleanor Gehrig, who died in 1984 without ever remarrying. She said the movie was all that she could have hoped for and that she was completely happy with it.

## NOTES

1. *Hollywood Reporter*, July 15, 1941, 4.
2. *American Film Institute Catalogue, Feature Films M–Z, 1941–1950*, executive ed. Patricia King Hanson (Berkeley: University of California Press, 1993), 1891. *Lou Gehrig, American Hero* is one title.
3. *American Film Institute Catalogue, Feature Films M–Z, 1930–1941*, executive ed. Patricia King Hanson (Berkeley: University of California Press, 1993), 3638.
4. *Ibid.*
5. James Curtis, *William Cameron Menzies: The Shape of Things to Come* (New York: Pantheon Books, 2015), 267.
6. *Ibid.*, 268.
7. Tom Shieber, *The Pride of the ~~Yankees~~ Seeknay*, Baseball Researcher, baseballresearcher.blogspot.com/2013/02/the-pride-of-yankees-seeknay.html, February 3, 2013, last accessed August 13, 2018.
8. A. Scott Berg, *Goldwyn* (New York: Alfred A. Knopf, 1989), 170.
9. *Ibid.*, 372.
10. Leonard Maltin, *The Great Movie Shorts* (New York: Bonanza Books, 1972), 206.
11. *Ibid.*, 219.
12. Eleanor Gehrig and Joseph Durso, "My Luke and I," (New York: Thomas Y. Crowell Company, 1976), 229.
13. Berg, 372.
14. Interview with Ted Spencer, Curator, The Lou Gehrig Collection, National Baseball Hall of Fame and Museum, Cooperstown, New York, "What He Left Behind," *The Pride of the Yankees*, directed by Sam Wood (1942; Burbank, CA: Warner Home Video), DVD.
15. "Pride of the Yankees," *Variety*, December 31, 1941.
16. Bosley Crowther, "'Pride of the Yankees,' a Film Biography of Lou Gehrig, With Gary Cooper and Teresa Wright, on View at Astor, *New York Times*, July 16, 1942: 23.
17. Berg, 372.

# Lost in the Wilderness

*The New York Yankees,
Corporate Ownership
and the Anti-Establishment Era
from 1964 to 1973*

RON BRILEY

The mystique of the New York Yankees relies upon an image of power and success reflecting America's largest city and most iconic sports franchise. With their 40 American League pennants and 27 World Series championships, the Yankees have dominated Major League Baseball while the nation's popular culture celebrates Yankee heroes, including Babe Ruth, Lou Gehrig, Joe DiMaggio, Yogi Berra, Whitey Ford, and Mickey Mantle. But the Yankees became one of the worst teams in the 1960s when the Columbia Broadcasting System (CBS) owned the team before George Steinbrenner led a group to buy it. He restored the Yankees to greatness in the late 1970s. This period of the Yankees as losers reflected in many ways the changing political and popular culture environment of the 1960s, when traditional institutions such as Major League Baseball were questioned by a rising counterculture and anti-establishment symbolized by the rise of the flamboyant Oakland A's and the muckraking *Ball Four* by former Yankee Jim Bouton.

The Yankees dominated the American League during the post–World War II period by winning the pennant every season between 1949 and 1964 with the exception of the 1954 Cleveland Indians and 1959 Chicago White Sox; both teams lost on the World Series stage. However, reports that Yankee owners Dan Topping and Del Webb were selling the club to CBS brought forth jeremiads from reporters and other baseball owners that corporate control and financial support would simply enhance Yankee dominance and threaten the future of baseball by destroying any sense of competitive balance. Under the leadership of Chairman of the Board William S. Paley, CBS was a corporate juggernaut expanding beyond radio and television to purchase Columbia Records, guitar-maker Fender, and a toy company. Theatrical investments included the Broadway show *My Fair Lady*. The complete package deal for the Yankees was reported by the press as totaling $14 million.[1] When the transaction was officially announced, Chet Huntley of NBC News quipped that it was "just one more reason to hate the Yankees," while New York Congressman Emanuel Celler, whose subcommittee on monopoly investigated allegations of antitrust violations against Organized Baseball, insisted that "baseball is big business" and called for a Justice Department investigation of the sale to CBS. Judge Roy Hofheinz, president of the National League Houston Colt .45's, proclaimed, "The day CBS finally acquires the New York Yankees will be a darker day for baseball than the Black Sox scandal."[2] In response to this outcry, CBS President Frank Stanton issued a statement that CBS would continue to carry the *Game of the Week*, while Yankee General Manager Ralph Houk reassured players that CBS ownership would not dictate baseball operations on the playing field. Paley concluded that "the great American game" would thrive under CBS.[3]

Nevertheless, the *Sporting News*, the self-proclaimed "Bible of Baseball," was alarmed; it called for a meeting of American League owners to approve the sale and clarify the issues raised by corporate ownership. The *Sporting News* editorialized, "The way baseball is threatening to become purely an adjunct of big business certainly should be cause for alarm. What would prevent General Motors from buying the (Detroit) Tigers? Would this be good for baseball? Who knows?"[4] Although a league meeting was scheduled, American League owners were less worried by the Yankee acquisition. During a meeting that went longer than five hours on September 9th in Boston, the owners approved the sale by a vote of eight to two despite a warning from attorney Paul Porter of Baseball Commissioner Ford Frick's office and National League attorney Lou Carroll that CBS involvement with the Yankees could trigger "an element of risk" for an antitrust violation.[5]

Kansas City Athletics owner Charlie Finley voted against the deal and expressed his concern to the Justice Department, telling reporters that other owners were intimidated by the Yankees, leaving Finley "disappointed, disgusted, disillusioned, disenchanted, discouraged, and depressed."[6] Meanwhile, the *Sporting News* continued to express concern over corporate control of baseball, insisting, "While CBS may be baseball-minded, the ownership of the Yankees can be only a tiny part of the daily business of the radio and television network. Baseball may not suffer immediately, but it can scarcely prosper."[7] The *Sporting News* also linked the Yankee sale to the franchise transfer of the Braves from Milwaukee to Atlanta, arguing that both transactions reflected a lack of transparency in Organized Baseball.[8]

In March 1965, the CBS acquisition of the Yankees was the subject of congressional hearings before the Senate Subcommittee on Monopoly chaired by Democratic Senator Philip Hart of Michigan. Testifying in favor of the CBS purchase were Baseball Commissioner Ford Frick as well as representatives from ABC and NBC television. Stanton described the Yankee transaction as justified "essentially because we thought it was a good investment. We have been trying to supplement our income from non-regulated and non-licensed businesses so that all of our eggs are not in the FCC (Federal Communications Commission) basket." The only testimony opposing the CBS expansion came from baseball owners Arthur Allyn of the Chicago White Sox and Charlie Finley of the Kansas City Athletics. An angry Finley told the subcommittee, "The position of CBS in baseball should be that of an observer, a reporter, a critic, just as other networks, magazines and newspapers. To me there is a tremendous conflict of interest in one unit obtaining the position where it is the bidder for rights controlled even partially by one of its subsidiaries."[9]

Despite such dire predictions of what CBS controlling the Yankees might mean to Organized Baseball, the reality proved to be that Finley transferred his club to Oakland and garnered three world championships in the early 1970s, while the once mighty Yankees struggled under the mantle of CBS leadership. After winning the American League pennant in 1963 and 1964, the Yankees lost the World Series to the Los Angeles Dodgers and the St. Louis Cardinals, respectively. The new management also failed to endear themselves to Yankee fans when they terminated the contracts of manager Yogi Berra and announcer Mel Allen following the 1964 season.

The Yankees slumped in 1965, finishing in sixth place with their first losing record in 40 years. And things only got worse the next year as the Yankees finished last in the American League for the first time since 1912 while losing 89 games.

There was little improvement during the 1967 season, but the Yankees returned to a winning record in 1968 with a mark of 83–79. Things looked rosier in 1970—the team reached 2nd place in the American League East with a 93–69 record. The Yankees barely hovered above .500 in 1971 with an 82–80 record, followed by 79–76 in 1972. Attendance at Yankee Stadium began to decline—the club drew under 1,000,000 fans for the 1972 campaign. In fact, a weekday makeup game with the Chicago White Sox drew only 413 spectators on September 22, 1966. Yankee historian and former team publicist Marty Appel attributes the firing of broadcaster Red Barber to his insistence that coverage of the game include television shots of the empty stadium.[10]

Under CBS ownership, the Yankee pipeline of young talent dried up. Horace Clarke, Bobby Murcer, Joe Pepitone, and Roy White were decent players but could hardly replace iconic figures from the club's past. Various explanations are offered to explain the decline in Yankee talent, which was apparent even before CBS assumed control of the club. Mike Burke, a CBS vice-president charged with developing new strains of revenue, had urged the corporation to purchase the Yankees. In September 1966, Burke became president of the club and served in management even after the Yankees were sold in January 1973 to Steinbrenner's group, although he resigned in April of that year following disagreements with the new ownership. CBS sold the team for approximately $10,000,000, with the City of New York picking up almost $2,000,000 of the price tag for parking garages and adjoining property owned by the Yankees. CBS suffered a loss of nearly $11,000,000 on its investment. A disappointed Burke commented, "The trouble was we didn't go in and feel the goods. We bought a pig in the poke." Burke's major accomplishment was reaching an agreement with the administration of New York City Mayor John V. Lindsay to keep the Yankees in the Big Apple and okay the city's refurbishing Yankee Stadium, a project that eventually cost more than $100,000,000.[11]

CBS took over the Yankees when the structure of the game was undergoing a major change with the introduction of the player draft. No longer could an affluent team such as the Yankees simply stockpile talent in their farm system. Teams would now make selections of unsigned talent at the high school and college levels based upon the team's record in the previous season. The clubs that finished last, selected first. The goal of the free agent draft was to reduce costs and maintain a sense of competitive balance. In December 1964, the *Sporting News* lauded the agreement for the draft, remarking, "This can be the most historic document ever passed by baseball. Its sponsors deserve credit for continuing their fight until they achieved their goal. All of baseball should be congratulated for a most progressive step."[12] But others saw the draft as discriminating against successful teams with well-organized scouting systems. Dodger General Manager Buzzie Bavasi denounced it as a form of socialism, proclaiming it "penalized the industrious" and allowed young athletes "to sell their talents in only one place."[13] The draft appeared to punish the successful Yankees for their extensive scouting system, yet as the quality of play on the field declined, the Yankees were rewarded with high draft picks, providing an advantage that the CBS management failed to exploit.

In reality, the move downward had started much earlier when the dynasty eschewed the signing of black players after Jackie Robinson shattered the sport's racial barrier in 1947 with the Brooklyn Dodgers. The New York Giants, Boston Braves, and Cincinnati Reds soon followed the example set by the Dodgers. However, the American League, with the exception of Bill Veeck and the Cleveland Indians, was reluctant to embrace black players, and the league's dominant New York Yankees franchise set the tone. Journalist David Halberstam wrote that the Yankees' management style was "to be blunt, racist." Halberstam further explained, "They were winning and winning consistently without black players, about whom the ownership believed many of the existing stereotypes that blacks were lazy and would not play well under pressure."[14]

George Weiss, general manager of the Yankees during the 1950s, was reportedly concerned that the recruitment of black players would draw black fans to Yankee Stadium and drive away the club's predominantly white middle-class clientele. Weiss lured one of baseball's best scouts, Tom Greenwade, from the Dodgers, but he placed limitations on Greenwade's recruitment of African-American talent. Greenwade had scouted Robinson for the Dodgers and discovered Mickey Mantle for the Yankees, but he wanted to sign far more black players for the New York franchise. Weiss, however, is quoted as telling Greenwade, "Now Tom, I don't want you sneaking around down any back alleys and signing any niggers. We don't want them."[15] Greenwade followed the instructions of his employer, but according to his son, regretted his collaboration with Weiss.

Greenwade's recruitment of Mantle seemed to reinforce the racial assumptions of Yankee management. Halberstam writes, "Ironically, Mantle's greatness increased the arrogance of the front office, for his exceptional speed and power convinced the Yankees that they did not need to change. He helped bring them an additional decade of dominance, and in so doing, he helped create the attitude among their executives that would lead to their eventual decline. As most of the other American League teams followed suit, the National League gradually began to pull away as superior, with better teams and more exciting young players."[16] Thus in the 1964 World Series, the St. Louis Cardinals with outstanding black athletes—Bob Gibson, Curt Flood, Lou Brock, and Bill White— defeated the Yankees.

The Yankee franchise's troubling legacy with African-American athletes is perhaps best exemplified by examining the career of Elston Howard, the first black Yankee. A loyal company man, Howard deflected charges of racism against the franchise, asserting that no one in the Yankee organization ever made him conscious of his color.[17] Nevertheless, when Howard joined the Yankees in 1955, management as well as the New York press demonstrated a somewhat condescending tone toward him. Before promoting Howard, however, the Yankees traded away another promising black player, Vic Power from Puerto Rico, who led the International League in hitting for 1953 with a .349 average. Power was considered too flamboyant for the Yankee organization. He would not back down from racial confrontations, was rumored to date white women, and loved to snag the ball one-handed as a first baseman. Lee MacPhail, who served as the Yankee farm director in 1953, denied in an interview with baseball historian Jules Tygiel that the club was racist in its treatment of Power, concluding, "I will agree that the Yankees may have perhaps dragged their feet a little bit. But I can't say there was any racial bias there at all. The Yankees were very anxious that the first black player that they brought up would be somebody with the right type of character whom they felt was ideal. Elston was the ideal."[18]

The belief that the first black Yankee could not constitute a threat to the more con-servative values of white middle-class Yankee fans was seconded by the team's head scout Paul Krichell who declared, "The Yankees have been criticized by racial agitators as anti–Negro because they got rid of several Negro players. The fact is any player turned loose by the Yankees was released because he didn't measure up to requirements, and that has nothing to do with color, creed, or race. Both as a man and a ball player, this boy Howard looks every inch a Yankee."[19] Of course, the boy referenced by Krichell was a 24-year-old man.

*New York World-Telegram* sportswriter Dan Daniel asserted that Howard was with the Yankees not only because he was an outstanding player, but also because "he was quiet, well-behaved, a fine asset to the off-the-field tone of the club." The reporter con-cluded his piece by observing, "The Yankees would like to find another Negro player. But they insist that he be of the Howard stamp, and this is not going to be easy. In fact, at the moment, it's impossible." Essentially, Daniel was suggesting that blacks might be capable athletes, but failed the test of character required to don the Yankee uniform.[20]

Howard would not respond to such comments, concentrating upon becoming a bet-ter player. He suffered, nevertheless, numerous indignities from Yankee management. The team's traveling secretary Bill McCorry expressed concern regarding accommoda-tions for Howard while the club was on the road. The Yankees finally insisted that Howard be housed in the same hotel as the other players, but because he was the only black player on the team, Howard was not initially assigned a roommate—although he eventually roomed with white first baseman Bill Skowron.

More disturbing were the racial attitudes of Yankee manager Casey Stengel, who sometimes called his only black player "eight ball," a reference to the black numbered ball in the game of pool. Stengel also reportedly used the N-word in complaining about Howard's lack of speed, "I got the only one who can't run."[21] Howard, however, never publicly registered any complaints, and Howard's widow, Arlene, insists that her husband did not perceive Stengel as a racist. According to Arlene, the manager was over 60 and simply the product of America's prejudiced past.[22]

Howard's attitude and work ethic made him a favorite among his teammates. And when a somewhat darker side of Mickey Mantle was revealed in former Yankee Jim Bou-ton's best-selling *Ball Four* (1970), Howard emerged as one of Mantle's most vocal defend-ers while castigating Bouton as an ingrate. A right-handed pitching prospect, Bouton joined the Yankees in 1962, and won 21 games while compiling a 2.53 earned run average in 1963. After another solid year in 1964, Bouton, who threw so hard that he knocked off his hat with many of his overhand deliveries, suffered a sore arm in 1965 with a won-loss mark of 4–15. After going 3–8 in 1966, Bouton spent part of 1967 with the AAA Syra-cuse Chiefs in the International League. He learned to throw a knuckleball in the Pacific Coast League with the Seattle Angels in 1968. During the 1969 season, Bouton appeared in 81 games with the expansion Seattle Pilots and the Houston Astros; his baseball memoir *Ball Four* was published the following spring. Bouton was an iconoclast who represented the growing anti-establishment mood in America by exposing the hypocrisy, anti-intellectualism, sexism, racism, drug use, and drinking that was part of baseball as well as the American experience.[23]

The baseball establishment denounced Bouton for violating the sanctity of the locker room and undermining public faith in one of the nation's cherished institutions during a troubled time in American history. Baseball Commissioner Bowie Kuhn summoned

Bouton to his New York City offices, but took no actions when the pitcher showed up with players' union head Marvin Miller. In his memoir *Hardball*, Kuhn later maintained that he confronted Bouton because he simply failed to believe the stories put forth in the book. But in hindsight the commissioner regretted providing Bouton with the publicity to sell more books.[24]

Many traditional baseball writers were even more caustic in depictions of Bouton and his book. Wells Twombly dismissed *Ball Four* as "an impudent betrayal of trust, good old rotten Hollywood-style keyhole reporting," while Joe Falls accused Bouton of revealing privileged information, and Dick Young concluded that the former player was now a social leper.[25]

Joining a chorus of critical players who appeared rather threatened by Bouton's journalism, Elston Howard expressed anger with his former teammate, asserting that Bouton was "a very self-centered and selfish man" who sought revenge against the Yankees for trading him after the right-hander became a losing pitcher. Though Bouton chronicled the truth, Howard portrayed him as a loser who was selling out his former teammates for 30 pieces of silver. Despite being traded to the Red Sox in 1967 at the end of his career, Howard remained loyal to the Yankees. He returned to the club as first base coach and entertained high hopes of becoming manager of the Yankees. But the call to manage the team never came, and Arlene Howard, although she never reconciled with Bouton, held the Yankees responsible for the death of her husband with a heart attack at 51. Writing of her husband's premature death, she asserted, "It was hard thinking about the years he sacrificed himself for the New York Yankees, he could have played for another team and been a star. Maybe if he had put up with the racism, maybe if they had made him the manager, he would still be alive today. Don't get me wrong. I consider myself blessed, we had great times together. Still, one thought has become increasingly clear to me. Baseball killed my husband."[26]

As with Howard, most of Bouton's critics seemed particularly perturbed by how Yankee and cultural icon Mickey Mantle was depicted in *Ball Four*. By contemporary standards, Bouton's description is hardly shocking. Mantle was a womanizer who drank heavily and loved practical jokes. But Bouton confessed to having "mixed feelings" about Mantle, writing, "On the one hand I really liked his sense of humor and boyishness, the way he'd spend all that time in the clubhouse making up involved games of chance and the pools he got up in golf matches and the Derby and things like that." Yet, Bouton was disappointed that Mantle sometimes shunned young boys wanting his autograph and made reporters "crawl and beg for a minute of his time." He admired Mantle's courage in coping with painful injuries, yet speculated whether "he might have healed quicker if he'd been sleeping more and loosening up with the boys at the bar less."[27]

Before his death, a sober Mantle acknowledged many of these criticisms and even reconciled with Bouton, although he always claimed he never read *Ball Four*. But when Bouton honestly described his former teammate in 1970, it was considered an attack upon an American hero during a divisive period when the post–World War II consensus was under assault in the streets and college campuses, while an unpopular war surged in Southeast Asia. To many Americans, Mickey Mantle, who emerged from the small town of Commerce, Oklahoma, to find success in New York City despite having to battle severe injuries, symbolized the American dream as economic prospects expanded for many citizens during the 1950s. Mantle's biographer Jane Leavy writes, "With his aura of limitless potential, Mantle was America incarnate. His raw talent, the unprecedented alloy of speed and power, spoke directly to our postwar optimism. His father mined Oklahoma depths for lead and zinc that supported the country's infrastructure and spurred its industrial growth. Mutt's boy had honest muscles. His ham-hock forearms were wrought by actual work, not weight machines and steroid injections.

"He was proof of America's promise: anyone could grow up to be president or Mickey Mantle—*even* Mickey Mantle."[28]

Mantle got a liver transplant in June 1995, but it was not enough to save him. After his death on August 13, 1995, sportswriters praised the slugger whose faults had been revealed, most pointedly by him, in the few years preceding his death. Journalist Paul White wrote, "He simply was the best ball player on the best team in a sport then still unchallenged by football and basketball for popularity. He was at the center of baseball's Camelot, a made-for-TV player as the Yankees dominated a decade of World Series."[29]

Seeking to explain why so many middle-aged males openly wept when they learned of Mantle's passing, baseball analyst and commentator Bob Costas observed, "To me there was something noble about him. I am aware of his weaknesses as a person, but I think as a player he had a noble quality, fighting through injuries, effecting grace and dignity on the field that he might not have had off it."[30]

Mantle as a symbol of America's promise was also evident in the letters he received from common Americans during his last days. For example, one man confessed, "Your illness has caused me to reflect on my life, especially my youth, of which you were such an integral part. Your illness saddens me and causes me to do something I've never done before, write a fan letter. For better or worse, you are an American Hero. A larger than life icon to whom I can point to my sons and say you can be anything you want to be…. You will always be my hero, my idol."[31]

The context of the 1950s cannot be ignored in discussing Mantle's impact on the culture. Halberstam maintained, "It was a good time to be young and get on with family and career: Prices and inflation remained relatively low; and nearly everyone with a decent job could afford to own a home. Even if the specter of Communism lurked on the horizon—particularly as both superpowers developed nuclear weapons—Americans trusted their leaders to tell them the truth, to make sound decisions, and to keep them out of war."[32]

Mantle seemed to reflect these confident values—at least for white Americans—and authored, with the assistance of journalist Phil Pepe, a memoir of his 1956 season when he was selected as the American League's Most Valuable Player after winning baseball's Triple Crown—batting .353 with 52 home runs and 130 runs batted in. Recalling his favorite summer, Mantle proclaimed, "It was a time of prosperity, a time of the baby boom and the exodus to suburbia. It was 1956. America liked Ike, but it loved Lucy. Huntley and Brinkley teamed up and Martin and Lewis broke up. We the people wondered where the yellow went and wrestled with the burning question 'Does she or doesn't she?'"[33]

In the 1950s and early 1960s, therefore, Yankee pinstripes and Mantle symbolized the promise of American life, but by the late 1960s cracks in this portrait of consumerism and prosperity were evident as the nation was plagued by political assassinations, campus unrest, racial conflict, poverty, and the Vietnam War. Many Americans were losing faith in their leaders and institutions. For baseball, this was apparent in the changing fortunes and perception regarding the Yankee franchise. Peter Golenbock observes, "In many minds the powerful Yankees were seen to be the embodiment of the Establishment—a fantastically successful corporation with everyone from the owners down to the batboys working together for the good of the firm. If you weren't willing to submerge your individuality and conform to the aristocratic Yankee mold, unless you had the talent of a Mickey Mantle, you were not welcome into the Yankee family."[34]

Yankee management wanted their players to be undemonstrative and conservative as Casey Stengel employed a platoon system in which the players were inserted as interchangeable parts of the Yankee machine. It is within the context of this anti-establishment or countercultural critique of the Yankees and other traditional institutions that Jim Bouton published *Ball Four*.

While many in professional baseball were alarmed by Bouton's revelations, the book's honest look at professional baseball launched it to the best-seller list. Its iconic status today is recognized by the New York Public Library's selection as one of the 100 most important books of the 20th century.

Bouton was an anti-establishment figure and made clear his opposition to the Vietnam War and support for campus protesters. He denounced racism, sexism, and anti-intellectualism both inside and outside of professional baseball. With all of the problems plaguing America in the 1960s, he could not comprehend how some people became obsessed with such issues as long hair for boys and men. Bouton's critique resonated well with many Americans who were beginning to question traditional values and institutions. For example, George G. Hill of *Christian Century* urged readers to examine Bouton's book as it constituted "a positive contribution to the needed moral reordering of America."[35] Other reviewers echoed the sentiments expressed by Hill. Writing for the *New York Times Book Review*, Rex Lardner acknowledged that for some traditionalists, *Ball Four* was an act of blasphemy, but he concluded, "In an era of sophisticated reappraisal, it is a gem of honest good-naturedly biased reporting."[36] David Halberstam perhaps best placed *Ball Four* within historical and cultural perspective when he observed that both Bouton and his critics agreed that baseball was "the great American game, a reflection of what we are and who we are."[37]

But rather than the virtues found by many establishment sportswriters, Bouton depicted baseball as a manifestation of American culture and institutions "more often than not run by selfish, stupid owners, men who deal with their ballplayers in a somewhat sophisticated form of slavery, that despite the reputation of a melting pot, baseball dugouts reek of the same social and racial tensions and divisions that scar the rest of the country, that the underlying social common denominator is fairly crude and reminiscent of nothing so much as one's high-school locker team."[38] Just as their handling of Elston Howard and reluctance to recruit black ball players indicated that the Yankees were out of step with changing times, Jim Bouton's *Ball Four* presented the majestic Yankees and the iconic Mantle as representations of an America based on illusions while the realities of American life were far more complex.

Another challenge confronting the CBS-controlled Yankees was the rise of the upstart New York Mets, who seemed to better depict the anti-establishment times as they surpassed the Yankee franchise in attendance and emerged in 1969 as the world champions of baseball. The Mets were established in 1962 to replace the Brooklyn Dodgers and New York Giants who departed for the West Coast following the 1957 season. Tapping many former Dodgers and Giants in the expansion draft, the Mets were a disaster in their inaugural campaign, winning only 40 games.

They also attempted to entice disgruntled Yankee fans by hiring George Weiss and

Casey Stengel, who were fired following the Yankee loss to the Pittsburgh Pirates in the 1960 World Series. And despite their losing ways, the Mets attracted nearly 1,000,000 fans in 1962 to the Polo Grounds, the former home of the Giants. Two years later the Mets moved into their new home—Shea Stadium in Queens. Shea was located along a Queens subway route, but the stadium also included ample parking spaces. In his history of the Mets, Peter Golenbock observes, "The team was located in a borough of New York City, but George Weiss knew his target audience were the men and women who had fled the inner city for Long Island suburbs to escape the hoard of immigrants and blacks flocking to take their place." The Yankee franchise also angered many fans by firing Yogi Berra after the club lost the 1964 World Series.

A disgruntled Berra joined the Mets as a coach and managed the team from 1972 to 1975. Golenbock concludes that by 1964, "the hapless Mets had become an institution. In their first year at Shea, 1,732,000 fans flocked to Queens to watch them. And in ballparks across America one could hear the chant of 'Let's Go Mets.'"[39]

Although the Mets were consistently outdrawing the Yankees by the mid–1960s, they continued to flounder on the baseball diamond, finishing the 1968 season twenty-four games behind the Cardinals. However, the baseball world was shocked in 1969 by the ascendancy of the Mets—the team won the National League pennant in the first season of divisional play and then defeated the heavily favored Baltimore Orioles in the World Series.

While the 1969 Yankees drew slightly over one million fans, the Mets attracted over two million to Shea Stadium; it was the first of four consecutive seasons in which atten-

Yogi Berra was fired as the Yankees manager after the World Series loss to the St. Louis Cardinals in 1964. He got another shot at the helm in the mid–1980s, but Yankees owner Steinbrenner fired Berra 16 games into the 1985 season. The Yogi Berra Museum and Learning Center (pictured above) opened at Montclair State University in 1998. It was the site of reconciliation the following year (courtesy Yogi Berra Museum and Learning Center).

dance exceeded the two million mark. The so-called Miracle Mets with their young players sporting sideburns and long hair inspired many traditionalists, including the *Sporting News*, began to take a second look at their opposition to the youth culture. The paper editorialized that young teams such as the Mets were "perhaps catching the spirit of a youth rebellion sweeping the world. If so, the sports version seems highly preferable to the forms of revolt available elsewhere, including college campuses. The Mets not only epitomize the revolution occurring on the field, they are pacesetters in wardrobe and hair styles as well. No wonder they are the darlings of the mod set."[40]

While the Mets attracted their share of younger fans, the dynasty of the Oakland A's in the 1970s best mirrored the anti-establishment and countercultural values of the era.[41] The 1972 World Series showcased the mustachioed, and long-haired A's, champions of the countercultural crowd, against manager Sparky Anderson's well-disciplined and groomed Big Red Machine from Cincinnati in an exciting series won by the A's in seven games. Many fans and critics perceived the World Series as symbolic of the cultural clashes taking place in American society. In his history of the Cincinnati franchise, Robert Harris Walker asserts that the Reds saw themselves as projecting a conservative working-class image, reflective of the dominant values in their host city. Journalist J. Anthony Lukas observed, "The Reds, with their neat red-and-white uniforms, the short hair, and clean shaves are sound, solid, and stable, full of the substantial virtues that the flacks in the commissioner's office love to associate with our national pastime, while the A's, in their flowing hair and bristling mustaches are bizarre and flamboyant." But Lukas wondered whether the A's "hip" image was only hair deep.[42]

The reign of the Oakland A's changed baseball—three consecutive World Series titles between 1972–1974—and set the stage for an environment in which players could more openly challenge management, paving the way for free agency and restructuring of the sport. The New York Yankees under the leadership of George Steinbrenner took advantage of these changes to restore the dominant role played by the franchise, beginning with a dip into free agency to sign Catfish Hunter and Reggie Jackson.

In 1976, the Yankees made it back to the World Series for the first time since 1964. They faced the Reds and got swept in four games. When Jackson signed a five-year deal beginning in 1977, the team notched two World Series titles against the Los Angeles Dodgers. They were underperformers with CBS ownership during the late 1960s and early 1970s, but their image trailed the anti-establishment and counterculture movement where established institutions were interrogated and challenged. Like many other traditional institutions, the Yankees survived the onslaught before reassuming a privileged status.

## NOTES

1. Marty Appel, *Pinstripe Empire: The New York Yankees from Before the Babe to After the Boss* (New York: Bloomsbury, 2012), 353–354.

2. Ralph Ray, "Bomber Sale Stirs Bees' Nest of Boos: Yankees Seek A.L. Meeting to Clear Air," *Sporting News*, August 29, 1964: 1. The Colt .45s and the New York Mets began with the National League expansion in 1962. Hofheinz had the title of Chairman of the Executive Committee when the Colt .45s formed. He was also an owner with R.E. "Bob" Smith, Craig Cullinan, George Kirksey, K.S. "Bud" Adams, John Beck, A.J. Farfel, Earl Allen, J.S. Cullinan, Harding S. Frankel, Jack Josey, and Leonard Rauch. By 1966, Hofheinz had accumulated 88 percent of the Houston Sports Association, which owned the Astros and the Astrodome. Mike Acosta, Manager, Authentication, Houston Astros, email message to editor, August 23, 2018.

3. Carl Lundquist, "Paley Sees Baseball Gaining 'Long-Range Benefits' from CBS," *Sporting News*, September 5, 1964: 4.

4. "Yankee Sale Demands League Discussion," *Sporting News*, September 5, 1964: 14.

5. "A.L. Affirms Yankee Sale: Government Inquiry Likely," *Sporting News*, September 19, 1964: 9.

6. C.C. Johnson Spink, "Finley, Allyn Carry Fight Against Yank Sale to Justice Dept.," *Sporting News*, October 10, 1964: 6.

7. "Alarming Trend to Corporate Ownership," *Sporting News*, October 24, 1964: 14.

8. "Crying Need for Strong Leadership," *Sporting News*, November 7, 1964: 14.

9. Dave Brady, "Senate Hearing Airs Support for CBS," *Sporting News*, March 6, 1965: 4.

10. For an overview of the Yankees-CBS days, see Appel, 347–383.

11. John McQuiston, "Michael Burke, Ex-Executive with the Yankees, Dies at 70," *New York Times*, February 7, 1987; and Appel, 384–387.

12. "Progressive Action at Winter Meetings," *Sporting News*, December 19, 1964: 14.

13. Bob Oates, "Free Agent Draft—Death of Salesman," *Sporting News*, January 30, 1965: 2. (*Sporting News* cites *Los Angeles Herald Examiner* as original publisher of the article).

14. David Halberstam, *October 1964* (New York: Villard Books, 1994), 54.

15. *Ibid.*

16. *Ibid.*, 85.

17. Leo Krantz, *Yankee Stadium, a Tribute: 85 Years of Memories, 1923–2008* (New York: It Books, 2008), 153.

18. Jules Tygiel, *Baseball's Great Experiment: Jackie Robinson and His Legacy* (New York: Oxford University Press, 1983), 298.

19. Paul Krichell, quoted in Peter Golenbock, *Dynasty: The New York Yankees, 1949–1964* (New York: Prentice Hall, 1975), 141.

20. Dan Daniel, "Ol' Professor Pegs Howard for Bigger Billing as Bomber," *Sporting News*, February 1, 1956: 19.

21. Robert W. Creamer, *Stengel: His Life and Times* (New York: Simon & Schuster, 1984), 282.

22. Arlene Howard with Ralph Wimbish, *Elston and Me: The Story of the First Black Yankee* (Columbia: University of Missouri Press, 2001), 40–41.

23. For background information on Jim Bouton, see Mark Armour, "Jim Bouton," The Baseball Biography Project, Society for American Baseball Research, www.sabr.org. (Last accessed July 5, 2016); Leonard Shecter, "Jim Bouton—Everything in Its Place," *Sport* (March 1964), 71–73.

24. Jim Bouton with Leonard Shecter, *I'm Glad You Didn't Take It Personally* (New York: William Morrow & Company, 1971), 68–79; Lowell Reidenbaugh, "Author Bouton Hits Jackpot—With Bowie's Assist," *Sporting News*, August 8, 1970, 7; and Bowie Kuhn, *Hardball: The Education of a Baseball Commissioner* (New York: Times Books, 1989), 72–73.

25. Wells Twombly, "Beware of Snoopy Colleagues," *Sporting News*, June 20, 1970, 20; Joe Falls, "A Blast at Bouton's Brand of Realism," *Sporting News*, June 20, 1970, 34; and Dick Young, "Young Ideas," *Sporting News*, June 20, 1970, 16.

26. Joseph Durso, "Elston Howard Replies," *New York Times*, July 16, 1970, 25; Howard with Wimbish, *Elston and Me*, 195.

27. Jim Bouton with Leonard Shecter, *Ball Four: Twentieth Anniversary Edition* (with a new Epilogue by the author) (New York: Wiley Publishing, 1970; Wiley Publishing, 1970), 29–31. Citations refer to the Twentieth Anniversary edition.

28. Jane Leavy, preface to *The Last Boy: Mickey Mantle and the End of American Childhood* (New York: HarperCollins, 2010), xv.

29. Paul White, "Mickey Mantle, 1931–1995," *Baseball Weekly*, August 15, 1995.

30. Bob Costas, "He Graced Our Youth with Subtle Dignity," *Sporting News*, August 21, 1995, 10.

31. Michael P. Terrizzi, in "Friends & Fans of Mickey Mantle," *Letters to Mickey* (HarperCollins, 1995), 70–71.

32. David Halberstam, preface to *The Fifties* (New York: Villard Books, 1993), x.

33. Mickey Mantle with Phil Pepe, introduction to *My Favorite Summer, 1956* (New York: Dell Publishing, 1991), ix. The tag line "Does she … or doesn't she" was a popular slogan for Clairol. It underscored the claim that the company's hair dye products would be so effective that nobody could tell if the hair color was natural or a dye job.

34. Golenbock, ix.

35. George G. Hill, "Down in the Dugout," *Christian Century*, September 23, 1970, 1126.

36. Rex Lardner, "The Oddball with a Knuckleball," *New York Times Book Review*, July 26, 1970: 8.

37. David Halberstam, "Baseball and the National Mythology," *Harper's Magazine*, Volume 241, September 1970, 22–25.

38. *Ibid.*

39. Peter Golenbock, *Amazin': The Miraculous History of New York's Beloved Baseball Team* (New York: St. Martin's Press, 2002), 154–155.

40. "Kids Are Sassing Their Parents," *Sporting News*, September 20, 1969, 20.

41. For information on the Oakland A's in the 1970s, see Ron Briley, "The Oakland A's of 1972–1975 and the Counterculture in Baseball: Undermining the Hegemony of the Baseball Establishment," *Nine: A Journal*

*of Baseball History and Social Policy Perspectives*, Volume 1, No. 2, 1993, 142–162; Herbert Michelson, *Charlie O: Charles Oscar Finley Vs. the Baseball Establishment* (New York: Bobbs-Merrill, 1975); Billy Libby, *Charlie O. and the Angry A's* (New York: Doubleday, 1975); Tom Clark, *Champagne and Baloney: The Rise and Fall of Finley's A's* (New York: Harper and Row, 1976); and Jason Turbow, *Dynastic, Bombastic, Fantastic: Reggie, Rollie, Catfish, and Charlie Finley's Swingin' A's* (New York: Houghton Mifflin Harcourt, 2017).

    42.  Robert Harris "Hub" Walker, *Cincinnati and the Big Red Machine* (Bloomington: Indiana University Press, 1988), 53–54; and J. Anthony Lukas, "Way to Go, Jonathan Seagull," *Saturday Review*, November 11, 1972, 35.

# The Yankee Brand

## Part 1:
## The Brand of Champions

### RON COLEMAN

It is no surprise that the organization that introduced the concept of championship dynasties to professional sports was also a pioneer—beyond the world of sports—in the projection, monetization and management of an institutional sports brand. Powered by the first personal sports superstar, Babe Ruth, the Yankees changed the game when they responded to being booted out of the Polo Grounds by the New York Giants by not only building an unprecedented palace to baseball just across the Harlem River, but naming it after the team itself. This was arguably the first act in the Yankees' development of an entirely new conception of brand power in sports.

Ensconced in the nation's commercial capital, New York City, the Yankees' sophistication and innovation in brand building, trademark protection, and exploitation paralleled the increasing nationalization and media-powered projection of brands in American life through the 1920s and '30s. The post–World War II environment of marketing and advertising traditionally associated with New York's globally influential Madison Avenue "ad men" coincided perfectly, and probably not by accident, with the Yankees' utter dominance of the American League and the World Series throughout the late 1940s, the 1950s, and the early 1960s. When wags said that "rooting for the Yankees was like rooting for U.S. Steel," they were enunciating a truth about competitive dominance that extended beyond results "in the field" to the maturing world of American brand building.

## The Yankee Name

The Yankees have registered innumerable trademarks with the United States Patent and Trademark Office, not all of them particularly well-known. These include stylized representations of the famous Yankee Stadium façade, line drawings of the Stadium itself, the name "Yankee Stadium," the Yankees name alone in stylized form and in combination with other words and designs, as well as subsidiary marks based on names and symbols related to the Yankees' storied history, for example, "New York Highlanders." Related enterprises ("Yankees Universe") and phrases associated with the team ("The House That Ruth Built") are other areas protected by trademark registrations.

To have a federally registered trademark gives the owner a wealth of remedies, but not complete protection, against infringers seeking to benefit from unauthorized use and exploitation. Trademark rights in the United States are based on use, not registration, but while a trademark can be protected under the common law without a USPTO registration, the latter is often sought and highly prized.

The most prominent Yankee trademark is, of course, the "Yankee" name. The plain-vanilla word "Yankees" for "Entertainment services, namely, baseball games, competitions and exhibitions" may be one of the most valuable word trademark registrations in sports. The received history tells us that the nickname was first bestowed, though not officially, on the club while it was known primarily as the Highlanders. The team was not officially called the Yankees until 1913, but it was not until 2007 that the team registered the word "Yankees" even though it had registrations for numerous other subsidiary products as well as other marks that included the word in them. Notwithstanding all these registrations, the strength of the Yankee mark—and yes, "Yankee" and "Yankees" are, as a matter of trademark law, identical—is to some extent based on the fact that "Yankee" was, of course, a word in common use as a reference to Americans, and specifically northerners, before it was the name of a baseball team.

Because the Yankees baseball club is named, however inaptly, after the same group immortalized by works such as Mark Twain's *A Connecticut Yankee in King Arthur's Court*, derided by Confederate troops during the Civil War, and immortalized in a bit of British doggerel known as "Yankee Doodle" even before the country gained its independence, the baseball Yankees can't "monopolize" the word. "Yankees" are still people from New England or, from an overseas perspective, Americans. As a result, there are a host of "Yankee" registrations for things having nothing to with baseball. Even more strange, there are now-defunct Yankees trademarks for now-defunct sports teams having no affiliation with the New York Yankees of baseball. Under current trademark and branding doctrines, this would be unthinkable, but because the Yankees brand is so old, it has seen it all.

For example, the New York Yankees were a professional football team in the All-America Football Conference and, later, the early National Football League in the 1920s. They even played at Yankee Stadium, thus implying tacit permission for their use of the name, but were not formally connected with or licensed by the baseball team. There were also the New York Black Yankees, a professional team in the pre–Jackie Robinson Negro National League, which played in various locations in and around New York, including Yankee Stadium, from 1936 to 1948. They also used the name, by all indications, with the tacit acquiescence of the New York Yankees of the American League, but without any affiliation or formal permission.

In the days before "brand equity," such "sharing" of trademarks was understood as a form of homage that benefited the dominant brand by virtue of the tribute paid to it. This concept has not died entirely. Even today, Little League baseball teams are permitted, through an informal arrangement, to use the names of Major League Baseball teams, including the Yankees. But Little League management strongly urges that teams only use uniform items "authorized and licensed by Major League Baseball." As a matter of trademark law, this advice would normally be dubious because the risk to the big-league trademarks does not come from the risk of consumer confusion about the source of licensed duds. It comes from the potential for confusion about the connection between the MLB teams and that of the Little Leaguers—or at least it would if everyone in America did not already understand exactly what is going on. It is to MLB's credit that it permits this practice to continue. Associating with big-league teams doubtless creates extra fun and excitement for young players. Just as in the "homage" days of the Black Yankees and the football Yankees, this unorthodox, low-key approach to brand management reflects well on the brand owners.

## The Interlocking "NY"

Because the Yankees name is younger than the team, it should not be surprising that the oldest trademark now associated with the Yankees goes back further than 1913. The famous interlocking "NY" emblem traces its origins to 1903, well before the team's brand equity began to build when Babe Ruth joined the team in 1920. That original Yankees' mark is the "N Y" where both letters are separate, not interlocking. The N on the right side of the chest and the Y on the left was nothing more than a depiction of the well-known abbreviation for New York, of course. As essentially a geographical description of the team's home city, this configuration of letters and space was probably not really a trademark—at least at the time.

On the other hand, this pioneering configuration of Yankee branding was emblazoned on the Highlanders' jerseys long before anyone ever dreamed of protecting team insignia through trademark registration anyway. When, in 1992, the Yankees finally applied to register the "N Y" with the USPTO in 1992, it had been generations since the Yankees stopped using it on the field. Presumably, they wanted the right to maintain control of the design for sale on licensed "vintage" reproductions or novelty merchandise. The team had to convince the Trademark Office examiners that the configuration had achieved trademark status, or "acquired distinctiveness," by virtue of long use, notwithstanding that it did not seem to have gotten much use at all since the Roaring Twenties. After a period of back-and-forth between the team and the USPTO, the registration issued in 1995.

But the "N Y" trademark, such as it is today, is little more than an historical curiosity, a transitional stage on the way to the famous interlocking "NY," best known for appearing on Yankee baseball caps. According to histories of the "NY" logo published by Richard Morgan of the *New York Times* and the official Yankees.com website, after a brief flirtation with interlocking, N and Y stayed separate until, in 1922, by which time the team had been known primarily as the Yankees for nearly 10 years, the two letters merged permanently.

The inspiration for the design was a feature in a Medal of Valor designed for the New York Police Department by Tiffany & Co. all the way back in 1877. Unlike the "N Y" insignia, the Yankees' adaptation of the Tiffany interlocking "NY" was not used on uniform jerseys until 1936, appearing only on the Yankees' uniform caps. The Yankees adapted the approach of the medal by stretching out what looks like a rather cramped "Y" in a distinctively obtuse fashion, room for which was made by also horizontally elongating the "N" and bending its arms so that the letter almost looks like a "backslash" character connected by two inverted parentheses.

This version, described by the Yankees in USPTO filings as first coming into use in 1910, was registered as a trademark by the team in 1977.

The original interlocking "NY" eventually metamorphosed into three different variations, each of which is registered as a trademark by the Yankees with respect to different products and services. First, the 1910 version became, in somewhat refined form, what is known as the "print insignia," and is used by the Yankees and the league in printed and online displays. Because of the close and easy manner in which these mediums are encountered, the print logo can fairly be considered the essential, "pure" version of the Yankees logo.

In contrast, the jersey logo, which has been embroidered on the upper left side, or "heart," of Yankee pinstripe home uniforms since 1936, provides better scanning from a distance. To achieve this, the stretching process that was applied to the old Tiffany medal, which first made room for a robust letter "Y" to fit between the goalposts of the letter "N," was extended that much further. This allowed more white space between the upper sections of the "Y," whose diagonal arms are not only splayed far apart but assume a slightly concave form. At the same time, the members of each letter—which, in the print logo, almost resolve into serifs on the "N" and actually do form serifs on the "Y"—merely taper gently instead of flaring out at their tips. The result is an "NY" design that looks superficially identical to the Yankee original but where, in fact, the letters are more clear and distinct when encountered from afar and superimposed on dark pinstripes, which would obscure the less linear presentation of the "pure" version.

Version three, the cap logo, takes the slimming-down process further. The tapering of the letters is far less noticeable. At the same time, the yawning gap in the arms of the "Y" in the jersey logo is gone; the members are as straight as their counterparts in the print logo, though less tapered. This adaptation, for a logo embroidered in white thread on the dark navy cap of the Yankee uniform, makes for even easier scanning. The somewhat more constricted "Y" shape, and the consequently less distorted sides of the "N," are presumably concessions to an overall narrower presentation on the cap. The modest amount of real estate occupied by the logo on the Yankee cap is consistent with the famously low-key uniform style of the Yankees, which in turn reflects the at once confident and conservative design sensibility that carries across the Yankee brand. Although each of these versions is registered separately, all three can safely be considered the "same" as a matter of trademark law because, notwithstanding the fine details observed here, the differences are legally trivial.

## The Top Hat Logo

It would be decades after the establishment of the Yankees name and the interlocking "NY" as valuable trademarks before the third of the major Yankee brand identifiers, the "Top Hat" emblem, came on to the scene. The Top Hat logo was, in many ways, emblematic—no pun intended—of the way that business, commerce, and sports were changing in the post–World War II environment. U.S. Steel, for example, reached an all-time production peak of 35 million tons in 1953, a decade after its payroll had swollen to over 340,000 employees. The company was so central to U.S. prosperity that the year before, in 1952, President Harry Truman attempted to essentially nationalize the steel mills to resolve a steel union strike, an effort blocked by the U.S. Supreme Court.

New York and its Yankees were also on a postwar roll. The city, now home to the "capital of the world," the United Nations, peaked in 20th-century population in 1950 and experienced an unprecedented construction boom. It became a global center of the arts and finance, all the while benefiting from its key role as central transit and shipping hub for the Western hemisphere. Night baseball came to Yankee Stadium in 1945, and under the co-ownership and management of Lee MacPhail, the Joe DiMaggio–led team began to promote attendance and affiliation in new ways: season tickets, new "luxury" box seats, the first-ever Stadium Club, a pioneering team newsletter, and other innovative promotional strategies.

MacPhail believed a corporate logo, separate and apart from insignia used on uniforms, was also called for, and commissioned designer Henry Alonzo Keller to make one. Incorporating the colors of the American flag, a baseball, a bat, a distinctive Yankee "script" that would later achieve its own trademark status, and an Uncle Sam top hat, the new logo was a home run, becoming what the *New York Times* would call, over half a century later, "perhaps the most famous logo in sports." It was even adapted for use by the football Yankees, which placed the logo inside a football rather than a circle. Like the other Yankee trademarks, registration of the Top Hat mark took place decades after it was first use, but the Yankees have made up for lost time, registering it in numerous trademark classes (categories) to cover a host of goods and services.

So say the Yankees. The official account of the logo's design was challenged in a 2011 lawsuit by the heirs of Tanit Buday, a Yonkers woman who claimed to have succeeded to the "common-law copyright" held by the logo's real designer, her uncle Kenneth Timur, who was deceased. The claim was dismissed on multiple grounds, not least the extreme passage of time as well as its utter implausibility and many legal deficiencies. But the publicity surrounding the dispute also brought to light the claim of family members of the late Sam Friedman. They asserted in a 2013 interview with the *New York Times* that Friedman drew the logo on a bar napkin at the famous 21 Club while tippling with Yankees co-owner Dan Topping. Corroborating the narrative, family members insisted that the "Yankees script" was readily recognizable by those who knew him as "Uncle Sam [Friedman]'s handwriting."[1]

The Friedman claim also had no legs, due to the passage of time, the lack of documentation, and the implausibility of the most famous sports team in America relying on such happenstance. The family's belief that success in the litigation would lead to a huge payday, moreover, was also based on an incorrect understanding of how logo designers are compensated. Even if their family legend could have been proven, a logo designer does not have any trademark rights in his design. Those belong to the provider of goods or services that the mark comes to be associated with. Alternatively, while royalties may be available if the designer secures copyright in the logo—which requires prompt registration of the copyright—businesses virtually never license a logo but buy it outright. They certainly do not agree to compensate a designer on a per-use basis, which would make their brand a hostage to a designer. No client seeking a logo would agree to such an arrangement, and certainly no client as sophisticated as the New York Yankees.

## After the Dynasty Years

As Mickey Mantle's knees failed him and the Yankees' ability to dominate the American League by pure economic power weakened, the Yankees / U.S. Steel analogy became a little too close for comfort in terms of both the Yankees on-field success and their brand image. Where Truman failed, John F. Kennedy succeeded, trimming the wings of U.S. Steel by pressuring it into reversing price increases. The company's and the country's share of industrial production began to shrink as developing economies abroad progressed and competed. The decline in industrial demand affected industrial cities such as New York, which had, beginning in the late 1950s, begun to feel the effects of labor costs on its increasingly uncompetitive shipping terminals, the loss of factory jobs, and the flight of middle-class residents to the suburbs. The city's fortunes plummeted when it was cast into darkness during a 1965 blackout and hit by a series of devastating municipal-worker strikes at the end of that decade. New York faced the prospect of bankruptcy by the mid–1970s.

Just as American industry began to feel the pressure from foreign competition, excessive costs, and lackadaisical attention to quality, the Yankees' success, and its brand, suffered too. The mid–1960s and early 1970s were as harsh on the Yankee brand as they were on the image of the country that the team was named for and the city in which it played. Competition from the once-barren West Coast, baseball expansion, and a dearth of superstars (who were personal brands themselves) resulted in serious hurt to the Yankees brand through the mid–1970s. That the Ruth-Gehrig-DiMaggio-Mantle tradition of excellence seemed to have come to an end during a period of ownership by CBS, one of the media giants responsible for forming the modern marketing and branding world, is a decided irony.

CBS's 1973 sale of the Yankees for $10 million to a group led by George Steinbrenner, however, saved the day. Grabbing the opportunities presented by free agency in the mid–1970s, Steinbrenner revisited the way to build a baseball team much in the way modern brand equity and merchandising would soon leverage the financial value of sports success into revenue as never before. Fueled in part by important legislative change in trademark law that made merchandising trademarks immensely more profitable, by the mid–1970's the retooled on-field Yankees in their restored, if somewhat diminished, Yankee Stadium came into their own just in time to maximize the economic value of their resumption of success and the comeback of New York City under the leadership of the unforgettable Mayor Ed Koch.

The unleashing of branding and co-branding as an economic engine was a boon for the Yankees, notwithstanding attempts by the Mets to win over hearts and minds from their Flushing, Queens, abode. Celebrities came to World Series games at the Stadium to see and be seen in a way they did not appear when the postseason visited locations such as Oakland, Baltimore and Pittsburgh, adding immeasurably to the team's brand prestige. By the first decade of the 2000s, rapper and entrepreneur Jay-Z could quite accurately boast that he "made the Yankee hat more famous than a Yankee can." By 2010, Jay-Z-branded Yankee gear was being sold in Yankee Stadium; in 2012, his Rocawear line of clothes collaborated on co-branding a line of authorized fashion offerings.

Thus, the trademark registration campaign that the team stepped up in the 1990s and 2000s was just a small measure, and extension, of the way it went about maximizing the value of its brand beginning in the late 1970s. George Steinbrenner recognized the connection between investing in the team's championship and brand equity outcomes by "co-branding" with the likes of Reggie Jackson. As a result, the Yankees again became a gold-plated sports franchise in one of the first northeastern industrial cities to emerge from the decline of U.S. heavy industry by repurposing itself as a center for media and finance.

It would make a great ending to draw a line from the "Reggie" era to the golden years of the Jeter championships in the late 1990s and early 2000s. The team's increasing sophistication in trademark and brand management, exploitation, and protection did follow historical curves in professional sports as well as the team's fortunes on the field and off. And it was stars such as Jeter that, once again, were the key to this success. Individual player brand power—from the Babe who was credited with "building" Yankee Stadium through the other human superstar brands that followed—have been inimical to the Yankee trademark of success.

That curve, however, is not quite so smooth. The late 1980s and early 1990s, as Yankee fans know, were periods when the team seemed committed to a model that became known as "buying championships" by buying stars. The model failed more often than it worked. The raft of often-rash free agent acquisitions that characterized the end of the George Steinbrenner era resulted in an extended period of poor results in the standings and a decided lack of luster for the franchise as a brand.

It was New York's unexpected continued economic dynamism—and the growth of unprecedented revenue from cable television and licensing—that allowed the Yankees to survive that period long enough to recast its team-building strategy. On the shoulders of New York's economic success, and taking every advantage of the brand equity that it had built over the course of a century, the team that CBS sold for $10 million in 1973 is now estimated to be worth $3.2 billion. That makes the Yankees the most valuable sports franchise in the world despite not being, even remotely, the dominant franchise it was during the dynasty years in the 1940s and 1950s. Management of the team's image, brand, and intellectual property were key components of that success, but so were the fortunes of their home city and its increasing dominance as the definitive capital of media and merchandising in the world.

And U.S. Steel? After decades of decline and restructuring, it remains intact, but focuses more on the energy business than steel manufacturing. It was removed from the S&P 500 in 2014 because of its declining market capitalization. Analogies only go so far. For the Yankees and their brand, that is a very good thing.

NOTES

1. Corey Kilgannon, "Counterclaim on Yankees Logo," *New York Times*, October 17, 2009: A16.

# The Yankee Brand

### Part 2:
### That Damn Yankees Cap

### Martin S. Lessner

"I am very glad to see such familiar faces here tonight—Cardinal Cooke, Mayor Koch, and so many other great New Yorkers. This is the only event I've ever attended where the dress was black tie and Yankee baseball caps,"[1] joked First Lady Nancy Reagan at the 1981 Al Smith Dinner.

A baseball cap is to its wearer like a wand is to a wizard in the world of Harry Potter. In that world, a wand is an object through witch (pun intended) a wizard channels and projects his or her magical powers. A wand is manufactured and sold by only a few wand-makers—but each wand chooses its own wizard and can switch allegiance. The Elder Wand, which many seek to own, respects only power. To own the Elder Wand is a statement to the whole magical world, not just a mere declaration of how a Gryffindor alumnus's or alumna's favorite Quidditch team played in the World Cup.

A Yankees cap, manufactured by a limited few under license, rests on the heads of very non-magical people around the world who, in their own way, seek to associate themselves with the perceived power and glory that comes to its most famous wearers.

From its early days, the Yankees cap has been associated with the baseball equivalent of the aggrandizement of power and casting of a curse on its adversaries. Since the year that the Yankees acquired Red Sox malcontent Babe Ruth for $100,000 in cash and a $300,000 secured loan, that damn Yankees cap has been on the heads of a score of World Series champions, while its curse plagued the Red Sox for 84 years.[2] The longest stretch of years without the American League represented in the World Series by that Bronx team wearing the interlocking "NY" baseball hat was 11 years (the same number of years that Harry Potter went without a wand). The Yankee drought started after the Phillies' collapse of 1964 foreclosed an October pinstripe rematch in the City of Brotherly Love; the last Phillies-Yankees World Series happened in 1950. Thus, having cast the curse on the Red Sox, the Yankees cap (like Voldemort's own Avada Kedavra curse), absorbed a deflected beam of the laser-like Phillies curse, ensuring that the Yankees cap did not make it to the October big stage until the nation's Bicentennial, when the Phillies themselves played their first postseason game since the 1950 World Series.

The surface-level reason for the cap's popularity is the association between Yankees and winning. No other team is even close to 27 World Series trophics, 40 American League pennants, and 51 total postseason appearances. Even Joey Chestnut, the greatest competitive food eater ever, has only 11 "Mustard Belt" victories in the Nathan's 4th of July Hot Dog Eating Contest. With the biggest payroll, and the most glamorous star players, from Ruth, Gehrig, and DiMaggio to Mantle, Ford, and Jackson to Jeter, Posada, and Judge, many mere mortals wish to identify with such winning excellence. As the British sports journalist Ryan Ferguson has noted, "The Yankees have the best players, ergo they win, ergo people want to associate with them, ergo ticket and merchandise sales are exponential, ergo the Yankees make money, ergo they can afford the best players, ergo they win some more. Rinse, wash, repeat."[3]

But a comparison of Yankee baseball fortunes to any other city in the nation is an unrequited exercise, an impossible task of comparing sticks of wood wrapped in Thestral tail hair. People wearing an interlocking "NY" on their headgear are not celebrating any on-field achievement, but rather wrapping themselves in the promotion of a particular world view—that New York is the center of power, prestige, fame, and winners. For almost 100 years, the Yankees have been synonymous with what New York City represents—a diversity of people, architecture, arts, theater, music, glamorous celebrities, gangsters, and rags-to-riches successes staying up all night climbing the ladder of their own ambition, ideas, and challenges. Think Yankees cap-wearing Madonna, Spike Lee, and a pre-fall 2018 line of interlocking "NY" Gucci gear by designer Alessandro Michele.[4] When Nelson Mandela came to the USA in 1990 as the new president of post-apartheid South Africa, he did not wear eventual World Series Champion Cincinnati Reds gear—he wore a Yankees cap and jacket. "You now know who I am. I am a Yankee."[5] Nothing against Cincinnati, but as Billy Joel sings about the Yankees and the Reds in his song "Zanzibar," the latter squad just can't compete with the Yankees for drama on and off the field, which is why newspaper headlines are dominated by pinstriped achievements.

The Yankee view of the rest of the world is accurately summed up by the famous Saul Steinberg illustration gracing the cover of the *New Yorker* during the tail-end of spring training in 1976, the season that broke the longest Yankee postseason drought. A Yankee fan looking out from underneath the bill of a Yankees cap sees a civilization extending only to the Hudson River, with the rest of the world merely consisting of some rocks and water.

The hit New York–based TV comedy *Seinfeld* had Yankee themes throughout its nine-year run from 1989 to 1998. The most prominent is George Costanza's front-office job, which allowed several scenes with Yankees owner George Steinbrenner—always seen from behind and voiced by *Seinfeld* co-creator Larry David in a fast-talking voice that lampooned the bombastic shipbuilder from Cleveland known to fans as "the Boss." An episode featuring Kramer's Yankees fantasy camp experience underscores the appeal of the Yankee brand, though it ended in a disaster. Though the audience never sees what actually happened, the explanation is detailed and compelling—a bench-clearing brawl began after Kramer brushed back Joe Pepitone for crowding the plate.[6]

The intersection of the Yankees and hats collides in the episode "The Letter."[7]

Elaine, George, and Kramer have seats in the owner's box behind the dugout at Yankee Stadium courtesy of Jerry's current girlfriend, whose father is the Yankees' accountant. While Yankees caps come in numerous colors and styles, George and one person in each of two rows behind him are wearing identical dark blue caps with the white interlocking "NY." Elaine is wearing a Baltimore Orioles cap for her hometown team. This show of loyalty is too much for the girlfriend's father, who insists Elaine remove the offending non–Yankees cap if she wishes to continue watching the game.

Elaine remains defiant, so he calls security to enforce the Boss's unarticulated will. George and Kramer join her, though reluctantly.

The episode highlights the self-imposed "respect" that must be shown the Yankees cap on its home turf and the deemed sacrilege if a rival cap competes for the loyalty of the crowd at a Yankees baseball game. The Yankee cap is treated (at least in the Bronx) as an icon, similar to the reverence shown other symbols.

It is hardly the only instance of headwear in *Seinfeld*: Elaine puts the Urban Sombrero on the cover of the J. Peterman catalog,[8] George wears a large Russian sable to impress a potential date,[9] and Kramer completes his ensemble of a stereotypical pimp when he finds a large hat on the street.[10]

As a symbol of urban, cultural, and baseball superiority, the Yankees cap generates hostility from those rural folks— anyone outside the five boroughs—who may unfairly be considered the cultural downtrodden, the intellectually inferior,[11]

Mickey Mantle played his entire 18-year career with the Yankees. For 16 consecutive seasons, he made the American League All-Star team. Knee problems plagued the "Commerce Comet" throughout his playing days. By the end of his career, it looked like he could barely make it around the bases after he hit a home run (National Baseball Hall of Fame and Museum, Cooperstown, NY).

and the last guardians of the lost cause. Even diehard Mets fans, though perhaps grimacing at the sight of a Yankees cap, will acknowledge their cross-town rivals' legacy of excellence.

This rural category includes certain southerners, past and present. Maybe this is why NASCAR fans rarely wear a Yankees cap. In her review of George Rable's 2015 book *Damn Yankees!: Demonization and Defiance in the Confederate South*, Dr. Susannah J. Ural of the University of Southern Mississippi highlights Rable's effort to understand the term "Damn Yankees" based on his reading of hundreds of letters, documents, and articles by "politicians, ministers, newspaper editors, farmers and planters, women of different social classes and educational backgrounds, and African Americans."[12] The "Yankees" labels in a post–Confederacy universe meant northerners wanting to trample on southern tradition. It lasted for decades and, on occasion, served as a platform for comedy.

In the episode "Hillbilly Whiz" on the 1950s sitcom *The Phil Silvers Show*, Dick Van Dyke plays Private Hank Lumpkin, a southern-bred pitching phenom. Seeing dollar signs, Silvers's character, Sergeant Ernie Bilko, seeks to represent him to the Yankees for a contract of $125,000. "Yankees" is not a term looked upon with kindness south of the Mason-Dixon Line. When Lumpkin learns this, he refuses to sign out of paternal loyalty and grudges left from the Civil War: "I'm sorry, sergeant, my pappy says General Lee give up too soon." To assuage his prospect, Bilko claims that the Yankees team is comprised of "southern mountain boys" with nicknames: Country Boy Slaughter, Hillbilly Skowron, Mickey Moonshine Mantle. When they go to New York, Bilko has a meeting set up with Yankees co-owner with additions to their monikers: Yankees co-owner Colonel Dan Topping, Colonel Philip Calhoun Rizzuto, Colonel Gilbert Beauregard McDougald, Colonel Whitey Stonewall Ford, and Colonel Yogi Ashley Berra.

Bilko's efforts are for naught. Hank's sweetheart, Lulubelle, uses her womanly charms to persuade the pitcher to return south and marry her instead of play baseball. In the episode's tag, it seems that she had another plan all along—Bilko and his squad watch a Yankees game on television and find Lulubelle joining Red Barber to announce a Yankees broadcast.[13]

Across the baseball world, that damn Yankees cap ignited fury and jealousy when the team signed Jim "Catfish" Hunter, who traded in his green and gold uniform of the Oakland Athletics for pinstripes—the price tag was a reported $3.5 million over five years at the dawn of free agency in the mid–1970s. Catfish was good: he pitched a perfect game in 1968, won three consecutive World Series with Oakland (1972–1974), led the major leagues in wins (25) in 1974, and led the major leagues in winning percentage twice (1972 and 1973). Catfish was so good, it seemed unfair that the Yankees could just open up their wallet and buy his services.[14] Such is the Yankee aura and mystique. Of course, in 1975, his first year in pinstripes, Catfish again led the majors in wins (23).

Somewhere off to the left of that *New Yorker* view is the city of Wilmington, Delaware. The State of Delaware is so small, the joke goes, that it shares its capital with Maryland. Delaware has no national park, no TV network affiliate, and its most popular day-trip tourist attraction (Longwood Gardens) is actually across the border in neighboring Pennsylvania. Route 1 runs from Canada through Times Square down to Key West and through every state that borders the Atlantic Ocean—except Delaware. There is no Delaware / New York equivalence on any measure of popular culture or image.

The only professional baseball team in Delaware is the Wilmington Blue Rocks, a Single A affiliate of the distant Kansas City Royals. The Blue Rocks came to Wilmington in 1993, and held a contest for the design of the logo the new team. Hundreds of entries were submitted, with the most popular being some variant of mining the blue rocks found in the quarries near Wilmington, from which the team name originates. Perhaps succumbing to the pull from that city 100 miles up the Amtrak line, the team chose, coincidentally or not, a baseball hat with a simple interlocking "BR"—hauntingly familiar, if not remarkably similar to that Damn Yankees Cap.

As far as major-league affiliation, Wilmington is in the Phillies fan orbit, only 30 miles from Citizens Bank Park; Delaware further connects to the Phillies because the Carpenter branch of the iconic DuPont family tree owned the team for more than 50 years; and Dallas Green, the Phillies' first World Series winning manager, was born, raised, educated, and played baseball in Delaware. Former Phillies star pitcher Curt Schilling was dismissive of the Yankees' supposed "mystique" and "aura," describing those magical qualities as nothing more than the names of "dancers in a night club. Those are *not* things we concern ourselves with on the ball field." As a topper, before the position was automated, the Phillies organist commuted from Delaware to Connie Mack Stadium, Veterans Stadium, and Citizens Bank Park to play "Take Me Out to the Ball Game" and "Charge" for the Philadelphia fans. Delaware is a red state; Phillies red, that is.

The largest retail sporting goods store in Delaware, Al's, moved to its current down-town Wilmington location a month before the Phillies won the 2008 World Series. Al's carries hundreds of different baseball hats, from every team, every league, and every sport. In the grip of Phillies Phever, which hat was most popular? That Damn Yankees Cap. According to the store manager, Al's sells twice as many Yankees hats as all other hats combined.[15] And not because the purchasers are all baseball fans. They are not.

The Yankee logo on the cap was born of a shooting. In the early morning of January 8, 1877, New York Police Officer John McDowell was walking down Seventh Avenue when he surprised three burglars at work in Courtney's Liquor Store. As the burglars tried to escape with their loot of $120 worth of cigars, one James Farrell attempted to rush past Officer McDowell, who made a baseball-like play on a runner attempting to steal and struck Farrell with his club. Farrell drew a revolver and shot McDowell behind his left ear. The seriously-wounded McDowell wrestled Farrell to the ground, and held on like a bowled-over catcher on a bang-bang play at the plate. Officer McDowell was rescued by his teammates and eventually recovered from his wounds. For his heroics, McDowell was awarded the New York City Police Department Medal of Valor, designed by Tiffany & Company, which had the now famous interlocking "NY." More than 30 years later, in 1909, the Yankees (then known as the "Highlanders"), put the same McDowell Medal interlocking "NY" on their hats, perhaps because one of the club's owners, Big Bill Devery, was a former NYC police chief. McDowell's "NY" Medal was last seen at the New York Police Museum, before the site moved to Governors Island in 2017.

That Damn Yankees cap has been associated with a badass image in our popular culture for those on the wrong side of the law.

Example one: On the 31st anniversary of the Phillies winning their first World Series, the cover of the *New York Post* featured a very dead Moammar Khadafy, shot with his own golden gun by a Yankee cap–wearing Mohamed El Bibi.[16]

Example two: The man who robbed more banks than anyone else in American history, Edwin Chambers Dodson, wore a Yankees cap during most of his 72 California bank robberies, including six on one day in 1983. Perhaps his death in 2003 signaled the end of the curse of the Yankees over the Red Sox a year later.

Example three: In the years between the Yankees' World Series victories of 2000 and 2009, more than 100 suspects charged with serious crimes in New York City wore Yankees apparel at the time of their crime, arrest or arraignment. According to a *New York Times* article on the subject, "No other sports team comes close."[17]

Hip-hop icon Jay-Z has famously worn in public a Yankees cap for years, and boasts about it in his hit song "Empire State of Mind" (while also wearing a Yankees cap in the video). In "Swagga Like Us," Jay-Z exclaims that he's a graduate of the school of hard knocks. While most graduates wear a cap and gown, Jay-Z substitutes the Yankees cap for traditional head garb.

In the southern Jordanian desert lies Petra, the remnants of the ancient capital city of the Nabataean Kingdom. It is the most visited tourist site in the country, by both Jordanians and international travelers. At the government-run gift shop situated on top of the Siq (walking path to Petra down a narrow gorge), visitors rest after their long walk, and can buy drinks, pictures of King Abdullah, and postcards. And Yankees hats. People may hate America in that part of the world, but they seem to like what the Yankees cap stands for, whatever that may be in their minds. As Yankee historian and writer Marty Appel explains the iconic symbol, tourists and locals alike have adopted Yankee merchandise as a NYC uniform, and "given the population of New York, and the success of the Yankees—it has made its way to the caps worn by thousands of tourists on the streets of almost every city in the world."[18]

Walk the streets of Lisbon on a summer day. People from all around Europe and the world flock to the Portuguese capital. And many wear Yankees caps. I interview several, asking only one question: "Excuse me, why are you wearing that Yankees cap?" Some don't speak English, and probably think I am about to assault them. Some don't know what I am even asking. "Who are the Yankees?" Some have the hat as a souvenir from a trip to the USA, or a gift from an American-centric friend. Nobody cites Jay-Z or Jeter. Nobody says that there's a desire to be associated with criminality. Most think it is just a cool symbol of wealth, power, and the American attitude of winning at all costs.

That "winning at all costs" paradigm is just the image some wish to project with a Yankees cap, even if that person is already famous for winning. Tom Brady is a hero in New England for taking the Patriots to the Super Bowl eight times and winning five. But you don't see him wearing a Pats hat. No, Brady has been photographed strolling the streets on Manhattan wearing that interlocking NY on his head, not because he is a fan, certainly not because he is from New York, but, most likely as a fashion statement.

Maybe the true power of Yankees cap lies not in its association with glamour, wealth, or criminality, but in its image as a symbol of excellence. This is the same geographic branding rationale behind "Philadelphia Cream Cheese," "Boston Consulting Group," or any entity using the word "Princeton." In 1935, the Negro National League had a team in Brooklyn for one year. They played in Ebbets Field and called themselves the Brooklyn Eagles. How to attract a crowd and brand the quality of their play? They made their baseball cap with the interlocking "NY." As quoted by the one place on the Internet selling replica Eagles caps: "You might think this is a cap from a certain New York American League ballclub. You would be mistaken."[19]

## NOTES

1. Speechwriting, White House Office of: Speech Drafts: Nancy Reagan: Al Smith Dinner, Oct. 22, 1981, Box 435, Ronald Reagan Library.

2. Andrew Mearns, "The Bambino Bargain: How the Yankees Bought Babe Ruth from the Red Sox 95 Years Ago Today," SB Nation—Pinstripe Alley, December 26, 2014, www.pinstripealley.com/2014/12/26/7416875/yankees-babe-ruth-red-sox-purchase-trade-harry-frazee-no-no-nanette-fenway ("[Red Sox owner Harry Frazee] saw an opportunity in Ruth, who despite his success on the field was already threatening a holdout in order to obtain a pay raise. And so on December 26th Frazee agreed to the terrible deed."), last accessed August 8, 2018.

3. "How the Yankees' Brand Became Universally Popular," *Suicide Squeezin': An Homage to the Finer Art of Baseball*, ryanfergusonbaseball.blogspot.com/2015/02/how-yankees-brand-became-universally.html, last accessed August 13, 2018.

4. Jacob Gallagher, "From Jay-Z to Gucci, How the Yankees Hat Became Bigger Than Baseball," *Wall Street Journal*, March 12, 2018, www.wsj.com/articles/from-jay-z-to-gucci-how-the-yankees-hat-became-bigger-than-baseball-1520871316, last accessed August 13, 2018.

5. Ralph Warner, "Stylin' on 'Em: The Pop Culture History of the Yankees Cap," June 21, 2011, www.complex.com/sports/2011/06/pop-culture-history-of-the-yankees-cap/, last accessed August 13, 2018.

6. *Seinfeld*, "The Visa," Castle Rock Entertainment, NBC, January 27, 1993, Peter Mehlman.

7. *Seinfeld*, "The Letter," Castle Rock Entertainment, NBC, March 25, 1992, Larry David.

8. *Seinfeld*, "The Foundation," Castle Rock Entertainment, NBC, September 19, 1996, Alec Berg and Jeff Schaffer.

9. *Seinfeld*, "The Chicken Roaster," Castle Rock Entertainment, NBC, November 14, 1996, Alec Berg and Jeff Schaffer.

10. *Seinfeld*, "The Wig Master," Castle Rock Entertainment, NBC, April 4, 1996, Spike Feresten.

11. Intellectuals seem drawn to the Yankees, and brag about their affiliation to the team in their writings.

See Josephine (Jo) R. Potuto, *Swinging at the Facts: How Baseball Informs Legal Argument*, *Louisiana Law Review*, Volume 78, no. 1 (2018): 245–265. "Casey Stengel and Yogi Berra—two of the best-known philosophers of modern times." *Ibid.*, 246. Potuto describes herself as "a lifelong New York Yankees baseball fan from a large extended family of Yankee fans." *Ibid.*, 245. Available at digitalcommons.law.lsu.edu/cgi/viewcontent.cgi?article=6655&context=lalrev.

12.  Dr. Susannah J. Ural, review of *Damn Yankees!: Demonization and Defiance in the Confederate South*, by George C. Rable, *Journal of Southern History*, Volume 83, no. 1, The Southern Historical Association: 174, Available at muse.jhu.edu/article/647317/summary, last accessed August 13, 2018.

13.  *The Phil Silvers Show*, "Hillbilly Whiz," Filmways, CBS, October 1, 1957, Coleman Jacoby and Arnie Rosen.

14.  Melissa Lockard, "Oakland A's History: Finley Attempts Fire Sale," 247sports.com/mlb/athletics/Article/Oakland-As-History-Finley-Attemps-Fire-Sale-104429934/ ("The richest clubs would take advantage of the new rules and they would sign the top talent available, leaving the smaller market clubs on the sidelines. This created a huge problem for Finley. Already burned by the loss of star pitcher Jim Hunter to the Yankees the previous season, there was no way for Finley to compete against the richer teams in baseball. Consequently, he decided to dismantle his championship A's club before free agency would.") Last accessed August 8, 2018.

15.  Interview with Al's store manager, 200 N Market St, Wilmington, DE 19801 (2017).

16.  "Khadafy Killed by Yankee Fan" was the front-page headline for the October 21, 2011 edition of the *New York Post*.

17.  Manny Fernandez, "Crime Blotter Has a Regular: Yankees Caps," September 16, 2010: A1.

18.  Douglas Greenwood, "Here's How the New York Yankees Logo Became a Bona Fide Fashion Statement," www.highsnobiety.com/p/yankees-insignia-became-sports-biggest-fashion-statement/, last accessed August 8, 2018.

19.  "Brooklyn Eagles 1935 Vintage Ballcap," www.ebbets.com/products/brooklyn-eagles-1935-ballcap?view=quick; "Brooklyn Eagles 1935 Vintage Ballcap," tiltedbrimsf.com/products/brooklyn-eagles-1935-ballcap.

# From Ruth to Rivera

*The Core Four, Yankee Dynasties
and the Making of Legends*

Erin DiCesare

## Come on Down to Derek Jeter's Taco Hole

Derek Jeter's Taco Hole is next to El Duque's Shoe Repair. When Jeter guest hosted *Saturday Night Live* less than three months after the 9/11 terrorist attacks in New York City and Washington, it was a perfect match that allowed fans to see his lighter side with great comedy material.[1] Willing to participate in popular culture, even if it takes him injuring the audience as he hits balls into the "stands" in his opening monologue or playing a fictional wife of a fellow Yankee, Jeter ranks as the number five funniest *Saturday Night Live* athlete hosts according to *Rolling Stone*.[2] Singing a song about tacos to the tune of the Beach Boys song "Kokomo," only Jeter can express the desire for the season to end so he can return back to his first love … his Taco Hole.

## Introducing the Core Four

What makes a team so popular? We see teams with all-star players, but a core changes the face of the organization. The Yankees' "Core Four" exemplifies a united and winning team, but their contributions go beyond championships. Derek Jeter. Jorge Posada. Mariano Rivera. Andy Pettitte. Starting and ending their career with one organization (except Pettitte), something rarely heard of today, this group of players added to the richness of Yankee history. This phenomenon started in 1995, with the Core Four making their major-league début; these players got drafted by the club, signed, and worked their way up through the farm system to become key players, identifiable in their respective positions, as the heart of the Yankees. Posada, Jeter, and Rivera played together for 17 consecutive seasons, the longest streak witnessed in MLB; Pettitte departed the team in the middle of his career to play for the Houston Astros, only to return three seasons later. Why is this important? They changed the dynamic of the game. These players were known for their positions and their drive, and they were also known as top performers. How many times had batters faced Rivera only to not be able to hit his cutter?

## Baseball Culture to Fandom

Yogi Berra, in the Foreword for Marty Appel's team biography *Pinstripe Empire: The New York Yankees from Before the Babe to After the Boss*, makes a clear statement about the Yankees organization and culture: "I learned once you're a Yankee, you're always in touch with that history. You sense it all around you, the pinstripes, the stadium, the tradition."[3] The Yankees have a strong culture around them, so much so that it reaches the masses and makes a claim on popular culture.

When you have Jay-Z, an iconic rapper, incorporating the Yankee hat into his infamous song "Empire State of Mind," the power of the Yankees in popular culture cannot be denied. While Jay-Z's claim about increasing the appeal of the Yankee hat is interesting, and perhaps true, Yankee culture stands alone. I grew up a Yankee. I was born in New York and my family moved to the south at a young age, but my roots were still firmly in the north. My dad and I watched the Yankees on television every chance we got.

Yogi Berra's statement that once you're a Yankee, you're always in touch with that history holds true for the fans, too. I grew up with the '90s Core Four: Jeter, Posada, Rivera (my favorite player for many reasons), and Pettitte. As a fan, I taught those around me to respect the pinstripes, to respect the game. Berra goes on to state, "What I like most about the Yankees is that connection, like we're all related."[4] It's another claim that holds true for the fans. When I see another Yankees fan, there is an instant recognition; we are part of the culture, we are related as fans.

So, what makes the Core Four special? They accomplished something that any baseball fan can appreciate. "The Core Four would play as Yankees teammates for 13 seasons, during which time they would make the playoffs 12 times, win the American League East title eight times, the American League pennant seven times, and the World Series five times."[5]

While this is a rather great accomplishment, they also did something else: by 2010, "Rivera, Posada, and Jeter became the first three teammates in any of the four major North American sports to play together on the same team for 16 consecutive seasons," with Pettitte being with the Houston Astros for three seasons.[6] A lifetime with one organization, who would ever imagine? But these guys made a name for the Yankees in the '90s and their accomplishments have not faded from baseball conversations.

I hear talk about Rivera and his cutter and I hear talk about Jeter getting his 3,000th hit with a home run. Why? Because these are part of the baseball culture. They are part of why people tune in. When we talk about drive, Jeter was the one who stood out being the kid from Kalamazoo watching the Yankees with his grandmother and making the claim he would play for them one day. "When I grow up, I'm going to play shortstop for the New York Yankees, stated Jeter to his nana."[7]

For as great a closer Rivera was, his start was in soccer and he played baseball for fun. Pettitte was built to be a pitcher. Posada's hero? Thurman Munson. It's ironic because they shared the same position on the team. Posada developed into a switch hitter and had a rocky personal road before he got to the Yankees organization. Of course, who wouldn't, given the fact that he came to the contiguous U.S. from Puerto Rico for baseball and knew no one upon his arrival. These guys created fans, young and old; they were the glue through the '90s and the early 2000s. When 9/11 hit, we looked to them. They represented the city many of us loved, and they did not fail us.

## Old Core Four

This exploration would be amiss if we did not pay homage to the past "Core Four" players. From 1920 to current, there has not been a lack of core players. What makes the '90s players so special is that they were the most successful and the group that stayed together the longest. We kick off in the 1920s with Babe Ruth, Bob Meusel, Lou Gehrig, and Waite Hoyt and move to the 1930s with Lou Gehrig, Tony Lazzeri, Bill Dickey, and Red Ruffing (although Ruth was still a prominent figure). In the 1940s, we see Joe DiMaggio, Charlie Keller, Tommy Henrich, and Phil Rizzuto. The 1950s were dominated by Mickey Mantle, Whitey Ford, Yogi Berra, and Hank Bauer.

In the 1960s, Mantle is back as a foundational player and is joined by Roger Maris, Elston Howard, and Bobby Richardson. Only a true Yankees fan and Mantle worshipper like Billy Crystal could make the TV-movie *61\**, which revolves around the 1961 season, when Maris and Mantle battled to break Ruth's elusive record of 60 home runs in a season. This infamous season was not without drama and worry. Maris was lambasted by the media and the fans for chasing the record of a '20s "Core Four" player. The House that Ruth Built was going to remain intact; if the record was to be broken, the conventional wisdom was that it should be Mantle, who had always been a Yankee. Maris came from Kansas City in 1960. Though he won the American League MVP that year, Mantle was still favored.

Maris hit 61 home runs in the newly created 162-game season. This gave him eight more games to break the record, which he did in the last game. Many considered it not a true record-breaker, so the asterisk was attached; Ruth's record, therefore, remained intact, to fan and media satisfaction. Mantle, a renowned Yankee, ended his run at 54. An injury sidelined him in September. Maris won the MVP Award again in 1961.

## 1970s Core Four

Thurman Munson, Roy White, Graig Nettles, and Sparky Lyle. Munson was drafted in 1968 and had such an enormous impact on the team that he was given the title of captain, the first Yankee to have the label after Gehrig. While his reign was short-lived because of a fatal plane crash, his poise and demeanor were what Yankees were made of. I would even go so far as to argue that there is a case to expand to a quintet: Ron Guidry boasted two highly successful seasons in 1978 with 25 wins and only 3 losses with a 1.74 ERA and 1979 with 18 wins and 8 losses and a 2.78 ERA. He won the ERA title twice and was a five-time Gold Glove winner. Guidry is one that ends the '70s and moves the organization into the '80s as a core player in my personal opinion as he logged winning seasons from 1977 to 1985, with the exception of the 1984 season, but he well made up for it the following year logging 22 wins and only 6 losses with a 3.27 ERA.

## 1995 Season: Core Four Introduction

The "Core Four" players of the New York Yankees each made his major-league début in the 1995 season. Also on this Yankees club were Tino Martinez, Paul O'Neill, and Bernie Williams. This Yankees team, led by manager Joe Torre, was nothing short of special. This was their introduction.

What many remember, fans and non–Yankees fans, is the date October 30, 2001—the third game of the World Series. President George W. Bush throwing out the first pitch is a moment that people remember because the Yankees were more than a team that night; they represented the United States and the city still recovering from the terrorist attacks on the World Trade Center. All eyes were on the Yankees, the home team, the one team that could bring an entire nation together. Love them or hate them, the Yankees were everything the United States needed to make the statement that we will not be destroyed. It may seem like a lot to put on one game and one team, but once President Bush threw that first pitch, the crowd erupted in a chant of "USA, USA, USA." And while the Yankees may have lost the World Series to the Arizona Diamondbacks, they reunited an entire nation through baseball.

## #2 Derek Jeter

Jeter led the team with grace and dignity. We remember Jeter's great plays, some I am still picking my mouth off the ground about. We do not remember the clash with owner George Steinbrenner about Jeter's nighttime activities; they did a Visa commercial with Steinbrenner's critique as the punch line. We remember the header into the stands and Jeter coming out bleeding as he chased after a ball; we remember his acrobatic moves

New Yorkers were reeling from the 9/11 attacks when President George W. Bush threw out the first pitch before Game Three of the 2001 World Series. Yankee Stadium was a cauldron of patriotism and adrenaline. Jeter and the president met before the ceremonial pitch—Bush 43 threw a strike (courtesy of George W. Bush Presidential Library and Museum).

from shortstop to first to get the runner; and we all remember his 3,000th hit. I remember it so well because I had to call my boss to tell her I was going to be late to work—Jeter was up and I wasn't missing it. News stations turned to the game and Jeter delivered: a home run for hit number 3,000.

Jeter's 3,000th hit was something special: He is the first Yankee to get this record and he is one of 11 players to get all hits with the same team. Plus, he got his 3,000th hit in Yankee Stadium. And we remember Jeter exiting in style at his last at bat: a walk-off single to right field. It ended a successful Yankees career on a high note. But Jeter did something else that defines his quality as a player: he was never ejected from a game.

Jeter's last season helped to boost the Yankees to #1 on *Forbes* 2015 list of team revenues. The increase in merchandise sales from his last season helped to move the team to a value of $3.2 billion and a revenue total of $508 million.[8]

## #20 Jorge Posada

Posada's road to the majors was not easy, and he bounced back and forth between New York and the team's AAA club in Columbus. But by 1998, Posada had taken over as the starting catcher. Posada was impressive during his time with the Yankees. By 1999, he solidified his position as the full-time Yankees catcher. His dedication is exemplary, considering his personal challenge: the Posadas' son was born with craniosynostosis, which resulted in multiple corrective surgeries.

What Posada did not do was immediately make his son's condition public. He did not let family issues interrupt his goal on the field. When Posada did announce his son's condition, it was not for sympathy but for awareness, further reinforced by his founding of the Jorge Posada Foundation, which supports families who have fallen victim to this pediatric deformity.

In 2017, Hurricane Maria's destruction in Puerto Rico, Jorge's native home, inspired the former Yankee catcher and his wife, Laura, to start a fundraising page for victims. It almost reached their $100,000 set goal in less than 24 hours.[9] While Laura appeared on television to engage the public in helping rebuild Puerto Rico, Jorge stayed mostly in the background. Being humble is one core characteristic of the '90s "Core Four" players and Posada still possesses this virtue.

## #42 Mariano Rivera

Yankees fans hear the song "Enter Sandman" and we start looking around for Mariano Rivera (a.k.a. Mo). His infamous cutter was famous for breaking bats. On Rivera's farewell tour, he was presented a rocking chair by the Minnesota Twins made from the bats his pitches had broken over the years. While some may question his statistics and argue against his greatness, many fail to remember he did all of this with one pitch. Just one. Players encountered it year after year, season after season. And they still did not know how to harness and attack Rivera's signature pitch.

Even David Ortiz in a "Players Tribute" piece, notes: "He threw one pitch, man. He threw *one pitch*. And it was so damn good that it didn't matter. That's why, to me, he's the most amazing pitcher in the history of the game. You knew the cutter was coming.

The ball would come out of Mariano's hand and you were sure it was going right over the plate. All of a sudden, you were hitting it with your finger. Jam sandwich."[10]

Talk that the pitch would soon take on the name of Rivera in some form shows that his talent is not unnoticed. Rivera did not have to worry about his stake with the Yankees. His legacy was firmly rooted as the reliever/closer, although he started as a setup man for John Wetteland. Even after his torn ACL in 2012, Rivera's return was expected. Who ends their career on an ACL tear shagging fly balls? He was still our closer. When he retired he would be replaced and not a moment sooner. Rivera declared, "I'm coming back" and continued, "Write it down in big letters. I'm not going out like this."[11] And he did come back, ending with a bang. I will never forget Rivera leaving the mound for the last time with Pettitte and Jeter coming to get him. The Sandman had ended an amazing career in Yankee Stadium with the crowd cheering.

In addition to receiving the broken-bat rocking chair, he was presented by the president of the Rock and Roll Hall of Fame, Greg Harris, and Indians president Mark Shapiro with a gold record of his theme song, "Enter Sandman," by Metallica. For Yankees fans, "Enter Sandman" is not a heavy-metal song, it is Rivera's fanfare announcing his entrance.[12] It is the song that gives you goose bumps and invokes memories of the greatest closer to date.

## #46 Andy Pettitte

Handy Andy was the only player of the Core Four to leave and return to the Yankees to finish his career. He left to play with the Houston Astros for good reason: family. Pettitte was able to play with his idol Roger Clemens as they both moved to Texas, but what drew the Yankees to Pettitte in the first place? He was getting attention, like Jeter, since high school. He probably could have gone to the free-agent draft in 1990 but as usual, parents had the final word and Pettitte went to college. It is where Andy learned the pickoff move that would be his weapon.

Pettitte was not an easy player to sign, as he knew his worth. And it paid off. Pettitte was part of a devastating pitching rotation that dominated during the reign of the Core Four. Pettitte had a great run with the Yankees. We were sad to see him go to Houston and we were glad to take him back. I always claim he was one of the few Yankees who could leave and return to welcoming fans. But in 2011 we had to say goodbye to him again, this time for retirement. Pettitte was a foundational pitcher.

## Old Yankee Stadium to the New Yankee Stadium

In 2009, the Yankees moved from "The House that Ruth Built" to their new stadium, and the Core Four led the way. But before the move, they had one more game to play: Posada caught the pregame ball thrown out, Pettitte pitched five innings, Rivera entered the game to his theme song one last time, and Jeter stayed in until the ninth inning. The Core Four players were the team's glue and they made Yankees fans feel a sense of home in the new stadium. It was hard for even the fans to leave the old stadium. In his speech, Jeter stated "…although things are going to change next year and we're going to move across the street, there are a few things with New York Yankees that will never change. That's pride, tradition, and most of all, we have the greatest fans in the world"[13] and those greatest fans in the world loyally followed the Core Four and the rest of the Yankees to the new stadium with pride. Stepping off the train or out of the subway, you still hear the cheers "Let's go, Yankees" as you walk into the stadium. The sense of community never left because the community wasn't created by the stadium, it was created by the players and the fans, and the Core Four never let the fans go unnoticed or underappreciated.

While the '90s Core Four were going to play in their new home, it was only fitting to start the season with an old member of the Core Four club: Yogi Berra threw out the first ball, and with that, the new Yankee Stadium was christened. While there were a few new faces joining the Yankee's roster that season—and they are important to the Yankee organization—the Core Four were front and center, solidified with Posada letting everyone know that his shoulder was just fine as he hit the first home run in their new home. Would the new stadium be home if the Core Four weren't there? Yes … but it wouldn't have been as cozy.

## Popular Culture

The impact that the Core Four had on popular culture is impressive. How many Yankees fans found the ESPN commercial with Posada and Ortiz to be a bit humorous? Ortiz put on Posada's hat "because it looked like new." This is because catchers don't wear their hats. When Red Sox mascot "Wally the Green Monster" walks by and sees the seemingly treasonous act, it is hilarious to some and even more so to Yankees fans. Posada represented the organization with class and was always part of the "friendly" rivalry. To partake in the banter of the rivalry makes this commercial golden.

Jeter had been featured on many local New York television commercials, but when he retired, Gatorade featured him in an homage. The fans were genuine in this commercial; Yankees fans loved El Capitan and it showed. Nike even got in on the action with its "tip of the hat" commercial honoring Jeter. Never have I experienced a player's retirement like that of Jeter's.

For the longest time, Jeter was the face of the Yankees; commercial endorsements, gossip columns, and a documentary followed him on his way to hit number 3,000. He was synonymous with the word "Yankees" and he kept a lot of his life private. The only criticism I remember are Steinbrenner's comments and the talk about town when Jeter decided to not attend the All-Star Game the same season he hit number 3,000. This was a decision that had supporters on both sides. He had finally made a decision someone didn't like and he received backlash for it. But Jeter skated out of this criticism quickly and fans forgave him.

We can never forget Derek Jeter playing Alfonso Soriano's wife in the infamous "Yankees Wives" sketch on *Saturday Night Live*. Who didn't think Jeter looked good in drag? Jeter calls to light the struggles of being a Yankees player and women throwing themselves at them. In a funny but straightforward way, the sketch calls out the many media/paparazzi claims that circulate about players. As the wives gossip, the best line comes from Jeter himself: "Oh no, Jeter does not do it for me. He looks like if the Rock had sex with a Muppet." Jeter was willing to have a few laughs and has appeared on many late-night talk shows along with *SNL*.[14]

Rivera's farewell tour was nothing to be balked at either. In every stadium he visited, he was received with open arms, even though they would be seeing his cutter shortly, and honored for his accomplishments. MLB produced a video tribute to him, showing that "he didn't know" that he would be the greatest closer the game has ever seen. It's another example of a Core Four member being humble.

These men were highly respected across the baseball nation for their work on the field and little controversy off the field. They were role models to fans. When you have a mimic of the Beatles *Abbey Road* album cover with the Core Four, you know they are fully engrained in popular culture. But, these players were human. They had slumps. They encountered hardships. They are not devoid of knowing a struggle or two.

## Core Values

Humility is one thing these Yankees players have in common. Rivera never stated he was the greatest closer in baseball. Jeter never went around making claims to his title of captain. Posada kept his life very private, played through the tragic news of his son's condition, and used his position to create a support opportunity for those going through the same thing. Pettitte, well, we remember his pitching, nothing more. Their desires for fame were not driven by individuality. They wanted to be good, but they wanted to be good as a team.[15]

Fan appreciation is yet another value that these core players had. They always mentioned that Yankees fans were the greatest fans.

## 2017: The Search for the New Core Four

With the last of the Core Four retiring in 2014 (Jeter), the Yankees have not lost what this group has built and some wonder, with Aaron Judge, Gary Sanchez, Greg Bird, and Luis Severino starting their careers much like the '90s Core Four members, could they be the ones to keep the tradition alive? With Judge's performance in April 2017, many wonder if he is the start of the new Core Four and the new Yankees. Is the Core Four, and the search for a group to replace them, what Yankees culture is about? Is this team popular and viewed as one of the "key" components of MLB because of a group of players identifiable not only because of their records or numbers, but because they played for the love of the game?

Judge did not step onto the playing field without trials and tribulations. It should be noted that he was a three-sport athlete in college: football, basketball, and baseball. But … he chose baseball. Or did baseball choose him? He was lucky to have a family who fostered his love for the game but he did not make it to the show easily: He started in the minors, was called up, went back down to the minors, and was called up again. This time, he would not go back. Instead, Aaron Judge started the 2017 season with statements in the form of home runs. And from his ability, we have witnessed catch phrases develop. Now, when you go to a game, when Judge comes up to bat we hear "All Rise" and note the "Judge's Chamber," where lucky fans get to wear judge's robes and cheer on their rising Yankees' star. Is he one of the new Core Four? How could he not be? Drafted by the Yankees and moved through the farm system, he has the potential to play his entire career with the Yankees and create an entirely new Core Four that holds the same abilities, drive, and passion for the game that the '90s Core Four had. Now, instead of the fans wearing #2, we see them wearing #99.

Aaron Judge accomplished a lot during his rookie year, both highs and lows to note: taking the record for obtaining a strikeout in 36 consecutive games, but also breaking a 96-year record held by Babe Ruth for most home runs hit at home in a season.[16] He has surpassed Mark McGwire's rookie home run record and led the American League with 52 home runs. Judge has had an astonishing start: being voted AL Rookie of the Month for April, May, and June and going to the All-Star Game in his rookie year.[17] While he was drafted by Oakland in 2010, he did not sign. It was a lucky call for Yankees fans.

Aaron Judge is much like the players set before him. While he was hitting rockets in the beginning of the 2017 season, he stayed humble, he focused on the fundamentals, opportunities to contribute, and a team mentality. Will Judge take the rank of captain, a highly cherished label in the Yankees world? Only time will tell, and it is still rather early, but Judge is proving to be an asset to the team. Currently, Judge has numbers like Mantle. No, I am not claiming he is just like Mantle, but the sheer power of Judge shows that the potential is there. Even with a slump, he batted .284 in his rookie year. Mantle, had a career average of .298 with 536 home runs and boasted two seasons with 50 or more home runs, four seasons with 40 or more, and nine with 30 or more.

In true Yankees form: Aaron Judge has taken the lead in terms of interacting with fans. In a segment on *The Tonight Show Starring Jimmy Fallon*, Judge, wearing only glasses to conceal his identity, interviews fans in Byrant Park about what they think about … well … Aaron Judge. When Judge inquires as to who their favorite player is, fans stream off a list of names, including Bret Gardner and Jacoby Ellsbury. One fan mentions Judge and comments that he will only get 40 home runs this year. The audience howls when the fan claims, "He can't keep up this pace." Judge even banters with a fan about how much he thinks Judge can bench and reaffirms that the fan is correct with 400 pounds. Another fan calls him Adam Judge. The laughs come out when Judge shows the interviewees the next cover of *Sports Illustrated* featuring him, and they finally realize they have been sitting next to the star the entire time. With one fan making note of the "gap" and mentioning "you and Strahan" in reference to the front teeth, Judge, in good fashion, just laughs.[18]

Another Yankees player who can be deemed part of the potential new Core Four is Gary Sanchez, who was signed as a free agent in 2009. He boasted two Rookie of the Month awards in 2016 and was deemed one of the most valuable hitters in the last half of the 2017 season.[19] While the media may want to pit players against each other, the dynamics of the Yankees do not allow it, especially when we have the chance to recreate the Core Four of the '90s. I equate Sanchez to Posada in that he is a stabilizing force, even in a slump. He isn't a flashy player, he's just a ballplayer.

The new era Yankees players are slowly coming into their own, but are still aware of the positions and expectations they have to fill to be labeled a "core" Yankee player. Hopefully, we will see these players end their careers like they started: with the Yankees. Their names are gaining popularity, all eyes are on them, and the value of the Yankees franchise is still sky high.

## Notes

1. *Saturday Night Live*, "Derek Jeter's Taco Hole," Broadway Video, NBC, December 1, 2001.

2. Rob LeDonne, "10 Funniest 'Saturday Night Live' Athlete Hosts," *Rolling Stone*, January 22, 2016, www.rollingstone.com/sports/lists/10-funniest-snl-athlete-hosts-20160122/derek-jeter-2001-20160122.

3. Yogi Berra, foreword to *Pinstripe Empire: The New York Yankees from Before the Babe to After the Boss* by Marty Appel (New York: Bloomsbury, 2013), xi.

4. *Ibid.*

5. Phil Pepe, introduction to *Core Four: The Heart and Soul of the Yankees Dynasty* (Chicago: Triumph Books, 2013), ix.

6. *Ibid.*

7. *Ibid.*, 27.

8. "Mlb Team Values 2015," *Forbes*, www.forbes.com/pictures/mlm45fkhjm/1-new-york-yankees/#577585464733, last accessed September 1, 2017.

9. Dan Gartland, "Jorge Posada and Wife Laura Launch Fundraising Campaign for Puerto Rico Hurricane Relief," *Sports Illustrated*, September 21, 2017, https://www.si.com/mlb/2017/09/21/jorge-posada-hurricane-maria-puerto-rico-fundraising, last accessed September 21, 2017.

10. David Ortiz, "The Five Toughest Players I've Ever Faced," *The Players' Tribune*, September 23, 2015, https://www.theplayerstribune.com/david-ortiz-red-sox-five-toughest-pitchers-ive-ever-faced/, last accessed September 23, 2015.

11. Pepe, 207.

12. Mark Feinsand, "Indians Honor Mariano Rivera with Framed Gold Record of Metallica's 'Enter Sandman,'" *Daily News* (New York), May 13, 2013, www.nydailynews.com/sports/baseball/yankees/indians-give-mo-golden-honor-article-1.1343067, last accessed May 13, 2013.

13. Pepe, 123.

14. *Saturday Night Live*, "Yankee Wives," NBC, December 1, 2001.

15. Wayne Coffey, "Yankees Core Four—Andy Pettie, Mariano Rivera, Jorge Posada, and Derek Jeter—Had a Humble Beginning," *Daily News* (New York), October 3, 2010, http://www.nydailynews.com/sports/baseball/yankees/yankees-core-andy-pettitte-mariano-rivera-jorge-posada-derek-jeter-humble-article-1.187822, last accessed October 3, 2010.

16. Mike Chiari, "Aaron Judge Breaks Record for Most Consecutive Game with Strikeout," *Bleacher Report*, August 19, 2017, bleacherreport.com/articles/2728443-aaron-judge-breaks-record-for-most-consecutive-games-with-trikeout?utm_source=cnn.com&utm_medium=referral&utm_campaign=editorial, last accessed, August 19, 2017.

17. "Aaron Judge," Baseball Reference, www.baseball-reference.com/players/j/judgeaa01.shtml, last accessed August 13, 2018.

18. *The Tonight Show*, "Aaron Judge Asks Fans About Aaron Judge," NBC, May 15, 2018.

19. Allison Case, "Gary Sanchez, Not Judge, Is the New York Yankees Most Valuable HR Hitter," *Elite Sports Ny*, August 22, 2017, elitesportsny.com/2017/08/22/gary-sanchez-not-judge-is-the-new-york-yankees-most-valuable-hr-hitter/, last accessed August 22, 2017.

# Paragon vs. Prodigy

## The Cultural History of Joe DiMaggio and Mickey Mantle as Yankee Brand Icons

### Duke Goldman

On October 1, 1932, a monumental baseball myth was set in motion. In the fifth inning of Game 3 of the 1932 World Series, Babe Ruth hit a home run off Chicago Cubs hurler Charlie Root to punctuate an eventual four-game series sweep by the New York Yankees. To this day, it is debated by historians and fans alike as to whether Ruth "called his shot" by pointing to the distant outfield bleachers indicating that he would hit the next pitch there for a home run, or merely was just gesturing that he had one more shot at Root, as he had two strikes on him.

Either way, the mythical blast that Ruth hit furthered the development of his storied tenure as the first icon of the initial set of dominant Yankee teams of the 1920s and 1930s. But another blast, a triple, was hit that same day—one that began the professional career of another great Yankee whose tenure would succeed Ruth's as the linchpin of the second Yankee dynasty, a 17-year-old Italian lad as the new shortstop for the Pacific Coast League's San Francisco Missions. Of local origins, he was pressed into duty when Missions owner Charlie Graham gave future major-leaguer Augie Galan permission to leave his team to go to Hawaii with Henry "Prince" Oana three games before the end of the season. That young shortstop, Joseph Paul DiMaggio, son of a Sicilian-born fisherman who emigrated to the San Francisco Bay Area, would become a New York Yankee superstar center fielder less than four years later, in essence replacing Babe Ruth as the dominant performer—and personality—on a dominant team.

On April 17, 1951, 19-year-old Mickey Charles Mantle, the son of a coal miner who hailed from Commerce, Oklahoma (though Mickey was born in nearby Spavinaw), made his major-league début batting third against the rival Boston Red Sox at Yankee Stadium. Mantle was one of five future Hall of Famers in the first six slots of that day's Yankee batting order, including cleanup hitter Joe DiMaggio. Like DiMaggio, Mantle also began his professional career as a 17-year-old shortstop, albeit in Class D, five levels below where DiMaggio started. Unlike DiMaggio, who spent three full seasons in the Pacific Coast League auditioning for his eventual center station as a Yankee idol, Mantle rocketed directly from Class C ball in Joplin, Missouri, 27 miles away from Commerce, to take his place in right field alongside DiMaggio on that April day. Mantle singled in his first major-league game and though his first year with the Yankees was interrupted by a 40-game stint at Triple-A Kansas City, that 1951 season was simultaneously the start of the meteoric rise of the Commerce Comet, as Mantle was sometimes called, and the last year of Joltin' Joe DiMaggio's classic tenure on the center stage of the Yankee dynasty.

Neither Mantle nor DiMaggio were outstanding performers in 1951, but in the end the Yankees still won the 1951 World Series. It was unsurprising that Mantle as a 19-year-old freshman from the low minors and playing outfield for the first time was not an immediate success as was the 21-year-old DiMaggio in 1936, seasoned by three campaigns of outfield play at the top minor league level. Nevertheless, the World Series triumph shared by Mantle and DiMaggio was the ninth in DiMaggio's thirteen major-league seasons in pinstripes, and the first of seven World Series crowns in Mantle's first twelve seasons as a Yankee.

While countless biographical treatments and magazine articles have depicted the careers of both men, relatively little has directly compared and contrasted perceptions of the two Yankee heroes. This essay will look at the development of both players as American heroes, through the creation of their images, the public perceptions of their personality, and their respective performances on the field and off. Both Joltin' Joe and the Commerce Comet became popular culture as well as baseball icons—and both remain established brands in 21st century America. As performers, the potency of Mantle—characterized by astonishing displays of power and speed—rivaled but did not erase the enduring memory of DiMaggio's grace, perfection, and dignity.

As media personalities, DiMaggio and Mantle followed career paths congruent with those images—the former as a reliable, reassuring spokesperson for Mr. Coffee and the Bowery Savings Bank, the latter as a charismatic and, at times, self-deprecating folk hero endorsing a wide array of American consumer products.

DiMaggio was selective in what he chose to represent while Mantle was ubiquitous as a spokesperson. As American cultural icons, Mantle portrayed a hero in the mold of Elvis Presley, another southern idol who dominated 1950s popular culture, complete with Oklahoma twang and a magnetic presence as a blond, blue-eyed specimen of American manhood. DiMaggio was clearly the greater presence in American art, feted in literature, song, art, and theater as a larger-than-life realization of American ideals of manhood and accomplishment.

Both Mantle and DiMaggio were and still are worshipped by Yankee and non-

In the 1970s and 1980s, Joe DiMaggio was a mainstay on television with his commercials for the Bowery Savings Bank and Mr. Coffee. DiMaggio's persona of sophistication gave him credibility with New Yorkers (National Baseball Hall of Fame and Museum, Cooperstown, NY).

Yankee (and even some non-baseball) fans. Mantle, in this author's view, was (and is) more beloved by individuals who could also see something of themselves in Mantle's down-to-earth country demeanor, even though they could scarcely perceive themselves capable of his prodigious output. In contrast, DiMaggio was (and is) revered for his classy, elegant, and superlative performance. The pursuit of perfection as embodied by DiMaggio left him greatly admired by fans, teammates, and sportswriters but not as beloved as the flawed Mantle.

## DiMag and the Mick—Image Building

### The Transformation from "Deadpan Joe" to "Joltin' Joe" (1933–1941)

After his cameo appearance in 1932, Joe DiMaggio emerged as a star ball-hawking outfielder for the 1933 San Francisco Seals, leading the Pacific Coast League with 169 RBI along with setting a Pacific Coast League record of a 61-game hitting streak eight years before he broke the major league record with his legendary 56-game skein. As he began a noteworthy professional career, the media, taking notice of a new presence in the pantheon of accomplished ballplayers, began to refer to DiMaggio as "Deadpan Joe." According to columnist Jack Kofoed, Joe was so nicknamed by his own teammates shortly after joining the team because he "had nothing to say."[1] Kofoed referred to DiMaggio eight times as "Dead Pan" in a column, so even if the nickname originated with teammates, writers like Kofoed clearly popularized it. Additionally, another press account suggested a different rationale for the sobriquet; a 1933 Associated Press report stated that he was called Deadpan "because his face is expressionless as he rifles baseballs to all corners of the lot."[2]

Because the press was still trying to figure out whether Joe's last name was de Maggio, de-Maggio, Di Maggio, or DiMaggio, it is not surprising that they were unsure of the precise origins of the Deadpan Joe label, but what they had already identified was, in the words of historian Richard Crepeau, that Joe D. was "the colorless superstar par excellence."[3] In an era before television, when baseball was the number one participant *and* spectator sport in America, sportswriters often created and/or employed "colorful" nicknames that mythologized players, for example, calling Babe Ruth the "Sultan of Swat" because of his home runs. But they also liked to use nicknames that described a ballplayer's personality, disposition, or key characteristic. Lou Gehrig, therefore, became the Iron Horse for his iron constitution and will exemplified by his 2,130 consecutive games played, while Charlie Gehringer became the Mechanical Man for his automatic success. In the case of DiMaggio, "Deadpan Joe" illuminated a personal characteristic that did not represent his burgeoning talent. The AP's use of the phrase clearly did so by describing DiMaggio's lack of affect in decided contrast to his demonstrable throwing skills.

Clearly, there was a need for a descriptive nickname that would elevate Joe DiMaggio in the eyes of a soon-to-be growing fan base. The dean of New York sportswriters, *New York World-Telegram* and *Sporting News* columnist Dan Daniel, was up to the task. *New York Times* sportswriter and DiMaggio biographer Joe Durso noted that Daniel called DiMaggio "the replacement for Babe Ruth" before Joe D. had even appeared in a Yankees exhibition game.[4] Daniel loved nicknames and he loved alliteration. He changed his own birth name, Daniel Margowitz, to Dan Daniel. And he wrote a daily column called "Daniel's Dope."[5] He liked to call Lou Gehrig "Larrupin' Lou" and was one of the sportswriters who sometimes referred to Mickey Mantle as the "Commerce Comet." According to baseball historian Paul Dickson, Daniel also coined the term "Bronx Bombers" in 1936 as a nickname for the New York Yankees.[6] In latter day terminology, Daniel was one of the "gee whiz" sportswriters, one who believed in making gods out of athletes.[7] Daniel was also the ghostwriter of Joe DiMaggio's first published autobiography, which appeared in six parts in the *World-Telegram* starting on May 11, 1936. The time was ripe for Daniel to coin a new moniker to go with the newspaper's serialization of the DiMaggio story.

In his May 11th report of the previous day's 7–2 Yankee win over the Philadelphia Athletics, Daniel waxed eloquent as he recounted Joe DiMaggio's first major-league home run, hit off St. Louis Browns pitcher George Turbeville: "Jolting Joe jounced George's first pitch—a ball far on the outside—into the right field bleachers to send the fast increasing DiMaggio Marching and Rooting Club into a frenzy."[8] To this author's knowledge, Daniel's May 11th column constitutes the first reference to Joe DiMaggio as "Jolting Joe." For the next two months, Daniel often peppered his columns with that nickname, although he also called him Giuseppe, and sometimes, the Little Bambino. As 1936 wore on, other sportswriters also started to call him Jolting Joe.[9]

Apparently, Daniel adapted Jolting Joe DiMaggio from championship boxer Joe Louis. Like DiMaggio, Louis had a multiplicity of nicknames, although in his case many were racially motivated. Starting in 1935, at first in black newspapers but quickly picked up in the white press, Joe Louis was often referred to as Jolting Joe.[10] The other nickname was also shared. In a 1936 *Collier's* article about DiMaggio entitled "The Frisco Kid," Quentin Reynolds stated, "In some ways he is like another Dead Pan Joe—Joe Louis."[11]

In early 1936, Louis was very much in the news as he prepared for his first bout against Max Schmeling, held on June 18th, only one week after Daniel first used "Jolting Joe." When one considers that Daniel named the Yankees the Bronx Bombers after Joe Louis, who was also known as the Brown Bomber, at around the same time,[12] it is easy to draw the conclusion that Jolting Joe DiMaggio emerged in Daniel's mind as he watched Joe Louis, known for his hard-hitting boxing style, approach his showdown with Schmeling. Although a jolt might seem more like an electric punch by the hard-hitting Louis than a long, arcing drive by a man with a lengthy batting swing as DiMaggio had, one could also see how Jolting Joe DiMaggio could fit a man with a "deadly arm snap of the bat."[13] Daniel's depiction added a dynamic component to the developing image of the brand icon of the perennial World Champion New York Yankees.

As the 1936 season developed, Joe DiMaggio developed from the ballyhooed phenom of the Pacific Coast League into a league-wide phenomenon remarked upon by sportswriters all over baseball. For example, the *Washington Post*'s Shirley Povich, while discounting the New York tendency to boast about its players, its transportation, and its food, acknowledged, "If there's anything that DiMaggio can't do on a baseball field, I dunno what it is."[14] While he detailed Joe D.'s fielding and hitting exploits, Povich also mentioned that Joe demonstrated poise and confidence on the ball field. According to Povich, Washington Senators manager Bucky Harris (who would manage DiMaggio for the Yankees in 1947 and 1948) expressed the belief that DiMaggio was the best rookie outfielder ever, while owner Clark Griffith said he was a wonder—and this, after only 25 games with a .383 batting average, 30 runs scored, and 26 runs batted in.[15]

At the time, New York City had 10 daily newspapers, all extensively covering DiMaggio, thereby filling the void created by Ruth's absence in the Yankees outfield in 1935 for the first time since 1919. In addition to Daniel, other notable New York sportswriters included Frank Graham, who wrote for the *New York Sun* and later the *New York World-Telegram*; Tom Meany, who wrote for the newspaper *PM* after a stint with the *World-Telegram*; Louis Effrat, a *New York Times* sports writer; Jimmy Powers, longtime sports editor of the (New York) *Daily News*; and Joe Williams, who was primarily associated with the *World-Telegram*. Powers was sued for libel for writing that Lou Gehrig exposed his teammates to his life-ending disease and Williams was the lone sportswriter to write about Babe Ruth's "called shot" immediately afterwards. By season's end, Jolting Joe's final .323 batting average, 29 home runs and 125 runs batted in were enough for Daniel to suggest that DiMaggio was "perhaps the greatest first-year ballplayer in the history of the major leagues."[16]

In Frank Graham's recounting of the 1936 season, he stated that DiMaggio was tremendously popular, especially drawing an outpouring of Italian fans throughout the American League.[17] Yankee attendance increased by 319,405 that season while American League attendance increased a total of 490,915, meaning that almost two-thirds of the league's boost at the turnstiles occurred at Yankee Stadium.[18] How much was directly attributable to DiMaggio is not known. Presumably, the Yankees winning their first AL pennant and World Series since 1932 was a major factor. In DiMaggio's first four seasons, the Yankees won the World Series title.

DiMaggio followed up his stellar rookie season with a spectacular sophomore year in 1937, smashing out 46 home runs and driving home 167 runners, both totals establishing career highs that he would not again reach in his remaining 11 seasons. The Yankees repeated their 1936 World Series triumph over the New York Giants and attendance remained strong, increasing slightly in New York but more significantly around the American league.[19]

The "Roosevelt recession" that hit in September 1937 and lasted two years apparently had a minimal impact on 1938 and 1939 AL attendance, which declined slightly each year, while Yankee attendance also declined a bit in 1938 but dropped more than 100,000 in 1939. The Yankees won the World Series over the 1938 Chicago Cubs and 1939 Cincinnati Reds; both contests were 4–0 sweeps. DiMaggio hit 32 home runs and drove in 140 runs in 1938 with a solid .324 batting average and led the American League in 1939 with his career-best .381 average with 30 home runs and 126 runs batted in. So, it is a bit surprising that home attendance did not hold up.

Despite his spectacular performances, did Jolting Joe play a part in the decline in Yankee fan turnout in 1938 and 1939? One argument is that DiMaggio's stellar performance combined with his quiet, dignified bearing contributed to the perception that Joe and his teammates were nowhere near as colorful figures as the Murderers' Row Yankees from the previous generation—Ruth, Meusel, Gehrig and Lazzeri.[20] During Ruth's peak years, the Yankees consistently attracted around a quarter of the American League's attendance, including a peak of 30.71 percent in the Depression year of 1932. DiMaggio's Yankees reached their high of 23.38 percent of American League attendance in 1936.

Joe McCarthy, whose approach was perceived as cold and business-like, had taken over as Yankee pilot from Bob Shawkey in 1931. He still had Ruth, whose last dominant year was 1932, whereas the DiMaggio-led Yankees under McCarthy were perceived as competent professionals without the flair and charisma of the Ruthian teams. Yet another factor depressing attendance could well have been DiMaggio's failed holdout of 1938, when he had to settle for a $10,000 salary increase to $25,000 rather than the $40,000 he held out for until after the start of the season. Initially adamant, he compromised. During those Depression years, such a salary request by a player with only two years of experience was perceived as selfish, and Joe D. was booed.

One could also argue that simply winning the World Series year after year had a depressing effect on Yankee home attendance. A's manager Connie Mack believed that a perennial pennant-winner was less appealing to the fans than a newly-contending team. Meanwhile, on the road, Yankee teams could potentially increase attendance as the team everyone wanted to beat might well bring out the fans.

DiMaggio decided not to hold out for higher salaries in 1939 and beyond after the negative publicity attendant to his 1938 contract dispute. In 1939, he picked up another nickname—Yankee sportscaster Arch McDonald began calling him "The Yankee Clipper." Some sources suggest that this nickname derived from the majestic Clipper ships of the 1800s, but more likely the immediate source was a new air shuttle developed by Pan Am called The Yankee Clipper.[21] Either way, this new nickname contributed to the image of DiMaggio as a regal, majestic ballplayer—one that produced consistently and was worthy of admiration.

He got the AL batting title in 1939 and followed with another one in 1940, a year when, for the first time in his career, the Yankees failed to win the pennant.

In 1941, Jolting Joe DiMaggio accomplished the feat that made him renowned throughout the land and cemented his status as a Yankee icon and a living legend—successfully hitting in 56 straight games. The backdrop to DiMaggio's daily pursuit of extending his batting streak was the growing likelihood of the U.S. being drawn into World War II. Although true heroism was taking place on the battlefields of Europe, North Africa, and the Far East, and ballplayers like Hank Greenberg and Hugh "Losing Pitcher" Mulcahy had already joined the American military, DiMaggio became an American ideal during this relentless pursuit of perfection, which only underscored the impeccable standard of play that Joe embodied.

It's become a part of baseball lore that Americans were obsessed with his daily attempt to continue to reach base safely. The question "Did he get one today?" is commonly mentioned in scholarship without attribution, such is its acceptance as fact. Whether someone was an avid baseball fan or not, DiMaggio was known and his streak was followed. The daily ritual of opening up the newspaper, listening to the radio, or asking one's fellow citizen to answer that question was a bonding experience for Americans looking for a masculine role model in a time of international strife. During that time, female role models largely evoked domesticity or sultry sexuality, although the war would bring on "Rosie the Riveter" types to accomplish wartime industrial tasks and, at least temporarily, elevate women as heroic figures to provide a sense of comfort and security.

The ennobling of Joe DiMaggio arguably was completed near the end of the 56-game hitting streak in July of 1941 when Les Brown and His Band of Renown immortalized the slugger in song with the slight alteration of his name: "Joltin' Joe DiMaggio." The minor change in DiMaggio's nickname took over. The alteration may appear cosmetic, but it elevated, in some sense, DiMaggio to folk hero status, along with the song itself. "Joltin' Joe" provided a lyrical, hip expression that transformed a quiet hero into a colorful, moving image of hipness with even a hint of swagger. One could argue that this imagery contradicted the character of DiMaggio's play to some degree. Roy Blount, Jr., a prominent essayist, suggested, "You don't hear of DiMaggio making diving tumbling circus catches.... He glided from wherever he was waiting to wherever the ball was going.... 'Jolting Joe' was a misnomer: never was there a player whose movements entailed fewer discernible jolts."[22]

Or maybe the nickname alteration actually *reconciled* DiMaggio's "smooth as silk" movements with the suggestion of power in the word "jolt"—as " joltin'" seems more like a rhythmic, danceable groove than the disjointed movement that could be "jolting." Blount's analysis, written long after the Les Brown song débuted, used the older version of DiMaggio's nickname.

The song's refrain emphasized that America had chosen sides in the worldwide conflict we were about to formally enter and it wanted the San Francisco native in their corner, whether it be in their foxhole, on their radio, live or in spirit.

## Mickey Mantle: From Commerce Comet to Bronx Bomber, 1950–1956

Mickey Mantle's origins, like those of Joe DiMaggio, were humble and remote from his final baseball destination of New York City. While Joe D.'s story was that of a son of a recent immigrant making good, Mantle's was that of a heartland American rising from poverty and the coal mines to a fast-paced life where he was adored, idolized, and envied. And in Mantle's case, he came with an authentic baseball name—one derived from a nickname. Gordon Stanley "Mickey" Cochrane, was a Hall of Fame catcher for the last Philadelphia Athletics dynasty (1929–1931). Elvin "Mutt" Mantle, a semipro player when he wasn't mining Oklahoma coal, named his first-born son after Cochrane.

Mickey Mantle was signed by Yankee scout Tom Greenwade as he graduated high school in Commerce for a relative pittance—a bonus of $1,150 and a $140 per month salary,[23] which was what Greenwade figured was roughly what Mantle would have made if he had worked at the mines while continuing to play local semipro ball. As a 17-year-old shortstop, Mantle first played in 1949 at Independence in the Class D Kansas-Oklahoma-Missouri league, establishing himself as an erratic fielder with immense potential in a community roughly 170 miles from Commerce.

At age 18, Mantle rose one level to Class C but moved even closer to Commerce, playing in Joplin, Missouri for the Joplin Miners of the Western Association, a mere 27 miles from Commerce. He scored a league-leading 141 runs and drove in 136, with 26 home runs. His .383 batting average led the WA. But he lacked a future at shortstop, following his .886 fielding average for Independence with an only slightly improved .908 average for the Miners. Mantle tallied more than 100 errors in the two seasons.

Fittingly, given Joplin's proximity to Commerce, the September 21, 1950, *Joplin Globe* included an article by sports columnist Porter Wittich on potential Yankee prospects for 1951 that referred to Mickey as "the Commerce Comet who helped lead Joplin to the Western Association title."[24] While acknowledging that Mantle would not be playing Class C ball in 1951, Wittich indicated that "probably the most prized prospect in the New York Yankee farm system" was not yet clearly better than all the other talent in the Yankee farm system, that he might be better suited to the outfield, and that it was unclear whether he was ready for Yankee pinstripes.[25]

For thirty years, Wittich wrote a daily column called the "Globetrotter," which appeared in the left-hand column of the *Joplin Globe*'s lead sports page.[26] When the Joplin Sports Authority's Hall of Fame inducted Wittich in 2008, writer Wendell Redden, whose first boss was Wittich, wrote a tribute to his old boss describing the column as "one of the most popular pieces in the newspaper."[27] Wittich, who was born in Galena, Kansas, seven miles from Joplin and 20 miles from Commerce, was a "prolific, colorful wordsmith" whose "favorite assignment was the Joplin Miners.... He always said that Mickey Mantle was his favorite player on the Joplin teams."[28]

It seems likely that Wittich, a popular local writer native to the border areas of Kansas, Oklahoma, and Missouri first called Mantle "the Commerce Comet."[29]

And it was not only Wittich who recognized Mickey's awesome potential in 1950. One first-hand account described Yankee director of player personnel (and future Hall of Famer) Lee MacPhail coming to see Mickey play at Joplin in April 1950 to decide whether he ought to stay there for the season, even though he was clearly ready for a higher classification. According to Bill Repplinger, a 13-year-old boy at the time, MacPhail pondered keeping him at Joplin, close to his home in Commerce and to his mentor, Mutt, even though he told Repplinger that "the guy playing shortstop right here in Joplin can run faster than any man in all of baseball and can hit a ball farther than any player, and that includes the ones in the big leagues."[30]

The Mantle tale continues with Mantle wowing Yankee brass in the lighter air and higher elevation of Phoenix, Arizona, where the 1951 Yankees held a prospects camp followed by a one-year switch with the New York Giants, meaning that they played their spring training games in Arizona while the Giants played in Florida. Mickey took advantage of the desert, to the tune of a .402 spring training average with nine home runs, leading to the surprise decision by Yankee brass to bring the 19-year-old Commerce Comet north to Yankee Stadium, to play five levels above Class C in the Yankee outfield, alongside Joe DiMaggio. Or maybe not so surprising, given that Yankee executives believed, as stated above, that Mantle had been ready to go beyond Class C in 1950. In the words of esteemed *New York Herald Tribune* sportswriter Red Smith, Mickey had just finished a "prodigious spring training tour."[31]

In his April 18, 1951, article describing Mantle's major-league début against the Red Sox the previous day, Smith added to the "volume of prose" that had already appeared about Mantle during spring training. He linked the Commerce Comet's first appearance in pinstripes to DiMaggio:

> Earlier, Joe DiMaggio had started a double play with an implausible catch of a pop fly behind second, as if to tell Mantle, "This is how it's done up here, son." Now Joe, awaiting his turn at bat called the kid aside and spoke to him.
> Mantle nodded, stepped back into the box and singled a run home. Dickey coaching at third, slapped his stern approvingly. When the kid raced home from second with his first big-league run, the whole Yankee bench arose to clap hands and pat his torso. He was in the lodge.[32]

In addition to all that was being written about young Mick in the newspapers, the rookie was swept into the New York media landscape before he even stepped onto the field to start his major-league career. Author Donald Honig, in his triple-biography *Mays, Mantle, Snider*, claimed that "even before having played a single major-league game, Mantle was being taken at face value; he was being asked to endorse baseball gloves, cigarettes, and bubble gum."[33] In addition, Honig described Mantle receiving invitations to appear on television shows in 1951—*The Ed Sullivan Show, Break the Bank, We the Peo-*

*ple*—while lengthy articles on the Oklahoma spring training sensation churned from the press box.[34]

While Honig provided no evidence to support his recounting of Mickey's appearances in advertisements and on commercials, Dan Daniel reported in the April 4, 1951, edition of the *Sporting News* that Mantle was offered a $1,500 fee by a large advertising company.[35] In the April 11th edition, Clarence Young mentioned that Mantle was to appear on Sunday, April 15th on NBC's radio program *The Big Show*, along with former Yankee outfield star and now Yankee coach Tommy Henrich. Ultimately, though, Mantle did not go on the program.[36] Clearly, Mickey Mantle had become a celebrity even before he demonstrated his worth in the games that counted.

Mantle was overwhelmed by the attention, the offers, and life in New York City. Commonly recounted in Mantle biographies and autobiographies is the sad tale of the rather unsophisticated slugger signing a contract mandating a 50–50 split of endorsement money with an agent named Alan Savitt. Mickey was all of 19 years old and without the business skills or street smarts to note that the deal was unconscionable. The Yankees backed up their player, beginning legal proceedings to extract Mantle from the contract, but not before Savitt apparently sold a quarter of Mantle's future endorsement potential to a showgirl named Holly Brooke, who was also a paramour of Mickey's in 1951. The sordid details of these transactions were not then reported, but they would come back to haunt Mickey in 1957.[37]

All the attention and attractions of New York, along with the attendant pressure of being the heir apparent to Joe DiMaggio, led to a slumping Mantle getting sent to Kansas City of the American Association in mid–July of 1951.[38] By current standards, Mantle hadn't been doing so poorly—though strikeouts were common, he was hitting .260 and driving in runs—but the impossible and unmet expectations of immediate stardom and the media storm around him led Yankee management to send him down to their top farm team for more seasoning. In one of Mantle's several ghostwritten autobiographies, *The Education of a Baseball Player*, Mickey expressed that "the newspapers were nearly my undoing."[39] Reflecting back on the pressure cooker atmosphere of 1951, Mantle related that the media suggested 1) he was DiMaggio's successor and 2) he was already headed to the Hall of Fame. In his estimation, this bred resentment among fans that loved DiMaggio and expected Mantle to deliver results comparable to what Joe achieved. This expectation resulted in pressure on him to succeed or he "would be done for" as a major-league player.[40]

Mantle initially struggled at Kansas City, but some tough love from his dad, who threatened to bring him back to the Oklahoma mines when Mickey suggested that he couldn't succeed at baseball, began a quick turnaround. He returned to the Yankees in late August. More important than Mantle's final season results—97 games, .267 batting average, 13 home runs, 65 runs batted in—was his severe knee injury in the 1951 World Series. When Mantle stopped short to avoid colliding with Joe D. on a fly ball hit by Willie Mays, he tore his right knee ligament. It was the beginning of a history of crippling injuries that would dog him throughout his career. He also found that he was about to lose Mutt, who was terminally ill with Hodgkin's disease.

Mantle came back from his knee injury to a Yankee team that no longer included Joe DiMaggio. The Yankee Clipper would be doing pre-game and post-game shows for Yankee television broadcasts, a job he was unsuited for, but he would no longer command center field. It was now Mantle's territory to cover.

DiMaggio's presence and guidance would not be missed by Mantle. There had been little interaction between the two of them in 1951. Reportedly, DiMaggio privately told writer Lou Effrat that Mantle was a "rockhead"[41] and Mantle was so awed by DiMaggio that he barely spoke to him. Perhaps their discord was exaggerated in later chronicles, but they were clearly not involved in supporting each other or even having a casually conversational relationship.

The Commerce Comet settled into a steady position in the center of Yankee success from 1952 through 1955. The Yankees won World Series championships in 1952 and 1953 and lost the American League pennant—even though they won 103 games, more than any other season of Casey Stengel's managerial tenure—to a juggernaut Indians team in 1954 and the World Series to the Brooklyn Dodgers (finally!) in 1955. Mantle was on a World Series championship team in his first three seasons, close to DiMaggio's record of winning the Series in his first four. While his performance steadily improved, it neither fulfilled the outsized expectations of the press nor rivaled Joltin' Joe's performance standards in the late 1930's. In those first four seasons, Mantle's average performance—.303 batting average with 112 runs scored, 27 home runs and 98 runs batted in—was far exceeded by the Yankee Clipper's .341 batting average, 130 runs scored, 34 home runs and 140 runs batted on average during the years 1936–1939.[42]

In late July of 1953, Daniel wrote a column explicitly comparing Mantle and DiMaggio—"Can Mickey Succeed Where Joe Failed?"[43] In the headline, Daniel asked whether Mantle could lead the Yankees to a fifth consecutive World Series title, something DiMaggio did not accomplish in 1940. Daniel acknowledged the age disparity in the comparison—Mantle was 21, DiMaggio was 25. In addition, Mantle was nearing the end of his third season at the time of the article's publication while DiMaggio had completed five seasons at the end of 1940. Daniel concluded that Mickey had yet to fulfill his early promise, and that he had not nearly equaled DiMaggio in his playing skills. He critiqued Mantle for being prone to injury, inconsistent in his fielding and throwing, and striking out too much. Implicit in Daniel's observations was a sense that Mantle was under constant pressure from the media to the point that it would have been quite difficult for him to live up to their expectations.[44]

Daniel referenced an astonishing feat accomplished by Mantle on April 17, 1953, exactly two years after his major-league début. Mantle's gargantuan home run in Washington's Griffith Stadium off Senators southpaw Chuck Stobbs was supposedly measured by Yankee public relations director Red Patterson as landing 565 feet from home plate in a neighboring back yard. The 83-year-old Senators owner, Clark Griffith, said that it was "the longest home run hit in the history of baseball."[45] Daniel expressed the belief that a great deal of publicity and many television appearances resulted from the home run, but that it was not necessarily a good thing for Mantle.[46] The occasional colossal poke (and there were many others of what were later called "tape-measure home runs") only underscored his tremendous potential and the frustration that both he and the fan base felt when he could not produce consistently. As late as 1955, Mantle was often booed at Yankee Stadium. Sports columnist Milton Gross described a game where, after the public address announcer introduced Mantle, "…the boos rolled across the huge ball park like thunder in a summer night."[47] As described by Randy Roberts and Johnny Smith in their 2018 book *A Season in the Sun*, Gross interviewed fans classifying Mantle as lazy, overrated, and uncaring about them while the press that Gross interviewed mocked Mantle for his lack of intelligence.[48]

In 1956, Mantle had his breakout season and truly fulfilled the promise that he displayed as a 19-year-old prodigy in the Arizona desert. The season that Mantle memorialized in another of his many ghost-authored books, *My Favorite Summer: 1956*, was the first Triple Crown season since Ted Williams accomplished the feat in 1947. It had the added mystique of being an achievement that DiMaggio could never claim. Mantle not only led the AL with 52 home runs, 130 runs batted in, and a .353 batting average, but he also led the league with a .705 slugging percentage; his .467 OBP was edged out by Ted Williams.

Robert Creamer was one of dozens of scribes writing about Mantle's feats, which were transcending even DiMaggio's, and the consequent status of a prodigy fulfilling his potential. In the June 18, 1956, edition of *Sports Illustrated*, Creamer describes the home run off Washington Senators hurler Pedro Ramos in Yankee Stadium on May 30th; the ball hit the right field façade and came a foot or two from clearing the roof and being the first ball hit out of the ballpark. It has become a seminal work for budding sportswriters to study, particularly Creamer's capturing the fans' visceral reactions to the mammoth home run and other Mantle achievements, including his home run pace surpassing Ruth's at the same point in the season when the Sultan of Swat hit 60 home runs in 1927, a single-season record until Roger Maris broke it in 1961 with 61 round trippers.[49]

Mantle turned another corner in 1956, becoming an endorsement king. In the immediate aftermath of his triple-crown season, he represented more than 10 companies in advertisements[50] and reportedly earned $59,000 in endorsement money, roughly double his 1956 salary.[51] It was his best year. In his sixth major-league season, Mickey Charles Mantle had truly become an American hero, just as Joltin' Joe DiMaggio did in 1941, his sixth major-league season, with the 56-game hitting streak. Mantle would still occasionally be booed, as he did not sustain the excellence of 1956 in subsequent seasons. He really became an eternally beloved Yankee brand icon in 1961, when he was greatly favored by fans to beat out Roger Maris for Ruth's single-season record of 60 home runs. Maris broke it on the last day of the season with his 61st home run, while an injury had forced Mantle to the bench for several games. Consequently, he dropped off the pace in September, ending the season with a career-high of 54 home runs.[52]

Yankee pitching coach Jim Turner, sensing Mantle's ascendance to hero status, summarized the essence of the Commerce Comet in 1956: "That Mantle is something that America has needed—and something America hasn't had since DiMaggio."[53]

## NOTES

1. Jack Kofoed, "Thrills in Sports: 'Deadpan Joe Dimaggio Prospective Baseball Great,'" *New York Post*, 1933; reprinted in Richard Whittingham, ed., vol. 1 of 2 (1932–1941), *The DiMaggio Albums: Selections from Public and Private Collections Celebrating the Baseball Career of Joe DiMaggio* (New York: G.P. Putnam's Sons, 1989), 28.

2. "Youthful S.F. Star Hits in 50th Game," Associated Press, *Oakland Tribune*, July 15, 1933: 11.

3. Richard C. Crepeau, *Baseball: America's Diamond Mind* (Gainesville: University Press of Florida, 1980); paperback ed. (Lincoln: University of Nebraska Press, 2000), 124. Citations refer to the paperback edition.

4. Joseph Durso, *DiMaggio: The Last American Knight* (Boston: Little, Brown and Company 1995), 67.

5. Richard Ben Cramer, *Joe DiMaggio: The Hero's Life* (New York: Simon & Schuster 2000), 80, 81.

6. Paul Dickson, *The Dickson Baseball Dictionary,* 3rd ed. (New York: W.W. Norton & Company, 2009), 137–38.

7. Warren Corbett, "Dan Daniel," Society for American Baseball Research Baseball Biography Project, www.sabr.org/bioproj/person/58a3764c, last accessed August 13, 2018.

8. Dan Daniel, "Yankees Headed for West Determined to Keep Lead," *New York World-Telegram*, May 11, 1936: 23, reprinted in Whittingham, 1:73.

9. Edward T. Murphy, "Dimaggio's Average Mounts: Jolting Joe, Now Hitting .340, May Set Highest Mark for First-Year Player," in *The DiMaggio Albums*, vol. 1., 99 (undated but appears to be late season 1933); Jack Cuddy, "Frisco Kid: Joe Dimaggio? As He Goes, So Go the Yankees?," *Washington Post*, September 30, 1936: X19 ("A lot of experts believe that Jolting Joe, with his rifle arm and his antelope gollop [sic] and his deadly arm snap of the bat, was the real spark plug behind the Yanks' thundering march to the pennant this year—that he was murder with a capital 'M' on murderers' row and suicide with a capital "S" on the suicide squad."). One example of the "Giuseppe" moniker appears in the *Democrat and Chronicle* recount of the 4–3 National League victory in the 1936 All-Star Game, though it's misspelled: "Note to the Mulberry Street Mob—Guisseppi [sic], a cool, calm, collected guy, got himself all tangled up in a mess of spaghetti in the fifth and practically cost Mr. Harridge's horde the ball game when DiMaggio tried to make a shoestring catch instead of playing it safe, and instead of a single it went for a double by [the Cubs' Billy] Herman." Jack Miley, "We Won!—Eh, Diz?," *Democrat and Chronicle* (Rochester, New York) July 9, 1936: 20.

10. "Joe Louis: When He Puts 'Em Down They Usually Stay," *Baltimore Afro-American*, September 7, 1935: 21 ("His flailing fists have earned him such titles as the Brown Bomber, Detroit Destroyer, Tan Thunderbolt, Jolting Joe, Dusky Dynamite, and many others in the thirteen months since he cast his lot with the professionals, and since that fight with Adolph Wiater, only two other men have stayed ten rounds with him."); "16,486 Watch Negro Pound Foe to Floor with Vicious Blows," Associated Press, *Washington Post*, January 18, 1936: 15 ("Charley Retzlaff, raw-boned North Dakota rancher, finished lying on his side, his glassy eyes staring at the ring lights, exactly 1 minute and 25 seconds after he raised his hands for his scheduled 15-round fight with Jolting Joe Louis [sic] in the Chicago Stadium tonight."); "Henderson works with Joe Louis," Associated Press, *Hartford Courant* January 14, 1936: 13 ("Otis Thomas, 190 pound negro, gave Louis his best workout. He faced Jolting Joe for two rounds and absorbed punches without hitting the canvas."); George Drape Davis, "As I See It," *Atlanta Daily World*, June 10, 1936: 5 ("On the night of June 18, in the famed ring of the 20th Century Sporting Club, under big bright lights, Jolting Joe Louis [sic], the pride of all fistiana, an answer to Promoter Mike Jacobs' prayer and Max Schmeling, the sturdy 'Black Uhlan' of the Rhine, are slated to square on in the most important and greatest ring contest since the old days when Jack Dempsey's mighty dukes were devastating the rank of the heavyweight division.)

11. Quentin Reynolds, "The Frisco Kid," *Collier's*, June 13, 1936, 29.

12. Dickson, 138.

13. Cuddy.

14. Shirley Povich, "This Morning...", *Washington Post*, May 31, 1936: X3, quoted in *The DiMaggio Albums*, vol.1, 80.

15. *Ibid.*

16. Daniel, "Daniel's Dope," *New York World-Telegram*, October 14, 1936: 35, reprinted in Whittingham, 1:119.

17. Frank Graham, *The New York Yankees* (New York: G.P. Putnam's Sons 1948), 226.

18. American League and New York Yankee attendance figures found in John Thorn and Peter Palmer, eds., *Total Baseball* (New York: Warner Books, 1989); 5th ed., John Thorn, Pete Palmer, Michael Gershman, and David Pietrusza, eds. (New York: Penguin Books USA Inc. 1997), 103. Citations refer to the 5th edition.

19. 1937 AL attendance increased another 13.3 percent from 1936 while Yankee attendance only increased 2.2 percent from 1936 after a jump of 48.6 percent from its 1935 Yankee total.

20. In his excellent book on Depression-era baseball, Charles Alexander states that baseball players were often measure by the "undefinable quality called 'color'" during those times. Sportswriters, Alexander opined, hoped that Joe DiMaggio was colorful but "as yet they had been disappointed." Charles Alexander, *Breaking the SLUMP: Baseball in the Depression Era* (New York: Columbia University Press 2002), 139.

21. Cramer, 152; Mel Allen, foreword to *The Men of Autumn: An Oral History of the 1949–53 World Champion New York Yankees* by Dom Forker (Dallas: Taylor Books, 1989); paperback ed., New York: Signet Printing, 1990), xii. Allen cites DiMaggio on the source of the "Yankee Clipper" nickname: "Arch McDonald who I broke in under, coined that name in 1939." Citations refer to the paperback edition.

22. Roy Blount, Jr., "LEGEND: How DiMaggio Made It Look Easy," in *The Ultimate Baseball Book*, eds. Daniel Okrent and Harris Lewine (New York: Houghton Mifflin, 1979), 194.

23. Jane Leavy, *The Last Boy: Mickey Mantle and the End of America's Childhood* (New York: HarperCollins Publishers 2010), 67.

24. Porter Wittich, "Globetrotter," *Joplin Globe*, September 21, 1950: 12.

25. *Ibid.*

26. "Porter Wittich," Joplin Sports Authority, www.joplinsports.org/hall-of-fame/entry/porter-wittich, last accessed April 23, 2018.

27. Wendell Redden, "Former Boss Inducted into Hall of Fame," *Joplin Globe*, June 30, 2008: 1B.

28. https://joplinsports.org/hall-of-fame/entry/porter-wittich.

29. This author found no references to that nickname before Wittich's usage of it in his September 21, 1950 column.

30. Bill Repplinger, "A Mickey Mantle Story," *Mound City Memories* (Cleveland: Society for American Baseball Research, 2007), 40.

31. Red Smith, "Opening Day, Yankee Stadium," Views of Sport, *New York Herald Tribune*, April 18, 1951: 31, reprinted in *Red Smith on Baseball: The Game's Greatest Writer on the Game's Greatest Years* (Chicago: Ivan R. Dee 2000), 117.

32. Smith, "Opening Day, Yankee Stadium," 119.

33. Donald Honig, *Mays, Mantle, Snider: A Celebration* (New York: MacMillan Publishing Company, 1987), 68.

34. *Ibid.*, 69.

35. Dan Daniel, "Mickey Signed to K.C. Pact, but New York Will See Him," *Sporting News*, April 4, 1951: 4.

36. Clarence Young, "Radio and Television to Salute Baseball Week, April 14 to 21," *Sporting News*, April 11, 1951: 18. *The Big Show* was a comedy-variety program hosted by Tallulah Bankhead. The April 15th broadcast was one of several shows promoting baseball that week. archive.org/details/OTTR_The_Big_Show_Singles?51–0415_ep24_Eddie_Cantor_Jack_Carson.mp3, last accessed July 25, 2018.

37. Leavy, 24, 176–77.

38. Daniel, "Mickey Signed to K.C. Pact, but New York Will See Him."

39. Mickey Mantle, *The Education of a Baseball Player* (New York: Benco Edition, published by arrangement with Simon & Schuster, 1967), 70.

40. *Ibid.*

41. Cramer, 301.

42. Of course, these raw numbers do not provide overall performance assessments that have been calculated prospectively using wins above replacement (WAR) or other advanced metrics. Because those measures did not exist, the raw totals were the only relevant comparisons when both played. Slugging percentages were computed in the eras of Mantle and DiMaggio but on-base percentages (OBP) were not generally available. Mantle had a slightly better OBP (.408 to DiMaggio's .397) in comparing their first four full seasons. DiMaggio had a much better slugging percentage, .622 to Mantle's .542. On-base plus slugging percentage (OPS), which did not exist during their playing days, has DiMaggio at 1.019 to Mantle's .950, a clear superiority for DiMaggio in this four-season comparison.

43. Dan Daniel, "Can Mickey Succeed Where Joe Failed?," *Sporting News* July 29,1953: 2.

44. *Ibid.*

45. "Mantle Poke Longest—Griff," *The Sporting News* April 17, 1953: 13.

46. Daniel, "Can Mickey Succeed Where Joe Failed?"

47. Milton Gross, quoted in Honig, *Mays, Mantle, Snider*, 78.

48. Randy Roberts and Johnny Smith, *A Season in the Sun: The Rise of Mickey Mantle* (New York: Basic Books 2018), 48–49.

49. Robert Creamer, "The Mantle of the Babe," https://www.si.com/vault/1956/06/18/620630/the-mantle-of-the-babe, last accessed April 25, 20184.

50. Roberts and Smith, 114.

51. Jonathan Light, *The Cultural Encyclopedia of Baseball* (Jefferson, NC: McFarland, 1997), 231.

52. 1961 was the first year for a 162-game season. Ruth hit 60 in 154 games.

53. David Condon, Condonsations, "'Mantle Something U.S. Has Needed'—Turner," *Sporting News*, July 4, 1956: 16.

# Joe DiMaggio, Mickey Mantle and the Cultural Impact of Yankee Excellence

DUKE GOLDMAN

## The Personality Brands of the Paragon and the Prodigy

Joe DiMaggio and Mickey Mantle became heroic figures in the hearts and minds of baseball fans, reporters, teammates, and even the general public that had a tangential interest and minimal knowledge concerning the National Pastime. Each developed a brand identity during their careers and after retirement. In some ways, the attributes of those brands remained true to their initial images—Joe D. as the perfect ballplayer who never made a mistake, Mickey Mantle as the player of unlimited talent and potential fulfilling expectations in mid-career but ultimately never reaching the Ruthian levels that were expected, especially by media commentators. Both players struggled with the unrelenting demands of their audiences to continually embody these images, especially in the aftermath of their careers.

### Joe D.

Joe DiMaggio's personality as a New York Yankee evolved from the "Deadpan Joe" who played in the Pacific Coast League from 1933 through 1935. Initially, Joe D. was known more for what he was not—an expressive, colorful ballplayer who not only displayed talents but also displayed emotion. But his Pacific Coast League identity was that of a quiet, efficient, expressionless yet successful practitioner of the ballplaying arts, one who drew attention to himself through his batting and fielding exploits only. When he arrived in New York, with breathtaking advance reviews as the "amazing paragon" of the Pacific Coast League,"[1] he immediately displayed refined talents and a style of play demonstrating dramatic aesthetic qualities that went along with the home runs, throws, and catches leading to Yankee victories.

DiMaggio was a graceful player who embodied perfection; he rarely made any mistakes, by throwing to the wrong base or getting thrown out on the basepaths. He also did not make flashy plays. In his book *Beyond DiMaggio* on Italian ballplayers, Lawrence

70

Baldassaro writes, "DiMaggio made everything look easy.... The Italians have a word for it: *sprezzatura*—the art of making the difficult look easy. But *sprezzatura* defines the *appearance* of ease and simplicity. In reality it is a mask concealing all the preparation and effort that precede excellence [Italics in original]."[2]

During World War II, when America was looking for male role models, DiMaggio became a heroic figure, even though his war service was stateside. The perception of fans, sportswriters, and teammates was that Joe was the best player they had ever seen. In 1941, Art Rust, Jr., was a 14-year-old fan who later became a sportswriter. He believed that DiMaggio was "the greatest player I ever saw.... But I was not alone. There were millions of Americans who identified with the spirit of the man. It was World War II, and perhaps all of us needed Joe for courage and at least diversion. We knew Joe could beat the unbeatable foe."[3] His Herculean achievement of hitting safely in 56 consecutive games in 1941 inspired belief by others that they could manage the immense challenges of wartime, through preparation and effort, even if they could not make it look easy, as did DiMaggio.

One could argue that Joltin' Joe could also have been called "Broadway Joe" as one of his best friends in New York was George Solotaire, a ticket broker who often supplied DiMaggio with tickets to Broadway shows. There is no doubt that DiMaggio, despite being a San Francisco native who did not live in New York for any significant length of time after his career was over, continued to be perceived as a quintessential New York figure. Joe D. was also a denizen of Toots Shor's restaurant, a meeting place for members of the sports world, athletes and reporters alike, where he was the most revered figure in the sporting crowd as well as a friend of owner Toots Shor.

DiMaggio was also greatly admired by teammates for playing through his various ailments. A famous DiMaggio declaration is that he always played hard because he never knew when someone was seeing him play for the first time. His teammates showed their reverence for him when they surprised him with an engraved silver humidor in 1941 to honor him for his 56-game hitting streak. At the same time, most teammates, with rare exceptions such as Lefty Gomez, Joe Page, and Billy Martin, had little to do with DiMaggio off the field. Tommy Henrich told sportswriter Maury Allen that "Joe was kind of a cold guy; everybody knows that. He never asked me out to dinner alone in all the years I was with the Yankees, but I never asked him either."[4]

Overall, Joe DiMaggio was considered a noble, regal performer. He was perceived as a player of impeccable skills, who always played under control and delivered consistently. Although he was not originally thought of as a sex symbol, he became one when he married Hollywood starlet Dorothy Arnold and later, bombshell actress and sex symbol Marilyn Monroe.

After his career, DiMaggio's personal behavior was seen a bit more critically. He became known as someone who expected absolute loyalty from any friends, with any "betrayal" meaning an end to the friendship. He felt that he was always being exploited by others, and resented being asked for favors or being surprised by an uninvited guest to any social event he attended.

DiMaggio became a heroic personality symbol to the average American during difficult times, first during the Depression, and then during World War II. He was perfect as a pre-television personality. He was very nervous about TV appearances, did not like being interviewed, and did quite poorly in his one year as a pre-game and-post game interviewer for the Yankees. Before television, he was able to control his image by careful management of his playing style as well as the complicity of newspapers in keeping most of his private problems with his wife Dorothy Arnold and any off-field "escapades" out of print.

## The Mick

In 1951, Mickey Mantle became a Yankee at a time when the television age was ascendant. He was photogenic—a blond, blue-eyed, well-built country boy landing on Broadway as the replacement for Joe DiMaggio.

The three games in the 1951 National League playoff between the Brooklyn Dodgers and the New York Giants were the first baseball games broadcast on the West Coast via satellite. They determined who would get to play the Yankees in the 1951 World Series,[5] which was also Mickey's first post-season appearance. The Giants won the third and deciding game on Bobby Thomson's bottom-of-the-ninth three-run homer, also known as The Shot Heard Round the World. The Yankees beat the Giants in six games to win the World Series.

Mickey was perceived as perhaps the most talented baseball athlete to ever appear on the scene. He was regarded as a player who could produce astonishing feats through his speed and strength yet was unassuming, running the bases with his head down when he hit a home run. At first, Mantle was considered to be shy and rather ignorant, a hayseed in the big city. Like DiMaggio, Mantle became an athletic hero who had a sports following in the New York bars, including Toots Shor, who also became pals with Mantle. But Mickey always was a bit of an outsider in New York, a visitor from Oklahoma who arrived to bring energy and dynamism to a "rocking" era, when celebrity in music, movies, and television especially took off—from Elvis Presley, James Dean, Marilyn Monroe, and Lucille Ball to attractive athletes like Mantle.

Along with being a prodigy, there was a feeling for the first half of Mickey's career that he was not always industrious in the fulfillment of his gifts, and that he was temperamental when he failed, in stark contrast to DiMaggio's careful control of his expression, where an outburst like kicking the dirt when Al Gionfriddo caught his homer bid in the sixth game of the 1947 Series became famous because it was so uncharacteristic of Joe D. Mantle, instead, was seen as being immature and lacking self-control.

Gradually, though, it became known that Mantle's family was cursed by Hodgkin's disease, and Mickey was heroically playing despite crippling injuries. His image improved, especially after he became a superstar in 1956 with his first 50-home run season and proved himself worthy of the worshipful assessments that he gathered early on in his career.

Mickey was always loved by teammates. He was not a loner like DiMaggio, but "one of the boys" who was a buddy as well as a team leader. Notoriously with Whitey Ford and Billy Martin, he also developed a reputation as a partier and playboy, which both titillated his fan base and further substantiated claims that he never completely reached his potential because of his own lack of commitment to keeping himself in good condition to play. He especially had difficulties with sportswriters, as he could be very cold and dismissive with them, resenting their intrusions and constant questions. Nevertheless, Mantle was a beloved figure for them and so many that he played with and played for. Mantle dazzled all those who watched him—he was not, in any way, seen as the essence of perfection, but rather as a Bunyanesque hero accomplishing feats that no one had seen before. He was more akin to Ruth, while DiMaggio was closer to Lou Gehrig for his quiet pursuit of excellence. Mantle produced home runs and strikeouts in impressive numbers, like Ruth, and also partied like him. Gehrig and DiMaggio produced runs, hits, and power with regularity but not with fireworks. They were more admired for their strength of character.

## Comparing Joe DiMaggio and Mickey Mantle as Performers

### Statistical Comparisons

Joe DiMaggio was the more successful ballplayer when his first four seasons as a major-league ballplayer are compared to Mickey Mantle's first four full seasons, excluding his partial rookie season of 1951. Mantle, though, was playing in the major leagues after two seasons of low minor-league ball at the age of 19; DiMaggio was a veteran of three seasons in the Pacific Coast League when he reached the majors as a fully developed ballplayer at age 21. Mantle reached his peak in 1956, his fifth full season, and had his best seasons from then through 1964, when he began his decline phase. In contrast, Joe DiMaggio was not the same ballplayer after his sixth full season, 1941, although he still had several outstanding years.

### Career Comparison

|  | R | H | 2B | 3B | HR | RBI | W | K | AVG | OBP | SLG | OPS | WAR |
|---|---|---|---|---|---|---|---|---|---|---|---|---|---|
| DiMaggio | 1,390 | 2,214 | 389 | 131 | 361 | 1,537 | 790 | 369 | .325 | .398 | .579 | .977 | 78.1 |
| Mantle | 1,676 | 2,415 | 344 | 72 | 536 | 1,509 | 1,733 | 1,710 | .298 | .421 | .557 | .977 | 109.6 |

*Key: R—Runs; H—Hits; 2B—Doubles; 3B—Triples; HR—Home Runs; RBI—Runs Batted In; W—Walks; K—Strikeouts; AVG—Batting Average; OBP—On-Base Percentage; SLG—Slugging Percentage; OPS—On-Base plus Slugging Percentage; WAR—Wins Above Replacement.*

DiMaggio hit for a higher average, walked, and struck out considerably less than Mantle, was outdone by him in home runs, but drove in a few more runs while scoring almost 300 less times. Although Mantle was considered to be a home-run slugger and DiMaggio more of an all-around power hitter, it is interesting to compare their home run percentages. Mantle did hit more home runs per at bat—6.6 per 100 at-bats as compared to DiMaggio's 5.3 per 100. If you divide their home runs by 100 plate appearances, the difference is even smaller—DiMaggio hit 4.7 per 100, Mantle hit 5.4 per 100. Mantle was the better home-run hitter, but not by as much as one would think.

An interesting statistical coincidence is that Mantle and DiMaggio had identical OPS for their careers—.977. One must acknowledge that these numbers were accumulated in different offensive contexts. Generally, DiMaggio played in an era of somewhat better offense than did Mantle. Mantle's WAR is significantly better than that of DiMaggio, 109.6 to 78.1, although he did play approximately four more full seasons than did Joe D. and WAR is a cumulative (counting) statistic.[6] The WAR figure takes into account offense, defense, base running and position played, so it suggests that Mantle was the better all-around player.

If one compares Joltin' Joe's first six seasons to the best six-season stretch of the Commerce Comet's career (1956–1961), we get the following:

|          | R   | H     | 2B  | 3B  | HR  | RBI | W   | K   | AVG  | OBP  | SLG  | OPS   | WAR  |
|----------|-----|-------|-----|-----|-----|-----|-----|-----|------|------|------|-------|------|
| DiMaggio | 735 | 1,163 | 214 | 69  | 198 | 816 | 336 | 160 | .345 | .408 | .626 | 1.034 | 42.6 |
| Mantle   | 734 | 981   | 127 | 28  | 253 | 618 | 717 | 657 | .316 | .443 | .619 | 1.061 | 54.6 |

Dramatic differences and some similarities in their best six seasons can be easily discerned from this data. Mantle and DiMaggio scored almost the same number of runs, were very close in slugging percentage, and were quite close in OPS, although Mantle's is slightly better. The most important contrasts are in RBI, with DiMaggio driving in almost 200 more runs. In batting average, DiMaggio fares almost 30 points better. In walks and strikeouts, Mantle has more than twice as many walks and four times as many strikeouts as Joe D. In home runs, there is a clear advantage for Mantle. And finally, in WAR, Mantle is still significantly ahead of DiMaggio.

Many teammates and commentators have observed how impressive it was that DiMaggio struck out so rarely—he K'd only 13 times in his streak season of 1941, and ended his career with only 8 more strikeouts than home runs. It is worth noting, however, that in Mantle's best seasons, he walked a bit more than he struck out, even as he consistently fanned about 100 times per season.

DiMaggio's significant advantage in RBI can be attributed to the better offensive context in which he played.[7] During several of Mantle's best years, managers Casey Stengel and Ralph Houk batted Bobby Richardson and Tony Kubek at the top of the batting order. In 1961, while both players batted more than 600 times, Richardson scored 80 runs with a below .300 OBP and Kubek scored 84 runs with an OPB barely above .300. Roger Maris, who batted third ahead of Mantle, led the league with 132 runs scored but drove himself in 61 times with home runs, making it much harder for Mantle to drive in anyone. Mantle still drove in 128 runs, two short of his career high in 1956, but 39 less than DiMaggio's career high of 167 in 1937.

Finally, if one compares Mickey Mantle's three peak seasons—1956, 1957, and 1961—to Joe DiMaggio's peak years of 1937, 1939, and 1941, we get the following data:

|          | R   | H   | 2B  | 3B  | HR  | RBI | W   | K   | AVG  | OBP  | SLG  | OPS   | WAR  |
|----------|-----|-----|-----|-----|-----|-----|-----|-----|------|------|------|-------|------|
| DiMaggio | 381 | 584 | 110 | 32  | 106 | 418 | 192 | 70  | .360 | .431 | .663 | 1.094 | 25.4 |
| Mantle   | 384 | 524 | 66  | 17  | 140 | 352 | 384 | 286 | .345 | .474 | .686 | 1.161 | 33   |

In their three best seasons, both put on outstanding performances, but Mantle has narrowed some areas where he trailed—RBI and batting average—and extended others where he led—OPS and WAR.

In conclusion, Mantle was clearly a superior ballplayer at his peak. In fact, many have concluded that he was also superior to contemporary Willie Mays at the peak of their respective careers. Just as Mays was generally considered a better all-around player than Mantle, DiMaggio was voted the best living player over both (and Hank Aaron, Stan Musial, and Ted Williams as well) when a vote of sportswriters was taken in conjunction with the centennial of professional baseball in 1969.

It is well known that DiMaggio often requested that he be introduced as the Greatest Living Ballplayer at events such as old-timers games. How much did DiMaggio benefit from his image of perfection and grace, while Mantle suffered for the outsized expectations many had of him and the profligate partying behavior he became known for? There is the potential for placing too much emphasis on one vote of sportswriters as an important benchmark of their relative worth as players. In contrast, one could point to Mantle being inducted into the Hall of Fame in his first try, while it took three tries for DiMaggio to be inducted. One should look at each of these votes as subjective assessments made within specific circumstances. The Greatest Living Ballplayer vote was made in conjunction with a celebration of the game's history when Mantle had just retired. The Hall of Fame votes "snubbing" DiMaggio occurred when the Hall was still working through a backlog of earlier stars yet to be inducted and the five-year wait after a player's retirement had not yet been instituted. Had DiMaggio been first voted on in 1957, there is little doubt that he would have gotten in immediately. DiMaggio biographer Joe Durso speculated that DiMaggio's initial low vote total in 1953 may have been due to a sense of resentment by non–New York sportswriters about Yankees being glamorized—putting in DiMaggio so soon after retirement when many other long-retired and highly qualified heroes had not yet been inducted would be moving Joe D. ahead of his turn at glory.[8]

When Joltin' Joe DiMaggio was voted the best living ballplayer in 1969, he was a living legend—a ballplayer admired for his seemingly peerless effortless play. But modern-day analytics suggest that he is a bit overrated by those who considered him the best. Official Major League Baseball historian John Thorn has expressed the view that many other Hall of Fame center fielders were better on defense than DiMaggio, if either the amount of plays made rather than never having to dive for a ball or, supposedly, never making a mistake is used as a standard.[9] The offensive production of DiMaggio certainly pales in comparison to that of contemporary Ted Williams, predecessors Babe Ruth and Lou Gehrig, and successors Mays and Mantle. But, Thorn eloquently states that "when you put it all together, the myth counts. The story counts. It's not just stats. The DiMaggio myth transcends history and you deny it at your peril."[10]

## Performance Myths of the Paragon and the Prodigy

The image of the complete ballplayer who never makes a mistake is a part of the brand of personality identified with Joe DiMaggio. Joe's first major-league manager, Joe McCarthy, said of Joe D. that "he never made a mental mistake. He never missed a sign; he never threw to the wrong base."[11]

While Joe's actual performance in the field was certainly stellar, he did make mistakes, in one notable instance during one of his best outfield plays. In late 1939, slugger Hank Greenberg hit a tremendous blast to the deepest part of Yankee Stadium, and, as described by pitcher Spud Chandler, "DiMaggio … took off with the crack of the bat, on a dead run going, at a kind of angle toward the fence.… Right at the fence, at the 460 mark, he just flicked out his glove, and caught the ball."[12] What Chandler did not mention to oral historian Donald Honig was that base runner Earl Averill was almost at third base when DiMaggio caught the ball. According to DiMaggio, "I pulled a rock. I thought there were three out, and I was running in with the ball before I saw Averill scrambling to get back to first."[13]

A review of the box scores of DiMaggio's 56-game hitting streak indicates that he made no fewer than seven errors or one for every eight games he played during that stretch.[14] In games 15 and 16 of the streak, Joe D. played in a doubleheader tilt with the Boston Red Sox at Fenway Park. DiMaggio had a stiff neck and a sore shoulder, which led him to commit four errors in the doubleheader—one in the first game, when he dropped a fly ball, and three in the second game, including a mishandling of a ground ball single by Ted Williams and two wild throws that ended up crashing into the box seat railings. His performance inspired a cartoon caption in a Gene Mack cartoon in the next day's *Boston Globe*: "[S]eldom on any field has anyone equaled his wild throwing."[15] While DiMaggio's performance that day was certainly the worst fielding day of his major league career, his error-filled afternoon showed that even a ballplayer known for his unerring performances could have an atrocious one.

Was Joltin' Joe's vaunted base-running ability exaggerated? Manager Joe McCarthy weighed in: "He wasn't the fastest man alive. He just knew how to run the bases better than anybody. He could have stolen 50 or 60 bases a year if I let him."[16] Although the suggestion that Joe D. could have successfully stolen more bases than Jackie Robinson's career high of 37 in one season seems doubtful, there is evidence that Joe was a smart base runner. In sportswriter Tom Meany's 1952 article "DiMaggio, As I Knew Him," he quotes DiMaggio as follows: "[I]n 1935, my last year with the San Francisco Seals, I stole 24 bases in 25 attempts."[17]

In his first three major-league seasons, DiMaggio stole a total of 16 bases, and was only thrown out one time. If the information is correct on his Pacific Coast League success rate,[18] DiMaggio was successful in 40 out of 42 steal attempts during four years of play, or 95.2 percent of the time. Not quite perfect, but almost.

The Mantle mythology centers on his unprecedented power/speed combination. According to DiMaggio biographer Richard Ben Cramer, Casey Stengel described Mickey thusly: "[H]e has more speed than any slugger and more slug than any speedster—and nobody ever has had more of both of 'em together."[19] Accordingly, there are many mentions throughout the voluminous Mantle literature of his incredible, unmatched speed running down to first base. There are various claims that Mantle ran from home to first in 3.1 seconds, 3.0 seconds, 2.9 seconds. Some sources indicate that he could run 3.0 seconds from the left side and 3.1 seconds from the right side. Even allowing that times of the past were less accurate as they relied on stopwatches, these times must be exaggerated. In 2016, Statcast determined that the fastest time (non-bunt) for a right-handed batter running to first base was 3.72 seconds by Byron Buxton, and the fastest left-handed was 3.61 by Billy Hamilton.[20]

Whitey Ford, unlike others who promoted this myth, at least gave specifics to his claim, stating that sportswriter Lou Miller timed Mickey with his stopwatch at "3.1 from home plate to first base. *On a bunt going to first base* (emphasis added)."[21] In an interview for John Tullius's oral history *I'd Rather Be a Yankee*, pitcher Eddie Lopat claimed about Mantle that "[O]n a drag bunt, he could get to first in 3.1 seconds. On the left side he could get there in 3.4 or 3.5. Right now there's no one as fast as Mantle was."[22]

It is therefore extremely doubtful that Mickey Mantle could run faster than about 3.5 seconds to first base without bunting. And in all likelihood, that was no longer true after his devastating knee injury in 1951.

The other great myth of Mantle's career was the 565-foot home run that he hit against Chuck Stobbs in Washington's Griffith Stadium on April 17, 1953. Yankee public relations man Red Patterson claimed that he found a 10-year-old boy named Donald Dunnaway [SIC—correct spelling later determined to be "Dunaway"] who was showing the ball to other children. Dunaway then showed Patterson the spot where he retrieved the ball.

Patterson then "produced the measurements for the Mantle homer as 565 feet, although Senators vice-president Calvin Griffith supposedly measured it later as 552 feet."[23] Author Jane Leavy did crack investigative work for her 2010 biography *The Last*

*Boy* and found Dunaway more than 50 years later. She discovered that Dunaway did find the ball but never showed a landing spot to Red Patterson.[24] In 1969, this story was turned into the "myth of the tape measure home run" as broadcaster Mel Allen did a re-creation of his home run call (which had not been recorded) in which he described how Red Patterson took out a tape measure and went to find the ball.

Patterson later admitted that he never used a tape measure and experts to this day can only estimate how far the ball travelled—certainly more than 500 feet but likely closer to 500 than 565. "(T)he number 565 is pure fiction,"[25] states Yale professor Robert Adair, the author of *The Physics of Baseball*.

The feats of Joltin' Joe and The Commerce Comet as Yankee icons and superstar ballplayers are scintillating in their verifiable versions. In the hero development of both players, hyperbole added to the mystique that each player carried with them as they developed images that they could sell to the American public.

## DiMaggio and Mantle: Endorsement Brands and Identities in Popular Culture

### Mr. Coffee

Joe DiMaggio became a recognizable brand during the early stages of his major-league career. After his 1936 rookie season, he became an investor in a restaurant to be run by his brother Tom in his hometown. "Joe DiMaggio's Grotto was located at San Francisco's Fisherman's Wharf."[26] Although Joe was, in no way, sophisticated about business at this stage of his development, he and Tom recognized that his name already had value as a brand.

Over the course of his 84-year life, DiMaggio built significant *brand equity*, a term that has been defined as "A brand's power derived from the goodwill and name recognition that it has earned over time."[27] Not only did Jolting Joe DiMaggio deliver powerful clouts, but his name now had power. Gradually, Joe cashed in on that value as a brand endorser. One example was the restaurant doubling its daily revenues in the days after the 56-game hitting streak magnetized the public's attention.[28]

In addition to the restaurant, Joe endorsed Wheaties early in his career, which was almost a given for any star baseball player of that era. He also endorsed Camel cigarettes.[29] There were print advertisements showing both DiMaggio swinging a bat and in a suit holding a Camel cigarette in hand. Camel apparently decided that its brand attribute of mildness was represented well by a ballplayer known for his gracefulness and fluidity of movement, one who could make challenging plays look easy.[30]

Not only did Joe D. appear in magazine ads for Camel, but he was featured in a mammoth billboard overlooking Times Square with his picture next to the words "Heavy-hitting baseball star Joe DiMaggio feels the same way about Camels as so many millions of smokers do…. Says Joe: …I stick to Camels. They don't irritate my throat or get my nerves jumpy…."[31]

Although Joe DiMaggio was not the only famous figure to appear as an endorser on a Times Square billboard, he was particularly resonant as a quintessential New York celebrity. New York restaurateur and DiMaggio pal Toots Shor was known to say about DiMaggio and New York that "[I]t's Joe's town."[32] In *Summer of '49*, writing about the

1949 season, when DiMaggio's Yankees knocked out the Red Sox in the season's final two games, David Halberstam noted that in New York "…there was no doubt who the ultimate celebrity was in those days: DiMaggio."[33]

He took advantage of that celebrity, as evidenced by a description of a ride that teammate Frank "Spec" Shea gave Joltin' Joe to the ballpark in the late 1940's. According to Shea, during that ride, Joe D. opened envelopes that contained $12,000 in endorsement checks, quite a hefty sum in those early post-war days.[34] DiMaggio biographer Richard Ben Cramer says that as DiMaggio neared the end of his career, he "had more endorsement offers than he could handle. He was already doing cereal and cigarettes, a line of toiletries, T-shirts, sport shirts, rubber balls with his autograph stamped on, baseballs, baseball gloves and bats."[35]

Overall, DiMaggio was preparing for a post-baseball career by being "fully involved in the business of being DiMaggio." In addition to endorsements, that included a weekly 15-minute radio show geared towards children on CBS radio, a new edition of his auto-biography *Lucky to Be a Yankee*, a recording of baseball stories called *Little Johnny Strike-out*, and negotiations to appear in movies, including a biography of his life.[36]

Despite these promotional activities, DiMaggio was not fully prepared for the new age that was dawning as he retired from ball playing—the age of television. Halberstam dubbed DiMaggio "the last great hero of the radio era."[37] But, as Halberstam points out, television could easily overexpose an athlete, and TV appearances could create an unpleasant contrast between the seemingly flawless athlete DiMaggio presented on the baseball diamond and the awkward and uncomfortable presentation he could make on a late-night talk show.[38]

DiMaggio nonetheless agreed to do a pre- and post-game TV show for the Yankees for $100,000 (his 1951 salary) in his first post-retirement year, 1952. The degree to which he disliked this job was demonstrated by his quitting it after one season.[39] At the time, Joe D. was beginning his star-crossed romance with Marilyn Monroe.

In the ensuing years, while DiMaggio romanced, married, divorced, attempted to reconcile with, arranged the funeral of, and mourned the loss of his beloved Marilyn, he worked in public relations for three years for the V. H. Monette Company, a merchandise supplier for military post-exchange stores.[40] Throughout the 1950s and 1960s, Joltin' Joe continued to make appearances at charity events, golf tournaments, old-timers games, and testimonial dinners, but he generally avoided doing television commercials.

In the early 1970s, DiMaggio crossed paths with songwriter Paul Simon, whose 1967 song "Mrs. Robinson" with partner Art Garfunkel included the famous refrain lamenting DiMaggio's absence. According to Simon, DiMaggio was perplexed about this line, saying that he had not gone anywhere, and was a spokesman for the Bowery Savings Bank and Mr. Coffee.[41]

When the line was written, though, Joe D. had not started doing these two iconic advertising campaigns, which reintroduced him to an American public that had not seen very much of him, except through the combustible "Marilyn and Joe" saga.

In his often-anthologized 1966 *Esquire* piece "The Silent Season of a Hero," Gay Talese writes that DiMaggio was a man in his early fifties who fiercely protected his privacy, deflecting all inquiries regarding his relationship with Marilyn Monroe. Talese depicted DiMaggio as "tense and suspicious," spending idle time at the family restaurant with loyal associates, and otherwise making spring training appearances for the Yankees, engaging in business dealings, and playing golf.[42] One later business endeavor was a bit surprising. It was reported in early 1970 that he was about to open a franchise restaurant specializing in Italian food, despite his dislike of being associated with his Italian heritage because of blatant stereotyping early in his career.[43] As no other references have been found to this enterprise, it is likely that it was very short-lived.

DiMaggio had only dabbled in TV commercials before Mr. Coffee and the Bowery Savings Bank. When the Bowery first approached him in the early 1970's, DiMaggio recalled his experience with a Brylcreem advertisement and said, "I didn't know what I was doing out there."[44] Despite his history of doing Camel cigarette ads, Joe D. made it known in agreeing to do the Bowery's advertising that he would not do beer or cigarette advertising or any other advertising that he thought could damage his image.[45]

Although DiMaggio was apparently stiff at the start, he eventually got better and became more involved in the conceiving and filming of the advertising. When Robert Spero, an Ogilvy & Mather ad executive, told his nine-year-old son that he had just signed a famous ballplayer for the Bowery advertising campaign, his son guessed that the ballplayer was Joe DiMaggio, showing that even a generation after he stopped playing, Joltin' Joe still had name recognition, even with people who were not born when he played.[46]

The Bowery stopped doing television advertising in 1984, but when it decided to resume in 1989, there remained a strong connection between the bank and DiMaggio in the minds of focus-group participants. They decided to run new advertising including DiMaggio because his integrity connected well with the Bowery's image as an honest lending institution, which could enhance the brand equity of the bank. It had recently been acquired by Home Savings of America, a Los Angeles banking enterprise.[47]

Even more iconic than DiMaggio's Bowery commercials, which aired only in the New York City area, were his nationally-advertised Mr. Coffee TV commercials. The business developer of Mr. Coffee, Vince Marotta, began to develop his coffeemaker in the late 1960s as an alternative to the old-style percolators and instant coffee that he loathed. In 1973, Marotta approached Joe DiMaggio, whom he believed would be the "perfect pitchman for Mr. Coffee" because he was "a great baseball hero … a class guy…. (H)e was a gentleman in every respect and had the mystique from his marriage to Marilyn Monroe. I thought that would give the product a lot of oomph."[48]

DiMaggio promoted Mr. Coffee for 14 years, simultaneously becoming known to a generation of TV watchers as "Mr. Coffee" while the product became synonymous with coffee makers. As one writer concluded, "DiMaggio had an instinct for associating himself with brands consumers could trust."[49]

In later years, Joe DiMaggio became a fixture on the autograph and memorabilia circuit. He sold his name for various items, including 1,941 baseball bats to commemorate the year of the hitting streak. During the 1980s, the mania surrounding sports cards and memorabilia enabled DiMaggio, Mantle, and other pinstriped Hall of Famers to cash in on their enduring status as Yankee brand icons to the tune of millions of dollars. Did Joe DiMaggio tarnish his brand by selling his image in this fashion? There is no easy answer to that question. Undoubtedly, by affixing his name to thousands of items, he diluted their eventual value. And there were people who felt that he "sold out." Yet his legacy endures, even as fewer people survive who remember his on-field accomplishments and his admirable image as a faultless performer who sacrificed for his team.

In his 2017 book *Dinner with DiMaggio*, podiatrist Rock Positano, a constant companion during Joltin' Joe's later years, wrote,

Joe took his own role in the business of being Joe DiMaggio seriously. He knew that working the crowd, admittedly a very select crowd, was an important aspect of letting the show go on, and contributing to the value of his brand. Joe DiMaggio could always satisfy people, and he viewed this as part of his business. The business of entertainment occurred off the field as well as on it.... Joe was adept at polishing his image and collecting loyal fans. His appeal was irresistible as was his desire to be as perfect as possible.[50]

Whether Joe DiMaggio was reaching a wide audience with television advertising, or a select audience at an autograph show or an awards banquet, he knew who he was and what the audience wanted. And he delivered.

## The Ubiquitous Mick: Mickey Mantle (Enterprises) Is Everywhere ... And Everyman

Mickey Mantle began his endorsement career and became a marketable celebrity even before he played his first major-league contest. From these initial exposures, Mantle began a 44-year excursion into the American consciousness. Justly or unjustly, particularly in the early stages of his career, Mantle was criticized for not giving his all on the playing field. But he certainly covered all the bases off it.

The simultaneous dawning of his career with television's birth as a mass medium enabled the development of the Mantle brand in multiple directions. Unlike DiMaggio, whose promotional messaging as a selective product endorser was separated from the profound impact he made as a virtuous hero of song, theater, literature, and art, Mantle embedded his many endorsement and business endeavors within an inclusive populist framework.

The constellation of brands that Mantle created and/or represented overlapped with his masculine folk hero/sex symbol cultural identity. Mantle was more relatable to the "average Joe" (average guy) yet less resonant in American cultural values than was Joltin' Joe. As expressed by Richard Lewis in the 2005 HBO special *Mantle: The Definitive Story of Mickey Mantle*,[51] he may have been Superman in Yankee pinstripes, "[B]ut the truth is ... he was just a regular guy. He had this aura about him that he was just one of us."[52]

The year 1951 was a propitious one for Mickey Mantle to arrive in the Big Apple. The Yankees were arriving at the midpoint of their unprecedented and never-to-be-repeated five-year run as World Series champions, televisions were selling like wildfire as they were now penetrating the American household market after several years of being more of a specialty product seen mostly at bars, and Frank Scott was looking for work. Scott had been the travelling secretary of the Yankees since 1947, but at the end of the 1950 season, Yankees General Manager George Weiss fired Scott, ostensibly because of his unwillingness to be a source of information for the Yankee front office on the private lives of Yankee ballplayers.[53] Building on his close relationship with Yankee players, Scott decided to start a business as a player agent for "radio, television, testimonials, and the like."[54] Almost immediately, Scott signed up Phil Rizzuto, Yogi Berra, Hank Bauer, and Eddie Lopat.[55]

While Mantle adjusted to the New York limelight in 1951 and 1952, he signed with the unscrupulous Alan Savitt, who convinced Mickey that they should split all deals 50–50. During the process of getting that deal invalidated, Mickey was already edging his way into the worlds of advertising and television. In 1952, Mickey made an appearance on the TV game show *I've Got a Secret*,[56] and he also made his first appearance on *The Ed Sullivan Show*,[57] with Yankee teammates Rizzuto, Berra, Bauer, Allie Reynolds, and Philadelphia Athletic and later Yankee teammate Bobby Shantz. Things really picked up for Mantle in 1953, when he joined the stable of clients represented by Scott.

A partial list of companies that Mickey did endorsements for in 1953 includes Gem Razor blades (including a side-by-side plug with Pee Wee Reese), Beech-nut Gum, Jo-Mar Dairy Products (advertising premiums containing the likenesses of Mantle and Hopalong Cassidy), Esquire Socks, Martin Firearms, Sears Cata-

Mickey Mantle succeeded Joe DiMaggio in center field. While the fans idolized Mantle, they revered DiMaggio (National Baseball Hall of Fame and Museum, Cooperstown, NY).

log (Mickey Mantle autographed baseballs), Vitalis Hair Tonic, Haggar Slacks, and of course, Camel Cigarettes (along with many other ballplayers).[58] In a particularly interesting brand endorsement, Mickey Mantle was employed to demonstrate the resiliency of Timex watches. The print ad showed him swinging a bat on the left, and on the right holding the bat with a Timex watch strapped to it—the advertising copy linked Mantle's performance to the brand: "50 times, he sent scorching drives to all corners of the park.... Mickey examined the Timex watch. It was still running—and still on time!"[59]

In 1953, Mantle also appeared on the game show *What's My Line?*[60] as a mystery guest; *The Jackie Gleason Show*[61] with teammates Bauer and Berra; *The Arthur Murray Party*[62] with teammates Allie Reynolds and Billy Martin, who was a drinking buddy of Mantle and Whitey Ford. Murray's show featured ballroom dance, comedy, songs, and dance contests.[63] If Mantle was still uncomfortable in front of TV cameras, he certainly gave himself plenty of opportunities to get used to them.

In 1956, the Mantle brand really took off. Mickey now had his own business entity, Mickey Mantle Enterprises. According to Scott, Mickey made $80,000 off the field that year,[64] including "well into five figures"[65] for a TV production sponsored by Kraft—*The Life of Mickey Mantle*,[66] a G-rated version of the story of his life so far, starring Mickey in the title role, dramatizing his early career struggles, and sanitizing his late-night escapades and domestic squabbles with wife Merlyn.[67] And Scott boasted that Mickey turned down an offer of $30,000 to make 20 appearances at supermarkets and department stores after the World Series and honorariums for banquet appearances. He accepted expenses and "in some cases they give him an award that has a lot of value" like the 1956 Hickok belt, a diamond-studded belt worth anywhere from $10,000 to $25,000 given annually to the best professional athlete in America, a slam-dunk for Mickey with his breakout triple crown season.[68]

The year 1956 also saw Mantle make appearances on a year-end TV show hosted by comedian Bob Hope,[69] *The Steve Allen Show*,[70] and another appearance on *The Ed Sullivan Show*,[71] where he joined with singer Teresa Brewer, who hit the charts that year with the song "I Love Mickey"—Brewer "pitches woo" to a clueless Mickey, who responds, "Mickey, who?" every time Theresa makes her intentions known.[72]

There was no doubt that "Mickey Mantle led the hit parade on and off the baseball diamond in 1956."[73] After all, Mickey now had a song written about him, even if it was not quite as compelling as "Joltin' Joe DiMaggio." And by early 1957, Scott had lined up $25,000 in commitments for "off-the-field services," including endorsements for a low-calorie soft drink and for Ford Motor Company.[74]

At the same time, DiMaggio was believed to be turning down speaking engagements worth $30,000 because he did not like talking to audiences.[75] Joe D. was ahead of Mantle at this juncture as a cultural icon, particularly in song, romance, and literature having already been referenced as "the great DiMaggio" in Ernest Hemingway's *The Old Man and the Sea*[76] and married to Marilyn Monroe. But Mantle was busily fashioning a brand with middle-American appeal and his own version of sexuality as a romantic figure.

Two "events" of 1957—the now-legendary Copacabana nightclub brawl that led to the banishment of Billy Martin in the form of a trade to the Kansas City Athletics and Holly Brooke's sensational and salacious *Confidential* magazine profile of her 1951 "relationship" with Mickey in the March 1957 issue—may have tarnished Mantle's image as a clean-living family man while helping to establish his image as a playboy partier. Sportswriters were not yet finished "godding up the ballplayers," in the immortal words of former *New York Herald Tribune* Sports Editor Stanley Woodward, but they were clearly moving in the direction of exposing the off-field antics of theretofore protected ballplayers. Later on, Mantle would get a lot of mileage out of his off-field life in a series of ghostwritten autobiographies and in Miller Lite commercials celebrating his drinking bouts with buddies Ford and Martin.

Mantle's brand portfolio grew as a result of the "M & M" home run duel of 1961. By the end of 1961, deals made for both Roger Maris and Mickey Mantle had surpassed $100,000.[77] Scott negotiated a fee of $7,500 apiece for both men to go on the *Perry Como's Kraft Music Hall Show*,[78] a fee characterized by Scott as "the highest price ever for a sports celebrity."[79] Mantle and Maris reportedly "burlesqued their eagerness for commercials and endorsements" on the show, as Mantle was shown shaving himself and declaring, "This is the tenth commercial I've shaved for today."[80]

And then, it was on to the movies. Both men starred in a movie called *Safe at Home!*, also starring a 10-year-old actor named Bryan Russell making up a friendship with Mantle and Maris, only to be found out by his friends. But he ends up, of course, becoming buddies with his idols and receiving batting tips while coach Bill Turner (William Frawley, famed as Fred Mertz in *I Love Lucy*) looks on.[81] Mantle and Maris signed for $25,000 apiece plus 25 percent of the profits split between the two of them.[82] The film's director, Walter Doniger, gushed that "Mantle and Maris were very, very, good. Not amateurish at all."[83] For a saner assessment, sports writer Dan Daniel, who usually aggrandized the ballplayers, indicated that they were prepared, but were not going to replace Clark Gable as Hollywood stars.[84]

In *Sports Illustrated*, Robert Creamer depicted the movie "as being like all movies starring nonacting celebrities: it's a guest appearance, designed to draw the crowds while the celebrity is still of red-hot interest to the public."[85] In 1986, Bert Randolph Sugar put the movie at the top of his list of the ten worst baseball movies.[86] Mantle and Maris, along with Yogi Berra, also made cameo appearances in the Cary Grant/Doris Day movie *That Touch of Mink* in 1962.[87] Neither would go on to extended careers as movie actors, although they both did appear as themselves in the 1980 Jill Clayburgh movie, *It's My Turn*.[88]

As his career wound down, Mickey Mantle continued to make appearances and receive endorsement opportunities. In 1965, Mickey reportedly received $7,500 plus residuals to do a Lifebuoy soap commercial.[89] Mickey Mantle Enterprises continued to bring in lucrative endorsement deals for the Mick, even after the hullabaloo of the 1961 home run chase had subsided. Unfortunately, much of the money Mantle earned from endorsements, along with his now six-figure salary, ended up being invested in non-returning assets, most of them sporting the Mantle name.

It is evident that the alliterative, rhythmic quality of Mickey Mantle's name—plus its evoking baseball past with the slugger being named after Hall of Fame catcher Mickey Cochrane and the prowess of Mickey himself—enhanced the Mantle brand as an asset that could be exploited. With the help of longtime friend and adviser Harold Youngman, Mickey started to affix his name to various businesses in the late 1950s. Mickey and his family moved to Dallas after the 1958 season, even though Youngman had previously tried to influence Mantle to stay around Commerce by giving him a house in Joplin, Missouri, where his baseball career first took off, and a 25 percent ownership stake in a Holiday Inn being built in Joplin. The Holiday Inn was called "Mickey Mantle's Holiday Inn" and it was "the only Holiday Inn in the U.S. of A named after an actual person, Mantle bragged."[90] In Dallas, Mickey "invested heavily" in the Mickey Mantle Bowling Center around the same time. But sportswriter Arnold Hano says that he neither made nor lost money on both of those enterprises.[91]

In the late 1960s, the Commerce Comet's launching of self-named businesses really "took off" as Mantle was looking to keep busy while replacing the baseball salary he gave up by refusing to continue his career after 1968. In 1969, Mickey invested in a chain of restaurants named "Mickey Mantle's Country Cookin'" with 45 franchises and a clothing business called "Mickey Mantle's Men's Shops" with 55 franchises. Both businesses failed miserably—"Mickey Mantle's Country Cookin'," a Southern cafeteria-style operation which reportedly had great food, lost more than $1,000,000 and ceased operations, while his menswear outlets went into reorganization.[92]

Mickey started one other business in the late 1960s, in tandem with "Broadway Joe" Namath—an employment agency called "Mantle Men and Namath Girls." The agency was backed by George Lois, a 1960s advertising guru with an innovative spark, who also recognized Mantle's folksy appeal and light-hearted, joking persona. Namath and Mantle "seemed to be having fun" doing TV commercials for their agency. Broadway Joe was shown typing in one commercial and another showed a young woman facing a camera listing her credentials and asking two men in suits with their backs to the camera, "Can you do anything for me?" The camera revealed the faces of Mantle and Namath as they said in unison, "Yes we can!" A voice-over intoned the tag line "Mantle Men and Namath Girls—the employment agency for the cream of the crop."[93] Like other Mantle-named ventures, this one looked promising at the start, with 500 placements of secretaries per week. But it ended up in bankruptcy by 1972.[94]

Working with Lois, Mickey Mantle became the first sports figure to be chosen as a pitchman for the children's breakfast cereal Maypo. In 1967, Lois decided that he wanted to broaden the appeal of what had previously been a baby cereal to reach the pre-teen crowd. Lois had what advertisers like to call "a big idea"—using "self-mocking wit" by macho athletes, and reaching youngsters through "a twisteroo on the unconscionable hustles by jocks who manipulated kids through hero worship."[95]

Mantle was doing another commercial for Lois, when the advertising guru asked Mickey to do him a favor and cry "on cue." Mickey was happy to oblige. The four-second cry "I Want My Maypo!" became what we would call a meme today. Sales of the brand tripled.[96] Lois called it "popular folklore, an iconographic image" that created an "indelible symbol" through, in this case, the combination of simple words and visuals. Mantle was a natural.[97]

Lois later recruited Willie Mays, Johnny Unitas, Wilt Chamberlain, Ray Nitschke, Oscar Robertson, and Don Meredith to do "I Want My Maypo." But according to author Allen Barra, Mantle's spot was the most popular of all, even with baseball's popularity relative to football—and Mantle's career—in decline.[98]

Another Lois creation was the 1967 ad presenting Mantle as the pitchman for a stock brokerage named Edwards & Hanley. Once again, self-mocking wit was the method—Mantle portraying himself as starting out in life as a "shufflin', grinnin', head duckin' country boy" who was now "still a country boy, but I know a man down at Edwards & Hanly. I'm learnin'. I'm learnin'."[99] The line "I'm learnin'. I'm learnin'." was a hit with Johnny Carson, and "became an au courant phrase among talk show denizens and stand-up comics all over America."[100]

Mantle appeared on many talk shows well after his retirement. In addition to *The Ed Sullivan Show*, he also chatted with other hosts on the circuit—Dick Cavett, Merv Griffin, Mike Douglas, Johnny Carson, David Letterman, and Arsenio Hall. Mickey made numerous guest appearances on *Match Game*, appearing on 25 episodes trying to match the contestants' choices in choosing a word to fill in the blank of a sentence. And in the 1980s, he appeared on *The White Shadow*,[101] *Remington Steele*,[102] and *Mr. Belvedere*[103]—always as Mickey Mantle. Given the relative lack of success of his business ventures, it certainly seemed that Mickey "learned" how to be a guest celebrity better than how to be a successful businessman.

For the rest of his life, Mickey continued to do television commercials. The swaggering sex symbol of his early days with the Yankees might have been replaced by an aging playboy, but Mickey was still telegenic and trusted. In 1973, Alan R. Nelson research discovered that Mickey Mantle was the second most trusted pitchman behind Stan "The Man" Musial.[104] Take that, Joe DiMaggio!

While one must look at any single research result with a degree of skepticism, Mantle ranking ahead of Joltin' Joe as a believable product endorser may be explained by his "regular guy" persona. Or maybe because Mickey was seen much more often in American homes, although this can lead to a loss of credibility by overexposure.

Ultimately, the most likely explanation for Mickey's being trusted was that he was self-deprecating. Mickey might not have carried himself with the dignity or nobility that Joe D. displayed, but his willingness to poke fun at himself read as being humble—which Mantle also demonstrated in the way he rounded the bases after hitting a home run by looking down as he trotted, betraying no sign of celebration of his accomplishment. In contrast, Joe DiMaggio was held in awe by everyone, but his rather humorless style, and later, his insistence on being introduced last at Yankee Old-Timers' Games as "The Greatest Living Ballplayer" indicated that he was a man who expected recognition and took himself very seriously. A person who draws attention to himself may well be perceived as promoting a brand for his own benefit, while one who is self-effacing may be expected to represent products that he would use and believes in as he does not come across as looking for rewards for himself.

In the mid–1970s, Mickey did a series of commercials for Miller Lite. In one well-known commercial, Mickey and his buddy Whitey Ford, who called each other "Slick" after Casey Stengel had labeled the drinkers on the team "whiskey slick,"[105] joked that they had "a beer or two" after every game. Mickey then asked Whitey a question: "…if we'd a had a great tasting beer that was less filling in the old days, can you imagine where we'd be now?" Whitey's response: "Yeah! The beer drinker's Hall of Fame!"[106] One could look back today on this advertising appeal and shudder at the casual alcohol consumption it promotes, but it also expresses an essential reality of Mickey Mantle's descent into alcoholism.

In his later years, as has been widely reported and discussed, Mickey Mantle embarrassed himself in a series of public escapades where he displayed vulgarity, misogyny, and other bad behaviors while under the influence of alcohol. Mickey quit drinking two years before he died of liver cancer and disavowed his profligate behavior. In the 1980s and 1990s, Mickey's brand, while tarnished by his ugly displays during the various celebrity appearances he made to earn his living, was especially successful in two areas— his final business venture and the business of memorabilia.

Restaurateur William Lederman opened Mickey Mantle's Restaurant on 59th Street and Central Park South in Manhattan. For the use of his name, Mantle received an annual fee of $80,000 plus a seven percent stake in the restaurant. He finally had a business that succeeded. According to Lederman, "the Mantles made more money from the restaurant than from any other business venture."[107]

There was another way for the Yankee icon to earn more money near the end of his life—the memorabilia business. In the early 1990s, Mantle signed a deal with Score Board, a New Jersey memorabilia company, for $750,000 a year. Mantle's deal allowed him to earn other money signing memorabilia at card shows, while Joe DiMaggio signed a two-year deal worth $3.5 million per year with Score Board that was more exclusive but also more restrictive than that of Mantle's. DiMaggio could sign baseballs and photos for charity or in public but otherwise was restricted to Score Board signings.[108]

After his Score Board deal ended in 1992, Mantle signed a more lucrative deal with the card company Upper Deck for $2.75 million per year. It required him to give the company 20,000 autographs and make 26 show appearances.[109] DiMaggio, though, upped the ante by signing a deal in the middle of his Score Board contract for more than $3 million to sign bats for Louisville Slugger.[110]

Why was Joe DiMaggio worth more than twice what Mickey Mantle was worth on the memorabilia market? There were two reasons. At age 78, Joe DiMaggio would, in theory, not be signing for very much longer, whereas Mickey Mantle was 17 years younger than Joe and could be expected to be around for some time to come. Nobody knew in 1993 that Joe DiMaggio would survive three-and-a-half years longer than would Mickey Mantle.

The other reason was that "Mantle did not have the magical allure of Joe DiMaggio, who had compiled a 56-game hitting streak in 1941, married Marilyn Monroe, and been immortalized in song by Simon and Garfunkel."[111] Mickey Mantle was ultimately more successful as a national advertising presence, despite DiMaggio's iconic Bowery and Mr.

Coffee endorsements, because "Mantle's public image, his brand, was representative of Middle America, the innocence and strength of the heartland…. His appeal derived from his small-town roots and folksy lifestyle…."[112] But Joe DiMaggio's mystique clearly overshadowed that of Mickey Mantle

## The Great DiMaggio

No sports figure has been celebrated in American pop culture with as much variety, meaning, and depth as has Joe DiMaggio. Starting with the 1941 song "Joltin' Joe DiMaggio," an array of powerful references to DiMaggio's character, heroism, skills, and overall presence in American culture has been made by artists, writers of literature and song, and makers of films and TV shows. DiMaggio, unlike Mantle, made relatively few appearances in popular culture, preferring to maintain a zone of privacy, especially in the aftermath of his publicly celebrated romance with Marilyn Monroe and the tragedy of her death in 1962.

It began with the 56-game hitting streak. In discussing *New York Times* sports writer Dave Anderson's description of that two-month period in which DiMaggio reigned supreme, game after game, Jack B. Moore indicates that "Anderson also recognized that when DiMaggio ultimately became a symbol of heroism whose symbolism extended beyond sports, it had been in large part 'the hitting streak' that 'shaped that symbol.'"[113]

Anderson describes how a 29-year-old disc jockey named Alan Courtney came to write the song at the time of the streak's end, scribbling lyrics on a tablecloth in a nightclub and then giving them to bandleader Les Brown, who deputized Ben Homer to do an arrangement.[114]

"Joltin' Joe DiMaggio" was the first widely popular recorded tribute to a baseball star.[115] And it was not the last. "Yankee Clipper" was another song paying tribute to DiMaggio, recorded in 1949 by Charlie Ventura and His Orchestra.[116] Simon & Garfunkel's song "Mrs. Robinson" highlighted DiMaggio's stature nearly 20 years later.

Joe D. heroically returned from his devastating heel injury to hit four home runs in three games against the Red Sox in 1949. That year, he was mentioned in the classic musical *South Pacific* when the skin of Bloody Mary was directly compared to the tenderness of DiMaggio's glove. It could be interpreted two ways—that her skin was truly as smooth as DiMaggio's graceful fielding or that it was rough, like the physically rough baseball glove that is made from an animal's hide.[117] The more likely interpretation would seem to be the first one, as it seems doubtful that Richard Rodgers and Oscar Hammerstein, the creative team behind *South Pacific*, would choose to represent a negative quality through an individual perceived as a hero.

After being celebrated in song and in theater, DiMaggio reached another level of resonance as a cultural hero when he became a "character" in Hemingway's Pulitzer Prize-winning novella, *The Old Man and the Sea*. Though Hemingway did not publish the novella until 1952, its genesis began in 1936 when he wrote a story for *Esquire* about a real fisherman that became the basis for the fictional struggle of Santiago.[118] Hemingway wrote *The Old Man and the Sea* in 1951, during DiMaggio's last season.[119]

In describing the protagonist Santiago's battle to hook a great marlin, Hemingway makes numerous "allusions to DiMaggio" in which Santiago "shows his identification with the Yankee star."[120]

In essence, DiMaggio is constantly referenced as a role model that the old man, San-tiago, wishes to emulate. Joe D. strove for perfection despite his own struggles, particularly the heel problem in 1949 that he overcame. He is repeatedly described as "the great DiMaggio."[121] Clearly, a whole new literary and at least partly non-baseball-fan audience became engaged with the story of a masculine ideal figure, a paragon of virtue that sym-bolized an ongoing battle to achieve excellence.

In the 1950s and 1960s, the cultural resonance of Joltin' Joe reached new heights. DiMaggio's relationship with Marilyn Monroe linked baseball nobility with America's ultimate sex goddess. Perhaps the most famous story associated with Monroe and DiMag-gio as American icons is Marilyn describing a time when she was cheered by thousands of GIs in Korea at a personal appearance during her honeymoon with Joe. Marilyn has been quoted as saying, "Joe, you never heard such cheering." Joe's response: "Yes, I have."[122] In the cultural zeitgeist of the era that spawned matinee idols Elvis Presley, James Dean, and the prodigious clouter Mickey Mantle, it is at least arguable that Joe DiMaggio remained unsurpassed as a heroic cultural figure, especially upon loving—and losing—Marilyn Monroe. In some sense, his failure to stay married to Marilyn or to interfere in the chain of events that led to her death only reinforced the virtue of a hero who knew total success on the field and suffered in a stoic fashion on those rare occasions when he failed.

The refrain asking about Joe DiMaggio in the 1967 Simon & Garfunkel song *Mrs. Robinson* brought him back into cultural relevance at a turbulent time in American his-tory. Upon DiMaggio's death in 1999, songwriter Paul Simon wrote an essay that originally appeared in the *New York Times* describing the meaning he intended in the lyrics. Simon said that he told Joe DiMaggio that he was someone "I thought of as an American hero and that genuine heroes were in short supply."[123] DiMaggio took umbrage at the idea that he had left the American stage, and Simon suspected that Joe D. thought that the song was depicting him as an anachronism, "the antithesis of the iconoclastic mind-expanding, authority-defying, sixties" when Simon truly thought him to be admirable not only in his values but also in his flaws, his sadness, and the quiet way he handled life's miseries.[124]

There is no doubt that if Joe DiMaggio was temporarily out of the public conscious-ness in the mid-to-late 1960s, Simon's lyrics, followed shortly thereafter by DiMaggio's becoming "Mr. Coffee" and the spokesman for the Bowery, saw a resurrection of his rev-erence by the American public.

As referenced earlier, DiMaggio was reluctant to make appearances in the visual media, especially after his disastrous year in 1952 doing Yankee pre- and post-game shows. He appeared in the movie *Manhattan Merry-Go-Round* in 1937 and sang in that movie. During the 1950s, he made a cameo appearance in the movie *Angels in the Outfield*. But he did not appear in any other movies until 1998, the year before his death. In the inde-pendent film *The First of May*, Joe D. plays himself, an old ballplayer who talked to young people finding out about baseball. Joe "observed that he played an 'old dude'" in the movie.[125]

To the end of his life, Joe DiMaggio remained a cultural touchstone. Though he fiercely guarded his privacy, he was constantly in demand and referenced.[126] Simon chose Joe DiMaggio to lionize in song, even though his favorite player was Mickey Mantle.[127] No doubt Simon's choice was influenced by Mantle not yet being missed. Simon likely bypassed his hero Mantle for DiMaggio especially because DiMaggio resonated as a model American character figure throughout his adult life. The famed evolutionary biologist Steven Jay Gould summarized what the Yankee Clipper meant to him thusly: "DiMaggio remained my primary hero to the day of his death, and through all the vicissitudes of Ms. Monroe, Mr. Coffee, and Mrs. Robinson."[128]

## NOTES

1. Dan Daniel, "DiMaggio Gets First Test," *New York World-Telegram* March 11, 1936: 29.

2. Lawrence Baldassaro, *Beyond DiMaggio: Italian-Americans in Baseball* (Lincoln: University of Nebraska Press, 2011), 215–216.

3. Art Rust, Jr., *Recollections of a Baseball Junkie* (New York: William Morrow and Company, Inc. 1985), 146.

4. Maury Allen, *Where Have You Gone, Joe DiMaggio? The Story of America's Last Hero* (New York: E.P. Dutton & Co., 1975), 94.

5. James Mote, *Everything Baseball* (New York: Prentice Hall 1989), 95. A "microwave relay system" was used for these initial coast-to-coast broadcasts.

6. Data for all the comparisons between Mantle and DiMaggio taken from https://mlbcomparisons.com/mickey-mantle-vs-joe-dimaggio-comparison/, last accessed August 14, 2018. Note that if one were to compare DiMaggio's career wins above replacement to Mantle's through 1964, excluding Mantle's declining seasons but roughly equalizing the length of their careers, Mantle's career WAR is closer but still exceeds that of DiMaggio by 97.8 to 78.1.

7. Branch Rickey believed that "as a statistic RBI's were not only misleading, but dishonest" as they were a function of opportunities. Keith Law, *Smart Baseball* (New York: HarperCollins Publishers 2017), 31.

8. Joseph Durso, *DiMaggio: The Last American Knight* (Boston: Little, Brown and Company 1995), 218.

9. John Harper, "How's This for a 100th Birthday Greeting? MLB Historian Says: Joe D Was Overrated!" *Daily News* (New York): 55. This article coincided with what would have been DiMaggio's 100th birthday.

10. *Ibid.*

11. Jack B. Moore, "Literature About Joe DiMaggio, 1936–1986" in *Joltin' Joe DiMaggio*, ed. Richard Gilliam (New York: Carroll and Graf Publishers, 1999), 309.

12. Donald Honig, *A Donald Honig Reader* (New York: Simon & Schuster First Fireside edition 1988), 181.

13. Tom Meany, "DiMaggio as I Knew Him" in *Mostly Baseball* (New York: A.S. Barnes and Company, 1958), 251.

14. Box scores found in Michael Seidel, "Appendix: Box Scores," *STREAK: Joe DiMaggio and the Summer of '41* (New York, Penguin Books 1989) 223–260.

15. Gene Mack, "Well, the Nightcap Was Okay," Cartoon, *Boston Daily Globe*, May 31, 1941: 6; Seidel, 82.

16. Durso, 77.

17. Meany, 251.

18. Sources of minor league statistics found by this author did not list caught stealing data for DiMaggio's 1935 season with the San Francisco Seals.

19. Richard Ben Cramer, *Joe DiMaggio: The Hero's Life* (New York: Simon & Schuster, 2000), 296.

20. Corinne Landrey, "Watch the Fastest Baserunning of 2016 According to Statcast," Major League Baseball, www.mlb.com/cut4/2016s-fastest-baserunning-feats-in-mlb/c-209340878, last accessed April 28, 2018.

21. Fay Vincent, *We Would Have Played for Nothing: Baseball Stars of the 1950s and 1960s Talk About the Game They Loved*, The Baseball Oral History Project, Volume 2 (New York: Simon & Schuster, 2008), 160.

22. John Tullius, *I'd Rather Be a Yankee* (New York: MacMillan Publishing, Jove Edition 1987), 227. Lopat goes on to say that Mantle was faster than Vince Coleman or Rickey Henderson, so his comment was probably made around 1985.

23. Dan Daniel, "Mantle Makes Home Run History at 21," *Sporting News* April 29, 1953: 13.

24. Leavy, 91–98.

25. *Ibid.*, 99.

26. Durso, 92; Cramer, 103.

27. "Brand Equity" definition, Business Dictionary, www.businessdictionary.com/definition/brand-equity.html, last accessed February 12, 2018.

28. Kostya Kennedy, *Joe DiMaggio and the Last Magic Number in Sports* (New York: Sports Illustrated Books, 2011), 217.

29. James Quiggle, "Joe DiMaggio Was Clutch as Baseball, Endorsement Star," *Investor's Business Daily*, www.investors.com/news/management/leaders-and-success/dimaggio-superstar-stats-and-humility-made-him-an-enduring-american-hero/, September 21, 2015, last accessed February 23, 2018.

30. Kennedy, 166–67.

31. Durso, 103.

32. Allen, 214.

33. David Halberstam, *Summer of '49* (New York: William Morrow & Co., 1989; New York: Harper Perennial Classics edition, 2006), 138. Citations refer to the Harper edition.

34. Don Harrison, *Connecticut Baseball* (Charleston, SC: The History Press, 2008), 96.

35. Cramer, 294.

36. *Ibid.*, 294–295.

37. Halberstam, 165.

38. *Ibid.*, 165–66.

39. Cramer, 328. Cramer states that, in addition to feeling like he looked bad on the show, DiMaggio hated that the show was sponsored by Buitoni, which only accentuated the Italian stereotypes he despised.

40. *Ibid.*, 385.

41. Paul Simon, "The Silent Superstar," in *Joltin' Joe DiMaggio*, ed. Richard Gilliam (Darby, PA: Diane Publishing), 1–2.

42. Gay Talese, "The Silent Season of a Hero," in *The Baseball Chronicles*, ed. David Gallen (New York: Galahad Books, 1994), 183–201.

43. Dick Young, "Young Ideas," *Sporting News* January 31, 1970: 14.

44. Allen, 219.

45. Allen, 212–13. In 1983, Journalist Tom Boswell reported that DiMaggio turned down $250,000 to hawk Grecian Formula and rejected an overture to promote Polident. Clearly, image mattered to him even though he said, "It isn't that I don't like money..." Thomas Boswell, *the Heart of the Order* (New York: Doubleday 1989), 5.

46. Allen, 211.

47. Isadore Barmash, "DiMaggio Bats Again for Bowery," *New York Times*, February 22, 1989: D19.

48. Steve Chawkins, "Vincent G. Marotta Dies at 91; Talked Joe DiMaggio into Pitching Mr. Coffee," *Los Angeles Times*, www.latimes.com/local/obituaries/la-me-0804-vincent-marotta-20150804-story,html, last accessed February 23, 2018.

49. Greg Johnson, "Even as an Endorser, DiMaggio Had an Instinct for the Home Run," *Los Angeles Times*, www.articles.latimes.com/1999/mar/09/business-fi-15347, last accessed February 23, 2018.

50. Rock Positano and John Positano, *Dinner with DiMaggio: Memories of an American Hero* (New York: Simon & Schuster 2017), 134.

51. *Mantle: The Definitive Story of Mickey Mantle*, HBO, July 13, 2005, Steven Stern.

52. Randy Roberts and Johnny Smith, *A Season in the Sun: The Rise of Mickey Mantle* (New York: Basic Books, 2018), 112.

53. *Ibid.* 114–115; Dan Daniel, "What Did Those 93,103 Mean?," Over the Fence, *Sporting News*, May 20, 1959: 10.

54. Dan Daniel, "Scott Quits as Road Sec to Become Player Agent," *Sporting News*, January 10, 1951: 6.

55. Roberts and Smith, 114.

56. *I've Got a Secret*, CBS, October 2, 1952.

57. *The Ed Sullivan Show*, CBS, September 21, 1952.

58. www.mickeymantle7.net, last accessed May 1, 2018.

59. www.pophistorydig.com/topics/keeps-on-ticking'1950s-1990s/, last accessed March 1 2017.

60. *What's My Line?*, CBS, May 17, 1953.

61. *The Jackie Gleason Show*, CBS, September 26, 1953.

62. *The Arthur Murray Party*, NBC, June 28, 1953.

63. www.imdb.com/title/tt0042078/, last accessed August 14, 2018.

64. Doc Greene, "Scott 10th Man on Team—as 10 Per Center," *Sporting News*, October 21, 1959: 10.

65. Harold Rosenthal, "'See Scott' Say 88 Major Players to All Outside Offers," *Sporting News*, October 24, 1956: 4.

66. *Kraft Television Theatre—The Life of Mickey Mantle*, NBC, October 3, 1956, Nicholas A. Baehr.

67. Roberts and Smith, 165–66.

68. Bill Roeder, "'Trophy Champ,' New Mantle Title—He's Far Ahead," *Sporting News*, February 13, 1957: 17.

69. *The Bob Hope Show*, NBC, December 28, 1956.

70. *The Steve Allen Show*, NBC, October 7, 1956.

71. *The Ed Sullivan Show*, CBS, August 5, 1956.

72. Roberts and Smith, 164–65.

73. Mote, 339.

74. Oscar Ruhl, "10,000,000th Spalding Ball for Majors," From the Ruhl Book, *Sporting News*, March 27, 1957: 15.

75. *Ibid.*

76. Ernest Hemingway, *The Old Man and the Sea* (New York: Scribner Classics, 1996), 18; 22; 54; 55; 74; 79; 80. First published 1952 by Charles Scribner's Sons. Page references are to 1996 edition.

77. Ray Gillespie, "Diamond Facts and Facets," *Sporting News*, October 11, 1961: 4. Gillespie has a "culled

by" credit. The information regarding Mantle and Maris is credited to Max Kase from the *New York Journal-American*. Other writers credited in Gillespie's amalgamation are Les Biederman from the *Pittsburgh Press* and Bob Addie from the *Washington Post*.

78. *Perry Como's Kraft Music Hall*, NBC, October 4, 1961.

79. David Condon, "Home-Run Mark Worth 500 Gs to New Champ," *The Sporting News*, September 20, 1961: 10.

80. "Roger, Mick Turn Gag Men on Como's Television Show," *The Sporting News*, October 11, 1961: 6.

81. Til Ferdenzi, "Yanks Go Hollywood for M-and-M Movie," *The Sporting News*, February 28, 1962: 6.

82. *Ibid.* Frank Scott claimed that they expected the film to make a million dollars, meaning that the M & M boys would each clear $125,000 in addition to their $25,000 up front. This author has no specific information on the film's success but in his review of baseball movies, Bert Randolph Sugar stated that the audiences stayed home. Bert Randolph Sugar, "Rating the Baseball Movies," in *The Fireside Book of Baseball*, Charles Einstein, ed. (1956; 4th ed., New York: Simon & Schuster 1987), 370. Citations refer to the 4th edition.

83. *Ibid.*

84. Dan Daniel, "Mick and Rog Old Smoothies in Film Roles," Over the Fence, *Sporting News*, February 21, 1962: 10.

85. Robert Creamer, "Mantle and Maris in the Movies," *Sports Illustrated*, April 2, 1962, 90; www.si.com/vault/1962/04/02/593549/mantle-and-maris-in-the-movies, last accessed 1/24/2018.

86. Sugar, 370.

87. Mote, 45.

88. *Ibid.*, *Everything Baseball*, 25–26.

89. Arnold Hano, "The Twilight of a Hero," in *The Baseball Chronicles*, ed. Richard Gallen (New York: Carroll & Graf, 1991), 318.

90. Leavy, 185.

91. Hano, 317–18.

92. Leavy, *The Last Boy*, 293. According to Allen Barra, most Mantle biographies are mistaken in saying 1) that the chains were fast-food outlets—they were versions of Southern places known as "meat and three" (meat and three vegetables with biscuits or cornbread) and 2) that they were called "Mickey Mantle's Country Kitchen"—the name "Country Kitchen" was owned by a Wisconsin company. Allen Barra, *Mickey and Willie: Mantle and Mays, the Parallel Lives of Baseball's Golden Age* (New York: Random House 2013), 372.

93. Barra, 369; For TV commercial, see https://www.youtube.com/watch?v=zq2s126iDf0.

94. Leavy, 293.

95. George Lois, *Sellebrity* (London: Phaedon Press Limited 2003), 60.

96. Leavy, 273.

97. Lois, 60.

98. Barra, 354.

99. Lois, 14.

100. *Ibid.*

101. *The White Shadow*, "Reunion: Part 2," CBS, October 23, 1980, John Falsey and Joshua Brand.

102. *Remington Steele*, "Second Base Steele," NBC, October 23, 1984, Rick Mittleman.

103. *Mr. Belvedere*, "The Field," ABC, September 16, 1989, Fredric Weiss.

104. Leavy, 302.

105. *Ibid.*, 181.

106. www.youtube.com/watch?v=R_m-Run4Vg. (An advertising executive once told this author that the key appeal of Miller Lite was that "you could fit more beers into you" because of its lower caloric content. No doubt Mickey appreciated that benefit as his alcoholism deepened.)

107. William Lederman, *Mickey Mantle's: Behind the Scenes in America's Most Famous Sports Bar* (Guilford, CT: The Lyons Press 2007), 14.

108. Pete Williams, *Card Sharks: How Upper Deck Turned a Child's Hobby into a High-Stakes Billion-Dollar Business* (New York: MacMillan 1995), 166.

109. *Ibid.*, 236.

110. Cramer, 455–56.

111. Williams, 236.

112. Roberts and Smith, 115.

113. Jack B. Moore, "Literature About Joe DiMaggio, 1936–1986" in *Joltin' Joe DiMaggio*, 293.

114. Dave Anderson, "The DiMaggio Years," in *The Yankees: The Four Fabulous Eras of Baseball's Most Famous Team*, Dave Anderson, Murray Chass, Robert Creamer, and Harold Rosenthal (New York: Random House, 1980), 78.

115. Mote, 333.

116. *Ibid.*

117. Jack B. Moore, *Joe DiMaggio: A Bio-Bibliography* (New York: Greenwood Press, 1986), 141.

118. Joy Lazendorfer, *11 Facts About Hemingway's "The Old Man and the Sea*," Mental Floss, www.

mentalfloss.com/article/64363/11-facts-about-hemingways-old-man-and-the-sea, May 27, 2015, last accessed May 6, 2018.

119. Ernest Hemingway, Biography, www.biography.com/people/ernest-hemingway-9334498, last accessed 5/6/2018.

120. Moore, *Joe DiMaggio: Baseball's Yankee Clipper*, 142.

121. William Simons, "Joe DiMaggio and the American Ideal" in *Joltin' Joe DiMaggio*, Gilliam ed., 33–34.

122. See, e.g., Cramer, *Joe DiMaggio*, 360.

123. Simon, "The Silent Superstar," in *Joltin' Joe DiMaggio* 2.

124. *Ibid.*

125. Michael P. Riccards, *The Odes of DiMaggio: Sports, Myth, and Manhood in Contemporary America* (Binghamton, NY: Global Publications 2001), 148.

126. The Wikipedia entry on Joe DiMaggio has over 5 pages of popular culture references that testify to his popularity as an American figure of great interest. Included among those references are artistic renditions such as paintings, sculptures, and caricatures of him; comic books in which he appears; and TV shows and movies where is played by someone or a fictional plot line involves him. en.wikipedia.org/wiki/Joe_DiMaggio, accessed March 14, 2018.

127. Simon, "The Silent Superstar," in *Joltin' Joe DiMaggio* 2.

128. Stephen Jay Gould, *Triumph and Tragedy in Mudville: A Lifelong Passion for Baseball* (New York: W.W. Norton & Company 2003), 130.

# The Yankees as a Metaphor for the 1970s

## LOUIS GORDON

Anyone growing up in the early to mid–1970s was part of an era that was radically different from the one that had preceded it. Changing attitudes towards marriage, dress, and women's rights, plus the long hair on men that started creeping over the ears around 1972–73, were just a few of the changes that marked the decade. In sports—captured in full color on television because the networks had completely transitioned to color broadcasts by the late 1960s—no team symbolized the cathartic changes sweeping American society in the "Me Decade" more than the New York Yankees baseball team.

The seventies attitudes in sports began when the Oakland Athletics beat the Cincinnati Reds to win the 1972 World Series. The A's sported that new long hair and mustaches, and a carefree style that seemed to come directly out of 1960s California. And they defeated Johnny Bench's Big Red Machine, which could be interpreted as a symbol of the establishment, in the World Series, 4–3.

Back in New York the following spring, the Yanks under manager Ralph Houk hoped to bring back the glory that had characterized the franchise since the 1920s but faded in the last half of the 1960s. The old Yankees had Babe Ruth, Lou Gehrig, Joe DiMaggio, Mickey Mantle, and Whitey Ford, to name just some of the stars. For a kid who was a Yankees fan in the early 1970s, it was easy to become a Yankee historian; many of the books in the sports section of the school library were about the Yankees, allowing for rapid accumulation of statistical knowledge about the team and its prior exploits. On television, *The Pride of the Yankees* was often replayed and became a favorite for sports fans and film buffs alike. In the new convenience stores with names like 7/11 and QuickChek, which sprouted up in the early 1970s, Topps baseball cards often featured historical throwback cards that recalled the Yankee exploits of yesteryear.

Despite the deep history that cloaked the franchise in a majestic aura, the new incarnation was something different. Though Oklahoman Bobby Murcer was a bona fide rising star and considered the heir to Mickey Mantle, the team boasted a more modest lineup. Felipe Alou from the Dominican Republic, Horace Clarke, Roy White, Mel Stottlemyre, and Thurman Munson were the core, but the team also featured a number of more quirky players. In the late innings, Houk would send a signal that he wanted Sparky Lyle, a former member of the Boston Red Sox; Lyle débuted in Beantown during the team's Cinderella season of 1967, which ended in a World Series loss to the St. Louis Cardinals in seven games. His tenure with the Yankees began in 1972. And the reliever would heighten the excitement upon getting Houk's call.[1] The 1974 Yankee Yearbook related, "The drama of a Lyle appearance, so much a part of the New York Sports scene, features this master of confidence and ability challenging hitters and defying them with his crafts. In a key situation—and that's the only time you see Sparky—he thrives on the game-in-the-balance moments that earns saves."[2]

That 1973 team also featured Ron Blomberg, a slugger from Atlanta, who moved into the role of the designated hitter—a new innovation which, like the decade itself, riled traditionalists, allowing a stronger hitter to bat in place of the generally poor-hitting pitcher without having the responsibility of taking the field on defense. The new position gave strength to the offensive lineup while drawing fans that wanted to see more home runs. Blomberg served as the DH for 56 games in 1973 and by early July, he had a .400 batting average. *Sports Illustrated* ran a cover story, "Pride of the Yankees," which featured Blomberg and Bobby Murcer on the cover.[3] The DH for that season of 1973 took the American League by storm.

In 1973, Ron Blomberg became baseball's first designated hitter. He walked in his first at-bat, went 1-for-3, and notched one RBI in the 15–5 loss against Luis Tiant and the Boston Red Sox (National Baseball Hall of Fame and Museum, Cooperstown, NY).

The Yankees had a number of gimmicks to get out the fans, like "Bat Day" and "Old Timers' Day," but one thing that sticks out in that era was the bizarre switch of wives by two Yankees pitchers, Fritz Peterson and Mike Kekich. Today, Peterson is intensely religious, but his trade with Kekich reflected the crumbling of traditional family life in the decade. There were others who symbolized the unconventional style of the team. George "Doc" Medich, a pitcher, attended medical school during the off season. Medich seems to have been an early forerunner of the multiple career paths that later generations would take. Despite later being traded by Billy Martin, he said that Martin was the best manager he had ever seen.[4]

In June 1973, the Yankees were in first place, and this author's recollection is that the *New York Post*, which had arguably the best sports coverage of the team of any newspaper in the New York area, printed on the back page where the sports section started, pictures of the two New York managers, Ralph Houk of the Yankees and Yogi Berra of the Mets, noting Ralph Houk's "first-place cigar,"[5] and "Yogi Berra's loser's look." But that was a long summer and the classic "Here Come the Yankees" song, would soon be replaced in the hearts of many by the Mets' theme, "Meet the Mets." Still, for a moment in the beginning of that summer it seemed that the 1973 Yankees would be the team to bring back the glory that had characterized Yankees teams in every decade since the 1920s. Yet, to the dismay of every Yankee fan in 1973, it was the Mets who won the National League pennant, captured attention from the media and the baseball community, and went to the World Series where they were beaten by the strong Oakland A's team that included future Yankees Catfish Hunter, Reggie Jackson, and Ken Holtzman. In the avalanche of media attention that Jackson would bring to the Yankees both during (1977–1981) and after his time with the Yankees, his efforts in helping the A's foil Mel Stottlemyre's attempt at a no-hitter during the summer of 1973 are long forgotten. The defeats, stagnation, and lack of energy that marked the Yankees' lackluster finish that year are not; in retrospect, the Yankees' late summer performance seemed to match the complacency that settled over the country after the 1960s unrest that included civil rights marches, the assassinations of Robert Kennedy and Martin Luther King, Jr., and protests against the Vietnam War. Americans were exhausted from the upheavals of the previous decade and many pined for a simpler, easier time including the pleasure of the Yankees dominating baseball. The team, however, finished the season 17 games behind the Baltimore Orioles, with an 80–82 record that revealed little about their earlier successes at the beginning of the summer, or the glimmer of hope for recapturing the glory of past decades.

But changes were underway. Negotiations between a Cleveland shipbuilder looking to assemble a group of businessmen to buy the team from CBS had become public. Before the start of the 1973 season, the group led by George Steinbrenner bought the team.[6] Steinbrenner called the Yankees "the best buy in sports today," vowing to let the team's daily operations be run by others.[7] Houk resigned, and his replacement, Bill Virdon, who had previously managed the Pittsburgh Pirates, seemed to bring a productive style to the team. Ray Negron, a former Yankee batboy, described Virdon as having:

> a strong physique—big arms, broad shoulders—of a state trooper and the personality to match.... The only time I ever saw him show any kind of passion was when Thurman struck out a few week after Bill took over. Frustrated, Thurman hurled his batting helmet. Bill pushed me out of the way so I wouldn't get hit and then turned to Thurman and yelled, "You're not that good!" Bill's attitude was that all the players were the same.[8]

Sparky Lyle recalled that Virdon "took his losses as hard as anyone. When something bad would happen in a game, you could almost see his stomach knotting up."[9] Phil Rizzuto, the former star Yankee shortstop who became an announcer for the game broadcasts, touted Virdon's attributes in his coverage of the team, implying as the 1974 season started, that it seemed the Yankees were headed for a better times. One of the new additions was Elliott Maddox, a former Texas Ranger, who grew up in Vauxhall, New Jersey, just a stone's throw from Manhattan. The Yankee Yearbook described Maddox as arriving with "one of the best credentials for defensive play in the American League."[10]

Virdon made Maddox's fielding abilities part of his strategy[11] and Rizzuto often praised his fellow New Jerseyan on the air. In 1974, Maddox started in center field, batted

.303 and led the team with 75 runs scored. But if Maddox's performance on the field symbolizes the beginning of the Yankees return to glory in the 1970s, an incident that occurred in a 1975 spring training game against the Texas Rangers offers insights into some of the controversies that would later haunt the team. Maddox, in an interview with a Fort Lauderdale journalist, stated that then Rangers manager Billy Martin had "a reputation of lying to all his players."[12] The next week, at an exhibition game between the Yankees and Rangers, a pitch by Jim Bibby hit Maddox and a scuffle between the teams broke out. Martin subsequently called Maddox "a coward who is a disgrace to the Yankee uniform," and Maddox told *Sport* magazine that the Rangers' manager "had used racial slurs when discussing me."[13] The exchange is eerily similar to some of the altercations that marked the bad blood between Martin and Reggie Jackson. But sportswriter Randy Galloway reported that Martin's response to Maddox at the time was, surprisingly, "turn the other cheek," and is illustrative of the inability of many powerful men at the time to acknowledge a new sensitivity towards racial issues in the U.S.:

> "I know the kid (Maddox) hates me, and for what I think are all the wrong reasons," he said. "I never disliked him, in fact, the short time I was around him I liked him very much. He said those things in Florida and yeah, I got mad as hell at the time. But that was then. Anyway, he feels that way, so that's the way it is. I'm not going to worry about it, but I'm not going after him either."[14]

In the meantime, Steinbrenner had undertaken a plan to rebuild the old Yankee Stadium, putting the Yankees at Shea Stadium for three years while the "House That Ruth Built" was being revamped to retain the images of Yankee glory while adding the amenities of a modern stadium. But the failure of the new team to live up to the heroics of Ruth, Gehrig, DiMaggio, Mantle, Ford, and Don Larsen in his perfect game during the 1956 World Series, was reminiscent of nothing so much as New York City's own inability during the same time frame to live up to past successes. Indeed, the Yankees' inability to create a winning team matched the inability of New York City to reduce the economic stagnation that had gotten worse during Mayor Abe Beame's administration; the new stadium in a deteriorating neighborhood in the South Bronx epitomized the dilemma of urban blight that had come to symbolize New York City.

George Steinbrenner was also as colorful as any of the players. Known as "the Boss," he had a short temper and little tolerance for losing games. But in 1974, before he was able to implement too many changes to the team, Steinbrenner was suspended from baseball ownership for two years, after he was indicted for illegal contributions to President Nixon's re-election campaign and a subsequent coverup. Only after 15 months was the suspension lifted and Steinbrenner allowed to return to the Yankees.[15] The "Boss" reflected the conservative side of American popular culture in the 1970s, which had given Richard Nixon the 1972 election and had allowed Jimmy Carter the narrowest of wins in 1976.

Right after the end of the 1974 season, the Yankees, to the surprise and pain of many of the teams' most ardent fans, traded "the franchise"—Bobby Murcer—to the San Francisco Giants for Bobby Bonds, a slugger whose son Barry would later become one of Major League Baseball's greatest players while creating controversy because of alleged intentional use of steroids. The trade of Murcer was a shock to Yankee loyalists who would have accepted the trade of anyone else. Not only was Murcer the dubbed heir to Mickey Mantle, he was the epitome of what a Yankee should be to all who rooted for him. It seemed as if the Yankees without Bobby Murcer, weren't really the Yankees. Ray Negron wrote:

As a boy growing up in Oklahoma City, Bobby lived and breathed the legend of Ruth, Gehrig, and DiMaggio. Humble and charming he wore the Yankee uniform with more pride than anyone I had ever known. Bobby went from Clark Kent to a trim Superman when he put on his pinstripes.[16]

Bonds was a bona fide star with the Giants, but despite his athletic abilities, he didn't seem to fit the shoes of Bobby Murcer. And the Yankees still needed additional help.

Yet a new direction for the team began to emerge in the free-agent draft, when Steinbrenner signed Oakland A's ace James "Catfish" Hunter to a contract on December 31, 1974, for the then unprecedented sum of $3.75 million over five years.

Hunter pitched a good season for the Yankees, going 23–14 and earning an ERA of 2.58 for an AL-leading 328 innings. However, neither his pitching abilities nor Bill Virdon's more-than-decent job managing the team to a third-place finish in the AL East produced a result that was good enough for George Steinbrenner. Rumors were rife during the season that the trades of other key players were in the works. Yankees president Gabe Paul had to dispel rumors that the Yankees were going to trade slugger "Sweet" Lou Piniella in the spring of 1975. Paul noted, "When you feel you have a good club, the worst thing you can do is start breaking it up." He also said that Piniella would not be traded.[17]

But while Piniella remained a Yankee, Bill Virdon was fired as manager. His replacement, Billy Martin, possessed a temper and flamboyance that were quite the opposite of Virdon's quiet persistence. Martin had been a Yankee star in the team's glory days of the 1950s and the kid who had grown up in the slums of Berkeley, California[18] drew fans in. Martin generated headlines, which boosted the ticket sales for the team. Yet his new job was not easy. Martin had become manager of a third-place team and his simultaneous responsibilities included studying the team, dealing with the press, and weighing the advantages of trading for players. The team however, did not do any better under their new manager than they did under Virdon.[19] The 1975 Yankees went 83–77 and finished third in the American League East.

When George Steinbrenner signed Catfish Hunter in 1974, it was the beginning of an array of free agents that the Boss lured to play in pinstripes (National Baseball Hall of Fame and Museum, Cooperstown, NY).

But the 1976 team under Martin was something different. The newly-configured club won the 1976 AL pennant, with first baseman Chris Chambliss and catcher Thurman Munson, perhaps the most prominent players, leading the charge in securing the team's success. It took the Yankees five games against the Kansas City Royals to clinch the pennant. Chambliss hit a bottom-of-the-ninth-inning home run off pitcher Mark Littell to give the Yankees their first American League title in more than 10 years. At the 2006 "Old Timers' Day," Chambliss noted that he had decided he would "swing at the first pitch"[20] and recounted, "I knew Littell would be disturbed by all the noise and the break in the action. I figured he would throw a fastball for a strike to get ahead quickly. That's what he did, and I hit it out."[21] Chambliss was not able to reach home plate in his first attempt to run around the bases as he was mobbed by the fans who has witnessed the Yankees' return to championship status. The crowd was so chaotic that Chambliss needed uniformed police to escort him to home plate so the victory would be official.[22] Thurman Munson was voted the American League's Most Valuable Player, batting .302 in 152 games. His stats included 17 home runs, 105 RBI, 186 hits, and 79 runs.[23] Equally important was his defensive work in handling the pitching staff, most of whom had "quality seasons."[24]

It was the first Yankee pennant since 1964; newer generations of fans had no recollection of the earlier great Yankee teams led by Mickey Mantle's hitting and Whitey Ford's pitching. Further, no one from the earlier era was still on the Yankee roster. It might also be noted that it was the first pennant since the massive culture changes took place within the United States during the 1960s and early 1970s. When the Yankees last won the pennant, segregation was still in place in some parts of the country. In the New York City area, there was a riot in Harlem that year and again in 1967, which also saw devastating unrest in Newark. And yet the crime that plagued urban neighborhoods in New York City had arguably been elevated in the public consciousness with the murder of 28-year-old Kitty Genovese in Queens some months before the Yankees won the 1964 AL pennant. What made the Genovese murder impactful was the alleged reluctance of witnesses to get involved. It was reported that Genovese was stabbed outside her Kew Gardens apartment, but neighbors and other people nearby did nothing because they thought that others would get involved. It became known as the "bystander effect," though research in the 2000s found that the story had been somewhat exaggerated regarding the number of witnesses and other factors. Winston Moseley (29 years old) confessed to the murder.

When the Yankees last won the World Series, ballplayers had short hair and college dormitories were single-sex. When Roger Maris chased Babe Ruth's single-season home-run record in 1961, his crew cut and the black-and-white pictures of that time seem now to be a throwback to ancient history compared to the Kodachrome-infused, long-haired era of 1976. Indeed, the country had come a long way culturally and the return of the Yankees to power coincided with a general sense of nostalgia that gripped the country through such films as *American Graffiti*, the Broadway play *Grease*, and the television series *Happy Days*.

The Yankees of 1976 in their easy capture of the American League's Eastern Division were reminiscent of the old Yankees. The team record for the year was 97–62, outpacing the second place Baltimore Orioles by 10½ games in the division. Of course, adding to the excitement was the début of the renovated Yankee Stadium, which now offered fans a true rival to the relatively new Shea Stadium in Queens for the Mets, and which allowed old New Yorkers the satisfaction of knowing that at least one of the three old-time New York ballparks (the others being Manhattan's Polo Grounds and Brooklyn's Ebbets Field) had been preserved. When the Giants and the Dodgers left for California after the 1957 season, questions were raised about the effectiveness of both ballparks and their potential obsolescence. The Polo Grounds served as the Mets' home for two years, before succumbing to the wrecking ball. Ebbets Field, a decaying structure, was also destroyed.

Though they were defeated by the Cincinnati Reds in four games in the World Series, the Yankees had returned to baseball's upper echelon. Much of the Yankees' success was attributed to Munson, whose legendary toughness and leadership induced Martin to appoint him as the first Yankee captain since Lou Gehrig.[25]

But how did the Yankees turn it around to beat the Los Angeles Dodgers and become World Series Champions in 1977 and 1978? What was the single factor turning the team from mediocre to competitive to championship-level? While the reasons are arguable, it may have been the acquisition of Reggie Jackson. The Philadelphia-area native and Arizona State University star was indeed controversial, and it cannot be said that he unified the team. Sportswriter Gene Schoor depicted him as "an intelligent man, a sensitive man, a moody man, and a loner" who was "particularly aware of the struggle of blacks for a respectful and respected place in the American scene."[26] But he also did not practice diplomacy. In the spring of 1977 he gave an interview to *Sport* magazine that caused so much controversy that acclaimed Roger Kahn—who added to the decade's nostalgia boom by recounting his days on the Brooklyn Dodgers beat with his early 1970s book *The Boys of Summer*—noted, "No other piece of journalism ever so isolated a great star from so many teammates," many of whom stopped speaking to the slugger.[27] According to Robert Ward, who wrote the story for *Sport*, Jackson declared,

> I'll wait and eventually he'll [Munson] be whipped…. I'm a leader, but leader isn't the right word … it's a matter of PRESENCE…. Let me put it this way: No team I am on will ever be humiliated the way the Yankees were by the Reds in the World Series!
> … Munson thinks he can be the straw that stirs the drink, but he can only stir it bad.[28]

Munson said that the *Sport* article showed that it was Jackson who was insecure, not himself.[29]

Other players had conflicts. After being replaced by Bucky Dent, veteran shortstop Fred Stanley told sports writer Moss Klein, "They should've talked to me. Said something. I did the best I could. I tried. It wasn't enough for them…. Let me play every day and we'll win. I'm a good shortstop. Let me play."[30]

These types of events permeating Yankee Stadium—nicknamed the "Bronx Zoo"— "were just part of the disorder in a deadly dysfunctional New York."[31] The heated mayoral campaign between Mario Cuomo and Ed Koch, union strikes that had "crippled municipal services," and the "Son of Sam" serial killer plagued the city.[32] Yankees fans absorbed the tension between George Steinbrenner, Reggie Jackson, and Billy Martin. But their conflicts were minor eruptions as long as the team kept winning. Jackson had an unparalleled World Series in 1977, hitting .450 including four home runs in two games. In the last game of the series, he hit three home runs, all on the first pitch and all by different pitchers—Elias Sosa, Charlie Hough, Burt Hooton. Of all the home runs that he hit in the World Series, he was proudest of the one smashed out of the park off of fastball pitcher Elias Sosa, who threw 95 miles per hour. Jackson later recalled, "I overwhelmed that baseball by the sheer force of my will."[33] While fans all around New York City celebrated the first World Series victory in 15 years, perhaps no greater celebration took place than the one in Harlem at 125th Street and Seventh Avenue. Harlem Congressman Charles Rangel commenting to kids dancing into the night, noted, "Why not? Who else do these kids have for heroes—Sammy Davis, Jr.? Of course, they love Reggie. He's the black Babe Ruth."[34]

During his single-season sojourn in Baltimore the year before he joined the Yankees, Jackson famously said, "If I played in New York, they'd name a candy bar after me."[35]

Years later, in the autobiography *Becoming Mr. October*, he recalled that he said it as a joke, but on Opening Day 1978, some 75,000 of the peanut, caramel and chocolate bar were passed out to the fans.[36] Catfish Hunter commented, "The Reggie! Bar. It's the candy bar that when you unwrap it, it tells you how good it is."[37] And yet another tie-in between the Yankees and popular culture during the seasons of 1977 and 1978 should not be missed. The rock band Queen released its song "We Are the Champions" on October 7, 1977, just before the start of the World Series on October 11th. Music journalist Greg Prato has noted that the song "remains among rock's most recognizable anthems," and that it's "nearly impossible to go to a sporting event and not hear either one of the tracks blaring through the sound system and excited fans clapping and singing along."[38] But for Yankee fans in 1977 and 1978 it seemed that the song had been written specifically for the team. Four years after Jackson's three-homer game, the Dodgers beat the Yankees in the 1981 World Series; the season had been shortened by the strike. In a bit of irony, the Dodgers offered their take on the song—Jerry Reuss, Jay Johnstone, Rick Monday, and Steve Yeager formed the Big Blue Wrecking Crew. They recorded the song, performed it on television, and gave the money to selected charities.

The 1978 Yankees persisted through more conflict, the most notable being the mid-season firing of Billy Martin. Bob Lemon took the helm and the team won the American League Pennant and the World Series again, largely because of the stellar efforts of Ron Guidry, who went 25–3 with nine shutouts in the regular season.[39] The man dubbed "Louisiana Lightning" was so impressive both on the mound and in caring for his mentally-challenged younger brother that a New Orleans native recorded and released a "Cajun-sounding tune" called the "Ballad of Ron Guidry."[40] The repeat success did not come easy for the team. Though the Yankees had entered the 1978 season confident that they would be able to produce another championship, it looked like the team would be pushed aside by the Boston Red Sox, who had a tremendous start. By July 19th, the Yankees were 14 games behind the Sox, who were 62–28. While he was under great scrutiny, Martin remarked about Jackson and Steinbrenner, "One's a born liar and the other's convicted."[41] After the comment, Martin was "forced to resign" and the mild-mannered Lemon had the immense responsibility of plowing through the chaotic aura surrounding the pinstripes.[42] There had been instances of behavior that had nothing to do with baseball capturing headlines in previous eras—Babe Ruth getting his stomach pumped, several players getting in a brawl at the Copacabana in the late 1950s—but journalists were less likely to cover up or soften stories in a post–Watergate time.

Then, the Red Sox faded, the Yankees played phenomenal baseball, and the rivals tied for first place on the season's last day. A one-game playoff in Boston was required to determine the AL East winner. The unlikely hero of that game was the soft-hitting shortstop Bucky Dent, who hit a three-run homer in the seventh inning to put the Yankees up 3–2 over the Red Sox. Though a Reggie Jackson home run would give the Yankees a 5–4 victory, it was Dent's home run that made the game a crucial and dramatic episode in Yankee history and one that would come to be known as "One Bucky Bleeping Dent Afternoon" in New England.

The Yankees defeated the Royals three games to one in the American League Championship and then faced the Dodgers in the World Series. The Dodgers beat the Yankees 11–5 and 4–3. But there was a bit of Southern California swagger that didn't sit right with New Yorkers. Lyle wrote that Davey Lopes would circle the bases pointing upward in the air with his finger, as if to say, "We're number one." It inspired the Yankees who wanted more than victory—Lyle said that they wanted "to really kick their ass."[43] With that sentiment in mind, the Yankees reversed the momentum when the series shifted to New York. The Yankees won the third game 5–1, based on the defensive play of third baseman Graig Nettles. Game Four went into extra innings; Lou Piniella won the game on a game-winning single. Game Five was a Yankee blowout as the Yankees won 12–2 with 18 hits. Game Six belonged to Jackson, who hit a 430-foot home run to cap the Yankees' comeback season.

It was a superb World Series performance. And while Dent is remembered for his home run in Boston, he hit .417 in the World Series.

If Reggie Jackson had a lot of things to say about Thurman Munson, so did Billy Martin. Lyle noted how Martin had chewed out the Yankee backstop, though Munson often played under physical strain. Munson said that if Martin didn't give him respect, he was not going to play when he didn't feel like it. Though Martin apologized, Lyle opined that Munson wouldn't forget about it for a long time.[44] Perhaps the most interesting portrait of Munson during the 1978 season is the one written by Jackson in retrospect years later[45]:

> And Thurman was finally wearing down. He'd caught more than a thousand big-league games by then, which is a lot for any man. His right knee was very painful all year. He couldn't hit for as much power; his arm was bothering him. Even so, he made adjustments and played through it. He still threw out almost half the guys who tried to run on him, even though he had to throw the ball to second almost sidearm. Still only missed eight games. It wasn't his best season, but it might have been his gutsiest, and he set an example for all of us.

The Yankees went into the 1979 season without Sparky Lyle, who had been traded on November 10, 1978, to the Texas Rangers. The first two months were mediocre. The Yankees went from second to third place twice and then dropped to fourth place.[46] The team was losing its edge to younger teams in the same way that the glitzy bands of the late 1970s were losing out to new wave and punk rock.

On August 1, 1979, Munson was hitting .288 with only three home runs and there was "talk of retirement due to balky knees and an aching right shoulder."[47] That night, the Yankees completed a road trip and Munson flew home to Canton, Ohio to see his family.[48] On August 2, 1979, he took off from Akron-Canton airport in his new Cessna plane with two local men, co-pilot David Hall and passenger Jerry D. Anderson. The Yankee captain had hoped to identify a flying glitch, but he flew the plane too low before it crashed. Though the others were relatively uninjured, Munson had failed to utilize the shoulder strap and when the plane crashed and he was "instantly paralyzed from the neck down." The others tried to pull Munson from the plane but when the jet fuel exploded, they had to "scramble for their lives" and Munson died from smoke inhalation.[49] Munson's death, which stunned the world, was front-page news throughout the country. Accolades poured in from players and management across the baseball world. Graig Nettles said that he had expected to be Munson's friend his entire life.[50]

The Yankees flew to Ohio for the funeral on August 6th. Bobby Murcer and Lou Piniella delivered eulogies and the team returned to New York that afternoon for a game against the Baltimore Orioles at Yankee Stadium scheduled that night for a *Monday Night Baseball* broadcast. This was not a "Win One for the Gipper" situation. The team was emotionally drained from losing their leader plus the physical toll of flying to Ohio and back in the space of a few hours. But they plodded through their mourning. "I just know that that's what Thurman would've wanted," said Murcer. "If he was sitting here and I said I couldn't play, he'd say, 'You're crazy.' I just know that's what he would've wanted me to do."[51]

The catcher's box was unmanned "when the Yankees took the field."[52] Phil Rizzuto said a prayer on the air during the pre-game show:

It's just something to keep you really from going bananas.
Because if you let this,
If you keep thinking about what happened, and you can't understand it,
That's what really drives you to despair.[53]

Murcer, who had been traded back to the Yankees in the middle of the season, drove in all five runs with a three-run homer in the seventh inning and a two-run single in the ninth to beat the Orioles 5–4. The exhilaration and exhaustion caused Murcer to almost faint.[54]

The memorials did not stop there. The Yankees wore black armbands for the remainder of the season. Munson's number 15 was retired. Only eight other Yankees had that distinction before Munson: Lou Gehrig, Babe Ruth, Joe DiMaggio, Mickey Mantle, Yogi Berra, Bill Dickey, Whitey Ford, and Casey Stengel. Munson was also honored with the erection of a plaque in Yankee Stadium's Monument Park, which read "Our captain and leader has not left us—today, tomorrow, this year, next…. Our endeavors will reflect our love and admiration for him."[55]

In the summer of 1979, my brother sent Munson a request for an autographed picture and he was thrilled when it arrived toward the end of July. For Yankee fans that were kids, the 1970s ended when Thurman Munson died.

## Notes

1. David Fischer, *Miracle Moments in New York Yankees History: The Turning Points, the Memorable Games, the Incredible Records* (Delaware: Sports Publishing, 2017), 113.
2. "Sparky Lyle," *1973 Yankee Yearbook*, 28.
3. Fischer, *Miracle Moments*, 99–100.
4. Richard Lally, *Bombers, an Oral History of the New York Yankees* (New York: Crown, 2002), 201.
5. *New York Post*, June 21, 1973: 80.
6. Gene Schoor, *Billy Martin* (New York: Doubleday & Co, 1980), 151.
7. Fisher, 95.
8. Ray Negron and Sally Cook, *Yankee Miracles, Life with the Boss and the Bronx Bombers* (New York: Liveright, 2012), 152.
9. Sparky Lyle and Peter Golenbock, *The Bronx Zoo* (New York: Crown, 1979), 22.
10. Robert O. Fishel and Martin Appel, eds. "Elliot Maddox," *1974 Yankee Yearbook* (New York: NY Yankees Inc.), 25.
11. *Ibid.*
12. Randy Galloway, "Beanball Warfare: Game Within a Game," *Dallas Morning News*, May 25, 1975: 4.
13. *Ibid.*
14. *Ibid.*
15. Fischer, 95.
16. Negron and Cook, *Yankee Miracles*, 148.
17. Jim Ogle, "Talk of Piniella Trade Lacks Substance—Paul," *Star Ledger* (Newark, NJ), May 14, 1975: 61.
18. Schoor, 9–15.
19. Roger Kahn, *October Men, Reggie Jackson, George Steinbrenner, Billy Martin, and the Yankees Miraculous Finish in 1978* (Orlando: Harcourt, 2003), 113.
20. Maury Allen, *Yankees World Series Memories* (Champaign, IL: Sports Publishing LLC, 2008), 154.
21. *Ibid.*
22. *Ibid.*
23. Christopher Devine, *Thurman Munson: A Baseball Biography* (Jefferson, NC: McFarland and Co., 2001), 128–129.
24. *Ibid.*, 129.

25. Kahn, 143.

26. Schoor, 181.

27. Kahn, 136.

28. Robert Ward, "Reggie Jackson in No-Man's Land," *Sport*, June 1977, 94; article cited in Kahn, 136–137.

29. *Ibid.*, 138.

30. Moss Klein, "But Nobody Beat Stanley for the Job," Baseball Notebook, *Star-Ledger* (Newark, NJ), April 7, 1977: 58.

31. Bill Pennington, *Billy Martin, Baseball's Flawed Genius* (Boston: Houghton Miflflin Harcourt, 2015), 271.

32. *Ibid.*

33. Allen, 75–76.

34. *Ibid.*, 80.

35. Kahn, 191.

36. Reggie Jackson with Kevin Baker, *Becoming Mr. October* (New York: Doubleday, 2013), 202–203.

37. *Ibid.*, 204.

38. Greg Prato, *Song Review*, *ALLmusic*, www.allmusic.com/song/we-are-the-champions-mt0006771275, last accessed August 1, 2018.

39. Fischer, 112.

40. Jimmy Hyams, "Guidry-Mania" Autographs, Handshakes, And Now There's the 'Ballad of Ron Guidry,'" *The Advocate* (Baton Rouge), January 15, 1979: 2-D.

41. Allen, 161–162.

42. *Ibid.*

43. Lyle and Golenbock, 248.

44. *Ibid.*, 90.

45. Jackson, 208.

46. Devine, 214.

47. Fischer, 123.

48. *Ibid.*

49. Devine, 223–224.

50. *Ibid.*, 226.

51. Murray Chass, "Murcer Drives in 5 as Yanks Win, 5–4," *New York Times*, August 7, 1979: C13.

52. Fischer, 123.

53. Tom Peyer and Hart Seeley, eds., *O Holy Cow!* (New York: Ecco Press, 2008), 14.

54. Fischer, 123.

55. *Ibid.*

# Mr. October

## Cheers, Reggie!
## Everybody Knows Your Name!

PAUL HENSLER

The pantheon of great Pinstripers includes Ruth, Gehrig, DiMaggio, Berra, and Mantle, all of them instantly recognizable and forever linked to the famed tradition of baseball in the Bronx. Another member of that elite gathering is one Reginald Martinez Jackson, who, unlike the above-mentioned, only spent a small portion of his major-league career in New York. In terms of playing ability and the intangible assets that he brought with him when he signed with the Yankees as a free agent in late 1976, Reggie Jackson crammed nearly a lifetime's worth of experience—for better or ill—into his five years of employment under George Steinbrenner.

The terms under which Reggie Jackson ascended to the pinnacle of the sports world and commandeered the attention of the media constitute a narrative as complex as the man himself. His big-league journey commenced in 1967, the final year of the Athletics' stay in Kansas City, and by the time of his arrival at Yankee Stadium in 1977, he joined one of his future fellow Yankee alumni by virtue of being known simply by one name, "Reggie," thereby achieving an iconic status worthy of other notable cultural stars or athletes such as Yogi, Elvis, Pelé, or, for that matter, John, Paul, George, or Ringo.

## The Pre-Bronx Years

The life story of Reggie Jackson has been well covered, both in full-volume works authored by baseball writers as well as autobiographically by the man himself. In fact, a cottage industry has bloomed over the years to disseminate the tale of his rise to stardom: *Becoming Mr. October; Reggie: A Season with a Superstar; Reggie: The Autobiography; Mr. October: The Reggie Jackson Story;* and, perhaps quite compellingly, *Reggie Jackson: From Superstar to Candy Bar.* This groundswell of literature caters to an audience ranging from the youthful reader to the adult, and explores the trials and tribulations of Reggie's earliest days growing up in Pennsylvania, his athletic accomplishments as a youngster and on the collegiate level, and his transition to the role of major league baseball player.

A foretaste of the greatness to come was evident in the first round of the 1966 amateur baseball draft, when Reggie's feats at Arizona State University drew the notice of the Kansas City Athletics, who took him as the second pick overall. Following a brief stint in the minors, he débuted with the A's the next year and then made his mark in the pitching-rich season of 1968 by clouting 29 home runs when the team relocated to Oakland. With this legend of the long ball now budding—and, along with it, a proclivity for abundant strikeout totals—he endeavored to eclipse the 50-homer mark in 1969, but finished three short of this milestone. Reggie anchored the third spot in the batting order and joined forces with other teammates to become Charlie Finley's "Swingin' A's," World Series champions from 1972 to 1974.

In Reggie's watershed year of 1973, when he won the American League's Most Valuable Player award as well as MVP laurels in that year's World Series, he was installed as the clean-up hitter, thereby gaining a crucial measure of trust from Dick Williams, the Athletics' manager, but also earning the respect and honor for holding down the key run-production place in the batting order. After Oakland's third straight World Series triumph, Reggie released his first autobiography, with a subtitle inviting the reader to learn about "a season with a superstar."

The spotlight on Reggie grew in intensity and the number of spotlights trained on him increased as well. And observers of the subject being illuminated are left with no doubt as to how Reggie wanted to impress them, as evinced in the self-absorbed opening of that autobiography: "My name is Reggie Jackson and I am the best in baseball" because "there is no one who does as many things as well as I do."[1] On the first page alone, the proper pronoun "I" is used twenty times.

As Oakland's dynastic roster was about to be riven by the departure of potential free agents to other teams after the Seitz decision of December 1975, Charlie Finley tried to avoid the full impact of player defection—in which he would gain nothing in return by the abandonment of a group of notables that included Reggie, Rollie Fingers, Bert Campaneris, Joe Rudi, and Sal Bando—by trading Reggie to the Baltimore Orioles in a multiplayer deal that also featured Ken Holtzman, Mike Torrez, and Don Baylor. In the spring of 1976, Reggie was mired in a contract dispute with Finley, who actually cut Reggie's salary when he automatically renewed the pact with a 20 percent reduction. Reggie held out for more money and did not report to the Orioles following his April 2nd trade, and although he brokered a better one-year deal with Baltimore—raising his Finely-dictated $112,000 salary to $190,000 courtesy of Oriole general manager Hank Peters—this latest round of negotiations lasted a full month.

The delay of Reggie finally donning a Baltimore uniform in early May was evident in his uninspiring .225 batting average, but he came alive in the last three months of the campaign as the Orioles desperately chased the Yankees in the American League East. Slugging 19 homers, driving in 57 runs, and hitting .309, Reggie attempted to reincarnate his "One-Man Wild Bunch" personage that had appeared on a 1974 cover of *Time* magazine, and had Peters granted Reggie's initial request for a five-year contract for a total of around $1.25 million, he would not have entered the inaugural free-agent sweepstakes. But Reggie professed to having evolved into "a full-fledged baseball mercenary" who was intending "to use the system itself" for his own financial benefit.[2]

Despite the laudatory comments in his second autobiography—published in 1984—on his one year playing for the Orioles, Reggie knew that Baltimore was to be nothing more than a whistle stop in his travels to a new home where the grass would be greener and the second-place finish that he had just endured with the Orioles a distant memory.

## "This is your kind of town!"

Offering his observations and analysis as a color commentator for the 1976 American League Championship Series televised on ABC, Reggie shared the airwaves with announcers Keith Jackson and Howard Cosell, witnessing a preview of what might await him should he select the refurbished Yankee Stadium as his newest address. In the fifth and deciding game of the ALCS against the Kansas City Royals, New York first baseman Chris Chambliss—batting in the clean-up slot—slugged a home run to lead off the bottom of the ninth inning and give the Yankees their first AL pennant in twelve years. Joyful fans flooded the field as Chambliss attempted to bull and stagger his way around the bases, the crowd making his journey nearly impossible. Under the leadership of tempestuous manager Billy Martin, here in his first turn at the Yankee helm, the Bronx Bombers took a major step in reclaiming the glory that they had held for so long during their dynasty from 1947 to 1964.

The Yankees' subsequent loss to the Cincinnati Reds in the World Series—a four-game sweep for the National Leaguers—indicated that one piece of the puzzle remained outstanding before New York could reclaim baseball's ultimate prize. And with free agency about to become a fixture of the National Pastime's landscape, Yankee owner George Steinbrenner trained his sights and copious financial resources on the biggest name to hit the inaugural open market. A union of Reggie and Steinbrenner was a distinct possibility, and the race among club owners to corral the prime members of the first group of free agents commenced in early November.

*New York Times* columnist Dave Anderson referred to the newly-won freedom of player movement resulting from the striking down of the reserve clause as "Baseball Lib," and with Reggie front and center among the new free agents, he was courted by a number of teams.[3] Among the serious bidders for his services were the San Diego Padres, whose owner, McDonald's mogul Ray Kroc, was in the process of playing his own version of "checkbook baseball" by inking a pair of Reggie's former Oakland teammates, Rollie Fingers and Gene Tenace. Another interesting suitor was John McHale, Founding President of the Montreal Expos—who, in turn, were backed financially by the Bronfman family, steeped in wealth from its ownership of the liquor icon Seagram's. And Reggie's most recent employer, the Baltimore Orioles ball club, was trying to retain his services. The Los Angeles Dodgers were also in the hunt, and although Kroc and McHale actually put bigger contract offers (about $3.6 million and nearly $5 million, respectively) on the table to lure Reggie to their National League teams, "Reggie feared the relative anonymity that would come with playing in Canada, [and] the Dodgers were slow to act and thus failed to cater to Reggie's ego."[4] Dazzled by the allure of Gotham's hurly-burly and even encouraged by a cabbie who recognized Reggie and George Steinbrenner strolling in Manhattan prior to Jackson's signing—"Hey, Reggie! Come on, man. This is your kind of town!" cried the driver—the outfielder ultimately cast his lot with the Yankees.[5]

By his own admission that there were other factors informing his decision to play in New York besides money, the 30-year-old Reggie sought to capitalize further on his existing business relationships and generate new entrepreneurial opportunities. In addition to his contract with ABC, he had ties to clothing and shoe manufacturers. By putting his baseball talents to work on the nation's biggest stage, which was further illuminated by its brightest lights, Reggie would be positioned to burnish the stardom he had already won for himself.

Upon his signing with the Yankees for $2.9 million, Reggie's formal introduction to his new hometown took place during "a gala press conference" at the Americana Hotel, with the *New York Times* opining that "the ritual ... should have taken place in the [hotel's] Imperial Ballroom because it was more a coronation than an unveiling."[6] Indeed, the regal reference enhanced the legend and lore accruing to a former league MVP and World Series champion, a six-time All-Star whose statistical averages up to that point were: .269 batting average with 31 home runs, 91 RBI, and 19 stolen bases. This said nothing of the degree of swagger that led him to proclaim that he didn't come to New York to become a star because "I brought my star with me."[7]

Egotism aside, Reggie was about to immerse himself in a situation combining two key elements, one from his days in Baltimore, the other from his previous years in Oakland. By signing with the Yankees, he swapped one feisty manager, the Orioles' Earl Weaver, for another, Billy Martin; Reggie's new sparring partner in the owner's box would be George Steinbrenner, with whom there would be conflict reminiscent of that with his old boss, the Athletics' Charlie Finley. Although neither Oakland nor Baltimore were media centers, news of troubles in the Athletics' clubhouse and player battles with their controversial owner found its way into the papers, just as Reggie's tiffs with Weaver drew an audience.

But having relocated to New York and now becoming subject to much more intense scrutiny by fans and the press alike, Reggie found few places to hide when he assumed his place on the 1977 Yankee roster. With the exception of his brief stay in Baltimore, Reggie had played almost his entire career with many players who, like him, had cut their teeth in the Athletics' farm system. Despite the famous roiling in the Oakland clubhouse, there was nonetheless a tangible camaraderie among players who were united in their distaste for Charlie Finley. When Reggie arrived in New York, he not only faced the pressure of producing on the field in order to live up to the terms of his generous contract—he soon discovered that life could be lonely at the top.

Reggie's new teammate, Yankee captain and 1976 American League MVP Thurman Munson, became the object of the outfielder's controversial remark—the infamous "I'm the straw that stirs the drink" comment—printed in *Sport* magazine in the summer of Reggie's first season in New York. Publication of the swipe at Munson fueled resentment that other Yankees held toward Jackson, and as Reggie sought an end to the pain of the mounting alienation by his teammates coupled with "bursts of sarcasm" by Billy Martin, he felt that a trade from New York might be his only way out of his demoralizing conundrum.[8] The irascible manager was never in Reggie's corner to begin with: As the first free agent class hit the market, Martin implored Steinbrenner to sign Reggie's former teammate Joe Rudi because "he's a better player."[9]

The straw that supposedly stirred the drink was also the personification of a lightning rod, as evidenced in his notorious Fenway Park dugout scuffle with Martin in June 1977. This *cause célèbre*, instigated by Reggie's failure to hustle after a base hit by Jim Rice, was a test of wills in which the manager asserted his authority by pulling his ostensibly loafing outfielder from the game in mid-inning. Having hardly endeared himself to his teammates even before the incident, Reggie found redemption through swinging his bat, which came alive, especially in the second half of the season when he hit 19 home runs and drove in 69 runs. Stymied by Kansas City's pitching in the ALCS—Reggie batted a mere .125, going two for 16—he erupted in the most dramatic fashion with his stupendous three-homer performance in Game Six of the World Series against the Los Angeles Dodgers.

This demonstration of slugging forever etched his name into the granite of baseball history as one of the game's indelible moments, and it seemed to validate Steinbrenner's purported comment made when the owner was courting Jackson in the fall of 1976: "See, everybody knows and loves you already in this town."[10]

## Be Careful What You Ask For

The adulation and fame bestowed on Reggie Jackson had its costs, but it also had its rewards. He followed up his fairy-tale ending 1977 campaign by helping the Yankees to a stunning comeback in 1978 against the Boston Red Sox and rematch victories over the Royals and Dodgers in the post-season, thereby cementing his nickname of "Mr. October" by batting .462 (six for 13) against Kansas City and .391 (nine for 23) versus Los Angeles. After two seasons wearing pinstripes, Reggie had contributed mightily to the pair of World Series rings that now graced the fingers of so many Yankee players and coaches. Another AL East pennant followed in 1980, and one more appearance in the World Series of 1981 rounded out Reggie's five-year tenure in the Bronx. This, however, is only a brief review of the highlight reel.

Littering the path to those playoff berths were the firing and hiring of three other Yankee managers—Dick Howser, Bob Lemon, and Gene Michael; the tumultuous media accounts of the rantings of Steinbrenner; a debilitating players' strike in 1981; and, tragically, the death of Thurman Munson in early August 1979. The *coup de grâce* for Reggie at the conclusion of his contract may have been Steinbrenner's ill-conceived "apology" to Yankee fans for the team's defeat in the 1981 World Series at the hands of the Dodgers. Cleaning out his locker for the last time at Yankee Stadium, Reggie knew that come 1982, he would find a new home with another American League team. But the stamp that he left on the city of New York and the image burned into the minds of Yankee fans had garnered him the laurels commensurate with the "coronation" that described his November 1976 press conference.

Given the unsavory aspects of various controversies that attended Reggie's five years in New York, it can also be observed that his mental makeup helped him to persevere in the face of battles with Martin and Steinbrenner as well as the distance at which some of his teammates held him. Reggie's performance at the plate held up for the most part—although his fielding ability deteriorated noticeably—but a player of lesser physical and psychological means would not likely have been able to endure the conditions to which Reggie was subjected. Self-proclaimed as a superstar long before he came to New York, he was able not only to bear the cross of upholding his reputation but also to add to his legacy through diligence. Spending far fewer seasons at Yankee Stadium than Ruth, Gehrig, DiMaggio, or Mantle, Reggie nonetheless carved a niche peculiar to his own circumstances and found favor in the eyes of many Yankee fans, thereby becoming every bit the icon that his notable predecessors were.

## The Background of an Icon

The path traversed by Reggie Jackson to reach the pinnacle of stardom was not an easy one when viewed in the context of his life's experience. The zeitgeist of the post–

World War II era when he grew up and that of the 1970s as he assumed the role of notable baseball player certainly provided the backdrop to his coming of age. Reggie's high level of intelligence, supreme athletic ability, and ethnicity—"I was a black kid with Spanish, Indian, and Irish blood who lived in a white, Jewish suburb of Philadelphia"[11]—only tell part of the story.

The pain of seeing his parents split up just as he was entering grade school affected Reggie deeply, and his own marriage to a Mexican-American woman ended in early 1972, less than four years after they had wed. His youthful days living in Wyncote, Pennsylvania, led him to develop a sensitivity to anti–Semitism, manifested in the umbrage that he later took at players who told Jewish jokes in reference to his teammate, pitcher Ken Holtzman, or insulted some of the Jewish sportswriters who covered the baseball beat. In the aftermath of a dispute with Mike Epstein, Reggie and the Oakland first baseman set aside their differences when they affixed black armbands to their jerseys in honor of the seven Israeli athletes who were murdered by the Palestinian terrorist group Black September in September 1972 at the Summer Olympic Games in Munich. Reggie's exposure to Jim Crow while playing with Birmingham in the Southern League in 1967 laid bare the evils of racism. Taken in total, these traits underpinned the complexity that formed the personality of Reggie Jackson.

Reggie Jackson won three World Series rings and played 10 seasons with the Oakland A's. His five-season tenure in the South Bronx yielded two World Series rings, the nickname "Mr. October" for his postseason performance, and a candy bar named after him. Jackson went into the Hall of Fame as a Yankee (National Baseball Hall of Fame and Museum, Cooperstown, NY).

After finding a place on the roster of the Oakland Athletics in 1968, Reggie never returned to the minor leagues, and over the next several years, he was among an ethnically diverse group of Athletic players that included Bert Campaneris, Blue Moon Odom, George Hendrick, Ramon Webster, Jose Tartabull, Allan Lewis, and Felipe Alou. By the time he won the American League Most Valuable Player award in 1973, he was among the Oakland frontrunners contributing to the team's success, but in this regard, his face is one of several core players who grew up together as they made their way through the Athletics' farm system. When Reggie signed with the Yankees, he confessed to being "clearly a new breed of black player in New York ... a black athlete who felt he did not need to respect authority, Yankee history, or even his new Yankee teammates."[12]

By supposedly bringing his star with him to the Bronx, he also cast a shadow over other former and current Yankees of minority ethnicity. Al Downing, Horace Clarke, Jerry Kinney, Roy White, Willie

Randolph, Mickey Rivers, and Paul Blair all may have been solid ballplayers, but none were credentialed with the stature of Reggie. Even the first black player to don a Yankee uniform, Gold Glove catcher and 1963 AL MVP Elston Howard, was cut from different cloth. A star in his own right who also was a victim of the indignities of Jim Crow, Howard shunned the limelight despite the fame he earned—"a true Yankee," according to reliever Goose Gossage—and held a conflicted view of Reggie.[13] According to Howard's wife, Elston "always admired his talent, but Reggie Jackson was a showboat in Elston's eyes."[14] The image of showboat or hot dog fitted well with a player who, despite the flashiness, was nevertheless able to deliver performance when it counted most, and Reggie's powerful display in the 1977 World Series was emblematic of why teammates and fans could be drawn to him in his role as a hero.

Many years after his retirement and using less bombastic wording, Reggie was more reflective about his earliest days with the Yankees and why he may have been viewed as "arrogant" and egotistical" by the press and the public. "It was a touchy social time," he wrote in 2013. "It was 1977; there were very few black players who spoke out."[15] And when Reggie did speak out, plainly evident was one of his most outwardly visible traits—his ability to communicate in a conversational manner of speaking that was a behavior instilled at an early age by his father and which served him very well in his stint as a television commentator and pitchman.[16] On a day-to-day basis, however, this speech enabled him to deal with the media that followed the teams for which he played.

More is at work here than simply the musings of a man gifted with an IQ of 160 and no small touch of solipsism. Reggie was also a survivor of personal squabbles with Oakland team owner Finley as well as a veteran of confrontations with several teammates in the Athletics' clubhouse. His level of intelligence set him apart from what sports psychologist Gary Sailes referred to as "the 'dumb jock' stereotype and the myth of athletic superiority among African-American athletes in intercollegiate and professional sports."[17] Reggie's pre-eminence among baseball players was no myth and he certainly did not lack for smarts.

While the love was in full flower after Reggie stepped to the plate and deposited a pitch into the stands for another home run, rivers of resentment ran concurrent to the adulation, especially away from the ballpark. "If I ever took out my billfold and counted how much I had left in it, I was 'flashy,'" he opined, yet his popularity was a bane that he addressed with often crude or boorish behavior when recognized in public.[18]

At times, he acquiesced to autograph requests by scrawling an obscenity, and for a man who sought privacy, contradictions abounded when he drove his white Rolls-Royce bearing a license plate that read "MVP 73" or made a scene in a restaurant even though he was seated at a secluded table. The burden of fame could prove to be a major inconvenience. In Reggie's first year with the Yankees, his taking a simple stroll down Fifth Avenue could evolve into "a real New York City celebrity ruckus" where "guys in business suits were acting like little kids at their first major-league game, trying to just get near the guy."[19]

A book published during Reggie's final season in Oakland furnished an interesting analysis of his conflicted persona. This "portrait of an enigma" outlines a series of paradoxes that defined him in the first portion of his career and followed him in his continuing years. Reggie was "egotistical—but humble … a super athlete—yet brittle … a superstar—but not really … a great human being—but a failure in marriage and personal relationships … a swinger—but lonely."[20]

Was this a ballplayer or simply another person possessed of tics and foibles—good and bad—just like anyone else? Youth groups were recipients of his charitable giving; he joined Willie Stargell of the Pittsburgh Pirates to raise awareness of the fight against sickle cell anemia; his business ventures outside of baseball were successful; his physical ability and success on the field were the envy of many an athlete; and his penchant for often rising to the occasion at the critical moment of a game set him apart.

Reggie's nickname of "Mr. October" was bestowed on him by Thurman Munson, the Yankee captain, who spoke the moniker with a pejorative twist. But coming when it did, there was undoubtedly substance to the phrase based on Reggie's post-season feats. By achieving a hero's status in New York through World Series wins in 1977 and 1978, Reggie, in the eyes of many fans, fulfilled Merriam-Webster's definition of "icon" in spite of the roiling with teammates, management, and ownership. That is, he became "an object of uncritical devotion," and peccadilloes and faults that could be ascribed to him were easily forgiven because Reggie had played the role of Moses in delivering the Yankees to the promised land of a world championship.

The astonishing efficiency of his three-homer performance on three consecutive pitches in the finale of the 1977 World Series did not go unnoticed by the fans in attendance at Yankee Stadium, who chanted "Reg-gie!" until their hero emerged from the home dugout for a curtain call, an honor reserved for the most special of moments. A year earlier, Chris Chambliss's clout won a pennant; this time around, Reggie's display of power won a World Series *and* created a legend.

In a case of unabashed self-lionization years later in a book co-authored with St. Louis Cardinals Hall of Fame pitcher Bob Gibson, Reggie overtly drew a parallel between his connection with the Yankee owner and other great sporting tandems of unmistakable dynastic timber. Just as basketball great Bill Russell would always be linked to Red Auerbach, football's Bart Starr to Vince Lombardi, and Roger Staubach to Tom Landry, so, too, did Reggie firmly believe that "Reggie Jax" and the man called "The Boss" were "bound together as part of the history of the 'Steinbrenner Yankees.'"[21]

New York City in the summer of 1977 had been subjected to the calamity resulting from a power blackout in mid–July, socio-economic conditions in the Yankees' home borough conspired to coin the phrase "the Bronx is burning," and a serial killer dubbed "Son of Sam" terrorized the metropolitan region. But dousing the flames of these ills was the return of the World Series trophy to the House That Ruth Built, recently refurbished in 1974 and 1975, and now, once again, the center of attention of the baseball world thanks to a feat by the latest in the line of future Hall of Famers to pass through the Bronx.

## The Rewards of Star Power

The iconic intonation of "Reg-gie!" at the ballpark conferred the honor of single-name recognition that is accorded few celebrities, but in terms of material gains besides a lucrative contract with his team, Reggie Jackson was in a position to capitalize on the next phase of glory that he had won for himself. His attachment to Manhattan facilitated access to marketing opportunities that landed him endorsement deals with Volkswagen automobiles, Pentax Sport 35 camera equipment, miniature Louisville Slugger baseball bats, Rawlings baseball gloves—a bit ironic considering that his fielding skills deteriorated rapidly when he joined the Yankees—Panasonic car stereo systems, Pony sports footwear,

Upper Deck trading cards, and a Sega Master Baseball video game. Following his stint with the Yankees, Reggie continued to appear on baseball telecasts in the postseason throughout the 1980s, and he was cast as himself in a number of roles for television shows and motion pictures. However, his biggest name recognition related to a personal product and was the realization of a self-fulfilling prophecy.

At the time that Reggie made his decision to sign with the Yankees in November 1976, a quote attributed to him at the time indicated that "If I played in New York, they would name a candy bar after me"—a reference to the fame and glory that he confidently anticipated bringing to the Yankee lineup.[22] However gloating and contrived the statement may have been, it is doubtful that many endorsements would have come his way had he underperformed or otherwise not lived up to expectations. Not least of these was a confectionary treat created by Standard Brands and originally known as the "Wayne Bun" in tribute to the city in which it was manufactured—Fort Wayne, Indiana.

Recast as a candy "bar" even though it was circular in shape, the new REGGIE! bar consisted of one and one-half ounces of "chocolaty covered caramel and peanuts" according to its bright orange-colored wrapper, which also featured the picture of a pinstripe-clad Reggie whose batting pose and facial expression indicate that he has surely connected for a home run. A strategic introduction for the treat was set for 1978's Opening Day at Yankee Stadium, at which time all fans would be given a free REGGIE! bar upon entering the ballpark. In one way, the ploy worked perfectly: The object of the confection—and affection of the hometown crowd—slugged a home run in his first at-bat. However, the unintended consequence was the reaction of thousands of those adoring fans hurling their candy onto the field of play and causing an embarrassing delay of game so that the diamond could be cleared.

While the REGGIE! bar actually had a relatively short production cycle, disappearing in 1981, the product held enough significance to be included among one hundred "artifacts that tell the story of the national pastime [sic]," according Josh Leventhal, author of the 2015 book *A History of Baseball in 100 Objects: A Tour Through the Bats, Balls, Uniforms, Awards, Documents, and Other Artifacts That Tell the Story of the National Pastime.* Reggie's name and image on the product's wrapper placed him front and center in the eye of fans and consumers of the bar, a marketing opportunity that would only have been staged for someone of his stature. This venture provided far more exposure for the latest Yankee hero than that for the first notable black Yankee, Elston Howard, back in 1964, when he was featured with a host of teammates and manager Yogi Berra in a print ad for Yoo-Hoo chocolate drink. Times had changed in the years since Howard's likeness was included to plug a beverage, and his ad was as understated as Reggie's candy bar was flamboyant.

Catering to taste buds was one way to attract fans of all ages, but Reggie was also the biographical subject of a host of authors who shared his story to a reading audience of young adults. During Reggie's 1975 season in Oakland, Scholastic Book Services published a frank account of his life that detailed some of the riches he had treated himself to—an extensive wardrobe, a luxury apartment high above the city, and a burgeoning collection of automobiles—yet *Reggie Jackson: Superstar* attempts to ground Reggie as an everyman who takes breakfast at a local restaurant and whose clientele suits the slugger because they consist of "a wide range of both blacks and whites, and Reggie gets along with them all."[23] As endearing as this portrait is, this book also indicates that Reggie enjoys "times when I do like to get special treatment," and his impatience with a reporter's "dumb question" could easily disappear when the same query is posed by a youngster, who may then receive a lengthy, thoughtful response.[24]

Some volumes focused on a younger crowd are tinged with hagiography, such as *The Picture Story of Reggie Jackson* (1977), the author of which describes him as "a hard contender" who has "done his best since his days at Cheltenham (Pennsylvania) High School and at Arizona State University," and another notes Reggie's "special talent for getting hits at important times" that enable him to become "everyone's hero."[25] While Maury Allen's short 1978 biography does not eschew the negative incidents of Reggie's life, it does include an account of a purported encounter that the slugger had with a black youngster in the days before signing with the Yankees during the stroll with George Steinbrenner in Manhattan. "I love you, Reggie. Please play in New York," the lad entreated the free agent, who then turned to the Yankee owner and said, "I think that kid convinced me."[26] Whether true or apocryphal, this episode made for a heart-warming story and was infused with the importance of Reggie's ability to relate to a new generation of fans who were just beginning to appreciate how great the sport of baseball could be.

In 1979's *Reggie Jackson: Slugger Supreme*, the protagonist is revealed to enjoy "a long bubble bath" and relish the book *Jonathan Livingston Seagull* "because it's a religious experience every time he reads it." Indeed, this profile cites religion as being "the most important thing in his life" because without it, "he couldn't have a peaceful life."[27] Reggie's own scrapbook, published in 1978 with expansive captions, attempts to smooth the rough edges from his tiff with Thurman Munson, who is now described as "an emotional person" but also "a fearless guy and a winner … my closest friend on the team."[28] One adoring fan even composed a poem for each member of that era's Bronx Bombers, with his paean to Reggie lauding him as "the spark plug, propeller of the Yankee Team."[29]

The release dates of these publications are significant in that they come immediately after Reggie's signing with the Yankees or, even more notably, shortly after he had completed his first two seasons in New York, thus capitalizing on the glory of his post-season derring-do and his team's World Series triumphs. Reggie's iconic status continued to take shape at this time, and the galvanizing of his reputation over the remainder of his career laid the foundation for his inclusion in Edward J. Rielly's *Baseball: An Encyclopedia of Popular Culture*, published in 2005; it informs the readers that two criteria were essential for a subject to be worthy of inclusion: "First, the item (person, place, thing, or something else) must have some importance within baseball" and secondly, "[t]he item must have significance beyond the diamond."[30]

Reggie meets these constraints not only by his stature as a Hall of Fame player but his impact on American culture is manifest in one-name recognition ("Reggie," of course), the commercial endorsements he brokered, and his work in the media industry (broadcasting, television, and movies). Embedded in Reggie's notoriety outside the game is what sports historian Neil D. Isaacs best explained as his "power of personality," which he viewed as Reggie serving as an apotheosis of a Prima Donna. "The Prima Donna may be characterized by the difficulties of dealing with him," wrote Isaacs, "but that is a function of his 'star quality,' which he displays on and off the field, *a charisma that exaggerates both positive and negative traits and is exhibited in the characteristically gigantic nature of his exploits.*"[31]

Although Rielly oversimplifies his second standard, Isaacs unequivocally drives home the point because of his introduction of a characteristic crucial to a person gaining iconic status: the oft-elusive aura of charisma. And perhaps the best example of this can be found in a quote from former Chicago White Sox owner Bill Veeck, who believed that when the first class of free agents marketed themselves at the conclusion of the 1976 season, Reggie was clearly the premier player in terms of star power. "Joe Rudi is a great player, but when one of our pitchers strikes out Joe Rudi, you hear only polite applause," explained Veeck. "When one of our pitchers strikes out Reggie Jackson, it brings down the house."[32]

Emblematic of the enduring legend of Reggie Jackson is a book aimed at a young adult readership—although thoroughly infused with mature topics. James W. Bennett's 2001 novel *Plunking Reggie Jackson* not only trades on the player's name but also casts him as an inanimate, indestructible figure. In the story, Reggie exists only in the form of a life-size, bronze statue, which has been sculpted to depict him in his typical stance in the batter's box. A man has purchased the figure and installed it in his backyard; years later, his sons use the statue as an aid to learn the craft of pitching. When practicing, the older boy discovered that "if you hit the statue just beneath its bronze rib cage, in precisely the right spot, there was a hollow resonance that produced a mellifluous *gonging* tone." When the younger sibling takes his turn, his weaker arm and improper hits yield only *clinks* or a thin kind of *pink*. No *gong*. But Big Brother had encouraged him by saying, 'Don't worry, your day will come.'"[33]

In the book's final scene, time has come to dispose of the statue. One of the sons wraps a chain around its waist to drag it by tractor to a nearby low bridge and unceremoniously dump it into a creek. The hollowness of the statue is sufficient to provide buoyancy, thereby allowing it to float in the rain-swollen stream and be carried away to a distant ocean. Thus, Reggie is not just immortalized in bronze to carry on his baseball legacy but he also proves unsinkable, a trait symbolic of his ability to hold up under pressure. And as the real-life Reggie had to be asked questions in a proper way to elicit a proper answer, the fictitious statue had to be dinged the right way to get the right tone. Surely, at least in this case, art imitated life.

## Reggie by the Numbers

The persona of Reggie Jackson in a Yankee uniform was, in itself, a sartorial statement, a visage of no ordinary ballplayer but one who was a past champion. For most fans at the ballpark, however, the salient trait of the player's uniform visible from a great distance is the number on his back, and to this end, Reggie employed these digits to great effect.

After wearing number 31 for his début in 1967, Reggie thereafter wore number 9 through the end of the 1976 season, years that spanned his time in Oakland and Baltimore. When he joined the Yankees, that number had long been worn by third baseman Graig Nettles, so with a switch now necessary, Reggie requested number 42 as a tribute to the late Jackie Robinson. But that number was also unavailable because it had been taken by pitching coach Art Fowler, so following a short usage of number 20—as an honor to recently retired Frank Robinson, who broke the color barrier for major-league managers in 1975—Reggie picked a number that endured for the remainder of his baseball career and beyond.

Settling to wear the same number as that of another recently retired player, Reggie opted for number 44, which adorned the uniform of Hank Aaron. The former Braves and Brewers slugger eclipsed the hallowed career home-run total of Babe Ruth; the setting of a new record for homers was a monumental achievement for both its significance as a baseball standard and the racial overtones of an African-American surpassing the most noteworthy deed set by one of baseball's all-time greats. Aaron's route to breaking Ruth's record was fraught with the peril of threats and hatred spewed by those who detested the thought of a black player becoming baseball's home-run leader, and the perseverance and class displayed by Aaron enabled him to rise above the vitriol directed his way. It has become an accepted part of Yankees lore that Reggie, to honor this legacy and perhaps draw some unseen spirit from Aaron—though some corners say Willie McCovey—chose number 44.

The meaning of why this uniform number was selected has surely been lost over the ensuing decades, but there is much gravity infused in Reggie's tribute to a black player whose talents were not fully recognized or appreciated as they perhaps should have been. Aaron undoubtedly placed his stamp on the National Pastime with his career, yet he never achieved the status of Ruthian proportions. By wearing number 44, Reggie vicariously made Aaron part of his presence when he played on the big stage in New York. Reggie further facilitated this legacy by having baseball merchandise available through his web site, priced not just with a dollar amount but also with 44 cents trailing as part of the cost of the item. To newer generations of baseball fans, that 44 will always be linked with Reggie, but the reason for its association with him runs far deeper.

When the Yankees retired Reggie's number in 1993, the occasion marked the second time that the team had so commemorated a player of color. Nine years earlier, the number 32 was posthumously retired in honor of Elston Howard, the former player and coach whose comportment was as reserved as Reggie's was bold.

## An Icon in His Immediate Post-Yankee Career

When Reggie Jackson's production slipped considerably in the strike-riven season of 1981, this may have been a signal that the stress of playing in George Steinbrenner's superheated crucible had, at last, taken its toll on even the most intrepid of souls accustomed to the pressure of that milieu. After placing second in voting for the 1980 American League MVP award and earning Silver Slugger honors—based on a .300 batting average, a league-leading 41 home runs, and 111 RBI—the now 35-year-old right fielder/designated hitter stumbled to a .237 average and the lowest power output of his career (15 homers, 54 RBIs, and a slugging average of .428). For Reggie, the bloom appeared to be off the rose in the Bronx.

Yet, the image of icon, slightly tarnished from that off-year performance, was rejuvenated in Anaheim when Reggie inked a deal to spend the next five years with the California Angels. Immediately recovering his stroke, he went on to bat .275, tie Gorman Thomas for the major-league lead in homers with 39, and drive in 101 runs. As if 1981 were simply an anomaly, Reggie and his bat seemed to pick up where 1980 left off, thus endearing himself to a new crowd in a new city. *Sports Illustrated* presaged his comeback early in the spring of 1982 with a feature story—HARK! THE HERALDED ANGEL SWINGS was the campy headline for Reggie's cover photo of the March 15th issue—but the real welcome back for the departed hero came during the Angels' first visit to Yankee Stadium on April 27.

Homerless and batting an anemic .173 entering the contest, Reggie broke a 1–1 tie in the seventh inning by launching a trademark clout off the right field façade that put the Angels ahead for good. Breaking into a chorus of "Reg-gie! Reg-gie!" for old time's sake and prompting a curtain call for the man of the hour even though he was clad in a visitor's uniform bearing the number 44, the crowd of more than 35,000 erupted next into a derogatory verse of "Steinbrenner sucks!" One of the latest free agents to sign with the Yankees, Roy Smalley, made an observation of Reggie's feat shortly after the game that pointed directly to the bolstering of his iconic image writ large: "That's the kind of moment that makes little kids baseball fans for life."[34] Even by playing for a new team, Reggie continued to burnish the reputation he had earned while in pinstripes, and his slugging display offered proof that Steinbrenner's dictum of switching the Yankees' style of offense from power-oriented to one now focused on speed was ill-informed.

Yankee fans recognized and appreciated the aura that imbued their legend and saw no need to disavow the loyalty to a cherished hero who had given them so many reasons to cheer, especially over the last five seasons.

## The One-Man Hall-of-Fame Class of 1993

As a capstone to any Major League Baseball player's experience, Reggie's induction into the Baseball Hall of Fame places him among the select group of those deemed to be the best in their craft. Although some selections continue to generate a fair degree of controversy, such as those by the Veterans Committee, little surprise is expressed when the candidate is an obvious choice to merit inclusion. When Reggie appeared on the 1992 ballot in his first year of eligibility, the only suspense surrounding that year's vote would be how great a percentage he would receive because it was already a foregone conclusion that he would be elected.

Polling 396 of the 423 votes cast by the Baseball Writers' Association of America, Reggie added another entry to his already lengthy list of awards. Unique to that year's vote, and as if to pay homage to his reputation and the impact that he had on baseball, Reggie was the only player to exceed the 75 percent of the vote necessary to be enshrined at Cooperstown. That he shared the spotlight at the induction ceremony with no other inductees on August 1, 1993—save for peers and predecessors of past induction classes— was as defining an iconic moment as the curtain call he received after his three-homer feat in the 1977 World Series. The accolades were his and his alone, a moment in which nobody's attention would be drawn to another baseball luminary who might detract from Reggie's latest triumph.

As chants of "Reg-gie!" roared from many of the approximately 10,000 fans present at the induction, the man of the hour delivered his speech in which he, like several other players of the modern era, paid special tribute to his father as a singular figure in helping him to scale the heights that he reached. Reggie Jackson, Sr., was instrumental in his son's upbringing by stressing the importance of past Negro League baseball, ensuring that education was central to success in life, and teaching him "to be an assertive, vocal black man."[35] Reggie told the gathered crowd that his presence that day in Cooperstown was a direct result of heeding his father's lessons in life and partaking of his wisdom, and as a result, he "developed a drive … to be someone more than a ballplayer."[36]

Whether he envisioned ultimately becoming an icon can be debated, but to solidify the standing that he now gained with Ruth, Gehrig, Mantle, and other standouts who called the Bronx home, Reggie's plaque at the Hall of Fame features his cap adorned with the iconic "NY." The opening words of the plaque's brief narrative describe him as an "Exciting performer," leaving no doubt as to the special quality that contributed to the aura of Reggie Jackson.

## In Conclusion

The figurative—and oft times literal—klieg lights of celebrity, controversy, and athletic stardom enveloped Reggie for both profit and loss. His career role as a baseball player was the first step in his journey to Cooperstown, yet to appreciate the man in full, one needs to consider other factors that turned this particular athlete into the iconic figure that resulted.

Reggie's relationship with fans seldom courted neutrality, as would be expected from a man possessed of extreme talent and complex personality. He had the ability to make the Hall of Fame regardless of his address, but his importance to the Oakland and New York lineups is compelling: Reggie was the only position player from the great Athletic teams of the early 1970s and those Yankee squads of later in that decade to eventually gain entry into Cooperstown. Surrounded by a host of able talent on both clubs—Sal Bando, Bert Campaneris, Joe Rudi, Thurman Munson, Graig Nettles, and Chris Chambliss come to mind—the collective World Series titles won by the Athletics and Yankees may not have been as large had Reggie not been a part of their respective rosters. Reggie's layover season of 1976 in Baltimore proves the point: The lineup of the Athletics still had its framework of regular players—with many about to depart for free agency—yet they were unable to capture the American League West pennant, and the Yankees also emerged from their 11-year slumber to advance to the World Series, only to be swept by the Cincinnati Reds. As painfully as the scenario played out at times in the Bronx during Reggie's first season there, his joining the Yankees was a huge factor in their return to the pinnacle of baseball's post-season glory.

The public adulation Reggie received compromised his private life, yet his ability to withstand the pressure of being in the eye of the storm, on or off the diamond, was his strongest asset. This ethereal, elusive quality of *je ne sais quoi* was what abetted Reggie's iconography and set him apart from Bando, Nettles, and the rest. In the literary world, where biographies and autobiographies of Reggie abound, his imagery can be succinctly expressed in terms of Ernest Lawrence Thayer's "Casey at the Bat" in that he swung and missed—quite often—but when he struck the ball, there could be magic in the air.

Reggie Jackson as an All-Star, American League Most Valuable Player, World Series champion, and Series MVP, as well as 1993's solo Hall of Fame inductee all bear testimony to the remarkable accomplishments of a man whom you wanted to see clad in the uniform of your favorite team. For baseball fans, especially those in the Bronx, Reggie was the man they wanted stepping to the plate at the crucial moment, and his name was one that everybody knew. Whether he brought down the house when he struck out or when he connected, Reggie could be the man of the hour. Any hour.

NOTES

1. Reggie Jackson, *Reggie: A Season with a Superstar* (Chicago: Playboy Press, 1975), 1.
2. Reggie Jackson with Mike Lupica, *Reggie* (New York: Villard Books, 1984), 115.

3. Dave Anderson, "Reggie Jackson's View from the Top," *New York Times,* November 6, 1976: 13.

4. Dayn Perry, *Reggie Jackson: The Life and Thunderous Career of Baseball's Mr. October* (New York: William Morrow, 2010), 168.

5. *Ibid.,* 169.

6. Murray Chass, "Jackson Signs Yankee Contract for Five Years and $2.9 Million," *New York Times,* November 30, 1976: 47.

7. Phil Pepe, "Steinbrenner 'Humanism' Won Reggie for Yanks," *Sporting News,* December 18, 1976: 41.

8. Roger Kahn, *October Men: Reggie Jackson, George Steinbrenner, Billy Martin, and the Yankees' Miraculous Finish in 1978* (New York: Harcourt, Inc., 2003), 138.

9. Phil Pepe quoting Martin, *Yankee Doodles: Inside the Locker Room with Mickey, Yogi, Reggie, and Derek* (New York: Sports Publishing, 2015), 96.

10. Perry quoting Steinbrenner, 169.

11. Jackson with Lupica, 15.

12. Reggie Jackson with Kevin Baker, *Becoming Mr. October* (New York: Doubleday, 2013), 64.

13. Arlene Howard with Ralph Wimbush quoting Gossage, *Elston and Me: The Story of the First Black Yankee* (Columbia: University of Missouri Press, 2001), 187.

14. Howard, 186.

15. Jackson with Baker, 66.

16. Jackson with Lupica, *Reggie,* 24. Emphasis in original.

17. Gary A. Sailes, "An Investigation of Campus Stereotypes: The Myth of Black Athletic Superiority and the Dumb Jock Stereotype," in *Sport in Society: Equal Opportunity or Business as Usual,* ed. Richard E. Lapchick (Thousand Oaks, CA: Sage Publications, 1995), 193.

18. Jackson with Baker, 67.

19. Don Baylor with Claire Smith, *Don Baylor—Nothing but the Truth: A Baseball Life* (New York: St. Martin's Press, 1989), 174.

20. Jon C. Halter, *Reggie Jackson: All-Star in Right* (New York: G.P. Putnam's Sons, 1975), 119–121.

21. Bob Gibson and Reggie Jackson with Lonnie Wheeler, *Sixty Feet, Six Inches: A Hall of Fame Pitcher & a Hall of Fame Hitter Talk About How the Game Is Played* (New York: Doubleday, 2009), 205.

22. Murray Chass, "Jackson Decides to Play for the Yankees," *New York Times,* November 28, 1976: 197.

23. Dick O'Connor, *Reggie Jackson: Superstar* (New York: Scholastic Book Services, 1975), 87.

24. *Ibid.,* 91.

25. Text on back cover of George Sullivan, *The Picture Story of Reggie Jackson* (New York: Julian Messner, 1977); Gary Libman and Paul J. Deegan, *Reggie Jackson* (Mankato, MN: Children's Book Company, 1979), 3.

26. Maury Allen, *Reggie Jackson: The Three Million Dollar Man* (New York: Harvey House, 1978), 51.

27. James and Lynn Hahn, *Reggie Jackson: Slugger Supreme* (St. Paul: EMC Corporation, 1979), 32.

28. Reggie Jackson and Robert Kraus, ed., *Reggie Jackson's Scrapbook* (New York: Windmill Books and E.P. Dutton, 1978), 44.

29. "Reggie Jackson," in Louis Krapin, *A Poetic Tribute to the 1978 World Champions New York Yankees* (Brooklyn: Copen Press, 1980), 15. There is a copy of this book at the A. Bartlett Giamatti Research Center, National Baseball Hall of Fame and Museum, Cooperstown, New York.

30. Edward J. Rielly, preface to *Baseball: An Encyclopedia of Popular Culture* (Santa Barbara, CA: ABC-CLIO, Inc., 2000), xiii.

31. Neil D. Isaacs, *Batboys and the World of Baseball* (Jackson, MS: University of Mississippi, 1995), 136, 137. Emphasis added.

32. Ken Denlinger quoting Bill Veeck, "Falling Angels," *Washington Post,* July 6, 1977: D1.

33. James W. Bennett, *Plunking Reggie Jackson* (New York: Simon & Schuster Books for Young Readers, 2001), 14. Emphasis in original.

34. Steve Wulf quoting Smalley, "This Time George Went Overboard," *Sports Illustrated,* May 10, 1982, 42.

35. Michele Schiavone, Ph.D., Marshall University, presentation (unpublished), "'There's one man that's not here': The Father-Son Theme in Baseball Hall of Fame Induction Speeches," 7, Session I, Voices from Baseball, Past, Present, and Future (Moderator: Tim Morris, University of Texas at Arlington), Sport Literature Association 16th Annual Conference, Westfield State College, Westfield, Massachusetts, June 23–27, 1999. A photocopy of the presentation is available at the A. Bartlett Giamatti Research Center, National Baseball Hall of Fame and Museum, Cooperstown, New York. The presentation title on the SLA program is "Black and White Fathers in Baseball Hall of Fame Introduction [sic] Speeches." Sometimes, academic conferences use the paper's title from the speaker's proposal even though the speaker may change the focus, tone, and title by the date of the presentation. See www.uta.edu/english/sla/program1999.pdf, last accessed August 28, 2018.

36. *Ibid.*

# How Do You Solve
# a Problem Like the Yankees?

### Jeffrey M. Katz

"It's been written that when the Yankees took the field in that decade of the 1950's [sic], they must have appeared seven feet tall to the opposing team and, to the opposing pitcher, even taller when they strode to the plate."[1]—Douglass Wallop, *The Year the Yankees Lost the Pennant*

"It's a swell show except for a conspicuous flaw in the plot. A man who wants the Yankees to lose doesn't have to sell his soul to the devil. Satan already owns him."[2]—Theophilus Lewis, *America*, June 4, 1955

In the 1936 Fred Astaire–Ginger Rogers motion-picture musical, *Follow the Fleet*, the character Bilge Smith (played by Randolph Scott) remarks to the object of his affection, Connie Martin (Harriet Hilliard, soon to be Harriet Nelson, spouse of Ozzie), "You can't beat the Navy."[3] In the year this line was uttered, and, in truth, at any time during the 45-year period between 1920 and 1964, it would have been possible, given a slightly different film plot, for Bilge Smith or any similar character to have substituted "New York Yankees" for "Navy." Indeed, this jaw-dropping 45-year stretch saw the Yankees amass a combined regular-season won-lost record of 4,292–2,643, with 20 World Series championships in 29 appearances and only two seasons where the team finished lower than third place in the final American League standings.

When describing the Yankees in newspapers, magazines, or books, writers often used such terms as "seemingly invincible," "unstoppable," "all-powerful," and even "iconic." The team's players, managers, and its home stadium were genuine baseball legends and, whether fans deeply loved or passionately despised the Yankees (as Rob Fleder says, when it comes to the Yankees, "extreme, even fanatical views are the norm"[4]), there was a clear respect for the commitment to excellence and tradition that the team seemed to represent and promote.

In a very real sense, the New York Yankees, perhaps even as early as the Babe Ruth decade of the 1920s, became a symbol of the United States itself. Baseball was the National Pastime and the New York Yankees certainly could be classified as "America's team." Consider, as an example, the 1949 Broadway musical *Gentlemen Prefer Blondes*. In the song "Homesick Blues," an American traveler in Paris pines for his native country, invoking many classic American images, such as Broadway, Al Jolson, the race horse Man O'War, and Times Square. Also mentioned, in a rhyme with Tin Pan Alley, is a Yankee rally—another wonderful American memory.

Moreover, when pioneer American choreographer Ruth Page needed iconic American symbols to sprinkle into her 1936 dance interpretation of George Gershwin's tone poem, *An American in Paris* (which she retitled *Americans in Paris* and which was restaged and slightly modified in 1950), one of the characters that she opted to include was a baseball player—a baseball player who was fully decked out in a somewhat exaggerated version of a New York Yankees uniform. Con Chapman, author of *The Year of the Gerbil: How the Yankees Won (and the Red Sox Lost) the Greatest Pennant Race Ever*, points out in the "New York and Boston" chapter—which is reprinted in the extraordinary 2005 collection *The Yankees vs. Red Sox Reader*, edited by Mike Robbins—"There is no *Damn Red Sox*, nor is one likely to be produced in the lifetime of any Boston fan living today."[5]

It is not surprising, therefore, that this veritable juggernaut of success would provoke people to wonder if it was possible that this Goliath of Gotham could ever be stopped and defeated in a convincing manner, especially by teams whose moments of glory and triumph were relatively rare or, at most, sporadic. The concept of beating/defeating/vanquishing the Yankees gradually became, throughout the 45-year period of astounding success, as part-and-parcel of baseball lore as the unfathomable, uncanny dominance of the very team that everyone else struggled and schemed and battled to dethrone. Such a notion led to the creation of a book that, ultimately, would turn into a stage and screen musical—a musical that, very quickly, would become a juggernaut in its own right. The book, published in 1954 (when the Yankees' dynasty was in full bloom), was Douglass Wallop's *The Year the Yankees Lost the Pennant*, and the musical, first produced as a stage show in 1955 and as a motion picture in 1958, was, of course, *Damn Yankees*.

If we take a long, hard look at the culture in which these three related works were produced, specifically mid–20th-century America, it is possible to understand better the overwhelming grip that the Yankees held on the nation's consciousness and identity. There were popular songs composed in honor of heroic players ("Joltin' Joe DiMaggio" and "I Love Mickey" are two examples); there was a (short-lived) television show hosted by Joe DiMaggio (*The Joe DiMaggio Show* on NBC); and a number of guest appearances on other television shows and in movies by some of Joltin' Joe's generally admired teammates, including Yogi Berra, Whitey Ford, Gil McDougald, Phil Rizzuto, and, most often, Mickey Mantle; and there was that well-known ode to the owner of one of the game's most celebrated records, the incomprehensible 56-game hitting streak, in Ernest Hemingway's *The Old Man and the Sea*, considered by more than a few readers and critics to be *the* Great American Novel.

Babe Ruth's two mammoth home run records, for single-season and career totals, stood like giant golden pillars in the temple of baseball, while Lou Gehrig, immortalized in the 1942 film, *The Pride of the Yankees*, was viewed as the ultimate role model by vast numbers of parents, sports coaches, teachers, politicians, and social commentators. Add to this the image of DiMaggio, the Yankee Clipper, as the personification of "class," possessing the ability, in the words of *Boston Herald* columnist Bill Cunningham, to "lift" his team "bodily" by "his very presence" on the field, a "pressure player, a money player and a clutch player" who can "turn" any game "around with a mighty swing of his mace,"[6] and what you have is something that can be described as not merely all-encompassing, but borderline otherworldly, super-human, supremely blessed. Or, from a different perspective, inhuman, robotic, monstrous, and a terrible, destructive tool of the Devil himself. In Wallop's book, Mr. Applegate, the Devil in disguise, states plainly, "My first allegiance really is to the Yankees."[7] There is a common denominator, though, and that is a powerful combination of ubiquity and dominance. In the United States and throughout the world, the Yankees in the 1950s were a team known by all and a team associated with *winning*. Don Larsen's perfect game in the 1956 World Series just served to seal the deal. "It is the hated Yankees who have the Midas touch," proclaimed sportswriter Bill Lee, in the *Hartford Courant* in 1959. "Everything that brushes against their pin stripe uniforms turns to gold one way or another."[8]

At the time that Douglass Wallop, a "frustrated Yankee hater,"[9] created his fantasy, the Yankees had just completed their fifth consecutive American League pennant victory—a fact that prompted Wallop to imagine a world faced with the startling reality of 10 straight Yankee championships. Joe Boyd, the middle-aged hero of *The Year the Yankees Lost the Pennant*, who would agree to sell his soul to the Devil in exchange for youth, personal glory, and a Washington Senators championship, ponders early in the book, "Could an aim so worthy as denying the Yankees a tenth consecutive pennant be evil?"[10] Correspondingly, near the book's climax, Lola, the beauteous, curvaceous, seductive, and ultimately tragic tool of Mr. Applegate, remarks to Joe (now transformed into the gargantuan Joe Hardy), "You know, it's ridiculous in a way, but everywhere I go there's such a real bitter antagonism against the Yankees. Even in Hong Kong. A little man asked me not long ago, 'When will the Yankees not win the pennant?' I said I did not know, perhaps never."[11]

Indeed, the need to make a bargain with the Devil to secure an American League berth in the World Series was not at all far-fetched for any non–Yankee fan, especially one whose object of devotion was a club as universally maligned as the Washington Senators. In the brief biography of Douglass Wallop that appeared in 1958 souvenir programs for the touring production of *Damn Yankees*, it is revealed that "[y]ear after year he [Wallop] sat up there in left field eating his heart out for the Senators."[12]

A fascinating, insightful *New York Times* article from 1957, written by Ernest L. Barcella, illustrates this notion with precision, tenderness, and plenty of humor. Following the success of *Damn Yankees* on Broadway (more than two years on two different stages, totaling more than 1,000 performances) and with the motion-picture version looming on the not-too-distant horizon, boasting a cast almost identical to that of the stage show, Barcella chose to enlighten and entertain his readers by training his microscope on the actual, flesh and blood Washington Senators, whose fairly miserable plight as the happy losers of Major League Baseball was, by this time, quite well established. "Life and Hope in Baseball's Cellar," published on September 22nd, probed the psyche and resolve of the typical Senators fan, the mindset and outlook of the typical Senators team member, and the facts and figures in relation to Washington's attendance, revenue, and talent.[13]

Prominent in Barcella's intimate portrait is the manager of the Senators, Cookie Lavagetto, who also spent seven years as a productive and popular player with one of the Yankees' two hometown rivals, the Brooklyn Dodgers. Lavagetto, described at various times by Barcella as "strong and silent," "patient," and even philosophical, talks almost lovingly about his snake-bitten crew, referring to them as the "Super Nats" and praising their "never give up" attitude. At the same time, in spite of the "big moments" and the fun and camaraderie that Lavagetto attempts to promote in the Senators clubhouse, he has to admit to Barcella that the plot of *The Year the Yankees Won the Pennant* and *Damn*

*Yankees* often rings true in his mind. To quote Barcella, "Many nights he [Lavagetto] sits up late, 'worrying about the club, wishing maybe some night when I'm taking a walk I could run into this guy Mr. Applegate ... and get transformed into a young man again so I could get up there and hit one when we need it.'"[14]

As for the passion, anguish, and undying hope of the fans, the emotions that drive the devoted Senators rooter, Joe Boyd, directly to Satan for a costly cure, Barcella cites examples that seem to jump straight from Wallop's pages or from the script created for *Damn Yankees*. Barcella mentions the fan who, in the spring of 1956, "climbed a sixty-foot scaffold and vowed to remain there until the (Senators) won three straight." Sadly, this dedicated, though unfortunate fan "had to stay aloft one month." Also mentioned is the President of the United States, Dwight D. Eisenhower, an unashamed Senators backer who made a point of expressing his feelings very publicly and with vigor when rumors of a move by the Senators from Washington to Los Angeles were floating in the air throughout Washington, D.C. To quote Barcella once again, "'They must not go!' the cry

President Dwight Eisenhower throwing out the first pitch on Opening Day for the Washington Senators. Eisenhower's administration in the 1950s coincided with the novel *The Year the Yankees Lost the Pennant* and the Broadway play and film version, both titled *Damn Yankees*. The story revolves around a fan of the hapless Senators making a deal with the devil to be an outstanding ballplayer for his favorite team (courtesy of Eisenhower Presidential Library & Museum).

went up.... When asked at a press conference about the reported move, he [Eisenhower] replied, 'I'm agin it.'"[15]

Last place finishes or not and sparse in number though they may be, the Boyd-like, Wallop-esque fans of the Senators continued to support the team. Ballpark attendance was low, but team revenue, somehow, was high (an "economic miracle," according to Barcella) and even the players, notwithstanding the frustration felt by constant losing seasons, seemed reluctant to shift allegiances. Star slugger Roy Sievers stated plainly to Barcella, "I'm happy here," while the veteran third baseman, Eddie Yost, confessed, "I have no desire to be traded. I think this club is going to improve and I want to be with it as it moves up." Wallop's profile in the *Damn Yankees* souvenir program from the 1958 touring production echoes this optimism. "[M]aybe the time is not too far away," proclaims the unnamed author of the profile, "when Wallop will realize his day dreams of having his team come out at the head of the league."[16]

Certainly, these varying, intense human emotions that co-exist at the "heart" of Wallop's populist tale—unwavering devotion, undying hope, existential bewilderment and anguish—were and are recognizable to all, particularly during the post–World War II period, when the U.S. and the world at large were experiencing such massive cultural and political shifts. The Yankees in the 1950s reflected two true, parallel—sometimes conflicting—American realities: the desire, on the one hand, to support the underdog and vanquish the "bully" (Stan Isaacs, in a 1959 *Newsday* article, uses the cringe-worthy phrase, "*Yankees Über Alles*"!)[17] and, on the other hand, the admiration of and passion for great talent, success, organization, and professionalism, as well as common decency. Even the slugging, Yankee-hating savior of the Senators in Wallop's story, Joe Hardy, marvels that, before they "beat your brains out," the Yankees always "courted you with good fellowship,"[18] while in his essay, "I Have Feelings for the Yankees," Roy Blount, Jr., also a member of the vociferous anti–Yankee army, heaps praise on Yogi Berra, whom he calls "a great player and a fine spirit," and who, according to Mr. Blount, once attended a Little League father-son banquet and chose to spend the entire event at a table comprised of orphan boys rather than take his place at the dais.[19]

It is not at all an exaggeration to observe that through the New York Yankees flowed the benevolent and malevolent desires and meditations of the vast majority of American citizens. On one side, it is possible to point to someone like St. Louis Cardinals admirer Bruce McCall, who writes in "Take Me Out to the Oedipal Complex," about how much, as a child listening to baseball games on the radio, he "hated" the voice of Yankee broadcaster Mel Allen, whom he describes as a "mellifluous homer,"[20] while, on the flip side, there is the example of Yankee devotee, Theophilus Lewis, quoted at the outset of this essay, who stated, in his June 4, 1955, review of *Damn Yankees* in the periodical, *America*, "A Yankee fan for better than forty years, your reviewer bleeds more profusely than Mel Allen at the mere thought of the Yankees not winning the pennant. A show that lionizes another team is hard to take."[21]

Even for people with no interest in baseball, the Yankees were a *symbol*, a *representation* of something profound and primal. Worth noting is the fact that, although the idea was scrapped after the earliest out-of-town previews, the original production of *Damn Yankees* depicted a New York Yankees player in a gorilla costume.[22] Talk about primal!

To be sure, it is hard to argue against the notion that, hate them or love them (and Dean Chadwin remarks, in *Those Damn Yankees: The Secret Life of America's Greatest*

*Franchise*, that, in American sports history, "no ballclub has been more loved or hated than the New York Yankees"[23]), the Yankees, in that glittering, miraculous 45-year stretch of baseball dominance, permanently stitched the sport of baseball into the essential fabric of American culture. Ruth and Gehrig and Murderers' Row helped to raise the game out of the swamp of corruption that nearly drowned it following the 1919 Black Sox Scandal. Four decades of Yankee glory ensued, unparalleled by any team in any professional sport, bringing awe and amazement and unceasing analysis. And then, like a Divine chisel descending onto the monument of American culture, landed *The Year the Yankees Lost the Pennant* and its astounding double-headed spawn, *Damn Yankees*. In spite of his distaste for the book's eponymous team and regardless of the voice that his work gave to the feelings of legions of Yankee detractors and deriders (dubbed "those poor birds" by Stan Isaacs),[24] Wallop actually helped to refine and expand the mystique of the team he so despised, which, in so doing, brought even more attention to and enthusiasm for the National Pastime.

In 1956, for example, NBC aired a nationally televised special to help celebrate the coming baseball season. This special, *Salute to Baseball*, was hosted by Art Linkletter and starred such entertainment luminaries as Art Carney, Gary Cooper, Dave Garroway, Eddie Fisher, Roy Rogers, and Ed Sullivan, along with baseball royalty, including Roy Campanella, Leo Durocher, Ford Frick, Carl Hubbell, Willie Mays, and Robin Roberts.[25] However, the highlight of the show, what Harry Harris of the *Philadelphia Inquirer* described as the show's most "loudly publicized" segment, was the "ballet sequence" performed by New York Yankees' catcher, Yogi Berra, during a short *Damn Yankees* skit.[26] Here was a genuine member—and a famous one—of the very team being accused of sorcery in the Broadway musical appearing in a skit taken from the musical in front of a national audience on live television and being applauded for it. Clearly, the producers of *Salute to Baseball* were convinced that a baseball special was something that American viewers wanted to see. And, just as clearly, these same producers understood that a *Damn Yankees* tribute, featuring an honest-to-goodness New York Yankee, was necessary to include in order to attract the largest audience possible. Also worth noting is the fact that another highly anticipated performance in *Salute to Baseball* was the re-enactment by Gary Cooper of Lou Gehrig's farewell speech from *The Pride of the Yankees*, the speech that made millions weep when first delivered on screen, 14 years before. This bit of Yankee iconography was saved for the show's finale and it cemented the Yankee brand on the minds of anyone and everyone who decided to tune in on April 15, 1956.

Furthermore, just a few days later, on April 19th, the CBS series *Climax!* paid homage to baseball's Iron Horse by airing an episode with the no-frills title, "The Lou Gehrig Story," starring Wendell Corey (Lou Gehrig), Jean Hagen (Eleanor Gehrig), Harry Carey, Jr. (Bill Dickey), and a host of baseball greats (including Dizzy Dean, Joe McCarthy, and Babe Ruth) appearing in archival footage.[27] Then, in October of the same year, NBC gave the American television audience a longer, closer look at the current icon of the Yankees, Mickey Mantle, when the network screened the documentary *The Life of Mickey Mantle*, as part of its *Kraft Television Theatre* series. Legendary announcers, Mel Allen and Red Barber, along with Joe DiMaggio and Phil Rizzuto, provided testaments to the greatness of The Mick.[28] Undoubtedly, along with Yankee lovers, these shows were seen by fans of the Indians and Pirates and Cardinals and even the Red Sox.

Media producers continued to wield the powerful mystique of the New York Yankees to lure viewers after 1956 and into the early 1960s. In 1957, Messrs. Mantle, Berra,

McDougald, Rizzuto, Barber, and Ford were recruited to play themselves on the October 1st installment of the popular CBS comedy series, *The Phil Silvers Show* (sometimes called *You'll Never Get Rich* or *Sgt. Bilko*).[29] In 1958, Mantle appeared as the baseball representative (alongside representatives of other sports, such as boxer Sugar Ray Robinson, basketballer Bob Cousy, figure skater Dick Button, and football quarterback Johnny Unitas) on Gene Kelly's sports/dance special, *Dancing—A Man's Game*. Kelly characterizes Mantle's form as a ballplayer—on the base paths, in the field, and at the plate—as "dancing … a beautiful, rhythmic thing to watch."[30] In 1962, Mantle teamed with new Yankees hero Roger Maris in two major motion pictures, *Safe at Home!* (with cameos by Ralph Houk, Joe Pepitone, and Mantle's son, David, as well as the camera-friendly Ford)[31] and *That Touch of Mink* (with a cameo by Berra).[32] Additionally, from 1953 to 1964, it was possible to see players from the Yankees on such popular evening fare as *The Bob Hope Show*, *The Jackie Gleason Show*, *Perry Como's Kraft Music Hall*, *The Steve Allen Plymouth Show*, *The Colgate Comedy Hour*, *Candid Camera*, *To Tell the Truth*, *The Arthur Murray Party*, *The Tonight Show*, and, of course, *The Ed Sullivan Show*.

Players and managers from other teams, most notably those from the Brooklyn and Los Angeles Dodgers, also had their moments on film and television screens. Who can forget Leo Durocher in 1963 on *The Beverly Hillbillies*[33]; Sandy Koufax, Willie Davis, John Roseboro, and Bill "Moose" Skowron, also in 1963, on *Mister Ed*[34]; or, once again in 1963, Koufax, Davis, and teammate Don Drysdale doing a delightful top-hat-white-tie-and-tails rendition of "We're in the Money" on NBC's *Bob Hope Variety Special*?[35] However, even in the world of the performing arts, the Yankees were able to prevail.

In much the same way, it seems quite safe to conclude that the producers of *Damn Yankees*—Frederick Brisson, Robert E. Griffith, Harold (Hal) S. Prince, and Albert B. Taylor (a high-powered theatrical agent and New Jersey native who is referred to as a former Weehawken High School baseball standout by journalist Bob Cooke in a 1955 *New York Herald Tribune* column[36])—as well as the show's director, George Abbott (whose previous Broadway endeavor, *The Pajama Game*, was a smash success), viewed this show as a near-perfect vehicle to attract not only die-hard theater aficionados, but also masses of non- or reluctant theatergoers—people very much like the central character of the story, Joe Boyd. Such novice attendees might come for the baseball and the allure of the Yankees (especially, in the case of Yankee haters, the allure and, in the words of Chadwin, "common joy" of witnessing a public drubbing and humiliation of the team they loathed)[37] and wind up being drawn in, entranced, and transformed into theater fanatics by the infectious songs, the eye-popping choreography and dancing, the clear and clever writing, and, of course, the sight of a scantily-clad Gwen Verdon doing her best to seduce a muscular Stephen Douglass in a live theatrical event. In his May 6, 1955, *New York Times* review of the Broadway production of *Damn Yankees*, critic Lewis Funke assures readers that "even the most ardent supporters of Mr. Stengel's minions should have a good time. And, as for that Dodger crowd, well you can just imagine."[38]

The *Damn Yankees* marketing and publicity team made this outlook unmistakably transparent by "playing up" the baseball angle. Front and center in newspaper and magazine advertisements was the sultry form of Ms. Verdon, holding a baseball glove, doffing a Washington Senators cap, and wearing a pin-striped baseball jersey (the number 39 visible to the camera) over sexy black tights, a high-heeled left shoe kicking backwards (one of the many authentically rendered baseball costumes, save for the high-heeled shoes and tights, created for the show by the husband and wife team of Jean and William Eckart).

Opening night tickets were "printed to resemble those of baseball, containing the usual rain check provisions, gate numbers and the games being played"[39] and the show's masterful choreographer, Bob Fosse, explained repeatedly to members of the media that dances created for the baseball sequences were based meticulously upon actual baseball movements and gestures.[40] Mr. Fosse, a well-known baseball fan who, in his teenage years, traveled across America as a vaudeville and burlesque performer, also revealed, after achieving show business success, that during sexual encounters with showgirls and strippers in his vaudeville and burlesque days (while still in his early teens), he would, in a near exact reflection of the lyrics of the Adler and Ross song, "The Game," think about his beloved Chicago Cubs, reciting their batting order and roster in his mind, over and over again.[41] One can only imagine how thrilling it must have been for Fosse, in the 1958 motion picture version of *Damn Yankees*, to restage the show's "most exciting" and "identifying" number, "Shoeless Joe from Hannibal, Mo.," on an actual baseball field, Wrigley Field, a minor-league park in Los Angeles. This "on location" shooting allowed "Shoeless Joe from Hannibal, Mo." to truly come alive. Howard Good describes the on-field dancing, choreographed by Fosse, very well:

> Fosse, a baseball fan, drew on the body language of the game for the choreography. The player-dancers flash signs, pound their mitts, and pantomime spearing line drives and stabbing grounders. They conclude by sliding en masse toward the camera in a cloud of dust.[42]

It is truly ironic to discover that, in the spring of 1955, immediately prior to its May 5th Broadway début (at the 46th Street Theatre), the stage musical version of Douglass Wallop's baseball-centered Faustian tale had its trial run in the very city where anti–Yankee passions are raised to the highest, most incendiary levels: Boston.[43] Casey Stengel, when asked about the book and the show, stated forcefully (in full-throated Stengelese), "I ain't gonna comment about a guy which made $100,000 writin' how this club lost."[44] Nevertheless, on April 15, 1955, the Yankees, who just happened to be in Boston, playing a series against the Red Sox, took the time to attend one of the preview performances of *Damn Yankees*.[45] To many, it may have seemed slightly crazy for the entire New York Yankees team to see this, of all possible shows, in a theater situated in the very heart of "enemy territory" (and it is more than likely that Mr. Stengel opted to spend that evening back in his hotel room). Yet, what this decision demonstrated with absolute clarity was the team's supreme confidence and, to use that phrase, cited previously, from *The Year the Yankees Lost the Pennant*, the "good fellowship" that seemed to exemplify the character of the players and the organization. The Yankees could laugh at themselves and the depiction of the team as the Devil's own because they understood their place in the world of baseball and in broader society and American culture.

Dr. John B. Henderson, a writer for Norfolk, Virginia's *New Journal and Guide*, one of America's oldest and most revered black newspapers, was well aware of this reality. In 1952, three years before *Damn Yankees* premiered in New York City, Dr. Henderson stated the following:

> I overheard a disgusted Dodger fan refer to Casey Stengel's four-time world champions as damn Yankees. I don't know how many of you are Dodger fans who feel like making a motion that that will be made a permanent prefix to the name Yankee, but whatever your feelings are, you will have to admit that the Yankees have the punch that's needed for the pinches. They always come through when they have to…. The matter of winning pennants and series has happened so often with the Yankees until it's almost a habit.[46]

It is not surprising to learn that the newly-recorded songs from *Damn Yankees* were played over the loudspeakers at Yankee Stadium in the latter part of the 1955 season.[47] Arthur Daley, in his "Sports of *The Times*" column in the *New York Times*, remarks that the playing of music related to vanquishing the Yankees—and the team's affiliation, in some way, with the Lord of the Underworld—did not seem to have any effect whatsoever on the players themselves.[48] In *The Year the Yankees Lost the Pennant*, Mr. Welch, the wizened, hopeful owner of the Senators, exclaims to the Commissioner of Baseball, "Why don't we investigate the New York Yankees? They're the ones who've won the pennant all these years. Not us. Not Chicago. Not Cleveland. But the Yankees."[49] Stan Isaacs, in his previously cited 1959 *Newsday* article, "Casey's Team Will Do Splendid," acknowledges the existence of this sentiment among "those who would like to see the White Sox or Detroit win."[50] Still, as Isaacs declares, "the players on the other teams put their pants on one leg at a time, the way the Yankees do, but that isn't what they pay off on."[51] The mystery, in other words, is not all that mysterious. Yes, it was possible to conclude, as so many were (and are) prone to conclude, that the "Yankees have too much quality 'for the good of baseball.'"[52] However, according to Isaacs, the Yankees continue to win because "nothing succeeds like talent."[53]

It is also not surprising to discover that, in spite of the fact that movie theaters in Milwaukee, screening the film version of *Damn Yankees* during the 1958 World Series, chose to add the words "Beat the" immediately before the film title on their marquees, the New York Yankees would go on to defeat the city's "beloved Braves" in seven games.[54] Criticism, outrage, diatribes, accusations, pleas, angry exhortations, emotionally-charged prayers—all of these projectiles, physical and spiritual, hurled at the intertwined "NY," the home pinstripes, the "banker's-gray visiting suits"[55] boasting the simply-rendered name of the team's city of origin, and the baseball bat crowned by a top hat emblazed with the stars and stripes. The Yankees, particularly in the extraordinary decade of the 1950s, were well aware of the massive target on their backs; yet, the team continued to roll on, occasionally outflanked, but, somehow, always in the mix, never put down permanently, forever ready to reclaim the top spot and their hard-earned glory, while packing ballparks and attracting enormous attention every step of the way.

Of course, the machine did come to a grinding halt after the 1964 season, the very same year that the toy company, Hasbro, released the board game "Challenge the Yankees" (an unvarnished attempt to take advantage of the team's reputation and worldwide popularity).[56] The great Mantle was still a member of the team in 1965, as were Whitey Ford, Elston Howard, Clete Boyer, Bobby Richardson, and Roger Maris. But age, injuries, and a deteriorating farm system were setting in. Soon, these sacred Yankee names and figures would be replaced in box scores and on the diamond by the likes of Ray Barker, Horace Clarke, Jake Gibbs, Andy Kosco, Charley Smith, and Fred Talbot. The question of solving a problem like the Yankees never did get solved completely by any of the other teams in Major League Baseball, but it was being answered quite effectively by the team itself. "Challenge the Yankees" was taken off toy store shelves after 1965 and the Yankees went into a rebuilding phase, both as a team and organization. Nevertheless, the Yankees brand was still very potent. People across the country and the world kept their eyes on this long-time giant of sports and waited for the time when the machine was brought back to life, when its force was restored, and it was possible, once again, to ponder the ways in which the problem of the Yankees could be solved.

It seems fitting to conclude this essay with a kind of supernatural, otherworldly epilogue, one which focuses our attention on the Broadway resurrection of *Damn Yankees* and its relationship to the team that lends its name to the musical. Over time, in the years that followed the original stage and screen productions of the Abbott-Wallop-Adler-Ross-Fosse extravaganza, it certainly can be said that *Damn Yankees* has been no stranger to the world of entertainment. Countless professional and amateur renditions were and are offered regularly all over the globe, some even featuring star performers, including a 1981 Jones Beach staging that gave audiences the opportunity, for better or worse, to watch former New York Jets football superstar Joe Namath give it the "old college try" in the role of Joe Hardy.[57] Yet, for decades, no full Broadway revival was attempted successfully by any group of producers. That all changed, though, in 1994.

The first Broadway revival of this "granddaddy" of baseball musicals in 1994 boasted another all-star lineup. In the roles of Lola and Applegate were two certified members of the Royal Family of Broadway, Bebe Neuwirth and Victor Garber (who were replaced, upon their departure, by the equally formidable team of Charlotte d'Amboise and, in his Broadway début, Jerry Lewis). Another veteran of the New York stage, Rob Marshall, contributed new choreography. The show opened at the Marquis Theatre on March 3, 1994, and the timing could not have been more perfect. With the notorious 1994 Major League Baseball strike looming, the subject of baseball was prominent in the public discourse and there was an eagerness to embrace an alternative to Opening Day. The critical reviews were almost universally favorable and the revival wound up running for nearly 600 performances, including previews, until its closing on August 6, 1995.

What is especially noteworthy and, as mentioned above, somewhat otherworldly (or at least intriguingly coincidental), is the fact that the rebirth of the show corresponded almost perfectly with the renaissance of the New York Yankees and the dawning of a new, powerful New York Yankees dynasty. When the revival of *Damn Yankees* premiered in 1994, the Yankees were entering their 13th straight year without a post-season appearance (the last being 1981, when the Yankees reached the World Series, only to be defeated in six games by their old nemesis, the Dodgers). The team, however, was poised to change that dynamic, thanks to a roster that was beginning to resemble those of the "glory years" of the 1950s, the decade that bestowed upon the universe the original production of *Damn Yankees*. A refurbished, fully fortified farm system was generating a new generation of legends and smart player transactions by the team's front office were bringing in all of the right puzzle pieces. The Yankees were actually sitting on top of the American League's Eastern Division, in sole possession of first place, when the 1994 season came to a crashing halt as a result of the great player strike. The team could not advance to the post-season (the strike lasted until the start of the 1995 season) but the "tide," most definitely, was turning for the New York Yankees.

Then, in 1995, it happened. The Yankees qualified for the American League playoffs, providing their battered star, Don Mattingly, with his first and only chance to appear and perform in the post-season before his retirement as a player. Although the Yankees were prevented from reaching the World Series by the surging Seattle Mariners, the stage was now set and in the year that followed, 1996, a new New York Yankees dynasty was inaugurated, fueled by players who would be worshipped in the New York Metropolitan Area and widely respected everywhere by fans and players alike for many years to come. In the next decade, the Yankees would appear in the World Series six times and emerge victorious on four occasions, while names like Derek Jeter, Bernie Williams, Jorge Posada, Mariano Rivera, Andy Pettitte, Paul O'Neill, Tino Martinez, Hideki Matsui, and Orlando

"El Duque" Hernandez would be discussed in earnest alongside the names of past Yankee greats.

The fact that all of this occurred on the heels of the Broadway revival of *Damn Yankees* is not to say that a new deal with the Devil had been hatched by a wise, but treacherous Yankee management team, nor is it to suggest that a more *Divine* type of intervention had taken place to bring the Yankees back from cellar dwelling to juggernaut status. But it certainly provides an observer with very tasty food for thought. And, if one makes an effort to peruse the pages of the two most famous New York City tabloids—the *Daily News* and the *New York Post*—from the two years in question, 1994 and 1995, it is possible to witness the shifting winds in full color, as well as black and white. While a full page of the February 15, 1994, issue of the *Daily News*, complete with color photos, is devoted to a Valentine's Day *Damn Yankees* backstage visit (with the show still in rehearsal) by members of the 1969 World Champion New York Mets (Ken Boswell and Ed Kranepool dancing with Bebe Neuwirth, Tug McGraw strutting his stuff with dancer Cynthia Onrubia, and Art Shamsky admiring a uniform bearing his name),[58] just one year later, on March 6, 1995, both New York newspapers offered fully-illustrated stories about the 73rd Annual Inner Circle fundraiser event at the New York Hilton Hotel, which featured not only New York Yankees representatives (owner George Steinbrenner being most prominent among them), but also the Yankee-loving Mayor of New York, Rudy Giuliani, cavorting with the new cast members of *Damn Yankees*.[59] Furthermore, we can see this phenomenon reflected in the television series *Seinfeld*. Although Mets star first baseman, Keith Hernandez, was cast in a pivotal role in two 1992 episodes, shows produced during and after 1994 were heavy with references to the Yankees and appearances by many real players and team personnel. As the title of the song by the ska band The Specials proclaims, it was the "dawning of a new era" in New York and in the entire baseball galaxy—a New York Yankees era and a new problem for all other teams and their respective fans to grapple with and attempt to solve.

## NOTES

1. Douglass Wallop, *The Year the Yankees Lost the Pennant* (New York: W.W. Norton & Company, 1954; New York: W.W. Norton & Company, 2004), 82–83. Citations refer to the 2004 edition.

2. Theophilus Lewis, "Theatre," *America*, June 4, 1955, 279.

3. *Follow the Fleet* (RKO Radio Pictures, 1936), written by Dwight Taylor and Allan Scott, directed by Mark Sandrich.

4. Rob Fleder, ed., Introduction, *Damn Yankees: Twenty-Four Major League Writers on the World's Most Loved (and Hated) Team* (New York: Ecco/Harper Collins, 2012), 1.

5. Con Chapman, "New York and Boston," in *The Year of the Gerbil: How the Yankees Won (and the Red Sox Lost) the Greatest Pennant Race Ever* (Danbury, CT: Rutledge Press, 1998), 62, quoted in prelude to *The Yankees Vs. Red Sox Reader*, ed. Mike Robbins (New York: Carroll & Graf, 2005), xxiv.

6. Bill Cunningham, "Sox Lack Lift Like Big Joe," *Boston Herald*, June 30, 1949: 24, quoted in Dave Anderson, "1949: The Joe DiMaggio Theater," *Pennant Races: Baseball at Its Best* (New York: 1994), 190.

7. Wallop, 213–214.

8. Bill Lee, "With Malice Toward None," *Hartford Courant*, February 19, 1959: 17a.

9. *Ibid.*

10. Wallop, 26.

11. *Ibid.*, 131.

12. The identical biographical text for Douglass Wallop appears in all souvenir programs produced for the 1958 touring company of *Damn Yankees*. The program consulted for this essay was produced for the South Shore Music Circus in Cohasset, MA, June 1958.

13. Ernest L. Barcella, "Life and Hope in Baseball's Cellar," *New York Times*, September 22, 1957: 43, 46.

14. *Ibid.*

15. *Ibid.*

16. *Damn Yankees* touring company, souvenir program, 1958.

17. Stan Isaacs, "Casey's Team Will Do Splendid," *Newsday* (Long Island, NY), April 6, 1959: 1C.

18. Wallop, 82–83.

19. Roy Blount, Jr., "I Have Feelings for the Yankees," in *Damn Yankees: Twenty-Four Major League Writers on the World's Most Loved (and Hated) Team*, 12.

20. Bruce McCall, "Take Me Out to the Oedipal Complex," in *Damn Yankees: Twenty-Four Major League Writers on the World's Most Loved (and Hated) Team*, 28.

21. Lewis, 278.

22. Kevin Winkler, *Big Deal: Bob Fosse and Dance in the American Musical* (New York: Oxford University Press, 2018), 51.

23. Dean Chadwin, *Those Damn Yankees: The Secret Life of America's Greatest Team* (New York: Verso, 1999), 7.

24. Isaacs.

25. *Salute to Baseball*, NBC, April 15, 1956, R.S. Allen (as Ray Allen), Harvey Bullock, Bill Dana, Tom Naud, Aaron Ruben. Information about *Salute to Baseball* may be found in Harry Harris, "Baseball Usurps Video Cameras," *Philadelphia Inquirer*, April 15, 1956: 21, 24; Shirley Povich, "This Morning…" *Washington Post and Times Herald*, April 15, 1956: C1; "Today's TV Programs," *Washington Post and Times Herald*, April 15, 1956: J5; Harry Harris, "'Baseball Salute' Fails to Register Home Run," *Philadelphia Inquirer*, April 16, 1956: 18; and Elizabeth Watts, "TV Notebook: Baseball's on the Air; NBC Steals on Ike," *Daily Boston Globe*, April 16: 24.

26. Harris, "'Baseball Salute' Fails to Register Home Run."

27. *Climax!*, "The Lou Gehrig Story," CBS, April 19, 1956, Mel Goldberg; Harris, "Baseball Usurps Video Cameras."

28. *Kraft Television Theatre*, "The Life of Mickey Mantle," NBC, October 3, 1956, Nicholas E. Baehr.

29. *Sgt. Bilko*, "Hillbilly Whiz," CBS, October 1, 1957, Coleman Jacoby and Arnie Rosen.

30. *Omnibus*, "Dancing: A Man's Game," NBC, December 21, 1958, Gene Kelly. The special was co-directed by William A. Graham and Gene Kelly. It's available in Jerome Robbins Dance Division, New York Public Library for the Performing Arts.

31. *Safe at Home!* (Columbia Pictures, 1962) written by Robert Dillon, directed by Walter Doniger.

32. *That Touch of Mink* (Universal Pictures, 1962), written by Stanley Shapiro and Nate Monaster, directed by Delbert Mann.

33. *The Beverly Hillbillies*, "The Clampetts and the Dodgers," CBS, April 10, 1963, Paul Henning and Dick Wesson.

34. *Mr. Ed*, "Leo Durocher Meets Mister Ed," CBS, September 29, 1963, Lou Derman, Michael Fessier.

35. *Bob Hope Variety Special*, NBC, October 25, 1963.

36. Bob Cooke, "Another Viewpoint," *New York Herald Tribune*, May 8, 1955: B5.

37. Chadwin, 7.

38. Lewis Funke, "Theatre: The Devil Tempts a Slugger," *New York Times*, May 5, 1955: 17.

39. Louis Calta, "'Damn Yankees' at Bat Tonight," *New York Times*, May 5, 1955: 40.

40. "Damn Yankees," *New York Times*, April 17, 1955: SM67.

41. Barry Rehfeld, "Fosse's Follies," *Rolling Stone*, June 19, 1984, www.rollilngstone.com/movies/features/fosses-follies-19840119, last accessed May 21, 2018.

42. Howard Good, *Diamonds in the Dark: America, Baseball, and the Movies* (Lanham, MD: Scarecrow Press, 1997), 87.

43. Lewis Funke, "Rialto Gossip," *New York Times*, April 17, 1955: X1.

44. *Ibid.*

45. Harold Rosenthal, "Red Sox Beat Yanks, 8–4, Piersall, White Belt Grim," *New York Herald Tribune*, April 15, 1955: 20.

46. Dr. John B. Henderson, "The Punch Needed for the Pinches," *New Journal and Guide* (Norfolk, VA), October 18, 1952, 14.

47. Arthur Daley, "Sports of *The Times*: Overheard at the Stadium," *New York Times*, September 14, 1955: 44.

48. *Ibid.*

49. Wallop, 184.

50. Isaacs.

51. *Ibid.*

52. *Ibid.*

53. *Ibid.*

54. Arthur Daley, "Sports of *The Times*: A Sudden-Death Finish," *New York Times*, October 2, 1958: 46.

55. Isaacs.

56. Bob D'Angelo, "Collecting Challenge the Yankees Game Cards," *Sports Collectors Daily*, July 6, 2015, www.sportscollectorsdaily.com/challenge-the-yankees-set-tough-make-grade/ (Last accessed July 30, 2018; Bob D'Angelo, "Challenge the Yankees Game Making a Comeback," *Sports Collectors Daily*, June 26, 2017.

57. Fred Ferretti, "'Damn Yankees' at Jones Beach: Joe Namath Hopes to Score in the Theatrical Arena," *New York Times*, June 28, 1981: D1.

58. "Miles of Memories," *Daily News* (New York), February 15, 1994: 19.

59. Jonathan Karl and David Seifman, "Rudy Gets Last Laugh at Annual Sendup of Pols," *New York Post*, March 6, 1995: 3, 11; "Rudy and the Vamp: Mayor Puts on a Show," *Daily News* (New York), March 6, 1995.

# Of Calzones and Costanza

## DAVID KRELL

The New York Yankees organization is a model of excellence. George Costanza, less so.

Played by Jason Alexander initially—and admittedly—as a character laden with Woody Allen neuroticism on *Seinfeld*, a situation comedy that aired on NBC from 1989 to 1998, George developed into a character worthy of abhorrence for his disregard of decorum, revulsion for his resistance to selflessness, and admiration for his keenness for schemes. There's no apparent boundary of behavior. At a birthday party for his girlfriend's son, George bolts out of the apartment when he thinks there's a fire because of smoke in the kitchen; it's later explained that greasy hamburgers caused the smoke. His escape includes shoving the girlfriend's grandmother—who's using a walker—and the kids out of the way.[1]

"He's the product of Jerry Stiller and Estelle Harris [who played Frank and Estelle Costanza] and that continual berating and insanity," explained Alexander in an interview with Charlie Rose a couple of weeks before the series finale, which aired on May 14, 1998. "At heart, you know, a guy who wants it all and has no tools with which to achieve it. But his saving grace is that he's aware of it and can laugh about it despite the fact that it frustrates and angers him to no end. And the end result of that is he kind of says and does all the unthinkable things that one might do in that situation."[2]

It is, therefore, a study in contrast when co-creators Larry David and Jerry Seinfeld take the self-absorbed, slightly maniacal, and superbly scheming George out of his employment misery—he failed at one job after another and had an extended unemployment phase—and put him in the executive offices of the sports world's most vaunted franchise. The New York Yankees.

It was a contrarian approach to life that lifted George from his miserable existence in jobs to the Yankees front office after years of self-loathing, deception, and insecurity. In "The Opposite,"[3] George realizes that every decision—big or small—has backfired, thereby rendering him hopeless with no job, no woman, and no apartment; he lives in Queens with his bickering parents. At Monk's Diner, the gang's hangout, Jerry posits the predication that if everything you try doesn't work, the opposite action must result in success. George, in turn, launches this approach by ordering chicken salad on untoasted rye, potato salad, and a cup of tea instead of his regular meal—tuna on toast, coleslaw, a cup of coffee.

When Elaine points out that a beautiful blonde at the counter looks directly at

George, the transformation continues. At Jerry's urging, George ignores his current situation, approaches the woman, and states that he noticed her looking at him. When she says that she ordered the same exact meal, he declares, "My name is George. I'm unemployed and live with parents." In a welcoming voice, she responds, "Hi. I'm Victoria."[4]

George's new stratagem results in a date, but he refuses to go upstairs to Victoria's apartment for a nightcap, stating, "I'm the opposite of every guy you've ever met." Victoria sets up an interview with her uncle, an executive with the Yankees. Her uncle—Mr. Cushman—meets with George, who summarizes the events of "The Red Dot"[5] (sleeping with the cleaning woman in his office) and "The Revenge"[6] (quitting a different job in a rage because he wasn't allowed to use his boss's private bathroom and then going back to work like nothing happened).

Cushman responds, "You are the complete opposite of every applicant we've seen."[7]

Upon a chance meeting with Steinbrenner, the "opposite" George rants against the Yankees owner's "Nice to meet you" greeting: "Well, I wish I could say the same, but I must say, with all due respect, I find it very hard to see the logic behind some of the moves you have made with this fine organization. In the past twenty years you have caused myself, and the city of New York, a good deal of distress, as we have watched you take our beloved Yankees and reduced them to a laughing stock, all for the glorification of your massive ego!"

"Hire this man!" orders Steinbrenner, seen by silhouette.[8]

And so, the "opposite"—a life strategy mentioned by George in the first episode[9] but not executed—becomes a lodestone for success.

When Steinbrenner led a group to buy the Yankees from CBS in 1973, he promised that his shipbuilding business was his priority. The purchase was a financial investment that others would supervise. Such was not the case—Steinbrenner's legendary hire-and-fire battles with manager Billy Martin, for example, became the stuff that newspaper editors dream of. "Being a Yankees fan with Steinbrenner as the owner is so frustrating," said David in 1996. "I was the kind of fan who even followed the minor leaguers in the system! I knew all the players coming up. But when Steinbrenner became the owner, they usually didn't come up. He traded them. Nobody would make it to the team."[10]

George's scenes at Yankee Stadium mostly took place in his office overlooking the field or in Steinbrenner's office; an actor played the Yankees owner, always seen from behind, and David voiced him. Dashes of realism were sprinkled in the show with real-life Yankees making guest appearances, including Derek Jeter,[11] Bernie Williams,[12] Paul O'Neill,[13] Danny Tartabull,[14] manager Buck Showalter,[15] and, in a scene that never made it to air, Steinbrenner himself.[16] George's impending marriage to his fiancée, Susan Ross, presents a problem for the unattached Elaine—she refuses to attend the nuptials and explains this to her friend in his Yankee Stadium office. Steinbrenner overhears her and declares, "Singles tables are for losers." Under the presumption that Elaine is a part of the Yankees organization, he will not allow a representative to go the wedding unescorted and in turn, states that he will go with her.[17]

"He was so awful. He was so bad," said David. "You couldn't use it. It was much better from behind with my voice than actually seeing the real guy doing it."[18] David's vocal depiction is a fast-talking version for comedic effect.

Being the Assistant to the Traveling Secretary for the most prestigious organization in sports does not alter the paradigm of mishaps for George, though they are largely due to misunderstandings rather than manipulation, lack of restraint rather than deficit of selflessness. A search for an assistant prompts George to reject attractive female applicants lest a professional relationship be infected by the possibility of sexual harassment. Working late one night, George is impressed by the bookish woman's ability to foresee problems and solutions, which leads to sex in George's office. Awed by her carnal skills, he screams out in passion, "I'm giving you a raise!" A slight problem emerges—George does not have the authority to increase her wages, no matter her performance at her desk or on his office floor.[19]

George's incompetence is evident when he suggests to Showalter that the team switch to cotton uniforms because the material breathes. It's an error of epic proportions—the uniforms shrink, thereby restricting the movements of the players.[20]

Ever the plotter to succeed in life and love without really trying, George creates scenarios to sate his needs, which are, to Ruthian degrees, steeped in both carnal and culinary pursuits. Lust for food marks George in "The Comeback."[21] During a Yankees executives meeting, he eats shrimp with a gluttony that that King Henry VIII would have applauded. It sets him up for an insult from his co-worker Riley: "The ocean called, it's running out of shrimp." George then suffers what the French call *l'esprit de l'escalier*, which means that you always think of a good retort once you've left the room. Riley gets a job at Firestone, in Akron, Ohio, but that does not stop George from pursuing vengeance with his line: "The jerk store called. They're running out of you."

Under the ruse of setting up a business deal with the Yankees and Firestone, George doubles down by stuffing shrimp into his mouth. With a new audience, Riley gives the same verbal lashing, then counters George's "jerk store" line with "What's the difference? You're their all time best seller." Remembering Kramer's suggestion from earlier in the episode, George exclaims that he had sex with Riley's wife, only to find out that she's in a coma.[22]

Paisano's, a pizza place near Yankee Stadium, is a favorite haunt because of its calzones. Steinbrenner gets curious about his underling's calzone filled with cheese, pepperoni, and eggplant and orders the calzone-loving executive to get him one. When George the employee fulfills the request of George the owner, the Paisano's cook catches the former retrieving a dollar from the tip jar. In fact, George was taking out his own dollar because the cook didn't see him put it in. He was waiting for the right moment to repeat the tip and get an acknowledgment.[23]

George's vocal manner changes in "The Jimmy"[24] when he talks about himself in the third person, a tic unknowingly embraced from the episode's title character. After a basketball game at the gym with Jimmy, Kramer, and Jerry, there's a potential financial boon for the balding, diminutive, stocky Yankees executive—Jimmy's product line of oddly designed training sneakers. They strengthen legs. George foresees a sideline business of selling the sneakers, though it's not clear whether he wants to buy them at a discount and sell them at a markup or partner with Jimmy.

While George takes a phone call in his office during lunch—Kung Pao chicken— from a potential buyer, his boss, Mr. Wilhelm overhears him talking about sneakers; the Yankees recently had a theft of sports equipment. In the interest of deference rather than obfuscation, George hangs up the phone when Wilhelm enters. George's sweating from the Kung Pao plus bits and pieces of the conversation lead Wilhelm to conclude that George is the culprit. The sweating is explained with a Jimmy-like declaration; "George likes his chicken spicy," claims the would-be sneaker mogul. The episode's tag features

George speaking to the Yankees owner in the third person. It leads Steinbrenner to think, naturally, that his employee is talking about him, which leads to comedic confusion.

Ignoring his focus on sex opens intellectual potential in "The Abstinence."[25] Jeter and Williams get a batting practice lesson as George breaks down the physics of hitting. When Jeter points out that they won the World Series, George snickers that it took six games. To get in extra sleep during the day, George hires Jerry's contractor, Conrad, an agreeable chap striving to please—he lets people decide whether to call him Conrad, Connie, or Con—to create a space under his desk at Yankee Stadium so he can take naps undetected.[26]

When George has an opportunity to become Head Scout for the Mets, there's a catch—he can only take the job if he gets fired from the Yankees. To boost his chances, he engages in activity sure to warrant a pink slip, including wearing Babe Ruth's uniform and smearing it with juice from the strawberries that he eats at a meeting. But defiling the Sultan of Swat's legacy backfires. Steinbrenner thinks it's a bold move: "I have to tell you it's exactly what this organization needed. We want to look to the future, we've gotta tear down the past. Babe Ruth was nothing more than a fat old man with little girl legs. And here's something I just found out recently. He wasn't really a sultan."[27]

George's job with the Yankees is not the only pinstriped link to the show. Joe DiMaggio, the epitome of proper demeanor, is mentioned in "The Note." Kramer claims that he saw the Yankee Clipper in the donut shop; he's more impressed with the slugger's comportment than his statistics—DiMaggio focuses on his donut and coffee without giving in to surrounding noise created by Kramer slamming the table and yelping. Kramer also emphasizes that DiMaggio dunks his donuts, an act that the group later witnesses at Monk's.[28]

Though advertisers could have unloaded enough cash to fill Yankee Stadium for Joe DiMaggio's endorsements, there are two companies with which he's synonymous. From the early 1970s to the early 1990s, DiMaggio appeared in television commercials encouraging people to save at the Bowery Savings Bank and buy Mr. Coffee for their morning caffeine routine.

Yankee broadcaster and former player Phil Rizzuto has his voice and likeness depicted in "The Pothole"[32]—Steinbrenner gives key chains with a likeness of Rizzuto's head to honor the "Scooter" getting inducted into the Baseball Hall of Fame. Squeezing the head triggers a recording of Rizzuto's trademark "Holy Cow!" phrase.

In "The Letter," Jerry dates an artist named Nina, whose father is the Yankees' accountant as well as Mr. Lippman's. He gives Nina four tickets for seats behind the dugout. Jerry is working out of town and Nina refuses to go without him, so she gives the tickets to George, Elaine, and Kramer. A Baltimore-area native, Elaine wears an Orioles cap to the game. When Nina's father sees this, he asks her to take it off. When she refuses, security removes the trio. Rizzuto's voice is also heard lamenting the disrespect shown by a Baltimore fan in the owner's seats.[29]

Kramer recounts how he punched Mickey Mantle in the mouth at a Yankees fantasy camp in "The Visa." Joe Pepitone was crowding the plate, so Kramer "had to plunk" him. The campers and the former Yankees get into a brawl. Someone pulls Kramer off of Pepitone. Without realizing that it's Mantle, Kramer hits him.[30] In "The Rye," Kramer pays homage to Joe Pepitone—while driving a horse carriage, he claims that Pepitone designed Central Park.[31]

In his 1975 autobiography *Joe, You Coulda Made Us Proud*, Pepitone expresses remorse for his legendary misbehavior after games. "It's always depressing to see people you love acting stupidly, showing no feeling at all for others. I know my family felt that way about me for years. I gave them ample reason to be concerned about me, about my self-destructiveness, and I'm sorry about that. Truly sorry that I brought them down so many times. I know now that you can't fuck over yourself without messing up the people you care about most, and with that knowledge comes the greatest pain of all. You do what you have to do, and you pay the price—but you pay it doubly when you see how it has hurt others you love."[33]

In an episode of *Seinfeld*, Kramer recounts pitching at a Yankees fantasy camp and hitting Joe Pepitone with a pitch for "crowding the plate." It set off a bench-clearing melee that included Kramer unknowingly punching Mickey Mantle in the mouth (National Baseball Hall of Fame and Museum, Cooperstown, NY).

David used Pepitone's name in an episode of his HBO show *Curb Your Enthusiasm* when the dry cleaners lose his Pepitone jersey.[34] *Curb* is a fictional parallel to David's life as the co-creator of *Seinfeld* after the show ends its broadcast run. Several celebrities have played themselves, including Richard Lewis, Ted Danson, David Schwimmer, and Mel Brooks.

Alexander has two connections to the Yankees beyond *Seinfeld*. In 2007, he altered the setting of *Damn Yankees* for a revival at the Freud Theater as Artistic Director of Reprise! Broadway's Best. Instead of the Washington Senators of the 1950s, the Los Angeles Dodgers of the 1980s become the bane and hope of Joe Hardy's existence. In 1987, he was in a Miller Lite commercial looking quizzically at Yogi Berra's linguistic maze-like description of the benefits of the "Less Filling, Tastes Great" beer.

There is no doubt that George's approach to life before, during, and after his pinstriped tenure, does not shift by even the width of a Yankee pinstripe. Working in an environment surrounded by tradition has no impact. But this steadfastness permeates the show, not just George's travails. Where other television often depict characters changing because of a crisis, David made sure that *Seinfeld* adhered to his "no hugging, no learning" edict. There was never a commercial with an announcer saying in a low baritone voice, "Tonight, on a very special *Seinfeld*…" Elaine Benes, Cosmo Kramer, and Jerry Seinfeld—upon whose life as a stand-up comedian the "show about nothing" is based—form the other quadrants of the show; David based George on himself.

Elaine, Jerry's ex-girlfriend and gal pal for most of the series—except for one episode where they resume being paramours[35]—is partly based on comedienne Carol Leifer, a

*Seinfeld* writer and story editor, who also wrote for the show. David based Kramer on Kenny Kramer, his neighbor when he lived in Manhattan Plaza, a federally subsidized housing complex for performing artists in Hell's Kitchen.

Failed romance is a hallmark; Jerry, George, and Elaine battle idiosyncrasies, misperceptions, and pickiness in their relationships with paramours. Sex and food are George's passions—and weaknesses. When he needs to buy a gift for Elaine in the episode "The Red Dot,"[36] he finds a cashmere sweater with a small red dot at the bottom; the defect triggers a severe discount, which upsets Elaine because George doesn't think enough of their friendship to pay full price. In turn, George gives the sweater to his office's cleaning woman, Evie, with whom he's having a sexual relationship on his desk at Pendant Publishing; Elaine, a Pendant editor, got him a job as a reader. Evie notices the red dot, too. Unknown is whether this influences her to disclose the affair to George's boss, Mr. Lippman.

When confronted, George professes a lack of knowledge regarding workplace governance: "Was that wrong? Should I not have done that? I tell ya, I gotta plead ignorance on this thing because if anyone had said anything to me at all when I first started here that that sort of thing was frowned upon, you know, because I've worked in a lot of offices and I tell ya, people do that all the time."

In "The Apartment," George experiments with the idea that women find men in other relationships more attractive. So, he wears a wedding ring to a party, approaches three women, and receives letdowns of epic magnitude when he learns about their lives— one woman works for Madison Square Garden and "can get free tickets to any sporting event in New York"; another woman says "I really have a thing for bald guys with glasses"; a third woman says, "I've never been able to be with just one person. I can, however, carry on strictly physical relationships which can last for years and years. It's a shame you're married."[37]

This turn of events causes George to label himself "Costanza, Lord of the Idiots."[38]

An exemplary storyline regarding culinary exploits takes place in George's post–Yankees life when he combines food (pastrami sandwich) with sex and television; Jerry dubs him Caligula.[39] George sneaks a pastrami sandwich into bed during coitus, then ups the ante for a "trifecta" by bringing a portable television set under the covers; disgust reigns when his girlfriend discovers the ruse.[40] George's connection to food goes beyond satiation—BOSCO is his ATM code. Kramer deduces that it's something in the chocolate family because George's vulnerability is food, specifically, "the cocoa bean."[41]

While sex is prominent fodder for laughter in *Seinfeld*, it is a prevalent goal for George. On his way to a job interview, he spots a gorgeous, auburn-haired woman on the subway. Attempting seduction by subterfuge, George claims that he's a successful investor. Faster than a Catfish Hunter fastball, the interview loses priority to potential sex with this striking, impeccably well-dressed creature who looks like she belongs on the covers of magazines by the grocery store checkout lines. But there's a twist—she's the predator. After luring George to a hotel room, she handcuffs him to the headboard, steals his wallet, and complains that it only has eight dollars.[42]

George's romantic schemes include converting to Latvian Orthodox[43]; convincing Elaine to take an IQ test so he can pass it off as his own to a girlfriend[44]; writing the instructions for a sexual maneuver on his hand because he can't remember them during sex[45]; preemptively breaking up so that he can have the power—also called "hand"—in the relationship[46]; sending a suggestive photo to be developed by an attractive clerk at the photo shop[47]; and wearing a toupee.[48]

It is not always George who ignites his ploys in pursuit of love and sex, however. Upon meeting an attractive woman named Diane from his and George's Queens College days at an ATM, Jerry claims that George is a marine biologist. Impressed, she agrees to go out with him. During a walk on the beach, they discover that a whale is stuck. Encouraged by Diane, George wades into the ocean to the delight of onlookers.

In the episode's tag, one of the longest laughs on the series comes when George explains to Jerry, Kramer, and Elaine in an elaborate fashion how he saved the whale. Harkening to another story line showing Kramer at the beach hitting golf balls and later saying that he only hit one that went far, George pulls a golf ball from his pocket and explains that it was the obstruction in the whale's blowhole. "Hole in one," says Kramer.[49]

"If he messed up with a girl, it's because he was trying to be all things to this girl," said Alexander in the Rose interview. "He didn't believe that he could possibly be enough. So, he would try to become whatever was expected of him and be hoisted on his own petard."[50]

George's lack of courage with women evokes the Cowardly Lion in *The Wizard of Oz*; parallels can be drawn with the other characters. The Tin Man has no beating heart and Jerry has no emotions, a trait noticed by a girlfriend, Patty, who wants him to change.[51] The Scarecrow has no brain and Kramer has no common sense, illustrated by his theory that the government has been experimenting with producing beings that are half-man and half-pig.[52] Elaine, of course, is Dorothy, always looking for the secrets to happiness, love, and fulfillment.

In "The Baby Shower," a second-season episode, George recounts a nightmare blind date that Elaine set up three years before with Leslie, a self-proclaimed performance artist who dumped chocolate on him in the audience during a show. George's red shirt is ruined but the collar escaped unscathed, allowing George to wear the shirt under sweaters.

Because Jerry will be out of town performing in Buffalo that weekend, he agrees to let Elaine use his Upper West Side apartment for Leslie's baby shower. When Jerry's show is canceled because of a blizzard, the pilot turns the plane back to New York. George picks him up, wears his shirt underneath a sweater, and convinces Jerry that they should crash the party so that he can confront Leslie with the shirt. Unable to do it directly, he leaves subtle hints. By the end of the episode, George's bravery remains sidelined—he subjugates himself to Leslie and schleps her gifts downstairs. The episode has a baseball-themed subplot. Though Jerry is reluctant to get illegal cable, Kramer persuades him by pointing out that the Mets have 75 games on cable that season.[53]

George finally gets the girl—Susan Ross—but kills her, accidentally. Susan dies from licking envelopes that George selected for the wedding invitations; the glue is toxic. Upon learning of Susan's death, there is no weeping from George *et al.* Rather, the feeling is one of indifference.[54]

When George is on the verge of his unemployment benefits ending, he pleads for an extension by making up a scenario—he's under consideration for a sales job at Vandelay Industries, a latex company. It backfires, of course. George gives Jerry's phone number in case the unemployment manager checks on the story's veracity, but Kramer is unaware of the plan—when he answers the phone, he says that it's a wrong number. In the bathroom, George hears the conversation and bellows for Kramer to say "Vandelay Industries." Half-finished in the bathroom, he sprints out with his pants at his ankles, then falls to the ground. At that moment, Jerry walks into the apartment and, with sarcastic disgust, says, "And you want to be my latex salesman."[55]

It has become commonplace to ask a friend starting a new job if he or she is working on the Pensky file, a tribute to George's new job in the episode "The Barber."[56] His strategy to avoid any real work is taking the file and putting the contents into an accordion-style red weld folder with different sections, which impresses Pensky, who offers George a job with an unfinished caveat that begins with "You are aware…." When George's boss, Tuttle, sees that, in fact, no real work has been accomplished, he ponders George's significance to the company. George quits to go work for Pensky, who gets arrested with other executives for fraud, thereby leaving George without a job.

In a story arc resting on a meta-filled premise, George and Jerry pitch an idea for a sitcom to NBC based on Jerry's life as a stand-up comedian with a group of eccentric friends. George, thinking he's a negotiator with aplomb, takes the reins to get a lucrative deal. The duo gets $8,000—about half of what NBC originally offered before George's involvement—to be split evenly. Although the pilot for *Jerry* shows promise, it gets shelved after one broadcast by the NBC executive succeeding Russell Dalrymple, the network chief who abandoned his job to join Greenpeace, an act meant to impress Elaine, the object of his affection. The action in the episode's tag suggests that he dies at sea after falling off a boat.[57]

David departed *Seinfeld* after the seventh season and returned to write the finale. "Personally, I felt when Larry left that George got a little less interesting," revealed Alexander. "I think that for the most part, and I still had a great time and I loved doing it, I mean I think they gave me some great story lines and some great things to play, but the complexity of the character, I think, got diminished and that the guys really had a better feel for Kramer and Jerry, and Elaine, to a large extent, than they did for George. And it was confirmed for me, although I can't, obviously I can't tell you much about it, when Larry came back and wrote the final episode, the finale, I felt a different character again. I felt something that hadn't been there for a while for me."[58]

*Seinfeld* had a reunion show-within-a-show on the seventh-season story arc of *Curb*. David's conception for a fictional reunion focused on George losing millions of dollars that he earned through iToilet—an iPhone app which gives the user directions to the nearest toilet via GPS—because he chose ponzi felon Bernie Madoff to invest his money. At the time, George was married; his ex-wife removed her money from Madoff's aegis after the divorce. She didn't trust the once-touted financial wizard because of how he wore a jacket. Her bounty is secure, to George's chagrin. The story line recalls a conversation in the second season episode "The Busboy"[59] when George claims that he knows the best bathroom anywhere in Manhattan.

"Everybody wants the *Seinfeld* reunion show. Larry says, 'Let's do it on *Curb*. Let's do a story line on *Curb* where we're going to the *Seinfeld* reunion show,'" explained Alexander in an interview for Archive of American Television. "And there's a lot of mixed emotions and some sense of foreboding. Mixed emotions on everyone's part and foreboding on my part. Mixed emotions are, you know, we got through our show and we kept all the emotions correct and the relationships are fine. But we haven't dealt with each other much. Now you want to throw us back together. Are things from the past going to emerge or are we going to be okay? That's the first thing. But that's secondary. Primary, you're going to put six of us in front of the camera at the same time, no script? It's one thing when we have a script. Now there's no script. Who knows who's supposed to speak?

Who knows what to do? How are we going to do this? Physically, how are we going to do this?

"Number two, we haven't worked as an ensemble in ten years. Just cause we had it years ago does not mean we still have it now. So, we don't even know if the four of us can work together. Number three, these characters were marginally cute in their thirties and forties. Now they're in their forties and fifties. And you want us to go back into these roles and not much has changed. This could be just depressing. This could be the best way to prove that it was a fluke the first time."[60]

During the "reunion" scenes, we learn that Jerry donated sperm so Elaine could have a child; her daughter is named Isabel.

*Seinfeld*'s co-creators belong to different fan bases—Jerry Seinfeld and the Mets, Larry David and the Yankees. In the first episode, stand-up comedian Jerry comes home after a performance looking forward to watching the Mets game, which he videotaped earlier. Kramer—then named Kessler—ruins the night by telling him what happened.[61] When Jerry's television has difficulty getting reception, Kramer persuades his neighbor to get illegal cable because nearly half of the Mets games are on cable that year.[62] In the two-part episode "The Boyfriend," Jerry and Elaine confront a dilemma in their friendship when the former befriends Mets icon Keith Hernandez and the latter dates him.[63]

*Seinfeld* was a cornerstone of NBC's prime-time lineup in the 1990s, marketed as Must See TV. It was the last decade of broadcast network prominence, before Tony Soprano took over the DiMeo crime family in northern New Jersey; before Vic Mackey blackmailed drug dealers to make extra cash and solid arrests in the fictional Farmington district of Los Angeles; before advertising genius Don Draper showed the dark side of reinventing an identity for a product and a person; before Jimmy McNulty revealed the intersection of Baltimore politics, drug lords, and police work; before President Laura Roslin and Commander William Adama led nuclear attack survivors on the Battlestar Galactica; before Dexter Morgan preyed on killers; and before the Fisher clan figured out how to deal with the loss of its patriarch and founder of the family's funeral parlor business.

NBC dominated Thursday nights with the force of rocket thrust, featuring characters in their 20s and 30s trying to navigate the complexities of careers, love, and friendships. Like *Seinfeld*, several sitcoms were based in New York City—*Friends, Caroline in the City, The Single Guy, Mad About You, Will & Grace, NewsRadio,* and the short-lived (14 episodes) *Union Square.* In addition, NBC planted *ER*, a drama set in Chicago's Cook County Hospital, on Thursday nights at 10:00 p.m. It was a turning point for another George—Clooney—who played womanizing pediatrician Doug Ross and leveraged his fame into a movie career during his five-year run. *Friends* and *ER* exploded in the ratings during their first season—1994–1995—making them water cooler shows, along with *Seinfeld.* In a tongue-in-cheek guest appearance, Clooney and Noah Wyle, who played intern John Carter, appeared on a first-season episode of *Friends* as doctors, but different characters.[64]

Jerry Seinfeld's tireless work ethic has made him the template for comedians, both veteran and emerging. Rather than dabble in his chosen profession at a relaxed pace after co-creating, writing, and producing a sitcom that brings in formidable syndication ratings more than 20 years after its last episode aired in 1998, Seinfeld treks to comedy clubs with the same enthusiasm that he showed in his tryout at The Comic Strip in the mid–1970s after graduating from Queens College. "If I don't do a set in two weeks, I feel it," said Jerry Seinfeld in a 2012 *New York Times Magazine* interview. "I read an article a few years ago that said when you practice a sport a lot, you literally become a broadband: the nerve pathway in your brain contains a lot more information. As soon as you stop practicing, the pathway begins shrinking back down. Reading that changed my life. I used to wonder, Why am I doing these sets, getting on a stage? Don't I know how to do this already? The answer is no. You must keep doing it. The broadband starts to narrow the moment you stop."[65]

On May 6, 1981, Seinfeld reached the pinnacle for stand-up comedians who, in the interest of honing their craft, schlep through small towns, perform at 1:00 a.m. for a half-dozen people, and barely get gigs lucrative enough to pay for a fast-food dinner. The sacrifice was rewarded when he performed on *The Tonight Show*, hosted by Johnny Carson, the national launching pad for comedians. If Johnny—the "King of Late Night," who hosted *The Tonight Show* from 1962 to 1992—gave the "OK" sign or, heaven willing, invited the comedian to the couch for light banter, then the bookings would get more lucrative. "You've seen him on *The Tonight Show*" would now be part of the introduction at the Chuckle Hut, the Laugh Room, and other similarly-named gathering places from Spokane to Savannah.

Seinfeld got the "OK" sign.

Jason Alexander né Greenspan, a native of Livingston, New Jersey, may be better known to children of the 1990s as the voice of the cartoon character Duckman than the portrayer of a misanthrope who worked in the House That Ruth Built during the Yankees' dominance of baseball in the Jeter era. He got cast in *Seinfeld* after Rob Reiner, whose production company Castle Rock produced the sitcom, saw Greenspan in the theatre anthology *Jerome Robbins' Broadway*.[66]

Michael Richards played Kramer, the slapstick-prone "hipster doofus" who garnered huge applause through his explosive entrances into neighbor Jerry's apartment, money-making schemes, and good-natured but blunt manner. When George dates a woman with an oversized proboscis approaching Durante territory and an undersized self-esteem fueled by self-comparing to other women, Kramer says, "You're as pretty as any of them. You just need a nose job."[67]

David knew Richards when they performed on ABC's *Fridays*, a short-lived, early 1980s attempt at sketch comedy to duplicate the success of *Saturday Night Live*, where David later worked with Julia Louis-Dreyfus during the 1984–85 season; David got one sketch on the air, which was squeezed in a few minutes before the end of the broadcast. A story that David repeatedly tells with fondness during interviews concerns his volcanic rant at *SNL* Executive Producer Dick Ebersol about the show's weakness before a broadcast; in full view of his cohorts, David quit. His neighbor, the real Kramer (Kenny, not Cosmo), told him to just go back to work like nothing happened. He did and later used it as the premise for the episode "The Revenge."[68] It was a common David technique to use instances from his life as comedy fodder.

On July 5, 1989, NBC broadcast the pilot, titled *The Seinfeld Chronicles*. NBC picked up the show—now dubbed *Seinfeld*—for four episodes, which aired in May and June of 1990. *Seinfeld*'s next batch aired in 1991, numbering 12 episodes about the comedian who lived at 129 West 81st Street—Jerry's real-life address when he was starting out—and his friends. When *Seinfeld* went off the air after a one-hour finale on May 14, 1998, it left a legacy of laughter that puts it on the Mount Rushmore of television sitcoms. Comedy scholars and buffs alike may differ regarding the other three spaces, but *The Honeymoon-*

ers, *I Love Lucy*, *Cheers*, *All in the Family*, *M\*A\*S\*H*, and *The Big Bang Theory* will likely be on the radar for selection.

A real-life Costanza sued Jerry Seinfeld for $100 million on the basis of false light, invasion of privacy, and defamation. Michael Costanza claimed that he was the inspiration for the George Costanza character. Like George and Jerry in the show, Michael went to Queens College with the real Jerry. He shared similar physical traits with the fictional Costanza: short, overweight, bald. The court ruled against him. It was a case about nothing.

## NOTES

1. *Seinfeld*, "The Fire," Castle Rock Entertainment, NBC, May 5, 1994, Larry Charles.
2. *Charlie Rose*, PBS, April 27, 1998.
3. *Seinfeld*, "The Opposite," Castle Rock Entertainment, NBC, May 19, 1994, Andy Cowan and Larry David and Jerry Seinfeld.
4. *Ibid.*
5. *Seinfeld*, "The Red Dot," Castle Rock Entertainment, NBC, December 11, 1991, Larry David. Elaine works as an editor at Pendant Publishing. She got George his job as a reader.
6. *Seinfeld*, "The Revenge," Castle Rock Entertainment, NBC, April 18, 1991, Larry David.
7. *Seinfeld*, "The Opposite." Cushman is played by Paul Gleason, who was a professional baseball player at the Class D level. Gleason played 13 games for the Selma Cloverleafs of the Alabama-Florida League in 1959 and 2 games for the Wytheville Senators of the Appalachian League and 2 games for the Rutherford County Owls of the Western Carolina League in 1960.
8. *Ibid.*
9. *The Seinfeld Chronicles*, "Good News, Bad News," NBC, July 5, 1989, Larry David and Jerry Seinfeld. IMDB.com classifies the episode as part of *Seinfeld*, though it was broadcast as *The Seinfeld Chronicles*.
10. Ira Berkow, "ON THE SET WITH/The 'Seinfeld' Steinbrenner; The Head Yankee, Deconstructed," *New York Times*, March 28, 1996.
11. *Seinfeld*, "The Abstinence," Castle Rock Entertainment, NBC, November 21, 1996, Steve Koren.
12. *Ibid.*
13. *Seinfeld*, "The Wink," Castle Rock Entertainment, NBC, October 12, 1995, Tom Gammill and Max Pross.
14. *Seinfeld*, "The Pledge Drive," Castle Rock Entertainment, NBC, October 6, 1994, Tom Gammill and Max Pross.
15. *Seinfeld*, "The Chaperone," Castle Rock Entertainment, NBC, September 22, 1994, Larry David and Bill Masters and Bob Shaw.
16. *Seinfeld*, "The Invitations," Castle Rock Entertainment, NBC, May 16, 1996, Larry David.
17. *Ibid.*
18. *The Rich Eisen Show*, DirecTV, October 17, 2017.
19. *Seinfeld*, "The Secretary," Castle Rock Entertainment, NBC, December 8, 1994, Carol Leifer and Marjorie Gross.
20. *Seinfeld*, "The Chaperone."
21. *Seinfeld*, "The Comeback," Castle Rock Entertainment, NBC, January 30, 1997, Gregg Kavet and Andy Robin.
22. *Ibid.*
23. *Seinfeld*, "The Calzone," Castle Rock Entertainment, NBC, April 25, 1996, Alec Berg and Jeff Schaffer.
24. *Seinfeld*, "The Jimmy," Castle Rock Entertainment, NBC, March 16, 1995, Gregg Kavet and Andy Robin.
25. *Seinfeld*, "The Abstinence," Castle Rock Entertainment, NBC, November 21, 1996, Steve Koren.
26. *Seinfeld*, "The Nap," Castle Rock Entertainment, NBC, April 10, 1997, Gregg Kavet and Andy Robin.
27. *Seinfeld*, "The Millennium," Castle Rock Entertainment, NBC, May 1, 1997, Jennifer Crittenden.
28. *Seinfeld*, "The Note," Castle Rock Entertainment, NBC, September 18, 1991, Larry David.
29. *Seinfeld*, "The Letter," Castle Rock Entertainment, NBC, March 25, 1992, Larry David.
30. *Seinfeld*, "The Visa," Castle Rock Entertainment, NBC, January 27, 1993, Peter Mehlman.
31. *Seinfeld*, "The Rye," Castle Rock Entertainment, NBC, January 4, 1996, Carol Leifer.
32. *Seinfeld*, "The Pothole," Castle Rock Entertainment, NBC, February 20, 1997, Steve O'Donnell and Dan O'Keefe.
33. Joe Pepitone with Berry Stainback, "Joe, You Coulda Made Us Proud" (Chicago: Playboy Press, 1975) 243.
34. *Curb Your Enthusiasm*, "The Anonymous Donor," Production Partners, HBO, September 16, 2007, story by Larry David.

35. *Seinfeld*, "The Deal," Castle Rock Entertainment, NBC, May 2, 1991, Larry David.

36. *Seinfeld*, "The Red Dot," Castle Rock Entertainment, NBC, December 11, 1991, Larry David. Elaine works as an editor at Pendant Publishing. She got George his job as a reader.

37. *Seinfeld*, "The Apartment," Castle Rock Entertainment, NBC, April 4, 1991, Peter Mehlman.

38. *Ibid.*

39. *Seinfeld*, "The Blood," Castle Rock Entertainment, NBC, October 16, 1997, Dan O'Keefe.

40. *Seinfeld*, "The Blood," Castle Rock Entertainment, NBC, October 16, 1997, Dan O'Keefe.

41. *Seinfeld*, "The Secret Code," Castle Rock Entertainment, NBC, November 9, 1995, Alec Berg and Jeff Schaffer.

42. *Seinfeld*, "The Subway," Castle Rock Entertainment, NBC, January 8, 1992, Larry Charles.

43. *Seinfeld*, "The Conversion," Castle Rock Entertainment, NBC, December 16, 1993, Bruce Kirschbaum.

44. *Seinfeld*, "The Café," Castle Rock Entertainment, NBC, November 6, 1991, Tom Leopold.

45. *Seinfeld*, "The Fusilli Jerry," Castle Rock Entertainment, NBC, April 27, 1995, Marjorie Gross.

46. *Seinfeld*, "The Pez Dispenser," Castle Rock Entertainment, NBC, January 15, 1992, Larry David.

47. *Seinfeld*, "The Package," Castle Rock Entertainment, NBC, October 17, 1996, Jennifer Crittenden.

48. *Seinfeld*, "The Beard," Castle Rock Entertainment, NBC, February 9, 1995, Carol Leifer.

49. *Seinfeld*, "The Marine Biologist," Castle Rock Entertainment, NBC, February 10, 1994, Ron Hauge and Charlie Lubin.

50. *Charlie Rose*, PBS, 1998.

51. *Seinfeld*, "The Serenity Now," Castle Rock Entertainment, NBC, October 9, 1997, Steve Koren.

52. *Seinfeld*, "The Bris," Castle Rock Entertainment, NBC, October 14, 1993, Larry Charles.

53. *Seinfeld*, "The Baby Shower," Castle Rock Entertainment, NBC, May 16, 1991, Larry Charles.

54. *Seinfeld*, "The Invitations," Castle Rock Entertainment, NBC, May 16, 1996, Larry David.

55. *Seinfeld*, "The Boyfriend," Castle Rock Entertainment, NBC, February 12, 1992, Larry David and Larry Levin.

56. *Seinfeld*, "The Barber," Castle Rock Entertainment, NBC, November 11, 1993, Andy Robin.

57. *Seinfeld*, "The Pilot," Castle Rock Entertainment, NBC, May 20, 1993, Larry David. George met Susan when she was an NBC executive in this story arc.

58. *Charlie Rose*, PBS, April 27, 1998.

59. *Seinfeld*, "The Busboy," Castle Rock Entertainment, NBC, June 26, 1991, Larry David and Jerry Seinfeld.

60. Jason Alexander interview, Archive of American Television, July 9, 2014, https://www.youtube.com/watch?v=9spg6o-wIWU.

61. *Seinfeld*, "Good News, Bad News," July 5, 1989, NBC, Larry David and Jerry Seinfeld.

62. *Seinfeld*, "The Baby Shower," Castle Rock Entertainment, NBC, May 16, 1991, Larry Charles.

63. *Seinfeld*, "The Boyfriend," Castle Rock Entertainment, NBC, February 12, 1992, Larry David and Larry Levin.

64. *Friends*, "The One with Two Parts," NBC, February 23, 1995, David Crane and Marta Kauffman.

65. Jonah Weiner, "Jerry Seinfeld Intends to Die Standing Up," *New York Times Magazine*, December 20, 2012, https://www.nytimes.com/2012/12/23/magazine/jerry-seinfeld-intends-to-die-standing-up.html, last accessed July 17, 2018.

66. Interview with Emmytvlegends.org, https://www.youtube.com/watch?v=Woi_aKsv69A, Published on July 9, 2014, last accessed July 17, 2018.

67. *Seinfeld*, "The Nose Job," Castle Rock Entertainment, NBC, November 20, 1991, Peter Mehlman.

68. *Seinfeld*, "The Revenge," Castle Rock Entertainment, NBC, April 18, 1991, Larry David.

# The Underworld to the Rescue

*Ban Johnson, Frank Farrell and the Installation*
*of the American League in New York*

BILL LAMB

In late January 1903, American League president Ban Johnson confronted a grim circumstance. With the start of a new baseball season on the horizon, the AL's bankrupt Baltimore Orioles franchise, currently in league receivership, was bereft of ownership suitors and a place to play. Only weeks earlier, things had been much rosier for Johnson. A peace parley in Cincinnati had yielded parity for his two-year-old circuit with the long-established National League; mutually-agreed upon disposition of disputed player contracts, and reinstitution of reserve clause recognition by both leagues. In addition, the upstart American League had been granted permission to place a club in New York City, the business, cultural, and sporting capital of the nation.

Although he had reluctantly signed the peace treaty, these developments did not sit well with John T. Brush, the most influential of National League magnates and a resolute Johnson antagonist. Particularly galling to Brush was his league's acquiescence in AL intrusion into New York where, only months earlier, Brush had achieved a longtime personal ambition: ownership of the New York Giants. By whatever means required, Brush was determined to keep the city solely for his Giants. In this endeavor, Brush had an important ally, Andrew Freedman, his predecessor as majority Giants owner and a powerful figure in the business and political affairs of Gotham. Using the powers attendant to his post as *de facto* overseer of the massive Interborough Rapid Transit project, Freedman stood ready to obstruct the acquisition of any city ballpark site that the American League might take interest in. And he had already done so once, quashing an AL bid to acquire an attractive and available location in Upper Manhattan. That demonstration of Freedman might had been demoralizing, unnerving would-be bidders for the moribund Baltimore franchise and leaving Johnson with a homeless, orphan ballclub on his hands as the new season approached.

Enter Joe Vila, a sportswriter for the *New York Sun* and a Johnson friend since the two had covered the celebrated John L. Sullivan–James J. Corbett heavyweight title fight as cub newspaper reporters more than a decade earlier. Accompanying Vila to Johnson's office in lower Manhattan was an improbable investor in AL fortunes, Frank J. Farrell. A sporting man, Farrell was active in the underbelly of local popular culture. From his base

143

in Midtown's iniquitous Tenderloin district, Farrell presided over a host of legal, quasi-legal, and illegal enterprises, all highly lucrative. In addition to having the financial where-withal needed for baseball club ownership, Farrell was also closely affiliated with Tammany Hall, the corrupt political machine that controlled the Democratic Party in Manhattan.

While not exactly the qualifications that the priggish Johnson had in mind originally, they were precisely what he needed now if New York was to be an American League venue in 1903. Once Farrell promised to absorb the cost of ballpark site acquisition/stadium construction and proffered a certified $25,000 check as a forfeit if he proved unable to get a New York team up and running for the coming season, the deal was struck. Johnson put his misgivings aside and admitted Farrell to the ranks of American League club owners.

## Ban Johnson and the Rise of the American League

Born in Norwalk, Ohio, on January 15, 1865, Ban Johnson was a college and law school dropout whose budding amateur baseball career was ended by a thumb injury.[1] Johnson entered the working world in 1886, taking a job as a sports reporter for the *Cincinnati Commercial Gazette*. In time, he rose to the post of sports editor. From 1891 on, a target of Johnson barbs was John T. Brush, principal owner of a newly reorganized National League club in Cincinnati. Among other things, Brush was skewered for the mediocre nines that he put on the field, paying low player wages, and, most pointedly, for

**Frank Farrell's wealth through questionable businesses and political clout through the notorious Tammany Hall gave him the platform to make New York City a venue for the American League. Farrell (left) had a partner, another Tammany beneficiary named Bill Devery (right), a corrupt but never-convicted patrolman who had previously ascended the ranks to NYPD's chief of police.**

being an absentee owner (as Brush, an Indianapolis department store owner, managed club affairs from afar rather than relocate to the Queen City).

Notwithstanding his disdain of Brush, Johnson developed a close friendship with Reds manager Charles Comiskey, a drinking companion. In early 1894, Comiskey was instrumental in the move that brought Johnson into the organizational side of the game, advocating for Johnson's appointment as president of the latest incarnation of the minor Western League. Brush, also owner of the WL's keystone Indianapolis franchise, was opposed but allowed Comiskey to persuade him that accepting Johnson as league boss would eliminate the constant criticism in the *Commercial Gazette* by getting Johnson out of the sports writing business.

The strategy backfired, as Brush soon tangled with president Johnson on a host of league issues, particularly the practice of revolving players from his NL Cincinnati club to his WL Indianapolis team, and back again.[2] At the close of the 1897 season and much to Brush's displeasure, Johnson and his WL allies prevailed upon the National League to outlaw simultaneous ownership of major-league and minor-league clubs by the same magnate. While never actually proved, Brush reputedly responded to the new dictate by ceding formal ownership of the Indianapolis Hoosiers to his wife Elsie, friend Bill Watkins, and/or other compliant parties, all the while retaining effective behind-the-scene control of Hoosiers destiny for himself.

By 1900, the National League, swollen to a 12-club circuit since the 1892 season, was ripe for competition on the major league level. At first, the principal threat to the NL's monopoly was perceived as a new American Association, then reportedly being revived by Cap Anson, Tommy McCarthy, and other erstwhile NL headliners with financial support from businessmen backers in various National League cities.[3] But the real threat came from Ban Johnson and his circuit, newly renamed the American League. Although the AL had played as a minor league during the 1900 season, it was no secret that Johnson intended to declare his circuit a major league shortly, abrogating Organized Baseball's National Agreement in the process, if necessary.[4] National League magnates, shortsighted and busy quarrelling among themselves, promptly played right into Johnson's hands. At their winter meeting in New York City that December, the NL owners left Johnson to stew in Philadelphia, declining him the opportunity to place his accommodations before the established baseball order and freeing Johnson to go his own way. During the same meeting, the NL further obliged Johnson by contracting to an eight-club circuit for the 1901 season and jettisoning major-league venues in Cleveland, Baltimore, and Washington that Johnson would quickly incorporate into his American League.

Tireless and visionary, Johnson thereafter upgraded the talent level of AL clubs through the unleashing of predatory and highly successful raids on NL player rosters. Cy Young, Nap Lajoie, John McGraw, and other NL stalwarts jumped to Johnson's circuit for its inaugural major-league campaign, and dozens more followed in 1902. The exciting, far-cleaner brand of baseball played in the American League rejuvenated fan interest, with AL attendance figures rivaling the senior circuit's in the first year of their competition, and surpassing them by a substantial margin the second. By the close of the 1902 season, reeling NL club owners were ready for settlement negotiations with Johnson.

Despite its rousing success, the American League was not without problems. Chief among president Johnson's headaches was the often-unruly conduct of John McGraw, manager of the financially shaky Baltimore Orioles franchise. McGraw chafed under the decorum edicts issued from league offices, and his numerous run-ins with AL umpires resulted in discipline imposed from on high. Of greater consequence than the friction between Johnson and McGraw on good behavior mandates was McGraw's creeping suspicion that Johnson intended to exclude him when the rumored transfer of the Baltimore franchise to New York came to fruition.

McGraw and Baltimore left fielder and first baseman Joe Kelley got hit with an indefinite suspension imposed by Johnson for abuse of umpire Tom Connolly and other antics that precipitated the forfeiture of a June 28, 1902, home game to the Boston Americans. With this, the tensions between the fiery McGraw and the often self-righteous Johnson neared the breaking point.[5]

Observing these developments with interest was Reds boss John T. Brush, then quietly in the process of acquiring the New York Giants from principal owner Andrew Freedman. Brush acted. First, he arranged for McGraw to pay a clandestine visit to Lombardy, the Brush mansion in Indianapolis.[6] There and with the approval of co-conspirator Freedman, he offered McGraw the position of New York Giants manager at the handsome salary of $11,000 per year. Once McGraw accepted, he was instructed to return to Baltimore and demand immediate reimbursement of the thousands that he had put into the Orioles franchise. When, as anticipated, the club's strapped ownership was unable to come up with the cash, McGraw demanded and received his immediate release from the Baltimore club. McGraw then trained to Manhattan where he was promptly invested as new Giants manager.

While this was going on, Brush and Freedman were busy orchestrating the purchase of a controlling interest in Baltimore franchise stock by Maryland politico John "Sonny" Mahon, the father-in-law of Orioles left fielder Joe Kelley and a Democratic Party ally of Andrew Freedman.[7] By mid–July, Mahon had accumulated a majority of club stock and, thus, had obtained control of the franchise. In short order, Mahon transferred the club stock to a local Freedman agent (Baltimore attorney Joseph France) who then conveyed the stock to Freedman, placing another Johnson nemesis—the AL president and Freedman had clashed repeatedly during the past two years—in charge of the teetering Baltimore operation.

The first act of the new Freedman administration was to release the Orioles' best players, freeing future Hall of Famers Joe McGinnity and Roger Bresnahan, as well as first baseman Dan McGann and pitcher Jack Cronin to sign Giants contracts. The Cooperstown-bound Kelley and slugger Cy Seymour, meanwhile, were also released and joined Cincinnati, with Kelley installed as Reds field skipper.[8] But the plotters had overplayed their hand. The gutting of the Orioles' roster left the club short of players and obliged a forfeit of the next-day game against St. Louis. Seizing upon provisions in the American League constitution, Johnson adroitly moved in, immediately stripping Freedman of Baltimore club ownership and placing the franchise in league hands. He then quickly re-stocked the club with players contributed by other AL owners. The cobbled-together club limped home, a last-place finisher. But the Baltimore franchise had been saved for the American League, leaving intact, if now more complicated, Johnson's intention to transfer the club to New York.

## The Fearsome Alliance of Andrew Freedman and John T. Brush

The two magnates could hardly have risen from more different surroundings. Born in Manhattan on September 1, 1860, Andrew Freedman was the son of well-to-do

German-Jewish immigrants and was raised in comfortable circumstance. Intelligent but an indifferent scholar, Freedman dropped out of CCNY after his freshman year, and began his working life as a clerk in a dry goods store. He soon gravitated toward real estate, the field where he would make the first of his several fortunes. To enhance his prospects, Freedman then took a fateful step. In 1881, he joined Tammany Hall, where he became a protégé (and later a close friend) of Richard Croker, the soon-to-be-anointed organization chief. For the remainder of his life, Freedman's conduct would often be connected in some way to the cold, shrewd, and unapologetically avaricious Croker.

Some 15 years older than Freedman, John T. Brush grew up impoverished in far-northern upstate New York. Orphaned as a four-year-old and brought up by a severe paternal grandfather, Brush spent his formative years tending to the grinding drudgery of farm work. He escaped the farm at age 17 and, after a brief college stint in Poughkeepsie, enlisted in the Union Army. Several years later, Brush emerged unscathed but Civil War–combat hardened.

Like Freedman, the course of Brush's early adult life was affected by a friendship, in his case with George Pixley, the co-organizer of a fledgling Troy-area retail clothing business. In time, Brush advanced from salesman to store manager to partner in Owen, Pixley & Company. In 1875, Brush was dispatched to Indianapolis as the company expanded westward. Brandishing an unlikely flair for advertising and promotion, Brush transformed a modest company outlet into the largest department store between New York and Chicago, severing the connection with Owen, Pixley along the way.

John T. was not an athlete but soon fixed upon baseball as a vehicle for promoting his store. And in no time, he became thoroughly smitten with the game. During the ensuing years, Brush progressed from founder of a municipal league in Indianapolis to owner of an Indianapolis minor-league team to president of the Indianapolis Hoosiers, a three-season (1887–1889) member of the National League.[9] A casualty of the Players League conflict of 1890—the NL had liquidated the weakling Indianapolis and Washington franchises as a preemptive wartime financial measure—Brush refused to be pushed out of baseball. He extracted stiff reparations from the league, retained his place in NL owners councils, and received his colleagues' commitment to be accorded the next available NL franchise. Brush was also among those magnates enlisted to bail out the wounded, near-destitute New York Giants franchise, agreeing to the conversion of a pre-existing $25,000 note from Giants boss John B. Day into a minority share of the New York club's stock.

In 1891, Brush outmuscled Players League angel Al Johnson for a new NL franchise in Cincinnati. But by now, he had set his eye upon a larger prize: acquisition of the still financially-ailing New York Giants. Yet as club ownership changed hands from Day to a group headed by Wall Street financier Edward B. Talcott, Brush remained inert in Cincinnati. Then in January 1895, Brush found himself beaten out of Giants ownership by Andrew Freedman, by now a real estate millionaire and a powerful behind-the-scene force at Tammany Hall but a complete stranger to John T. Shortly thereafter, a fierce antagonism between the two men was touched off by heavy-handed Brush overtures to buy out Freedman, a proud and imperious man whose personal wealth dwarfed that of Brush. Later, the two would reportedly come to blows in the tap room of a Manhattan Hotel.

A far more able and accomplished man than the one-dimensional ogre portrayed in the sporting press, Freedman was nonetheless a disaster as a club owner. During the eight-season Freedman regime, the once-proud Giants were a pennant contender only once (1897), a year when Freedman virtually ignored the club to focus on Tammany's upcoming election prospects.[10] Things only worsened when he returned his attentions to the Giants. Abrasive and intolerant of criticism, Freedman fought—at times literally, as he was bad-tempered and pugnacious—with everyone: his players, club managers, fellow NL owners, and especially, the New York press corps. Taking the lead of Charles Dryden of the *New York American,* the press retaliated by referring to Freedman as "Andy"—a familiarity that the haughty Freedman detested[11]—and printing imaginary interviews of Freedman replete with oxymora and malapropisms designed to portray the articulate, cosmopolitan club owner as an ignoramus.[12] The estrangement of Freedman from his NL owner colleagues deepened following the league's failure to adequately redress an anti–Semitic slur publicly directed toward Freedman by Orioles outfielder Ducky Holmes during a July 1898 game at the Polo Grounds. The league's rescission of the suspension imposed on Holmes was based on a due process technicality, but Freedman viewed the ruling as nothing less than NL countenance of a gross personal insult. And Andrew Freedman would not abide it.

Over the next two seasons, Freedman administered a punishing financial lesson to his fellow magnates. He degraded the league's most valuable asset, his own New York Giants franchise, driving baseball fans away from the gates in droves and depriving other team owners of the much-needed revenue ordinarily derived from games against the big-draw Giants.[13] Freedman, with a personal fortune reputedly in excess of that of the other NL club owners combined,[14] was unconcerned. He did not require baseball income. He drew an annual $100,000 salary from one of his insurance underwriting ventures and received large investment returns from various other commercial enterprises. Indeed, to Freedman, ownership of a major-league baseball team, like his collection of French landscape paintings, opera patronage, and yachting, was a diversion, not a livelihood. Fellow club owners like roofing contractor Arthur Soden (Boston) and brewer Harry von der Horst (Baltimore) could not be so cavalier. They were all prosperous capitalists, but hardly in a position to operate their baseball teams at a loss for an indefinite period.

The league's distress gave the embittered Freedman no end of satisfaction. As the Giants' dismal (60–90) 1899 season drew to a close, Freedman announced, "Base ball affairs in New York have been going just as I wished and expected them to go. I have given the club little attention and would not give five cents for the [best] ball player in the world."[15] And as even his detractors knew, Freedman meant it. With their prospects bleak and certain of Freedman's ruthlessness, NL owners entreated for peace, acceding to various Freedman demands. An unexpected byproduct of the mollification process was the emergence of an alliance of purpose between Freedman and John T. Brush, heretofore the leader of Freedman opposition in NL owners ranks. Although they never became friends, the two forged a cordial working relationship, joining forces on several initiatives (including NL contraction and the Base Ball Trust scheme) that culminated in the attempted destruction of the American League operation in Baltimore, described above.

By 1902, however, baseball had lost its charm for Freedman. Of more consequence, his time was now consumed by the endless demands attending his oversight of the mammoth subway construction project. That summer, Brush set in motion a change in New York Giants ownership by divesting himself of the Cincinnati Reds, selling the club to a consortium of local politicians headed by youthful Cincinnati mayor Julius Fleischmann, heir to his family's yeast manufacturing fortune. This enabled Brush to accept appointment as managing director of the Giants that August. A month later, he succeeded Freedman as principal owner of the New York franchise, buying out all but a tiny fraction of Freedman's interest in the club. Freedman declined a seat on the Giants' corporate board, and ostensibly withdrew from baseball. But as upcoming events would soon demonstrate, the Freedman-Brush alliance was far from over.

## Frank Farrell and Bill Devery, Comrades in Infamy

The Freedman-Brush combo was not the only odd couple on the turn-of-the-century baseball scene. Indeed in terms of color, the unloved magnates paled in comparison to prospective AL club owners Frank Farrell and Bill Devery, a notorious pair of New York City rogues. The two were born in Manhattan about 10 years apart, shared Irish-Catholic working-class roots, became great friends, and accumulated considerable wealth via service to Tammany Hall and catering to the Gotham citizenry's appetite for illicit amusement. But otherwise, Farrell and Devery were vastly different men. Devery was the first to attain public notice, working his way up from bartender to prize fighter to New York City patrolman—an occupation entered via provision of the standard $200 Tammany admission fee. As he worked and paid his way up the police ranks, Devery proved an adept collector of the "honest graft" contributed to Tammany coffers by the dive bars, pool rooms, gambling dens, brothels, dance halls, and other outposts of the mid–Manhattan demimonde. Having demonstrated his worth to Tammany boss Richard Croker and Manhattan state senator Big Tim Sullivan (a Tammany sachem second in stature only to Boss Croker himself), Devery was elevated to supervisory positions. A modern-day Falstaff in size (about 6-feet, 260 pounds in his prime, later much heavier) and enthusiasms (for food, liquor, and late-night revelry), Big Bill was soon a target of reform politicians and indignant *New York Times* editorial writers. Hauled before a legislative committee empanelled to investigate alleged police payoffs in his precinct, Devery famously informed his inquisitors, "Touchin' on and apertainin' to that, there's nothing doing."[16]

For the next several years, Devery was almost constantly under either indictment or administrative charge for extortion, bribery, or other misconduct, but always managed to beat the rap.[17] Unpretentious, outgoing, and cheerfully corrupt, Big Bill was a larger-than-life figure and almost irresistibly ingratiating. Even the reform crusaders who deplored Devery's existence found it difficult to dislike him personally. Commenting upon his later appointment as NYPD chief, muckraking journalist Lincoln Steffens remarked that Devery "was a disgrace, no more fit to be chief of police than the fish monger is to be director of the Aquarium. But as a character, he was a work of art, a masterpiece."[18]

The short, stocky (about 5-feet-7, 180 pounds) Frank Farrell was an altogether different sort of man, calculating, closed mouthed, and shadowy. During the height of his unsought celebrity as a Manhattan wheeler-dealer, the press and public were not even privy to where exactly Farrell lived.[19] As befits a man of such mystery, Farrell's origins, including the date of his birth (probably sometime in 1866), remain indistinct. All that can be said with any degree of assurance is that Frank was the son of an Irish immigrant boilermaker and grew up in the same Lower West Side Manhattan neighborhood that spawned future New York Governor and 1928 Democratic Party presidential candidate Al Smith, a lifelong friend of Farrell.

By age 13, Frank was working as a store clerk. While still young, he took his first step on the ladder of upward mobility by becoming a bartender at a saloon near Tammany headquarters. As he poured drinks, Farrell cozied up to the Wigwam foot soldiers patronizing the establishment and soaked up the practical and political wisdom that they dispensed. In time, he accumulated the funds needed to open his own saloon at Sixth Avenue and 30th Street, near the heart of midtown's infamous Tenderloin district and less than a block away from the police precinct stationhouse commanded by [then] Captain Bill Devery. It did not take long for Farrell and Devery to find each other, and soon thereafter the pair became personal friends and later business partners, a relationship that thrust Farrell into the orbit of Big Tim Sullivan.[20]

By means now impossible to confirm but easy to surmise, the astute Farrell parleyed his association with Devery, Sullivan, and other Tammany operators into a quick fortune. By the turn of the century, ex-bartender Farrell had evolved into New York City's "Pool Room King," with a reputed 250 off-track betting spots under his control.[21] He also received a cut from the Tenderloin protection racket, now raking in an estimated $3 million per year.[22] In addition, Farrell became a high-stakes racetrack bookmaker (then a legal profession) and a noted plunger in his own right, sometimes wagering thousands on the outcome of a single race. Farrell's immersion in racetrack affairs was a natural pursuit, for thoroughbred horseracing was the passion of his adult life. First with Julius Fleischmann and later with once-renowned hustlers like Sim Diemel and Davy Johnson, Farrell operated his own racing stables, with intermittent luck at the finishing wire. But the enterprise that would eventually bring disagreeable attention to Farrell was his association with the luxuriously-appointed but well-fortified gambling casinos that dotted midtown, strictly illegal but favored haunts of Manhattan society high-rollers and ignored for a price by certain factions of the NYPD.[23]

Although Farrell had become notable in Eastern horseracing circles and within the confines of Tammany Hall, he remained largely unknown to the public. All that changed during the New York municipal election campaign of 1901. The myriad scandals of the Croker-dominated Van Wyck administration had inspired Republicans, reformers, and other Tammany foes to combine forces. The soapbox star of their fusion ticket was the candidate for Manhattan District Attorney, William Travers Jerome, a sitting justice on the borough bench and a blue nose acutely agitated by gambling and other vice. During a large Fusion Party rally at the Murray Hill Lyceum, Jerome pilloried his Tammany-sponsored opponent Henry V. Unger as a pawn of "Frank Farrell, the head of the gambling combine in this city."[24] The Jerome charge was then endorsed by the *New York Times* in a blistering editorial captioned: "The Case Against Mr. Unger."[25] "It is not Tammany, merely, the patron and protector of the vicious: it is vice itself in the person of FARRELL that has brought about the nomination of Mr. Unger," the *Times* raged. Then, to enlighten its readership about this theretofore obscure villain, the editorial declared that "MR. FRANK FARRELL is a gambler, the chief gambler of New York City, we suppose. The business to which he owes his bad eminence, and in which he gains his living is carried out in violation of the law. His gambling places have enjoyed the protection of the law [because] he is an intimate, personal friend of Mr. W.S. Devery, the Deputy Police Commissioner of New York."[26] Farrell's purpose in arranging the Unger nomination was obvious to the *Times:* Farrell "wants a District Attorney who will not make trouble for him."[27]

Not to be outdone by *Times* editorialists, the Citizens' Union of New York subsequently published a widely circulated pamphlet that recounted the misdeeds of the often-accused but never-convicted Devery, adding his now-exposed connection to gambling honcho Frank Farrell to its bill of particulars.[28] Such rhetoric had the intended effect. In the November 1901 elections, Tammany was swept from office. And the previously veiled activities of Frank Farrell had now become an object of press interest.

The outcome of the New York City elections was not without ramifications in the baseball world. Shortly after the results were posted, Richard Croker resigned from Tammany Hall and sailed for his estates in the British Isles, far beyond the subpoena reach of incoming District Attorney Jerome. The fall of Croker undermined the power of his subordinates, most notably Andrew Freedman. It took some months, but once Charles F. Murphy had gathered power, Croker loyalists like Freedman were consigned to the back benches and the Tammany banquet circuit. A taciturn political genius, Murphy also embarked upon re-shaping the organization's public image, bad news for Big Bill Devery, the living embodiment of the crass Tammany hack caricatured in editorial cartoons. Murphy soon saw to it that Devery's star waned.[29]

Although most partial to horseracing, Frank Farrell was also an ardent baseball fan. At times during the 1902 season, it was rumored that he was interested in backing an American League club in New York, with the team to be managed by John McGraw, whose acceptance of New York Giants' job obviously kyboshed that plan. But it did not put an end to Farrell's desire to enter Major League Baseball.

## The Events That Brought American League Baseball to New York

A lifelong Midwesterner, Ban Johnson had little insight into the vicissitudes of political and sporting affairs in New York City. But events seemed to be turning his way. The fall of Richard Croker and the resulting evisceration of the political clout of Andrew Freedman loosened the National League stranglehold on Manhattan. The sale of the New York Giants to an out-of-town Republican like John T. Brush[30] also brightened Johnson's prospects of gaining access to the New York market. And the January 1903 NL-AL peace agreement sanctioned American League placement of a club in greater New York. Still, Freedman's opposition would prove a formidable obstacle to AL entry into the city.

Although reviled in the baseball press, Freedman was widely respected by New York City's business and financial elites. And while his political influence was now greatly diminished, Freedman's power base had never been confined exclusively to Tammany Hall. As the 20th century dawned, he assumed an even greater role in the civic affairs of Gotham as catalyst-in-chief of the massive city subway project. As he had in politics, Freedman preferred to wield his influence behind the scenes, bringing together the financiers (headed by Wall Street banker August Belmont, Jr., a close Freedman friend), the engineering experts, and the construction company men who would finally turn the long-stagnant project into a reality.

Thereafter, Freedman kept his eye on the property acquisition, underground construction, subway station designation, railway car manufacture, and the other details that held the privately-financed (at a staggering $35 million) colossus on schedule and up and functioning by early 1904. When he died a little more than a decade later, Andrew

Freedman's glowing *New York Times* obituary declared that he "did more than perhaps any other man to make possible the subway in this city."[31]

While ostensibly removed from the game and immersed in the subway project, Freedman also took pains to keep the American League out of New York City. Because he never explained himself, Freedman's motives can only be speculated on. Perhaps Freedman, a man of principle by his own lights, felt some sense of obligation to new club owner Brush. Or opposition to the AL might have constituted Freedman payback for disparaging public remarks made about him by league president Johnson.[32] Or he may have been acting entirely for his own perverse satisfaction. Whatever the case, Freedman was bent on making things difficult, if not impossible, for the American League to place a club in New York.

In the beginning, Freedman maintained a low profile. Following a transfer-of-power meeting with Brush, Freedman said no more than that he doubted the American League would try to place a club in New York, but if it did "the team Mr. Brush has secured will beat them out a mile. I'll bet on that."[33] In the meantime, speculation abounded regarding the identity of likely backers of the much-anticipated new AL club in Gotham. Most newspapers adjudged the front-runner to be James C. Kennedy, a local boxing promoter and the man who had brought the six-day bicycle races to Madison Square Garden. Kennedy had bona fide baseball credentials—he had managed the sad sack American Association Brooklyn Gladiators in 1890; had subsequently backed minor-league clubs in Newark and Jersey City; was presently the business partner of Eastern League president Pat Powers; and was a native New Yorker. Most important, Kennedy was a schoolboy friend of Big Tim Sullivan, still a power in Tammany Hall.

Kennedy did little to play down the speculation, allowing that he would lead an AL franchise in New York, but only if a suitable ballpark site "could be obtained on Manhattan Island. If the grounds were to be in the Brox [sic], Brooklyn or Jersey, [he] would have nothing to do with the club."[34] Shortly thereafter, Kennedy gave out assurances that could "secure accessible grounds" in Manhattan, and passed judgment on the worth of some of the ballplayers rumored to have been acquired by president Johnson to stockpile an AL New York nine.[35] Soon thereafter, the Kennedy bubble was burst by Big Tim himself. In unequivocal terms, Sullivan declared: "Kennedy is a friend and I think well of him, but I do not know anything about his baseball plans. I am not a backer of a proposed American League club here, nor have I exerted my influence to have the New York baseball club turn over Manhattan Field[36] to the new league. I have other matters to occupy my attention without getting into baseball."[37] With that, Kennedy's name disappeared from the news.

While Kennedy had been attracting most of the press notice, Ban Johnson had also been at work. With American League financier Charles Somers and Cleveland club president John Kilfoyl acting as his emissaries, Johnson made discreet overtures to the public figures associated with the ongoing New York City subway project. Armed with data showing how baseball park traffic had increased transit revenues in Boston and Philadelphia and brandishing the promise of crowded subway cars filled with fans coming to and from a new Manhattan ballpark during off-peak subway hours, the American League envoys intrigued the Interborough Rapid Transit corporation. Soon, the AL had important subway allies, including lead banker August Belmont, Jr., and John B. McDonald, the project's general contractor.[38] In time, a complex plan was developed for IRT acquisition of ballpark-suitable grounds on the Upper East Side at Lennox Avenue and 141st

Street and a long-term lease of that property to an American League ball club.[39] When the IRT Board of Directors met to review the proposal, the same was presented by no less a subway project eminence than McDonald himself. Approval of the plan seemed assured.

Then without warning, Andrew Freedman struck from behind closed doors. Using his intimate friendship with Belmont to malevolent advantage, board member Freedman turned the baseball-ignorant banker against the proposal.[40] And as Belmont went, so went the Board. The all-but-done deal was rejected. Freedman publicly denied engineering the reversal, innocently maintaining that "Someone has been stringing these Western men [along] and it is time that it was stopped. It is simply brutal."[41] But the enjoyment that Freedman so plainly derived from events told a different story. This demonstration of Freedman muscle was more than merely impressive in its own right. It prompted rumor that the sale of the Giants to Brush had been a sham, and that Freedman remained in charge of club affairs.[42] He was not, but did little to dispel the notion, much to Brush's chagrin. The IRT board action also had a sobering effect on others perhaps disposed to invest in an American League beachhead in New York. Few wanted to cross swords with Andrew Freedman.

The unexpected collapse of the Lennox Avenue property deal stunned Johnson. Worse yet, it left him with a cadre of signed ballplayers but bereft of a franchise venue and new club investors. As the advent of the 1903 season approached, Johnson made brave noises about the inevitability of American League presence in New York, often identifying property nearby in The Bronx as available for construction of a new league park.[43] In private, he searched frantically for a solution to the dire predicament his circuit now faced.

Although his name had occasionally been mentioned as a suitor for the American League club ticketed for New York, Frank Farrell appeared preoccupied with other endeavors: the acquisition of Empire State Racetrack in Yonkers, the opening of a new casino on West 46th Street, and avoiding the clutches of relentless Manhattan District Attorney Jerome. In January 1903, it was reported that Jerome had targeted Farrell for gambling-related indictment by a New York County grand jury.[44] Nothing ever came of it, but the local climate had changed and Farrell was not heedless of the necessity to diversify his income portfolio. Thus, the Tammany/underworld-connected sporting man was ready and willing to come to American League rescue.

Farrell's intermediary with AL president Johnson would be influential *New York Sun* sportswriter Joe Vila, a good friend of Johnson and an ardent hater of Andrew Freedman, often the recipient of Vila newsprint abuse during his tenure as Giants boss.[45] Escorted by Vila to Johnson's new satellite office in Manhattan's Flatiron Building, Farrell presented himself as a candidate for stewardship of an American League ballclub in New York. To establish his credibility, Farrell tendered Johnson a certified check for $25,000, a quasi-performance bond that Johnson could keep as a forfeit if Farrell did not make good on his commitment to have a Gotham nine up and playing in short order. Impressed with Farrell's confidence and bankroll—and with no other viable club sponsorship option— Johnson cast aside misgivings and allotted the AL's Baltimore franchise to him. The purchase price was only $18,000, it being understood that the real expense would arise from relocation of the club to New York, acquisition of a Manhattan ballpark site, and the erection of a stadium.[46] Agreement between the league and its newest magnate had been reached, but there were obstacles yet to be overcome.

As if Farrell's reputation were not a sufficient public relations negative, his financial partner in New York club ownership was even more unsavory, old friend Bill Devery. But a solution for both the image and ballpark problems of the new regime was near at hand: Joseph Gordon, a genial Manhattan coal merchant and former state assemblyman. At least in the beginning, proposed club president Gordon would serve as the public face of the New York franchise. A Tammany insider of long acquaintance, Gordon was a comfortable front man for Farrell and Devery. As one-time president of the 1884 American Association champion New York Mets and a longtime member of the New York Giants corporate board, Gordon was also an experienced baseball man acceptable to Johnson, the New York sports press, and Gotham baseball fans. And as a bonus, Gordon was Manhattan real estate–knowledgeable.[47] Indeed, it was Gordon who located what would become the site of the American League ballpark, a desolate mesa owned by the New York Institute for the Blind in the far north Manhattan neighborhood of Washington Heights. Once a 10-year, $10,000 per season leasehold on the property had been secured, the Greater New York Base Ball Club of the American League was ready for public unveiling.

At a press conference conducted on March 12, 1903, Ban Johnson introduced Joseph Gordon as New York Highlanders club president.[48] Also lending his presence to the occasion was John B. Day, the respected founder of the New York Giants.[49] Conspicuous by their absence from the conference were Frank Farrell and Bill Devery, their ownership of the franchise kept secret for the time being. When the club subsequently filed incorporation papers in Albany, now-forgotten New York businessmen were listed as club principals. But within weeks, the identities of the true club owners were ferreted out by the press.

During the press conference, Johnson also revealed the location of the new American League ballpark: West 165th Street and Broadway, or less than 10 blocks from the Polo Grounds. While affording scenic views of the Hudson River and New Jersey Palisades, a less hospitable site for a ballpark would have been difficult to imagine. As described in a doubtful *Sporting Life* report, "The ground starts in a low swamp. It rises into a ridge of rocks perhaps twelve to fifteen feet above the level of Broadway.... As the property is today it will be necessary to blast all along the ridge.... There are [also] about 100 trees to be pulled up by the roots."[50]

With Opening Day optimistically set for April 30, general construction contractor Thomas McAvoy, a former New York police inspector and local Tammany district leader, loosed some 500 men on the site, with digging, dynamiting, and carting away debris continuing on a near around-the-clock schedule. In no time, Andrew Freedman intervened, orchestrating neighborhood opposition to the ballpark. Petitions submitted to the Washington Heights Board of Improvement maintained that residential property values would be diminished by the riff-raff attracted to ball games. The area would be better served by the cutting of a city street through the ballpark construction site. But McAvoy proved more influential with the Board than the Freedman surrogates. The petition was denied by a 3–2 vote.[51]

All the while, progress continued on the new ballpark. Eventually, some 12,000 cubic yards of bedrock were excavated by the construction crew, replaced by 30,000 cubic yards of fill. Once the trapezoid-shaped grounds were reasonably level, a crude baseball diamond was laid out. Surrounding the ample playing field dimensions (the right-center field power alley was a gargantuan 542 feet from home plate) were hastily constructed wooden grandstands and bleachers. In a remarkable six weeks, the McAvoy construction force had converted a picturesque but forbidding landscape into serviceable, if not-quite finished, grounds for major-league baseball popularly called Hilltop Park.[52] But the transformation had not come cheaply. The project had cost approximately $275,000—the bulk for clearance and leveling the site and $75,000 for construction of the ballpark—most of which was borne by Farrell.[53]

In the run-up to the home opener, Farrell was inconvenienced by a court appearance, being the defendant in a civil lawsuit instituted by one Rogers I. Barstow, Jr. The suit alleged that Barstow had been swindled out of $11,000 at a Farrell casino. The accused prided himself on running an honest house and bristled at the charge. But on the witness stand, he would play it dumb, professing total ignorance about casino gambling. Why he had never even seen a roulette wheel, Farrell maintained with a straight face. The Barstow lawsuit was ultimately dismissed.[54]

It would take more than nuisance court dates to keep Frank Farrell from Opening Day at Hilltop Park. By first pitch, he was seated quietly next to Devery in a front row box near the Highlanders bench. A 6–2 New York victory over the Washington Senators sent Farrell home a happy man. And led by future Hall of Famer Clark Griffith, the Highlanders would play competitive ball, finishing a respectable (72–62) fourth in final AL standings. But home attendance (a lackluster 211,808) in the club's initial season proved a disappointment, and Hilltop Park would constantly require costly repair and renovation.

Until operation of the franchise bled him near-white,[55] Farrell persevered, taking a vigorous role in guiding club fortunes as acting general manager.[56] Without much success on the field and with their finances drained, Frank Farrell and Bill Devery sold the franchise to Jacob Ruppert and Til Huston in January 1915, and they would not share in the Babe Ruth–fueled glories that lay ahead. Still, New York baseball history may well have taken a different course had not an underworld-connected sporting man and his corrupt crony come to the American League's rescue in the dark spring of 1903.

## NOTES

1. The definitive biography of Johnson is Eugene C. Murdoch, *Ban Johnson: Czar of Baseball* (Westport, Connecticut: Greenwood Press, 1982). An excellent thumbnail profile of Johnson by Joe Santry and Cindy Thomson can be accessed in the Society for American Baseball Research Baseball Biography Project, sabr.org/bioproj/person/dabf79f8, last accessed August 14, 2018.

2. Although rarely credited, Brush effectively pioneered the farm club system refined into standard baseball practice by Branch Rickey a generation later.

3. The revived American Association was stillborn in early 1901.

4. The National Agreement was the mutual pact that specified the rights and responsibilities of the National League and the various recognized minor leagues, including the American (nee Western) League.

5. Charles C. Alexander, *John McGraw* (New York: Viking Press, 1988; paperback ed., New York: Penguin Books), 89–91. Citation refers to the paperback edition.

6. The mansion was named in honor of Brush's second wife, the former stage actress Elsie Boyd Lombard. With the physically frail Brush unable to meet McGraw at the train station, Elsie swept him to the Brush estate in her personal carriage. Warm-up time spent in the private company of the vivacious and sophisticated Mrs. B. may well have been intended to dazzle the far-less-worldly McGraw, leaving him in the frame of mind to accede to whatever Brush proposed. See Joseph Durso, *Baseball and the American Dream* (St. Louis: The Sporting News, 1986), 64–66.

7. Another successful Freedman venture, the Maryland Casualty Company, did extensive municipal bond and insurance underwriting in Baltimore and enabled Freedman to forge ties with local Democrat politicos like Mahon.

8. For more detailed accounts of the gutting of the Baltimore Orioles, see Mike Sowell, *July 2, 1903: The Mysterious Death of Hall-of-Famer Big Ed Delahanty* (New York: Macmillan, 1992), 129–133, and Burt Solomon,

*Where They Ain't: The Fabled Life and Untimely Death of the Original Baltimore Orioles, the Team That Gave Birth to Modern Baseball* (New York: Doubleday, 1999), 226–231.

9. In a late-life remembrance, daughter Natalie Brush de Gendron maintained that her father was also the principal owner of the one-season (1884) Indianapolis club in the major-league American Association. See Rick Johnson, "The Forgotten Architect of Indiana Baseball," *Indianapolis Star Magazine,* May 4, 1975. But the historical record suggests that Brush was unconnected to that Indianapolis club, "beaten out by a local liquor dealer named Joseph Schwabacher." J. Taylor Spink, "World Series Fire Started by J.T. Brush," *Sporting News,* October 10, 1939. Accord, an informative unpublished Brush bio by Guy M. Smith contained in the John T. Brush file at the Giamatti Research Center, National Baseball Hall of Fame and Museum, Cooperstown, New York.

10. Among other things, Freedman served as treasurer of the successful mayoral campaign of Robert A. Van Wyck, a Croker vassal then sitting on the state bench.

11. When ex-umpire Watch Burnham made the mistake of inviting *Andy* to join his railway club car party for a friendly drink, he unwittingly provoked a fist-fight with an enraged Freedman, as reported in *The Sporting News,* July 20, 1900.

12. The most enduring of these yarns is the supposed Freedman threat that Dryden "was standing on the brink of an abscess and if he ain't careful, I'll push him in." Although almost certainly apocryphal, later baseball historians repeated the tale as if it were gospel. Frank Graham, *The New York Giants: An Informal History of a Great Baseball Club* (New York: G.P. Putnam's Sons, 1952), 19–20; Mark Alvarez, "The Abominable Owner," *Sports Heritage,* Nov/Dec 1987, 45.

13. In two seasons, attendance at the Polo Grounds plummeted from an NL-leading 390,808 (1897) to 121,384 (1899), with even more dramatic fall-off for Giants away games.

14. According to Mrs. John J. (Blanche) McGraw, *The Real McGraw* (New York: David McKay Company, 1953), 177. Distinguished baseball historian David Quentin Voigt is less dramatic, merely describing Freedman as "a reputed millionaire" and the National League's "wealthiest owner" in *The League That Failed* (Lanham, MD: The Scarecrow Press, 1998), 219, 220.

15. "That New League: Freedman Not Hostile—Who Delegate Buckley Is," *Sporting Life,* September 30, 1899: 6.

16. Oliver E. Allen, *The Tiger: The Rise and Fall of Tammany Hall* (Reading, MA: Addison-Wesley Pub., 1993), 197.

17. Devery's acquittal on an earlier bribery charge came courtesy of an alibi supplied by Frank Farrell, as reported in "Devery Jurors Locked Up," *New York Tribune,* March 27, 1896: 1. See "Alibi for Devery," *New York Herald,* March 26, 1896: 4.

18. Regarding ill-concealed news reporter affection for Devery, Steffens added that "I think we never printed a paragraph against that crook that did not betray our liking for his honesty, courage, and character," quoted in Jim Reisler, *Before They Were the Bombers: The New York Yankees' Early Years, 1903–1915* (Jefferson, NC: McFarland, 2002), 12.

19. According to a front-page profile of "The Poolroom King" published in the *Watertown (NY) Times,* June 21, 1901.

20. Big Tim (Timothy Daniel) Sullivan (1862–1913) is not to be confused with his cousin, Little Tim (Timothy Patrick) Sullivan (1870–1909), another influential but less publicly prominent Tammany powerbroker.

21. Off-track horserace betting was a lucrative, if facially unlawful, source of revenue for those like Frank Farrell. In return for police indifference to their operation, pool-room proprietors kicked in the regular protection payments that forestalled police intrusion and comprised a substantial portion of the graft that kept the Tammany machine well-oiled.

22. "This City's Crying Shame," *New York Times,* March 9, 1900: 1. This front-page story encompassed a systematic breakdown of Tammany's annual protection booty.

23. The most celebrated of the Farrell casinos was located at 33rd Street and Fifth Avenue, footsteps from the Waldorf Astoria Hotel. Designed by the noted architect Stanford White, it boasted floor-to-ceiling tapestries, red velvet carpets, and oak-tabled game rooms for high-stakes roulette, poker, and baccarat. The most arresting feature of the premises, however, was its magnificent 15th century Italianate bronze door. Not only did this portal give the casino the outside look of a bank vault, it proved impenetrable by uncorrupted police raiders and political do-gooders. For more, see "Gambling Behind the Bronze Door: NYC's Posh Casino," *Bowery Boys History,* April 23, 2010.

24. Justice William Travers Jerome, Speech, Citizens' Union of the Eighteenth, Nineteenth, and Twentieth Assembly Districts, Murray Hill Lyceum, October 11, 1901, quoted in "Big Fusion Rally at Murray Hill Lyceum," *New York Times,* October 12, 1901: 1.

25. "The Case of Mr. Unger," *New York Times,* October 13, 1901: 6.

26. *Ibid.* Emphasis in original. In reaction to Devery's antics as NYPD chief, the state legislature in Albany had abolished the chief of police position, placing governance of the department under a newly-created NYC Police Commission. Unfazed, the ever-reliable Mayor Van Wyck thereupon installed Devery as a police commissioner.

27. *Ibid.*

28. "The Citizens' Union and Mr. Devery's Life," *New York Times*, October 28, 1901: 2. The article summarizes the organization's charges.

29. The Tammany *coup de grâce* was administered to Devery at the Democratic Party State Convention in Fall 1902 where the Murphy forces (with the acquiescence of Big Tim Sullivan, Devery's longtime patron) declined to recognize Big Bill's recent election as a local district leader and casted Devery into the political wilderness.

30. Brush had been an Indiana delegate to the Republican National Convention in 1896, but had no connection to the Republican-Fusion combination that had taken control of NYC government on January 1, 1902.

31. "Andrew Freedman Dies of Apoplexy," *New York Times,* December 5, 1915: 19. The obituary devotes paragraphs to recital of Freedman's civic, business, and charitable endeavors. His ownership of the New York Giants is noted in passing.

32. Johnson was given to personalized public criticism of Freedman, a proud, thin-skinned man with, as noted by one Giants historian, an enormous capacity for resentment and a ferocious vindictive streak. See James D. Hardy, Jr., *The New York Giants Base Ball Club, 1870–1900* (Jefferson, NC: McFarland, 1995), 159.

33. "Baseball: Change in the Directorate," *Cleveland Leader,* November 11, 1902: 9.

34. "New York Americans," *Trenton Times,* September 27, 1902: 11.

35. See "New York Team for American League," *Ann Arbor* (Michigan) *Daily Argus,* October 24, 1902: 4. The players later named as being under contract to play for the fledgling New York club included such notables as Willie Keeler, Jack Chesbro, and Jesse Tannehill, plus some lesser lights. See "Swat for Ban Johnson," *Baltimore Sun,* January 8, 1903: 9.

36. Aside from the Polo Grounds, the only ready-made baseball park located in Manhattan was Manhattan Field (née the New Polo Grounds), the former home field of the New York Giants and situated next door to the Polo Grounds. The two ballparks were separated by only a 10-foot wide alley and their stadium walls. But Manhattan Field (and the long-term lease to the real property on which the Polo Grounds and Manhattan Field sat) remained an asset of the New York Giants, and thus unavailable to the American League.

37. "Baseball: Denies Backing American Team," *Cleveland Leader,* November 11, 1902: 9. Only a week before, Sullivan had reportedly expressed confidence that placement of an American League team in Manhattan was an all-but-accomplished deal. See "Versions of the New York Invasion," *Sporting Life,* November 8, 1902: 3.

38. As reported in various sources, including "The New York Grounds," *Cleveland Leader,* February 3, 1903: 7; "Latest Phases of New York Invasion," *Sporting Life,* February 14, 1903: 4.

39. The intricacies of the property transactions were handled by Douglas Robinson, a Manhattan real-estate heavyweight and the brother-in-law of ex–New York Governor and current President Theodore Roosevelt, as subsequently reported in the *Boston Herald,* March 13, 1903. The AL was to pay the IRT the sum of $23,000 per season for the leasehold of the Lennox Avenue ballpark property. "New York American League Club Gets Grounds on West Side of Manhattan Isle. Racing at New Orleans and Oakland Tracks; Lively Night on the Alleys," *Boston Herald,* March 13, 1903: 10.

40. Without a trace of irony, the ex-Giants owner apparently persuaded Belmont that the construction of a baseball stadium would degrade Manhattan property values and was, therefore, not in the greater interests of the subway project.

41. Glenn Stout, *Yankees Century: 100 Years of New York Yankees Baseball* (Boston: Houghton Mifflin Company, 2002), 9–10.

42. Freedman also used his influence as an IRT board member to steer location of a planned subway stop away from Washington Park, then the home grounds of the Brooklyn NL club, another old Freedman adversary.

43. See, e.g., "Grounds Are in the Bronx," *Cleveland Plain Dealer,* March 9, 1903: 8; "Johnson Gets New York Field," *Evansville* (Indiana) *Courier,* March 9, 1903: 5. The most frequently mentioned Bronx ballpark site was the former Astor estate on Jerome Avenue and 161st Street, later the construction grounds for Yankee Stadium.

44. See "Now for Farrell," *Boston Herald,* January 27, 1903: 3.

45. Vila regularly worked references to Shylock and other repugnant anti-Semitic stereotypes into his copy about Freedman. The proud and easily-offended Freedman responded by instituting a welter of defamation-based lawsuits against the *Sun,* all of which he lost.

46. At the time of Farrell's death years later, Joe Vila published a firsthand account of the sale of the franchise. See Joe Vila, "Baseball and Racing Men Mourn Death of Frank J. Farrell, Founder of the Yankees," Setting the Pace, *New York Sun,* February 11, 1926: 45. For a slightly different version, see Frank Graham, *The New York Yankees: An Informal History* (New York: G.P. Putnam's Sons, 1943), 5–7.

47. Until swept out of office in the anti-Tammany election tide of November 1901, Gordon had served as NYC deputy commissioner of buildings.

48. The team nickname *Highlanders* was not an official one and its derivation is unsettled. At times, it has been attributed to the location of the club's ballpark, popularly, if erroneously, believed to be the highest

spot on Manhattan Island. At other times, the moniker was connected to club president Gordon and viewed as a play on the Gordon Highlanders, a famed Scottish regiment. Whatever the case, the more headline-friendly nickname *Yanks* or *Yankees* appeared in newsprint as early as 1904.

49.  Absent from the major-league scene since February 1893, Day made press-conference remarks suggesting an official connection to the new American League club. But Day played no further part in Highlanders history.

50.  "The Gotham Citadel," *Sporting Life*, March 21, 1903: 4.

51.  See "No Streets Through Baseball Grounds," *New York Times,* April 10, 1903: 10 (misreports the vote as 4–3).

52.  The official title was the American League Park of New York.

53.  At the time, Farrell's net worth was approximately $750,000, according to Steven A. Riess, *Touching Base: Professional Baseball and American Culture in the Progressive Era* (Champaign: University of Illinois Press, 1980), 80. Devery was not anywhere near as well-off, and his inclusion as a club partner was most likely a gesture of friendship by Farrell. It has also been maintained that AL president Johnson partially reimbursed Farrell for ballpark construction costs with league funds. See Stout, 13–14.

54.  As reported in "Farrell Once Saw Roulette," *New York Evening World,* March 18, 1903: 1. The performance was not without precedent. Only four months earlier in another courtroom, New York's Pool Room King had testified that, while he had an interest in horseracing, he had never been inside a pool room in his life. See "Frank Farrell on the Stand," *New York Times*, November 27, 1902: 14; *New York Evening World,* November 28, 1902 (Front page has a brief missive accompanied by a drawing titled "Artist Powers Shows a Modern Pool-Room to Frank Farrell, Who Says He Never Saw One.") Press coverage of such shameless Farrell testimony generally affected an amused, rather than an indignant, tone.

55.  In particular, finance of a sinkhole-plagued new stadium project in 1912 had a crippling effect on Farrell coffers.

56.  Apart from Opening Day and other ceremonial appearances, Bill Devery was uninvolved and nearly invisible during the dozen years that he and Farrell co-owned the New York club.

# Ruthian by Design

## *The Shared Monumentality of Yankee Stadium and Babe Ruth*

### ROLANDO LLANES

"Monumentality is enigmatic. It cannot be intentionally created. Neither the finest material nor the most advanced technology need enter a work of monumental character for the same reason that the finest ink was not required to draw up the Magna Carta."[1]—Louis I. Kahn, Architect

It can be said that Babe Ruth and beams and girders of the original Yankee Stadium, built in 1923, are forever intertwined in a timeless embrace that has survived not only the passing of time, but also the inevitable effects of change. Their collective impact on the history of professional baseball has been lasting and profound. Both emerged at a time when the game was redefining itself on the field and off. Ruth helped usher in the greatest dynasty in American sports history and was part of the 1927 Yankee team that many consider to be the greatest of all time. He revolutionized the game by exhibiting a legendary ability to hit home runs at a pace far beyond his peers, and at a time when hitting balls out of a ballpark was considered a rare and monumental feat.

In reciprocal fashion, the original Yankee Stadium possessed its own unique monumental qualities that set it apart from the ballparks that preceded it. Like other turn-of-the-century baseball venues, such as Shibe Park (1909), Forbes Field (1909), Fenway Park (1912), and Ebbets Field (1913), Yankee Stadium's architecture also underscored the growing understanding that professional baseball venues were emerging as vital constituents of a city's civic and urban life, taking their rightful place along with theaters, libraries, museums, and other public buildings. Yet, the monumental virtuosity of Yankee Stadium surpassed that of its predecessors not only by virtue because of its scale and architectural grandeur, but, more importantly, as a result of its association with the larger-than-life personality who famously christened the first game ever played there with a home run.

Over 12 epic seasons (1923–1934) and beyond, the "The House That Ruth Built," as it came to be known, and the legendary Ruth were inextricably and forever woven together into the fabric of baseball history and American culture. Ruth didn't *build* Yankee Stadium, and if we are to believe that the outfield dimensions were specifically tailored for his left-handed swing, the geometry could have been *friendlier* still. Instead, the more profound association between Ruth and Yankee Stadium rests in the less measurable traits of both. Together, they forged a distinct, timeless and almost perfect union of personality, edifice, and monumentality that has never been duplicated in American sports history.

## Ruth

"The combination of great skill on the field and a shared flaw off the field made him the most admired and theatrical man in the game"[2]—Marshall Smelser

Babe Ruth's legendary career with the Yankees, commencing at the heels of the "Black Sox" scandal of 1919, re-focused the attention of the public away from the game's off-field problems at a crucial moment in baseball history. Ruth quickly became baseball's central figure, a bigger-than-life personality that transcended his on-field dominance to a figure that single-handedly rescued the sport in its most perilous moment. In the iconography of the game, Ruth remains central, and in the lexicon of American culture, his name occupies a lasting place. To this day, to be *Ruthian* is to exhibit the very qualities of prodigious greatness.

Babe Ruth's association with on-field greatness and his reputation as the game's paramount personality were well-earned. At the conclusion of the 1920 season, New York Giants manager John McGraw sought to terminate the New York Yankees' status as decade-long tenants of the Polo Grounds. In addition to having outdrawn (and almost outplayed) their landlord, the Yankees had overextended their welcome with the Giants. The Yankees' owners, Jacob Ruppert and Tillinghast (Cap) Huston, had another reason for which to seek a new home—his name was Babe Ruth, who was acquired from the Boston Red Sox after the 1919 season.

Ruth's accomplishments on and off the field, as well as his charismatic presence, quickly made him one of the most popular sports figures of his time. As a result of the Giants' growing disdain with their more popular tenant and the rise of Ruth's celebrity, Ruppert and Huston were motivated to seek a new home for the Yankees after the 1920 season.

By 1921, Ruppert and Huston had purchased a 10-acre property within sight and immediately across the Harlem River from the Polo Grounds. Ruth was the main attraction and it was Ruppert's and Huston's intent to combine his power at the plate with his power to draw fans. As Donald Honig wrote, "The man was a combination of ball playing talent, personality, magnetism, show business drama, and innocence that had been hand-crafted by some celestial artisan who is probably too pleased to want to stop himself and too wise to try."[3]

When the Yankees acquired Ruth from the Red Sox after the 1919 season, he was already a proven talent and on the verge of greatness. By 1919, Ruth had begun his transition from pitcher to everyday position player. That season, while sporting a 9–5 record as a pitcher, he also led the major leagues in home runs with 29. By 1920, at the age of 25, he shared the baseball spotlight with more seasoned players, such as Tris Speaker (32), Joe Jackson (33) and Ty Cobb (34). That was until it soon became clear that he was in a league of his own. Ruth's slugging statistics were so staggering in comparison to the rest of the league that it is no wonder he quickly became a living legend. His 54 home runs in 1920 were 35 better than the 19 hit by runner-up George Sisler. That season, Ruth averaged one home run every seven at-bats. Sisler averaged one every thirty-three. As Robert Creamer wrote of fans in those days, "…they thrilled vicariously to the surging erectile power of the *Ruthian* home run. They wanted more. They wanted hits and they wanted runs, lots of hits and lots of runs. They wanted homers."[4]

In a span of 14 years (1919–1932), Ruth led both the American and National Leagues in home runs eight times and tied for the lead twice. This all but assured Yankee fans that in a single homestand, Ruth was certain to hit a few balls out of the park. His every at-bat was an electrifying event. During those 14 years, Ruth batted .315 or better 13 times, including the 1927 season, when he hit .356 while belting a record 60 home runs. Of his 192 total hits that historic season, 97 were for extra bases. He singlehandedly hit more home runs that year than the Athletics (50); Tigers (49); Browns (47); Red Sox (24); and Indians (16). No baseball player before Ruth or since can claim that level of dominance in their respective sports. Of his 714 career home runs, Ruth hit 259 in Yankee Stadium, solidifying his inextricable link to the place that would be forever known as the House that Ruth Built.

The combination of skill, endurance, and grace defined Ruth's 22-year career, and to this day, his achievements remain the standards against which many of the game's great home run hitters are measured. This fact proved to haunt the Yankees' Roger Maris who, in 1961, chased and ultimately surpassed Ruth's single-season home run record. Maris needed all 162 games of the season to hit 61 home runs and eclipse Ruth's record by the slimmest of margins. The effort left Maris bitter, disillusioned, and under severe stress as he chased a record that many felt he was unworthy to possess. Adding to Maris's woes was the debate about the very legitimacy of the record. While Maris needed all 162 games of the regular season to hit 61 home runs, Ruth achieved his feat over the course of a shorter 154-game season—some factions thought that Maris's home-run total was illegitimate further separating Maris from Ruth's legendary persona. While Maris's achievement might have been *Ruthian*, alas, he was no Babe Ruth.

> Like the air, Babe Ruth is all around us. Like a book or a snapshot, he endures. Nearly 44 years after his death, the Babe still breathes in movies and music and literature, as if he retired his pinstripes only yesterday, not 1935. As if he was less a ballplayer than a historical figure or an idol of pop culture—slugger, hero, myth.[5]—Pat Calabria

There is no question that Babe Ruth earned his iconic status in baseball by way of measurable and quantifiable achievements. On the field, he was a statistical colossus, maintaining an unparalleled level of performance over the course of a long 22-year career. Not only were his 714 home runs a monumental achievement for his day, Ruth had a career batting average of .342—a spectacular statistic for a home run hitter who also struck out more than 1,300 times. And if his hitting prowess wasn't enough to grant him his well-earned mythical status, for six of those 22 years, Ruth was predominantly a dominant pitcher who never posted a losing season.

But there is also a kind of monumentality and prominence that Ruth earned not only by virtue of his statistical greatness, but as a product of who he was both on and off the field. His "larger-than-life" personality was on public display throughout his baseball career and beyond. Legendary stories about his on-field and off-field personas abound.

Ruth famously promised a seriously injured boy that he would hit a home run for him in Game Four of the 1926 World Series, and did. The reality or myth of his "Called Shot" in Game Three of the 1932 World Series remains, to this day, one of the game's greatest tales and, if true, a remarkable example of Ruth's fearless confidence. Ruth was not shy about exploiting his on-field success into an off-field persona that lived life with reckless abandon. He had a well-known prodigious appetite for countless vices, appeared in movies during and after his career (playing himself in *The Pride of the Yankees*), and had numerous commercial endorsement deals and public appearances. Ruth was also very generous with causes that benefited children, a personal interest that extended beyond his playing days. The totality of Ruth's personality—the good, bad, and ugly sides of it; the athlete and the rabble-rouser; and the braggart and the humble servant—would propel him into the rarified air reserved for mythical figures.

On June 13, 1948, the New York Yankees celebrated the 25th anniversary of Yankee Stadium and the retirement of Babe Ruth's iconic uniform number 3. By then, Ruth had been out of the game for 13 years and was battling the ravages of cancer, a disease that would take his life two months later at age 53. The most lasting image from that day is credited to photographer Nat Fein of the *New York Herald Tribune*. While other photographers on the field during the pre-game ceremonies positioned themselves facing Ruth, 33-year-old Fein placed himself behind The Babe and took what would become one of the most famous photographs in the history of sports.

The image would become the first sports-related photograph to win a Pulitzer Prize. The photo captured a remarkable scene, depicting the architectural grandeur and monumentality of Yankee Stadium's grandstand together with the image of the man credited with changing the course of both the New York Yankees and the game of baseball. By virtue of Fein's serendipitous decision to photograph Ruth from behind, the sickly former slugger, leaning on a baseball bat for support, still seemed larger-than-life among the future Yankee greats in the background. Ruth's monumental, albeit frail figure (compositionally) stood taller and seemed larger than the likes of future Yankee greats DiMaggio, Berra, Mantle, and Rizzuto, and was matched only by the majestic sweep of the stadium's three-tiered grandstand and iconic frieze, adorned with the banners of championships past.

While the extraordinary image captures the unfolding sadness of Ruth's physical demise, his legendary achievements and mere presence transcended the moment by virtue of his mere presence. From that day forward, no Yankee player would wear Number 3 and, perhaps more fittingly, none would dare. Fein's photo also captures the shared monumentality between edifice and man, between The Stadium and Ruth, and the promise that the place he had become synonymous with was poised to remain the backdrop of future greatness for many years to come.

## The Stadium

"'The House that Ruth Built' was the first park referred to as a 'stadium'....
Instead of titling the site a 'park,' 'field,' or 'grounds,' rural metaphors enforc-

ing the arcadian ideology of baseball, the new terminology indicated an identification with the urban milieu."[6]—Steven Riess

Baseball's increasing popularity at the turn of the century resulted in a surge of new ballpark construction that marked the beginning of one phase of ballpark history and the end of another. The era of wood construction that made many structures susceptible to fire gave way to ballparks built primarily of steel and concrete. Places such as Washington Park in Brooklyn, Columbia Avenue Grounds in Philadelphia, and Hilltop Park in New York were abandoned by the Dodgers, Athletics, and Yankees, respectively, for newer, more lasting structures. By 1913, the Dodgers were playing in Ebbets Field; the Athletics had moved into Shibe Park; and the Yankees began had begun their 10-year stint at the Polo Grounds after a fire had destroyed its predecessor in Washington Heights, a neighborhood in Manhattan.

The game's growing appeal with the surging middle class in major-league cities put pressure on team owners to accommodate the spectator in more refined and formal environments. In the case of Ebbets Field, Shibe Park and Forbes Field, owners invested heavily in an external architectural style that reflected qualities of permanence, stability, and grandeur—attributes more aligned with turn of the century civic architecture. Attending professional baseball games had become more than a mere past time and the venues that hosted the games more than just ballparks.

In the book *City Games*, author Steven Riess best summarizes the evolution of ballpark construction at the turn of the century:

> The early baseball parks were dangerously constructed wooded structures with small seating capacities, but beginning in 1909, as major league baseball became very profitable, expensive modern fireproof grandstands were built. These edifices were semipublic monuments that testified to the forward-looking character of their cities.[7]

And while the structural make-up of the grandstand went from wood to steel, another architectural evolution was contributing to the transformation of ballpark design from rural to more urban typologies. The exterior characteristics of ballparks such as Forbes Field, Shibe Park, and Ebbets Field resembled the classical architectural language of ancient stadia and borrowed from the ornamental style of Beaux-Arts architecture.

The architectural character of these structures recalled the splendor and scale of neo-classical architecture, usually reserved for the important civic buildings of turn-of-the-century America. Culturally, baseball was fast becoming a unifying part of American culture. Baseball, according to Riess, was "rationalized and bureaucratized in cities, where the spirit of nationalism, wholesomeness, excitement, and drama made it the national pastime."[8] This national fervor for the game played a key role in the development of ballpark architecture. The fact that ballparks were beginning to exhibit the architectural properties of contemporary civic institutions represented a collective belief that baseball was not only the nation's most popular sport, but also one of its most essential cultural institutions.

It was within this period of transition that Yankee Stadium emerged—an architectural colossus worthy of the title. As has been well documented, Yankee Stadium was the first major-league baseball venue to be formally titled a "stadium." Up to that point, most ballparks bore the terms *field, grounds,* and *park* in their names—rural metaphors, as Riess notes, that reinforced "the arcadian ideology of baseball."[9] And while the design of places such as Forbes Field (1909), Shibe Park (1909), and Ebbets Field (1913), reflected a newly found architectural sophistication, the masterminds of the Yankees' new home aspired to a scale and grandeur that would exceed all that preceded it. Perhaps this need to make an architectural statement that far surpassed all prior examples was driven by numerous factors: from the great metropolis the stadium represented to the team's acquisition of Babe Ruth—arguably, the game's greatest draw—to the realization of the game's growing importance. According to Riess, Yankee Stadium was aptly titled for a building whose architectural expression was consistent with baseball's newly-found appreciation among contemporary urban society. By the 1920s, many ramshackle wooden ballparks had given way to more prominent structures, underscoring the belief that the sport of baseball had entered a new era of social and cultural prominence.

The design of Yankee Stadium is attributed to the Osborn Engineering Company of Cleveland, Ohio. Osborn Engineering was founded in 1892 by Frank C. Osborn, an engineer, who had developed an expertise in the design of steel bridges and other similar structures. Over the following three decades, as the design of sports facilities transitioned from wood to steel construction, Osborn Engineering evolved into the preeminent designers of new ballparks. In addition to Forbes Field in Pittsburgh, these facilities include places such as Forbes Field in Pittsburgh, Comiskey Park in Chicago, League Park in Cleveland, and Fenway Park in Boston. But it was Osborn Engineering's design of the Polo Grounds (1911) for the New York Giants that set the stage for the architectural direction the firm would employ at Yankee Stadium 12 years later, particularly with respect to the interior of the grandstand.

While the word *design* is often used in conjunction with Osborn Engineering and the firm's most famous stadium projects, Osborn's true technical prowess was in the *engineering* of sophisticated structural solutions to the challenge of multi-level steel grandstands. In fact, the design of ballparks such as Forbes Field, Comiskey Park, and the Polo Grounds was the collective creative product of Osborn's engineers working in tandem with associated architects. For example, the architectural designs of Forbes Field and Comiskey Park are credited to Charles Wellford Leavitt, Jr. (1871–1928) and Zachary Taylor Davis (1869–1946), respectively.

With respect to the version of the Polo Grounds that opened in 1911 after fire destroyed its predecessor, the architect credited with its design is Henry Beaumont Herts (1871–1933). Herts was a prominent New York architect whose partnership with Hugh Tallant had produced many famous theatre designs in the city such as the New Amsterdam and the Lyceum theatres, both built in 1903 and both exemplary examples of Herts & Tallant's brand of Beaux-Arts architecture.

Herts studied architecture at the École des Beaux-Arts in Paris, one of the most influential schools of architecture in the world during the late 19th century. Many prominent American architects such as David Adler and Richard Morris Hunt trained at the school—and became proponents of neo-classical architecture during the turn of the century and well into the 1920s and '30s, influencing many of their American peers. Herts's theatre designs were exemplary examples of Beaux-Arts–inspired architecture and were clearly an influence in the design of the Polo Grounds' grandstand. Elements of Herts's design for the Polo Grounds are described in great detail by Stew Thornley:

> [The grandstand] was faced with a decorative frieze on the façade of the upper deck, containing a series of allegorical treatments in bas relief, while the façade of the roof was adorned with the coats of arms of all National League teams…. The box seats were designed upon the lines of the royal

boxes of the Colosseum in Rome with Roman-style pylons flanking the horseshoe-shaped grandstand on both ends.[10]

Yankee Stadium was to be Osborn's signature stadium design, eventually rivaled in scale and architectural character by Municipal Stadium in Cleveland, another Osborn creation, which opened in 1931. For that project, the firm teamed up with the architectural firm of Walker and Weeks. Both Frank Walker (1877–1949) and Harry Weeks (1871–1935) were MIT-trained architects whose work reflected the same Beaux-Arts-inspired design practiced by Henry Herts and others.

Evidence of a similar collaboration with an established architect is harder to find in the case of Yankee Stadium. In his book *Babe's Place*, Michael Wagner attributes the creative leadership for the Yankee Stadium project to Bernard Green, a civil engineer who had been employed by Osborn since 1919. Wagner refers to Green as Osborn's "chief architect" who "designed and supervised the construction of Yankee Stadium."[11] While Green's role is well documented, it is unclear if the Osborn team also included formally trained architects, as was the case with the Polo Grounds (Henry Herts), Comiskey Park (Zachary Taylor Davis), and years later, Cleveland Municipal Stadium (Walker and Weeks).

By virtue of Osborn's three-tiered grandstand design, aimed at achieving a seating capacity far larger than recent ballparks, Yankee Stadium was about one-third taller than its most recent predecessors—such as Forbes Field, Polo Grounds, Shibe Park, Comiskey Park, and Ebbets Field.

The architectural intent of Yankee Stadium's external appearance was clearly meant to convey a sense of solidity, permanence, and monumentality. However, if one had watched the construction of Yankee Stadium take place from the beginning, the artifice of its architecture would have been clearly evident. While the predominant component of the stadium's structure was the vast steel frame that formed the unique three-tiered grandstand, the exterior concrete cladding was designed to convey a radically different architectural intent.

The stadium's street-side façade was composed of two distinct elements. The first reached a height of approximately 65 feet above street level and contained miscellaneous back-of house and front office program, as well as the ramps that led to the lower mezzanine levels of seating. The second step in the building's elevation reached a height of approximately 100 feet and stepped back about 30 feet from the lower element. This component acted as the exterior façade of the upper deck grandstand.

Internally, the vast three-tiered grandstand was an overwhelming sight, recognizable and distinct given its scale and the ever-present metal frieze. The approach of elaborating the interior of the grandstand with intricate metal work and decorative elements recalls similar techniques found in the interior architecture of theatres and playhouses at the turn of the century. And while it is not clear how much of Herts's architectural influence may have found its way into the 1923 plans of Yankee Stadium, there is no doubt that the appearance of the now-famous frieze (or *façade,* as it came to be known) is derivative of a similar design approach. The frieze, which would become Yankee Stadium's signature architectural motif, was composed of flat-arched metal panels spaced 24-feet on center. A flagpole was attached at the joint between each panel, helping to reinforce the rhythmic march of the frieze around the full length of the grandstand. The practical reason for the iconic panels, similar to that of the Polo Grounds design, was to conceal the raw edge of the trusses that made up the roof of the stadium's signature third tier.

Early drawings of Osborn's design for Yankee Stadium reflected a completely enclosed grandstand, projecting an even more singular overall structure. The pressures of getting the stadium ready for the 1923 season opener and subsequent financial limitations prevented that idea from becoming a reality. Instead, the stadium's configuration from foul pole to foul pole evolved over the following decades into a collection of idiosyncratic elements that, inadvertently, became part of the accepted fabric of its architecture. It remains an example of how the vision of the stadium as a staid, hermetically sealed box yielded to the vagaries of the time and resulted in a place where the imposing formality of the main grandstand coexisted with the endearing informality of the outfield enclosure.

The major renovation of Yankee Stadium undertaken between 1974 and 1975 forever altered the physical attributes of both its interior and exterior. The primary intent of the renovation was to modernize the 50-year-old structure to include amenities consistent with those of more contemporary ballparks. One of the most significant changes made to the original design was the removal of the columns that supported the upper deck in an effort to increase the rows of seats and eliminate the obstructed views of the seats in the lower decks. In doing so, the structural engineers developed a system of tension cables to support the upper deck. One end of the cables was attached to the back of the new concrete beams of the reconstructed upper deck, and the other end was connected to the new support columns that ran along the existing façade.

The cleverness of that structural solution not only resulted in eliminating obstructed view seats, it also necessitated the removal of the roof that covered the original upper deck seats. The roof that was removed supported the stadium's signature façade, the most visually significant victim of the renovation. As an acknowledgment of its historical importance, a replica of the façade was installed along the outfield to be a constant reminder of the original. And yet, regardless of the less-than-subtle reconstruction of the original bones of Yankee Stadium, the aggressive nature of the changes would not erase the stadium's connection to the events that shaped it over the previous 50 years.

While the controversial modernization project gave an additional 30 years of life to Yankee

Babe Ruth inaugurated the original Yankee Stadium by smashing a three-run home run in the Yankees' 4–1 victory over the Boston Red Sox on April 18, 1923 (National Baseball Hall of Fame and Museum, Cooperstown, NY).

Stadium, many consider the end result both lamentable and necessary. Albeit altered, the renovated stadium was still the same *place* that was home to Ruth, DiMaggio, and Mantle, and it was still home to its memories. As Bruce Kuklick writes in his book about Shibe Park, *To Everything a Season*, "Memories do not exist in the mind's isolation but are connected to objects and stored in them."[12]

There is no question that the renovation forever transformed the 50-year old edifice, but there was still enough there to remain the repository of the original's memories, albeit with a slightly altered backdrop.

Even after the reconstruction, Yankee Stadium possessed most of the stately monumentality that Osborn purposely *engineered* into its architecture. However, its lasting monumental qualities were not solely the product of scale, ornament, style, and (post–1975) its modernization. Instead, the stadium's enduring significance was, to paraphrase Louis Kahn, the product of an enigmatic monumentality, one not intentionally created; and one that could not have been anticipated by the engineers and architects that created it in 1923 and recast it in 1975.

The brilliance of Yankee Stadium's iconic grandeur is not that it was an ideal and beneficial setting for its left-handed home run hitter (i.e. the *short-porch* in right field); or that it was designed larger, taller, and more opulent than any of its contemporaries (arguably, the architectural characteristics of Forbes Field, Shibe Park, and Ebbets Field were more elaborate than Yankee Stadium's exterior). Those qualities and factors were the intentional construct of those that could never have imagined that the *monument* they were erecting would, indeed, become monumental.

As Louis Kahn said, true monumentality cannot be intentionally created. But for what happened on June 6th, 1944, the coast of Normandy would be just another collection of beaches along the northern coast of France. Without Ruth and the events that transpired within it, Yankee Stadium may have been just another ballpark, a *stadium* in name only notable for its physical and architectural attributes, yet falling short of the timeless monumental character that we now attribute to its memory.

Yankee Stadium's greatness, its true monumentality, its very importance, are the unintentional products of the real (not imagined) events that transpired within it and the traditions that it fostered over its lifetime. Like no other venue in American sports, Yankee Stadium transcended its original intent and became an integral part of the culture. It was the setting for the dynastic greatness of the teams that called it home, and the player that would change the game forever. Yet, over the course of more than 80 years, Yankee Stadium was more than a ballpark. It was a shrine to success, to be sure; but it was, more importantly, a place of reverence and a backdrop for events of national and international importance.

Yankee Stadium and Babe Ruth would share one last collective and historical moment that brought to a close the unique and powerful relationship between man and edifice. On August 17th and 18th, 1948, one day after 53-year-old Babe Ruth succumbed to the ravages of cancer, his body lay in state in Yankee Stadium's rotunda. The public viewing attracted over 75,000 visitors, many of which waited long hours outside the stadium for a glimpse of the Yankee great. Over the course of those two days, the stately palace of sport, setting of many of Ruth's on-field exploits and home to the game's most celebrated franchise, had transformed itself into a place of mourning. The stadium's architectural grandeur, associated with spectacle and celebration, provided an equally suitable backdrop for the veneration and reverence of the man most associated with its glory. While this final trip home for Ruth brought to a close the physical relationship between him and Yankee Stadium, it can also be understood as the genesis of their unique and inseparable bond.

Together, the *presence* of Yankee Stadium and the *ghost* of Babe Ruth linger in ways more profound than the memory of their statistical greatness. In fact, while most of Ruth's on-field records have fallen, he remains the game's iconic figurehead—an irreplaceable steward of a game now clinging to remain our nation's pastime. And although the original and reconstructed Yankee Stadium no longer stands, its *presence* is still equally profound, so much so that during the ceremony to retire Derek Jeter's uniform number in May 2017 at the new Yankee Stadium, one of the announcers commented on how *this place* (the new stadium) had seen many great events over the years. It was an understandable mistake and one that underscored the fact that even though physically absent, the events that gave meaning to the original and then renovated stadium (demolished in 2009) were transferable to its successor, seemingly giving the new stadium a head start as it (hopefully) builds its own legacy of greatness.

NOTES

1. Louis I. Kahn, *Louis I. Kahn: Essential Texts,* ed. Robert Twombly (New York: W.W. Norton & Co., 2003), 22.

2. Marshall Smelser, "The Babe on Balance," in *The American Sporting Experience: A Historical Anthology of Sport in America,* ed. Steven Riess (New York: Leisure Press, 1984), 299.

3. Donald Honig, *The New York Yankees: An Illustrated History* (New York: Crown Publishers, 1987).

4. Robert Creamer, *Babe: The Legend Comes to Life* (New York: Simon & Schuster, 1974).

5. Pat Calabria, "Larger Than Life: The World Hasn't Forgotten Babe Ruth," *Los Angeles Times.* http://articles.latimes.com/1992–04-17/sports/sp-566_1_babe-ruth (Last accessed, July 31, 2018).

6. Steven Riess, *City Games: The Evolution of American Urban Society and the Rise of Sports* (Champaign: University of Illinois Press, 1989), 221.

7. *Ibid.,* 257.

8. *Ibid.,* 65.

9. *Ibid.,* 221.

10. Stew Thornley, "Polo Grounds (New York)" Society for American Baseball Research Ballpark Biography Project, sabr.org/bioproj/park/58d80eca, last accessed, July 31, 2018.

11. Michael P. Wagner, *Babe's Place: The Lives of Yankee Stadium* (48HrBooks, USA, 2012), 31.

12. Bruce Kuklick, *To Everything a Season: Shibe Park and Urban Philadelphia, 1909–1976* (Princeton: Princeton University Press, 1991), 193.

# Yankee Stadium as the People's Cathedral

Dashiell Moore

The subject of Yankee Stadium—The House That Ruth Built—has been well covered in academic scholarship, with many historians accounting for the glamour of its construction, its relationship with its eponymous hero, Babe Ruth, and its status as the epitome of New York's "cultural capital." It mirrors, in a way, the manner in which the Yankees have dominated the MLB landscape, and yet, as the years pass, the subject seems to still resonate with us. Its properties are transportative, carrying its attuned historians, sports fans, and media alike into an era of nostalgia where the meteoric rise and change of attitudes in New York can be reflected back.

Yankee Stadium has functioned as a cultural symbol, a catalyst to, and a measure of popular culture. Its construction influenced and disrupted forms of culture outside of baseball, including popular forms of entertainment, sporting events (football, soccer, boxing), religious gatherings, political protests. It also served as a crucible for race relations within sport. Through this multi-faceted analysis, we can come to an understanding of the disparate logics that held the cathedral of baseball together; a motley-crew of symbolic meanings that defy its singular use among the Yankee faithful—predominantly understood as an upper-class, white audience.

By exposing historical accounts of Yankee Stadium's greatness and its hold on the baseball landscape—and in the North American imaginary—we can disrupt how nostalgia might influence our remembrance of Yankee Stadium, redubbing it the House That North America Built.

Just as New York was seen to be the epitome of North America, and yet be entirely different as a cultural symbol than the rest of America itself, so too does the flawed symbolic logic underpinning Yankee Stadium come undone—revealing the contradictory, diverse, and rich history of North America in the 20th century.

Yankee Stadium is typically titled by well-worn monikers, as the House That Ruth built, or the cathedral of baseball, a mythic mirror to the Mecca of Basketball in Madison Square Garden. And, as Philip Lowry writes, it is about as far away from resembling Fenway Park, the home of the Boston Red Sox, as can be—"no one can ever mistake Fenway Park for Yankee Stadium, as they might Busch Stadium for Riverfront."[1] It is said to be the embodiment of the character of New York. The sheer size of the Stadium intoned a sort of New York exceptionalist mentality that flooded into and radically altered the

North American sporting landscape, simultaneously symbolizing a new future for base-ball and North America. As Neil J. Sullivan imagines the moment:

> The Yankees had built the first true baseball *stadium*—a structure intended to accommodate massive crowds and make a progressive and confident statement about baseball's future: Big was good; inti-mate was obsolete; and nostalgia had no warm memories yet to summon.[2]

Yet, as we shall see, the hint of nostalgia would always dominate our knowledge of Yankee Stadium, a cultural necessity that we must investigate. The opening of the Stadium was a spectacle very much in keeping with the people of New York or more accurately, the style, the gesture, the patois, the walk and the talk of the everyday New Yorker. *New York Post* columnist Cindy Adams characterizes the boosterism of New York well in an article on tourism in New York, hinting at the dependency on material wonders such an attitude evokes:

> We are the capital of the world.… We are Attitude City.… We've got it all. If we ain't [sic] got it, you don't need it.… The boonies have Motel 6. We have The Plaza, Pierre, Waldorf, St. Regis, [and] Four Seasons.… They have Main Street. We have Wall Street.[3]

And at the center of it all, the mythic ballpark, the first ballpark in America to be named as a stadium. The means of the Stadium's fictional construction itself is a classic "New York story." As Robert Trumpbour writes, the ballparks built before Yankee Stadium could not seem to match the city's establishment as the center of the universe. Only the stadium could satisfy the masses:

> With the lustre of NY, the ballpark that came before YS was expected to reflect the grandeur of the city. New stadiums were regarded as an index of progress in other cities, but in New York, the sta-dium appeared to be considered an expected part of commercial sport, not a tangible symbol of progress.[4]

Thus, the relationship between New York and Yankee Stadium bears all the hallmarks you might expect. Its meaning to an audience member, to a participant, to a fan, to a punter, to an American citizen is as essential and immaterial as the luster of New York's financial sector itself—up in the air, confined to a set of abstract, ever-changing values. The Stadium is more than the sum of its parts; more than the celebrity of its inhabitants, the scale of its physical architecture or the spectacle on the field. It is not only the "colour of the pinstripes," as it were, but the ambition undergirding the Stadium's physical struc-ture that characterizes the Yankees.

On Opening Day in 1923, Yankee Stadium set a record that seems, even now, unbreakable for baseball, getting 74,200 punters into seats to begin the season; an estimated 10,000 were turned away because of excess capacity. If you are to read an account of the meaning of Yankee Stadium, you will doubtlessly hear the *New York Times* account of that day, an account that will live in public memory for a long time. The headline reads, "74,200 See Yankees Open New Stadium; Ruth Hits Home Run," although mostly what is quoted from the article are the audience's reaction to the sta-dium.

The *Times* article describes: "towers high in the air … a skyscraper among baseball parks" with some fans of the upper deck boasting that they had broken "all altitude records short of those attained in an airplane."[5]

Fittingly, the day's play lived up to the hyperbole—Babe Ruth punished a clutch home-run "well inside the foul pole about eight or ten rows above the low railing in front of the bleachers" to win the game and give Yankee Stadium an inaugural victory.[6] As Sullivan writes, seeing such a spectacle allowed spectators to profess faith in the exceptionalist myths of the American Century:

> The 1920s were a time to find comfort in American fables: a nation secure in splendid isolation; a land of opportunity for all; a place where heroes could rise from the most unlikely settings. Opening Day was a wonderful opportunity to profess this faith.[7]

With so much swell, the high watermark was set that day, and while the surrounding crowd would eventually subside and ebb away, the Stadium would remain.

Such a story enriches many scholarly reports on the Stadium's nostalgic hold on the sporting landscape, assessed almost as if it is a part of "American Dream" fable itself, epitomizing the impossible, fantastical dream of economic, political, and social success at the dawn of the North American century, while equally standing for how far one could fall, the risk of reaching for the stars. The financial strength of the Yankees owes itself to such cultural capital. This is evident now in the Yankees having the highest payroll. To investigate the place of this myth, it is worth scrutinizing how the Stadium's construction affected popular culture, and in turn, how its continual needs of renovation and reconstruction tested New York's needs of a symbol of progress.

As Andrew Gordon Harrington writes in his popular article, "The House That Cultural Capital Built: The Saga of the New Yankee Stadium," the means of the Stadium's construction in South Bronx uprooted several blocks of housing and community centers. Alongside this displacement, Harrington points out quite usefully the contradictions underlying the justifications for the stadium's construction; the argument being that the stadium would create new jobs in the community and enrich the area by having a "luxurious new ballpark in the vicinity of a lower-income neighbourhood." As Harrington alludes, this was an argument that never fleshed out in reality, as the income from the Stadium largely benefited the local treasury, rather than the economy itself.[8]

Further, the people surrounding the ballpark did not directly benefit from the immediate impact of the stadium, as the jobs given to the community were largely seasonal. Harrington sums it up best: "As we will see in the case of the new Yankee Stadium, while many sought to gain from a new sports complex in the Bronx, the people of that borough were an afterthought."[9]

The sizeable gap between the dream of a luxurious ballpark that would give back to the local neighborhood and the ballpark's costly reality extended into future turmoil. In the 1970s, as New York struggled on all fronts in fiscal crisis, the renovation of Yankee Stadium spiraled up to $70 million.

The stadium reopened on April 15, 1976. In the 1990s, and in the burgeoning New York's rent crisis, the Yankee's tenancy in South Bronx again came under review, and by 1993, the Stadium was under threat of being moved to New Jersey as the city claimed that the team owed as much as $6.1 million. While this debt was debated by the Yankees, who claimed that the city owed them $8.7 million "because of the costs of maintaining Yankee Stadium," the debate signals a discrepancy between the stadium's symbolic nostalgia and the needs of the ongoing present.[10]

As the ultimate exclamation point on the debate, a 500-pound steel beam collapsed in 1993 from the roof of the stadium, crushing a seat below. The need for Yankee Stadium's repair could not be clearer. The then New York City Mayor, Rudy Giuliani, attempted to resolve the issue by announcing "tentative deals with the New York Yankees and the New

The original Yankee Stadium lasted 50 years. In 1974 and 1975, the Yankees played their home games at Shea Stadium while the iconic facility was renovated. It reopened on April 15, 1976, and served as the Yankees' home field through 2008. The present incarnation of Yankee Stadium opened the following year (National Baseball Hall of Fame and Museum, Cooperstown, NY).

York Mets to build stadiums for a combined $1.6 billion in the backyards of the teams' current ballparks."[11]

However, in the aftermath of the terrorist attacks on the World Trade Center and the sizeable debts needed for the reconstruction of the city, as well as Giuliani's departure from his position, the Stadium's reconstruction came to a standstill. Renowned for its excess, particularly its luxurious distinction of being the first "stadium" in the MLB landscape, Yankee Stadium remained a quixotic oddity until its demolition in 2008. In the new Yankee Stadium, the luxury and allure of the Yankee's history is still upheld, as Aaron Judge dents a (probably in need of repair) door casement with his 28th home run of the 2017 season. Spectators can buy a "Legends' Seat" at Yankee Stadium for $600 to $6,000 dollars.[12] Looking forward, and in a curious return to the mythology of the Stadium's creation, it will be NYC citizens who will largely pay for the stadium's renovations and reconstructions to come:

The team, which does not expect to pay rent for the land, has asked the city and state for about $300 million in "infrastructure work," including about $160 million for new garages, a ferry terminal on the Harlem River, a Metro-North train station and 16.7 acres of new parkland to replace Macombs Dam Park.[13]

New Yorkers have had to come to terms with the Stadium's dubious place in the mythology of the city, its meaning in popular culture, and the relevance of its symbol in the 21st century. It is within this field that the cultural legacy of the Stadium must be re-evaluated for what it meant in popular culture; its legacy among the punters, in the cheap seats and further back. It is significant that Babe Ruth (the "Bambino") fulfilled the New York people's image of the American Dream, not enamored with fine society or the luxury of the Stadium around him, having come from a working-class section of Baltimore.

Peter Carino posits, "Ruth was not a sophisticate in any sense of the word, he exemplified the dream of the man of simple background to enjoy, for better and worse, what the modern American city, symbolized by the stadium, had to offer."[14] Such characteristics, as well as a phenomenal batting average, helped to capture a public's imagination. Whole swathes of the Stadium's seating were known under his name. As Sullivan romantically enthuses:

> The short porch in right field was designed to take advantage of Ruth's power for the fans' enjoyment, and this feature of the Stadium became one of its most distinctive as the right field stands quickly became known as "Ruthville."[15]

Ruth's significance to the popularity of Yankee Stadium crystallizes a truth of popular culture that disrupts its mystique—king among ballpark—and highlights the more esoteric reality of the Stadium's audience. In these early days, while most New Yorkers could afford the nickel commute to Yankee Stadium, this accessibility made it only the premier location for the upper classes; the admission prices charged for entry alienated the majority of the population. Tickets for the bleachers in 1923 sold for 75 cents, and grandstand tickets sold for $1.10, whereas popular entertainments such as vaudeville shows, where the price of admission was around ten to twenty cents, and in film, where admission to the nickelodeons was a nickel, were considerably cheaper. Such shows were predominantly based around Times Square, a space now well known for its embodiment of the glamour of the city, but could also be found across Manhattan.

The nickelodeon was an indoor exhibition space dedicated to the showing of projected motion pictures, sometimes set up in storefronts or in modestly decorated theatres. Its name came from its five-cent coin cost (a nickel) and its place, the theatre, or music-hall, the "odeon." These event spaces were often to be seen as disreputable, as places of vice where the poor would gather. However, as recent research has shown, the audiences of these "popular forms of entertainment" ranged from its working-class audiences to a middle-class audience throughout the nickelodeon era and well into the decades to follow.[16] Alongside the nickelodeons, other forms of entertainment such as vaudeville, a form of a variety show, were highly popular in this period. The nickelodeon would not run as a cinema might today, running regular shows, but a program that one could enter in and out of at your leisure; for example, one could see a "peep show," where audiences could see a pornographic show through a small hole or magnifying glass that would run sequentially for a few hours or more, after which it would begin again.

In a period when the separation between the rich and poor only grew larger and more entrenched, the vaudeville show and the nickelodeon were two of the most popular types of entertainment in North America among many classes and cultural groups.[17] These forms of entertainment, while being subjected to criticism as a puerile or vulgar outlet for Manhattan's poor, cannot be dismissed when considering the cultural resonance they had on the citizens of Manhattan. The democracy of the peep-show and the vaudeville act were scenes for the people, a great leveler of people in which to converse, gather, and "get off." In comparison, Yankee Stadium was a spectacle almost purely for those who could afford it, a physical structure for the economic elites to advertise, display and produce wealth, a selectivity that revealed the centrality of wealth in New York; Yankee Stadium couldn't have been built without it. In considering the costs of reconstruction, the prices of admission, as well as its contrast to other popular forms of entertainment, it is possible to see that Yankee Stadium was a contradictory symbol of a national pastime just as New York's skyline, or the Statue of Liberty, could stand for America, and yet be immediately representative of New York.

The meaning of the Stadium in popular culture also owes to its spread across multiple sports, not simply baseball, and to its being the center of numerous historical events that led to the formation of the so-called "New York State of Mind." While its eponymous forerunner, Ruth, will probably retain the title of Yankee Stadium's man far after the end of this article, it is worth enumerating the significance of many sporting and cultural events taking place in the Stadium that depart from baseball tradition.

Often in this context, Madison Square Garden is a more popular choice considering its multi-purpose stature as "the greatest arena on earth" and being the venue for any number of sporting and cultural events such as boxing, hockey, basketball, concerts, ice shows, professional wrestling, etc. Indeed, while the modern "Garden" opened its doors on February 11, 1968, there were three predecessors in 1879–1890, 1890–1925, and 1925–1968, respectively. The second was in use around the time that Yankee Stadium was thought of and first attended. But the fact that Yankee Stadium was not built for any of these events, but still supported and put them on says something of its ever-changing purpose and function as a cultural symbol.

One humid night in June 22, 1938, Joe Louis defended his heavyweight title with a first-round knockout of German boxer Max Schmeling in Yankee Stadium, immediately following Adolf Hitler's annexation of Austria. The fight's significance in history is well understood—built up as a contest between representatives of not only North America and Germany, or democracy and fascism, but also the Caucasian and African American peoples themselves. As Schmeling was heralded by Nazi propaganda efforts, the fight drew a symbolic resonance amongst the peoples of New York, alienating Schmeling and the cause he represented. Famously, a few weeks before the fight, Louis came to the White House to visit President Franklin Roosevelt, who, according to the *New York Times*, said: "Joe, we need muscles like yours to beat Germany."[18] As the Rev. Jesse Jackson remembers:

> Hitler was killing people and declaring superiority…. And he had put forth his pure specimen, Max Schmeling, who said he did not mean to be that, but the fact is he became that symbol…. And when he put forth his Philistinian giant, in a sense, he said to America and the Western world: "You put forth someone more superior. We have a superior race." It was bigger than athletics. Bigger than politics, really. Politics with a capital "P."[19]

Within the crucible of Yankee Stadium, the scale of the fight became legend—one can imagine the scale of the event as it crosses political and geographical boundaries. Fifteen years from the Stadium's opening, here was Nazi Germany and the United States at war in America's most iconic stadium. Reportedly, according to the *New York Times*'s figures, 70,043 people jammed in to watch the fight, while many more heard the fight broadcast on radio. The vitriol in the American media against Schmeling might have taken a toll—Schmeling threw just two punches in the fight. The Stadium's prestige as a national American landmark increased with the Louis-Schmeling bout—it became a place for American citizens to gather and unite in their hatred of an enemy. This was particularly emphatic for groups within the largely monotheistic population at Yankee Stadium, such as the African-American population around the Bronx. Other famous fights at the stadium include Muhammad Ali's dubious victory over Ken Norton on September 28, 1976. More recently, after 34 years of absence, a boxing match was put on between Yuri Foreman and Miguel Cotto in the New Yankee Stadium on June 5, 2010.

The history of football is also linked to the Stadium's prestige. Some of the more memorable collegiate and professional football games date back to 1923, the début year, when Yankee Stadium hosted its first football game played and became the fixture of the annual Army-Navy game. The use of Yankee Stadium to uphold these militant traditions underpins its relationship with North American normativity—a stronghold guarding the image of a nation.

Five years later, the phrase "win this one for the Gipper" became popular after George "The Gipper" Gipp died of a streptococcal throat infection at 25, five days after leading Notre Dame to a win over Northwestern. Reportedly visited on his hospital bed by Coach Knute Rockne on November 10, 1928, "The Gipper" provided the motivation for the Irish to win 12–6.[20] The phrase later entered the national arena when Ronald Reagan portrayed Gipp in the film, *Knute Rockne, All American* (1940). From this point, the term, "the Gipper" became synonymous with Reagan and the Republican campaign. Famously, at the Republican National Convention in 1988, Reagan told Vice-President Bush to "go out there and win one for the Gipper."[21]

The history of football is immutably linked to the luster of Yankee Stadium, the location of various, ubiquitously known phrases that conjure up the memorable games played. Yankee Stadium was the birthplace of well-chronicled moments in football such as "the tackle," a game-saving effort by John Lujack's in the historic 0–0 tie between Notre Dame and Army in November 9, 1946, "the kick," a 49-yard field goal made by Pat Summerall in a swirling snowstorm to give the NY Giants the playoff edge over the Cleveland Browns, and "the greatest game ever played," the 1958 NFL Championship Game, an overtime game that introduced the television age in American sport. The Stadium played host to some of the more bizarre conditions that football has ever been played in—"on ice" for instance, referring to the 1956 NFL Championship where the Giants defeated the Chicago Bears on an icy field, and "in which the Giants wore sneakers instead of cleats, shades of 22 years earlier when the Giants also wore sneakers to play on an icy Polo Grounds gridiron in what became known as 'The Sneakers Game.'"[22] The final football game played at the Old Yankee Stadium was on September 12, 1987, when Central State University of Ohio defeated Grambling in a Whitney Young Urban League classic. The game was a blowout.[23]

With the establishment of Harlem's black professional baseball team, the Lincoln Giants in 1911 playing at Olympic Field at 136th Street and Fifth Avenue, the question of race in baseball began to gain traction in conversations around Manhattan. Yankee Stadium was invested in such a question, being the ballpark where a number of African-American baseball teams began to play in the late 1920s. This was at a time when not many other major ballparks were offering such opportunities. On days when an African American player or team was playing at the stadium, it is reported that crowds of several thousands of African-American baseball fans would attend the games, claiming "temporarily, spaces within the city for blacks."[24]

The forging of a cultural space amidst Manhattan is a fecund direction for future study, particularly when thinking of the modern ballpark. The sports editor of the *New York Age* wrote in 1920 that a parade of automobiles followed the African-American Bacharach Giants, from Harlem to Dyckman Oval, "filling the streets around the stadium with vehicles driven by blacks." While such writing can be read with a grain of salt, for doubtlessly, the readers of the *New York Age* would not read such a statement and think of inclusivity, the writing resounds of a shock tactic designed to evoke fear in Manhattan's middle-class that the "blacks of Harlem were taking their ballpark from them."

Such an interest in the game among African-American communities capitulated in 1930, as the Yankees owner, Jacob Ruppert, allowed the Lincoln Giants to play the first game between black teams at Yankee Stadium, in a "benefit for the Brotherhood of Sleeping Car Porters that drew a crowd of around 20,000."[25] This moment would set the tone for the Negro Leagues to come that played throughout the 1930s, during World War II and for some time after, whereupon Negro League teams would play at the stadium in the Yankees' absence. That day in 1930, John Henry Lloyd, affectionately referred to as Pop, went four-for-eight stole a base, and was credited for playing errorless defense. In 2011, baseball historian Lawrence D. Hogan analyzed Lloyd's achievements in the *New York Times*:

> Lloyd was elected to the Baseball Hall of Fame by the Negro leagues committee in 1977. His plaque in Cooperstown recognized that he was "instrumental in helping open Yankee Stadium to Negro baseball in 1930." It essentially became the House That Ruth Built and Pop Opened. The Yankees, who take wonderful care of baseball's significant historical record, included a temporary Negro leagues exhibit in their museum when their new Stadium opened in April 2009. But this remarkable part of the original Stadium's history is not permanently commemorated.[26]

For a team renowned for opening their stadium to the Negro Leagues, the Yankees refused to have an African-American player on its roster for the first 52 years of its existence, a stretch of time longer than every Major League Baseball team, with the exception of the Tigers, the Phillies, and the Red Sox.

In 1946, the MLB set up a "steering committee" chaired by its owners following the infamous signing of Jackie Robinson in 1945. The steering committee reasoned together that "the preponderance of Negro attendance in parks such as Yankee Stadium, the Polo Grounds, and Comiskey Park could conceivably threaten the value of the major league franchises owned by these clubs."

This finding was in spite of the fact that the Yankee organization took $100,000 a year from renting their space to the Negro Leagues and from the concessions in connection with Negro League games at Yankee Stadium.[27] Putting aside the economic surplus that the Yankees enjoyed, a surplus that allowed them to reinforce their reputation as the marquee baseball franchise in North America, we can only wonder (and yet implicitly know) what "value" the steering committee had in mind.

Perhaps the real impetus behind such a statement is more understandable in the context of then General Manager George Weiss's comments on the debate. In defense of his upper-class supporters, Weiss was reported to have said: "I will never allow a black man to wear a Yankee uniform. Box-holders from Westchester don't want that sort of crowd. They would be offended to have to sit with niggers."[28]

The public defamations of African-American players like Vic Power (accused of "dating white women," that he was "unintelligent" and "hadn't hustled in the minors"), and Jackie Robinson ("With the *exception* of Jackie Robinson we have been interested in just about every Negro player who has come up to the majors") only further tarnish the progress made by the Yankees to use Yankee Stadium as a place for all Americans to enjoy the national game.[29] But what does such a contested cultural meaning illuminate to us as we consider Yankee Stadium's place in popular culture?

Thirty one years after the owners' "steering committee" judged that Negro attendance in Yankee Stadium would tarnish the Yankee's reputation, the cathedral of baseball was privy to another whirlwind of interracial relations in New York City. In Game Two of the 1977 World Series at Yankee Stadium, the proximity to the ravaged areas of the South Bronx called the media's attention to the world outside of baseball. Recurringly throughout the game, as ABC cameras cut to a helicopter shot of the surrounding neighborhood that seemingly depicted a large fire burning out of control in Public School 3, announcers Howard Cosell and Keith Jackson described the sight as a building fire in an "abandoned apartment building." As retired Bronx firefighter Tom Henderson remembers in an interview with the *New York Post* commemorating the event, "The smell is one thing I remember.... That smell of burning—it was always there, through the whole borough almost."[30]

Their comments led to the now ubiquitous phrase "Ladies and Gentlemen, the Bronx is burning," a phrasing spun on the *Man Alive* documentary series released in 1972 entitled "The Bronx is Burning," an hour-long episode featuring the impact of austerity measures on the fire services in the Bronx.[31] Three decades later, the phrase would inspire the title of Jonathan Mahler's non-fiction chronicle of 1977, *Ladies and Gentlemen, the Bronx is Burning* (2005), a layered account of several narrative threads surveyed the fiscal and spiritual crisis of New York in the mid–1970s. The phrase helped to solidify Yankee Stadium as a vantage point to witness the destruction of the real and imagined New York.

With that said, not all of the Bronx was burning. Yankee Stadium remained safe, although the smoke probably got in the lungs of those travelling to and from the game. The phrase is now a metaphorical one, calling up the year of 1977 in the Big Apple's memory, a year infamous for the serial murders by the "Son of Sam" (David Berkowitz), a city-wide 20-hour blackout that led to major looting and the largest mass arrest in New York City's history, widespread purse snatching—crises that were partly caused by the fiscal crisis overwhelming the city. It was in this time that Yankee Stadium's reconstruction was finally completed after multiple years of costly building, with the eventual cost of the reconstruction totaling more than $70 million. It was, once again, the city that paid the bill.

From this standpoint, the World Series coverage influenced the cultural meaning of the Stadium once more. As we witness the fires burning out of control in the Bronx, the heartland of Yankee Stadium and yet now the place hit hardest by austerity measures, we are able to see the watermark of 1923 shining brilliantly—a capitalist dream that was finally grounded. It was clear, through the smoke, to see that the Stadium had returned to face the means of its creation, a violent gutting of the surrounding neighborhoods to make room for the supreme artifice of the American pastime.

The multitude of truths, frailties, and outlets of the American Dream conjured up in Yankee Stadium's construction is stretched further considering its extra-curricular purposes, that is, its life aside from baseball and sport overall. It is no small thing when considering the significance of Yankee Stadium in popular culture that the single-biggest record for attendance at baseball's cathedral is not for a sporting event. Each year from the 1950s until the late 1980s, a Jehovah's Witnesses Convention has taken place at the stadium, attracting as many as 123,707 people in a single day in 1958. These weren't Yankees fans hoping to see Mickey Mantle or Yogi Berra, but there to attend a yearly Divine

Will International Assembly, which was split between Yankee Stadium and the nearby Polo Grounds in Manhattan.

This was a day that almost doubled the number of punters that paid the 75-cent entrance fee marking the Stadium's Opening Day in 1923. Infamously, as the Stadium's capacity stretched thin to the point of breaking, ladies were asked to remove their heels, people were brought to sit in the outfield, and a temporary camp was set up with a broadcast to listen to for the uncounted masses outside the venue. There is a historical plaque commemorating the feat today, inscribed in the sidewalk outside the modern Yankee Stadium.[32] By having such a high-profile place of worship, the Jehovah's Witnesses attendees were able to promote the growth of their religion in a national sphere. Within this mass event, there would have been innumerable conversations regarding the religion's practice, song and prayer, family life, politics, and an opportunity to see the power of religion. Such a sentence could probably also describe the conversations echoing around a baseball game. In a 1990 article regarding the most recent Jehovah's Convention at Old Yankee Stadium, Donatella Lorch writes:

> Clutching umbrellas and fans and hiding from the sun under tarpaulins, tens of thousands of people at Yankee Stadium yesterday watched Jehu and Jezebel fight a war of biblical proportions. When Jezebel was pushed in pantomime to her death, the crowd broke into enthusiastic applause. In the stands, Nancy Kennedy, who had her three children in tow, said, "I come here to get revitalized."[33]

The battle of titans was watched by a surrounding, utterly transfixed, enthusiastic crowd— the convening of Jehovah's Witnesses are not so far from the moment of Joe Louis's knockout of Max Schmeling a decade previous. The people attending the Jehovah's Witnesses convention, and particularly those living in the Bronx around the Stadium, would doubtlessly remember that a year earlier, the famous television evangelist Billy Graham played host to a crowd of 100,000 in a nationally-televised event at the Stadium, part of his week-long crusade in New York City, a feat that was proclaimed by the *New York Times* as "the largest crowd in Stadium history," and remaining so for another twelve months.[34] It is significant that Graham's feats were divided between Yankee Stadium and MSG, two cathedrals of cultural and sporting significance in Manhattan, each resonant and enriched in the history of a North American pastime. Each would exist outside of the evangelical movement, and yet be forever marked by the gathering of more than 200,000 people over the course of a week. The relationship between the National Pastime and a national religion was never clearer, as when the premonitions of baseball's first church were proven correct in 1957–1958. In the years to come, Yankee Stadium would play host to the first visit by a Catholic Pope in the history of the United States. In 1965, Pope Paul VI gave mass before a crowd that exceeded 80,000. In 1979, the Stadium received Pope John Paul II.

The relationship of New York's baseball cathedral to the dominant attitudes and perceptions in popular culture cannot be understated, as a location where conversations could take place that debated the mundane, the everyday, but also important issues affecting the New York citizen, such as religion or politics. Such an ideological reach extended into the Yankee's club-house in the post-war period, when the Yankees were becoming synonymous with the upper-class, the Establishment. The controversial memoirs of ex-Yankee pitcher Jim Bouton are instrumental when considering this relationship. Often a text known and read for the illuminating information Bouton chose to reveal about Mickey Mantle, Bouton also puts forward a valuable counter-cultural viewpoint on the

Yankees. Specifically relevant to the way religiosity was constructed in baseball's cathedral, Bouton makes an allusion in his book, *Ball Four,* to the way in which a locker-room culture was established within Yankee Stadium that was built upon an esoteric, archconservative bastion of past generations. For an example of this, a road trip back to New York City gives Bouton a moment to write:

> There is always a flood of memories when I come back to New York. Like all the trouble I used to get into with the Yankees. One time nobody in the bullpen would talk to me for three days because I said I thought Billy Graham was a dangerous character. This was after he had said that Communists were behind the riots in the black ghettoes.... My heavens, you'd think I had insulted Ronald Reagan.[35]

While the autobiographical account of Bouton may be seen as immaterial given the politically conservative nature of Major League Baseball, the contexts of his departure from the Yankees, and the vitriolic tone of his memoir—cited by William C. Bishop as "pathological if not for his wry humour on the subject"—Bouton nonetheless provides an insight into the construction of Yankee folklore as it was related to socio-political issues, such as the relationship of the Stadium to the evangelical movement. Less than 12 years after the stadium's attendance records were shattered by Graham and the evangelical movement in America, it is not surprising that such a sentiment existed.

To get a sense of the metaphorical implications of the union between church and ballpark, consider the relationship of a fan to the game, or a worshipper to the church. The game is embossed in ritual, a certain sound, a certain smell, and a sense of the divine—with fans often poring over the hymnal sheet, filled with stats that record their favorite player's feats the week before. This fact was never more clear than at the cathedral of baseball, decked out with the Hammond Organ installed in 1967 and played by Eddie Layton from its introduction until his retirement after the 2003 season. The paraphernalia of faith were exerted in both baseball and the church. This can also be thought of in terms of the familial, geographical, socio-political ties of respective worshippers. As Doris Kearns Goodwin describes the importance of a "tradition" among baseball fans in the post-war New York metropolitan area, "team affiliation was passed on from father to child, with the crucial moments in a team's history repeated like the liturgy of a church service."[36]

The Stadium has also enjoyed being the center of music culture, hosting a great many concerts and other cultural events. It was first used as a concert space in 1969, almost two decades after its usage as a religious gathering place, when an ensemble R&B show was put together by the Isley Brothers. The live album created from the concert, *Live at Yankee Stadium,* showcases a range of musical acts on that night, featuring Judy White, the girl group Sweet Cherries, the gospel group the Edwin Hawkers Singers, and the soul group the Five Stairsteps, along with many of the audience members who were brought up on stage.[37]

In another famous performance at Yankee Stadium, the U2 gig in 1992, Bono sang a famous lyric that mentions Joe DiMaggio and Marilyn Monroe. It reiterated the multifaceted nature of the stadium as a public space and showed that Bono was attuned to the cultural production of America's cathedral. This helps to glean for us its resonance across cultural borders. While functioning as a reflective metropolitan space in each of its uses, it still brimmed with the nostalgia of its past, speaking in steel beams of the grandeur of its making, the celebrity of its audience, and the cultural revenue of the. Such a statement also brings to light the fact that despite its cultural activities, Yankee Stadium still reflects the men who brought it together, of Ruth and his bat, John Henry Lloyd, George Weiss, Billy Graham, and Bono. The inherent multiplicity underlying such a motley crew of people speaks to the nuance of the Stadium's cultural prestige, as something more than a ballpark and representing the evolution of New York and its people.

NOTES

1. Philip Lowry, *Green Cathedrals* (Reading, MA: Addison Wesley, 1992), 11.
2. Neil J. Sullivan, *The Diamond in the Bronx: Yankee Stadium and the Politics of New York* (Oxford: Oxford University Press, 2001), 1–2. Emphasis in original.
3. Cindy Adams, "How Can Those Tourists Squawk About Noo Yawk?" *New York Post*, July 8, 2001: 12.
4. Robert Trumpbour, "The New Cathedrals: The Sports Stadiums and Mass Media's Role in Facilitating New Construction," Ph.D. diss., The Pennsylvania State University, 2001, 314.
5. "74,200 See Yankees Open New Stadium; Ruth Hits Home Run," *New York Times*, April 19, 1923: 1, 15.
6. *Ibid.*, 15.
7. Sullivan, 2.
8. Andrew Gordon Harrington, "The House That Cultural Capital Built: The Sage of the New Yankee Stadium," *NINE: A Journal of Baseball History and Culture*, 19.2 (Spring, 2011), 80.
9. Harrington, "The House That Cultural Capital Built: The Sage of the New Yankee Stadium," 80.
10. Richard Sandomir, "Made-for-TV Mystery: What, If Anything, Do Yanks Owe the City," *New York Times*, June 13, 1993: 6.
11. Jennifer Steinhauer and Richard Sandomir, "In Bottom of 9th, Guiliani Presents Deal on Stadiums," *New York Times*, December 29, 2001: A1.
12. Brenden Monroe, "Life of Luxury: An Inside Look at Yankee Stadium's Legend Seats," Bleacher Report, July 18, 2009, bleacherreport.com/articles/219857-life-of-luxury-an-inside-look-at-yankee-stadiums-legend-sea, last accessed August 4, 2017.
13. Charles V. Bagli, "What the Teams Want and What the City Gets," *New York Times*, January 16, 2005: 1.
14. Peter Carino, "Reciprocal Grandeur: Babe Ruth and Yankee Stadium," *NINE: A Journal of Baseball History and Culture*, 3.1 (Fall, 2004), 54.
15. Sullivan, 9.
16. Ben Singer, "Manhattan Nickelodeons: New Data on Audiences and Exhibitors," *Cinema Journal* 34.3 (Spring, 1995): 5–35.
17. For further insight into popular forms of entertainment in this period, see Trav S.D., *No Applause—Just Throw Money: The Book That Made Vaudeville Famous* (New York: Faber & Faber, 2006).
18. Joe Lapointe, "The Championship Fight That Went Beyond Boxing," *New York Times*, June 19, 1988, www.nytimes.com/1988/06/19/sports/the-championship-fight-that-went-beyond-boxing.html, last accessed August 26, 2018.
19. *Ibid.*
20. "History of Football at Yankee Stadium," *The New York Yankees*, newyork.yankees.mlb.com/nyy/history/football_history.jsp, modified 2017, last accessed August 15, 2017.
21. James Gerstenzang, "Reagan delivers 'last hurrah' to GOP". Los Angeles Times, August 16, 1988.
22. *Ibid.*
23. *Ibid.*
24. Stephen Robertson, "Harlem and Baseball in the 1920s," *Digital Harlem Blog*, digitalharlemblog.wordpress.com/2011/07/27/baseball-1920s-harlem/, July 27, 2011, last accessed August 14, 2017.
25. *Ibid.*
26. Lawrence D. Hogan, "The Negro Leagues Discovered an Oasis at Yankee Stadium," *New York Times*, February 12, 2011, www.nytimes.com/2011/02/13/sports/baseball/13stadium.html, last accessed August 14, 2017.
27. "Report of Major League Steering Committee for Submission to the National and American Leagues at Their Meetings in Chicago," in *The Jackie Robinson Reader: Perspectives on an American Hero*, ed. Jules Tygiel (New York: Dutton, 1997), 129–133. The report is dated August 27, 1946. It is reprinted in the chapter titled "The Race Question."
28. Burton A. Boxerman and Benita W. Boxerman, *George Weiss: Architect of the Golden Age Yankees* (Jefferson, NC: McFarland and Company, 2016), 122.
29. Steven Goldman, "On Jackie Robinson Day, the Yankees Must Answer for Jim Crow Baseball," SB Nation, *Pinstripe Alley*, April 15, 2013, www.pinstripealley.com/2013/4/15/4228172/jackie-robinson-day-new-york-yankees-vic-power-elston-howard, last accessed August 14, 2017.
30. Joe Flood, "Why the Bronx Burned," *New York Post*, May 16, 2010, nypost.com/2010/05/16/why-the-bronx-burned/, last accessed August 11, 2017.

31. *Man Alive*, "The Bronx Is Burning," BBC, 1972, www.bfi.org.uk/films-tv-people/4ce2b6d212415, last accessed August 14, 2017. Jeremy James was the narrator for this episode.

32. "Yankee Stadium History, New York Yankees," *The New York Yankees*, newyork.yankees.mlb.com/nyy/ballpark/stadium_history.jsp, modified 2017, last accessed August 14, 2017.

33. Donatella Lorch, "Jehovah's Word at Yankee Stadium," *New York Times*, July 23, 1990: B2; www.nytimes.com/1990/07/23/nyregion/jehovah-s-word-at-yankee-stadium.html, last accessed August 15, 2017.

34. George Dugan, "100,000 Fill Yankee Stadium to Hear Graham," *New York Times*, July 21, 1957: 1; www.nytimes.com/books/97/07/06/reviews/graham-yankee.html, last accessed August 14, 2017.

35. Jim Bouton, ed. Leonard Shecter, *Ball Four* (New York: Simon & Schuster, 1970), 214.

36. Doris Kearns Goodwin, *Wait Till Next Year* (New York: Touchstone Books, 1997), 61.

37. *The Isley Brothers: Live at Yankee Stadium*, T-Neck Records, October 18, 1969. The album is a recording of the June 21, 1969 concert. Author's description based on observation of film of the concert. A film of the concert is in the Motion Picture Collection, UCLA Film & Television Archive: *It's Your Thing*, Isley Brothers and Medford Film Corp., produced by Ronald Rudolph, directed by Mike Gargiulo, 1970, Inventory Number VA20475M, VHS; Inventory Number M17160, 35 mm. safety print; Inventory Number M69539, ¾ inch tapes (two videocassettes).

# Mystique and Aura in the Zeitgeist

RICHARD PIORECK

A Paul Simon lyric reminds us that every generation has its heroes. Beginning with Babe Ruth, every generation of Yankee fans has thrown heroes up the pop charts: Lou Gehrig, Joe DiMaggio, Yogi Berra, Whitey Ford, Mickey Mantle, Thurman Munson, Reggie Jackson, Don Mattingly, Derek Jeter, and Aaron Judge. For almost 100 years, the mystique and aura surrounding the New York Yankees have made the team the most popular—and most hated baseball team in the United States,[1] valued at $2 billion, second among team sports only to the Dallas Cowboys.[2] General Manager Brian Cashman declared, "The one thing the Yankees have always stood for, and do stand for, is the effort to try to become a superteam."[3]

This attitude about team success contributes to the Yankees' place in popular culture. The New York Yankees possess significance beyond baseball, firmly established in the cultural zeitgeist. As Birdie Tebbetts observed, "The myth is that you put a Yankee uniform on a player and he becomes great."[4] The myth of mystique and aura often is greater than the play on the field, despite Curt Schilling's denial during the 2004 playoffs.[5]

Yankee paraphernalia is seen throughout the country—caps, shirts, jackets, and license plates. Yankee caps are overwhelmingly preferred by the suspects arrested in New York City, as well the variously colored caps being the favorites of the Bloods, Crips and Latin Kings.[6]

While many people are responsible for creating—and adding to—the Yankees' place in popular culture, six men have played an inordinately large part in carrying it: Babe Ruth, Joe DiMaggio, Yogi Berra, Mickey Mantle, Derek Jeter, and George Steinbrenner. Their actions can be found in more than one area.

Babe Ruth was seminal in building the Yankee brand; others advanced and expanded it. In 1933, Lou Gehrig became the first athlete featured on a Wheaties box endorsing the Breakfast of Champions. Joe DiMaggio was the second Yankee endorser for the cereal giant, followed by more than a dozen others, including Lefty Gomez, Bill Dickey, Phil Rizzuto, Yogi Berra, Mickey Mantle, Bobby Richardson, Tom Tresh, Dave Winfield, Bernie Williams, Tino Martinez, Mike Mussina, and Derek Jeter. Even Ruth graced the Wheaties box in 1992, 44 years after his death.[7]

While many myths about the Yankees feature Babe Ruth, from curing Little Johnny Sylvester by hitting a promised home run to calling his shot during the 1932 World Series to the latest myth of a Ruth autographed baseball placed in the cornerstone of Bloomingdale's flagship store in New York,[8] not every myth is Ruth-centered.

Take the myth of Fidel Castro's major-league tryout with the Yankees. While it never happened, if Castro was offered a tryout, it was more likely to be with the Washington Senators or the New York Giants. But Fidel liked the myth and never dispelled it because only the Yankees of the great DiMaggio were good enough for Cuba's leader to play for.[9]

Besides the playing field and the sports pages, the Yankees have dominated popular culture in all forms: vaudeville, movies, radio, popular music, theater, advertising, television, books, and fashion since the (New York) *Daily News* assigned a photographer to cover Ruth every day of the year.[10] Beginning with vaudeville, the nation's then popular entertainment, Ruth was already a cultural phenomenon by 1922 when Ring Lardner's *The Bullpen* starring Will Rogers débuted in *The Ziegfeld Follies* at the Ambassador Theater in New York.

He certainly had hero credentials. Towns had Babe Ruth's appearance stipulated in the contracts with the Yankees on their pre-season barnstorming tours. Banks and stores closed at game time. Newspapers ran the syndicated column "What Babe Ruth Did Today" to satisfy the public's hunger for information about the most popular man of his day.[11] Hall of Fame sportswriter Fred Lieb reports that once Ruth was stopped for going the wrong way on a one-way street. Instead of rebuking or ticketing Ruth, the officer said, "Oh, it's you, Mr. Babe," and with the lights and siren on, led Ruth safely to an intersection.[12]

Perhaps the pinnacle of cultural aura and mystique for Ruth lies in the story of the 1926 World Series, Johnny Sylvester, and the belief of the slugger's curative powers and ability to perform heroic deeds. It began at the Essex Fells, New Jersey, estate of Sylvester's father, Horace C. Sylvester, a vice president of National City Bank. While horseback riding, Johnny was kicked in the head when he fell from his horse. By the time Horace vowed to fulfill Johnny's last request for a baseball autographed by Ruth, most accounts gave Johnny only 30 minutes to live. The Sylvesters sent telegrams to the Yankees in St. Louis. An airmail package contained two balls, one autographed by the Cardinal team and the other with the signatures of several Yankees and a special message from Ruth: "I'll knock a homer for you on Wednesday."[13]

Ruth hit three home runs in Game 4 of the 1926 World Series, and if those three home runs did not cure Johnny Sylvester, they did no harm. Johnny lived and spent the next 60 years telling people what Ruth did for him until his death at 74.[14]

Since Babe Ruth joined the Yankees in 1920, they have had a national fan base like no other team, particularly because other fans are focused against them: "I imagine rooting for the Yankees is like owning a yacht"[15]; or they expect the Yankees to win: "Rooting for the Yankees is like rooting for U.S. Steel."[16] Hall of Fame Yankee owner, Jacob Ruppert, who ensured that Ruth would become a Yankee, described the perfect afternoon at Yankee Stadium as "…when the Yankees score eight runs in the first inning, and then slowly pull away."[17]

According to cultural icon Lisa Simpson, "Symbols can cause strong emotions, symbols like the swastika or the New York Yankees emblem."[18] Chicago newspaper columnist Mike Royko explained, "Hating the Yankees is as American as pizza pie, unwed mothers, and cheating on your income tax."[19] Charging Japanese troops in World War II shouted, "To hell with Babe Ruth!" to insult and bring shame to America's most popular figure and icon who, in their eyes, was equal to the Japanese emperor.

As in real estate sales, "location, location, location" is related to the Yankees' importance. In the late 1910s and early 1920s, a name change from the Highlanders to the Yankees, and a move to an eponymously named stadium out of the shadow of the Giants at the Polo Grounds, henceforth known without ado as "the Stadium," put the Yankees on the cultural map, especially as Yankee Stadium was tied to its iconic Bunyanesque star Babe Ruth as "The House That Ruth Built."

The "greatest drawing card in history of baseball," according to his Hall of Fame plaque, joined the team about the time that the Jazz Age begins. The glamour and glitz that fashioned New York in the twenties had the same pizzazz Ruth had. The October 21 issue of *Baseball Magazine* declared him a national idol.[20] Designating someone or something the "New York Yankees of ___" or "Babe Ruth of ___" became the oft-used superlative and the gold standard for success, fostered by the Yankees penchant for winning multiple championships. In John Sayles's film *Eight Men Out* in 1988, Al Austrian, Charles Comiskey's lawyer, introduces the legal team representing the Black Sox, calling the lawyers "the Ty Cobb, Tris Speaker and Zack Wheat of the legal profession." When Buck Weaver asks which one is the Babe Ruth of the legal profession, Austrian replies that he is.[21]

The Yankees served as the definition of the worthy adversary, the cultural opponent against which all underdogs are measured. Between 1921 and 1943, the Yankees appeared in 14 World Series, winning 10 of them, becoming the very standard of champions while winning an additional 17 World Series out of 26 since 1947, not counting playoff berths that did not lead to winning the pennant.

In his 15 years with the Yankees, Ruth established the team's iconic brand. Whether hitting "Ruthian" home runs, or catching a baseball dropped from an airplane at nearby Mitchell Field on Long Island,[22] "[H]e was entertaining, he was fun. He filled the room when he came into it."[23] Boys and men followed in the street everywhere he went just to be near the Babe.[24] His teammates liked him, too. As Waite Hoyt said, "God, we loved that big son of a bitch."[25] New York sportswriter Jimmy Cannon observed, "He was a parade all by himself, a burst of dazzle and jingle."[26]

Ruth's popularity was such that he could make $1,500 to $2,000 for each post-season barnstorming game. After the first Subway Series in 1921 was won by the Giants—actually, the entire Series was played in the Polo Grounds—Ruth went barnstorming, as he did after most seasons.[27]

Unfortunately for Ruth, the owners had a rule against members of World Series teams barnstorming, feeling it would diminish the value of baseball's premiere event.[28] Commissioner Landis vigorously enforced the anti-barnstorming rule because he said that a rule is a rule, but some thought Landis did so more because of racial prejudice— he did not want a black team to beat major-league players from the season's best teams.[29] Babe Ruth disagreed with the rule and barnstormed anyway, explaining that he had been poorly advised about the confrontation that led to the clash with the new commissioner over the barnstorming rule. This led to Ruth's first vaudeville tour.[30]

It was only natural for Babe Ruth to step into the spotlight on the vaudeville stage, the prevailing entertainment of its time. That the man for whom songs were written should take to singing songs was logical—for Ruth was a combination of Blondel to his own Richard the Lionhearted.[31] Ruth had a "really fine baritone voice."[32]

Faced with forfeiting the barnstorming money as well as being fined the amount of his 1921 World Series share, and also facing suspension for the 1922 season—another part of the fallout from the clash with Landis—Babe Ruth signed to play the B.F. Keith vaudeville circuit for 20 weeks. Ruth was not the first ball player to play vaudeville, but he was the first one signed to "hit home run laughs" for $3,000 a week.[33] Ruth was not unfamiliar with performing outside the ballpark. Marshall Hunt of the *Daily News*, said that he often performed with Ruth at charity shows in Palm Beach during spring training.[34]

The producers were eager and enthusiastic about Ruth's performing, and were looking for the best way to advertise him. As they were trying to decide on Ruth's billing, one of the producers' friends cabled George Bernard Shaw—who, besides being a playwright and a critic, was regarded as a boxing expert and, thus, knowledgeable about sports—with the question, "Would it be quite proper to bill Babe Ruth as the superman of baseball?" Shaw's immediate reply was, "Sorry never heard of her. Whose baby is Ruth?"[35] The front-page story about Shaw's ignorance of Babe Ruth generated free publicity for Ruth's vaudeville début.

This occurred at the Proctor Theatre in Mount Vernon, New York on November 3, 1921, at the beginning of a 16-week tour. Billed as "the King of Swat," Ruth was teamed with veteran vaudevillian Wellington Cross in the sketch "That's Good: A Satirical Home Run." Armed with his easy way with the public and his "really fine baritone voice," Ruth sang a song written for the show: "Little by Little and Bit by Bit, I Am Making a Vaudeville Hit!"[36]

According to the *New York Times*,

> The act [was] … chiefly jocose patter … and the Babe, concealing any new nervousness that may have affected him, held up his end very well, indeed…. He got the jests and jibes over well, too, the chief outburst occuring [sic] when, after the Babe had received a stage telegram from Judge Landis and had been asked by Cross, "Is it serious?" Ruth answered, "Should say it is: 75 cents collect."[37]

Opening Night in Mount Vernon was a success even before Ruth performed. The crowd broke into spontaneous applause when he appeared. Ruth proved to be a trouper from the start, for "despite a cold the slugger unblanketed a not unpleasant baritone voice."[38]

Ruth and Cross next played Boston on November 7th, and less than two weeks after opening at Proctor's Theater in Mount Vernon, Ruth made his New York début at the Palace Theatre—a record for getting to play the Palace.[39]

Ruth "packed the Palace like he did the Polo Grounds during the baseball season…. His first appearance on the stage evoked applause that went on continuously for more than a minute while Ruth bowed back his thanks time and again."[40] According to the *New York Times* reviewer, Ruth was not a polished performer, but he was better by far than other baseball stars who had played vaudeville. As a matter of fact, "Ruth has good stage presence, a winning smile and he gets away with the singing part."[41]

That was not the only example of Ruth's stage presence. At one Palace performance, Ruth was singing his solo when his Yankee teammates watching the show from down front frantically waved at him. Ruth waved back and edged toward the footlights to share his "really fine baritone voice" with the audience. Someone in the front row began laughing. Then the nudging began, and soon the laughter spread throughout the audience, gathering volume and gusto. Babe finished "Little by Little and Bit by Bit, I Am Making a Vaudeville Hit!" and backed into the wings to rollicking applause, only to find that his trouser fly was completely unbuttoned.[42]

Overall, the vaudeville tour was much more successful than the barnstorming tour that had gotten Ruth into trouble with Landis. While he was performing in Washington on December 5th, Landis announced that Ruth and his Yankee teammates who had violated the barnstorming rule would forfeit their World Series checks and be suspended for the first six weeks of the 1922 season.[43]

Before the game at the Polo Grounds on May 20, 1922, the day his suspension was lifted, the National Vaudeville Association presented Ruth with an award commemorating his successful vaudeville tour, which grossed almost $50,000.[44] This more than compensated Ruth who had been fined the amount of his 1921 World Series check ($3,362) for barnstorming.[45]

Ruth barnstormed during the next four post-seasons, returning to vaudeville after the 1926 World Series, perhaps because he had been branded the goat of the Series for being thrown out attempting to steal second, which ended the seventh game of the 1926 World Series against the St. Louis Cardinals.[46] This time, Ruth played the Pantages vaudeville circuit in Minnesota and California as a headliner.[47] The tour was very successful in Minnesota. As always, everywhere Ruth played, the crowds were large, loud, and lionizing. One day, the hail and snow were falling so hard that Ruth told Marshall Hunt that he didn't think they could play the show. As Hunt and Ruth looked at the falling snow in the empty village square, the village band arrived and began playing for Ruth. According to Hunt,

> … This hail was coming down so hard you could hear it through the window, hitting the metal instruments. But the thing that the Babe and I loved was this tuba player, absolutely bald, blowing his guts out just playing…. [And] so I said, "Babe…. Reverence is being paid…. The mayor has welcomed you…." [And] the Babe said … "Okay, kid…." And Ruth did the show.[48]

On the California leg of the Pantages tour, the crowds were just as adoring as those in Minnesota, but the public officials were not as welcoming. Along with the patter and the songs in his vaudeville act, Ruth brought children from the audience onstage to josh with them, ask them questions, and then give them baseballs. The California Deputy State Commissioner of Labor charged Babe Ruth with violating the child labor law concerning employing children in theaters because he did not have a permit for children to appear in his vaudeville act. The newspapers erroneously reported that a bench warrant had been issued for Babe Ruth's arrest.[49] The case was settled as a misunderstanding because Ruth was unaware of the child labor law. The judge also ruled that children were not hired but "there was every reason to believe that any child in the audience could have responded to Ruth's general invitation."

That did not stop the publicity-seeking government bureaucrat from exploitation and filing charges against Ruth—who was in Hollywood making a movie entitled *Babe Comes Home*[50] with Anne Q. Nillson[51]—under another section of the law.[52] This case was also dismissed. Having had enough of legal troubles with the vaudeville tour, Babe Ruth met with Yankees owner Colonel Jacob Ruppert on March 2, 1927, and signed a three-year contract for $70,000 a year. Colonel Ruppert declared, "the Babe is a sensible fellow."[53]

Ruth's movie career suited him. As soon as he joined the Yankees in 1920, *Headin' Home,*[54] based on the mythology of Ruth's life, was released. *Babe Comes Home* and *Speedy*[55] were released in 1927 and 1928. Unfortunately, no print of *Babe Comes Home* survives, and *Speedy* is more remembered for Harold Lloyd's comic genius than Ruth's acting, but these popular films quickly capitalized on Ruth's popularity. Ruth paved the way for silver screen opportunities for other Yankees. Joe DiMaggio appeared in *Manhattan Merry-Go-Round*,[56] where he met his first wife, Dorothy Arnold.[57] Mickey Mantle and Roger Maris starred in *Safe at Home!*[58] Reggie Jackson was a California Angel when he attempted to assassinate Queen Elizabeth II in *The Naked Gun*,[59] but would he have had the opportunity without becoming Mr. October in New York?

And Derek Jeter, star of the modern media age, has 90 film and TV appearances—more than any other Yankee. Like most Yankees, Jeter plays himself. In the 2010 movie *The Other Guys*, the reference to Jeter shows how embedded in the culture the Yankees are. Jeter was a plot point as well as appearing in *The Other Guys*,[60] where Mark Wahlberg's NYPD character, Terry Hoitz, is tagged with the sobriquet "the Yankee Clipper" (originally Joe DiMaggio's nickname for the effortless way he seemed to glide across the outfield making plays) for accidentally shooting Jeter during the seventh game of the World Series.[61]

Not all films with Yankee stars have a positive cultural impact. Perhaps the worst film to ride the Yankee coattails to prominence is *Safe at Home!*, filmed and released after Maris and Mantle's chase of Ruth's single-season home run record in 1961, is an awful movie, but an interesting cultural artifact. *Safe at Home!* is the *magnum opus* of Yankee kitsch movies, rivaling the filmmaking art of Ed Wood, Jr. The producer of *Safe at Home!* said that the idea for the movie came to him during the summer of 1961: "Every headline you saw said M & M…. You couldn't buy that kind of publicity for a million dollars." Unlike the rest of the films, which annexed things Yankee as a cultural tie-in, *Safe at Home!* was "designed for cheap, quick filming, an April release date and a fast buck." It went into production during spring training in 1962 and released that April.[62]

William Frawley, best known as Fred Mertz on *I Love Lucy*,[63] was a lifelong Yankee fan, and had it written into his contract that he got off work early to attend Yankee home World Series games. With *Safe at Home!*, Frawley envisioned a starring project for himself as a Yankee coach and an opportunity to work with his favorite baseball team.[64] And while *Safe at Home!* might be the ultimate in cinematic Yankee kitsch, *The Pride of the Yankees*[65] is the ultimate Yankee film. But one that stands on Yankee gravitas is *The Old Man and the Sea*,[66] based on Ernest Hemingway's Nobel Prize-winning novel.[67] Throughout *The Old Man and the Sea*, Santiago holds up DiMaggio to himself and others as the paragon example of how to conduct yourself like a man—"What would the great DiMaggio do?" is Santiago's philosophical touchstone.

It wasn't only the Japanese Army and Commissioner Landis who held the Yankees as cultural opponents. Douglass Wallop's novel *The Year the Yankees Lost the Pennant*[68] had the Yankees in cahoots with the devil to deviously obtain Joe Hardy, the league's best player. George Abbott adapted *The Year the Yankees Lost the Pennant* as *Damn Yankees* for Broadway. A movie version premiered in 1958.[69]

Santiago in Hemingway's *The Old Man and the Sea* sees the Yankees and Joe DiMaggio on the side of the angels, counseling Manolin, "Have faith in the Yankees, my son."[70] While the Yankees' position in *Damn Yankees*, in Michael Shaara's *For Love of the Game*, and David S. Ward's *Major League* is not as lofty as in *The Old Man and the Sea,* they are presented as the Goliaths of the American League. In *Major League*, Bob Uecker's character, announcer Harry Doyle, exclaims that a Yankee slugger is "leading the league in most offensive categories, including nose hair."[71] This attitude towards the Yankees may stem from the imperial squads of 1947 to 1956 who won seven of 10 World Series.

Television programs and advertising involving the Yankees have been ubiquitous because "the true measure of Yankee greatness is marketability."[72] From Ballantine blasts to the Money Store to Visa credit cards, scores of products have been pitched with the Yankee connection. In one commercial for Colonial Brand Yankee Franks in 1979, newly acquired hurler Luis Tiant proclaimed, "It's great to be with a wiener!"[73] And wieners could be had with a Ballantine beer in the 1950s and 1960s.[74] In the 1970s, a Miller Lite could be paired with that wiener as Mickey Mantle, Whitey Ford, and Yogi Berra pitched the beer. Using the ad's tag line, Billy Martin and George Steinbrenner famously debated if the brew would be a "less filling" or "tastes great" beverage with the meal.

As for anyone, kids included, wanting a soft drink, Yogi Berra had a Yoo-Hoo for you. A New Jersey company close to Berra's Montclair home, Berra became involved with Yoo-Hoo in 1955 because he liked its taste. In a shrewd business move, he was a vice-president of the company, taking stock rather than a salary.

Berra was more than a figurehead at Yoo-Hoo. Besides appearing in commercials, he often visited the company's Carlstadt headquarters. One time, he answered a phone call from a woman who wanted to know if Yoo-Hoo was hyphenated. Berra replied, "No, ma'am, it's not even carbonated."

Jim Bouton remembers that the Yankee clubhouse had a cooler just for Yoo-Hoo. In the mid–1950s, when Yoo-Hoo was having trouble getting distributed, Berra went on sales calls, often bringing teammates like Mickey Mantle and Whitey Ford along. Berra also got his teammates to appear in Yoo-Hoo commercials. Needless to say, Yoo-Hoo got distribution throughout the Northeast and beyond. In an era when few sports figures had product endorsement deals, Berra made a fortune.[75]

Animation giant Hanna-Barbera cashed in on Yogi Berra when it introduced Yogi Bear on *The Huckleberry Hound Show*[76] in 1958. While Yogi Bear was based on Art Carney's character Ed Norton on *The Honeymooners,* complete with personality and trademark porkpie hat, the name similarity boosted the cartoon character's popularity. In 1961, Yogi Bear had his own TV show.[77] Berra announced a lawsuit against Hanna-Barbera, which he eventually did not pursue. "Television is big enough for me and Yogi Bear. I was going to sue the Yogi Bear program for using my name, until somebody reminded me Yogi isn't my real name—it's Lawrence."[78]

And in addition to inspiring a cartoon character's name, Berra was "undoubtedly a cultural icon" for his many malapropisms.[79] Who hasn't invoked Berra's probably most famous saying, "It ain't over 'til it's over"? The iconic cultural nature of Berra's quotes from "It's déjà vu all over again," to "Nobody goes there anymore, it's too crowded" to "You can observe a lot by just watching" to many more raise Berra's profile above association with baseball and into general usage.

Another piece of ubiquitous product association with the Yankees is the Boston-based Gillette Company. Beginning in 1910, Gillette used ads featuring John McGraw of the New York Giants. Since the 1939 World Series, Gillette razor blades used Yankees to pitch their product, as Gillette was the World Series sponsor when the Yankees were participants 20 times between 1939 and 1964. The relationship took hold before the Yankees-Red Sox rivalry became what it is today. But Gillette wasn't happy during the years that the Yanks swept the World Series, causing half of Gillette's advertising time to go unused.

Gillette was the sole World Series advertiser until 1959, when it sold half the advertising time to General Motors. Joe DiMaggio, Whitey Ford, Mickey Mantle, Red Rolfe, Eddie Lopat, Allie Reynolds, Phil Rizzuto, and Derek Jeter are just a few of the Yankees to appear in Gillette commercials. This relationship was especially powerful in the 1950s, when the Yankees represented excellence in baseball.[80]

Billy Martin was a cornerstone on some of those Yankee teams. While a brawler his entire life, Martin's two best-known fights occurred while he was a Yankee and found their way into Yankee lore. In 1957 at the Copacabana nightclub, Yankee legends Mantle, Berra, and Ford, along with Hank Bauer and Johnny Kucks and their wives, joined Martin to celebrate his 29th birthday. While only Bauer was arrested for a Copacabana patron's broken nose and leg, Martin was implicated for his penchant for fighting. Yankee President Dan Topping fined the players $6,000 collectively, the largest single-incident fine in baseball history to that time.

Because it involved the Yankees, the Copacabana incident overshadowed Mayor Wagner's meeting with Walter O'Malley and Horace Stoneham to prevent the Dodgers and Giants from leaving the city for California.[81] Casey Stengel's take on the incident was, "They're trying to make a big scandal over this because we're the Yanks."[82]

Twenty years later, Martin's next Yankee fight at Fenway Park with Reggie Jackson was nationally televised. Martin, the Yankee skipper, replaced Jackson with Paul Blair in the sixth inning without telling Jackson, who then confronted Martin in the dugout in full view of the fans and on the NBC *Game of the Week* cameras. Elston Howard separated the men. Jackson reportedly said, "You're a SOB … you're too old. Do you want to fight?" With that, Yogi Berra and Dick Howser restrained Martin while Jimmy Wynn held Jackson.

Joe DiMaggio knew where to get the best cup of coffee to start your day. The great DiMaggio became the spokesman for Mr. Coffee and the Bowery Savings Bank while fellow Yankee Phil Rizzuto reminded us that the cash we needed for our dreams, up to $50,000, was waiting at the Money Store for home improvements, debt consolidation, or a new car.[83] And if work force help were necessary, Mantle Men and Namath Girls, the second largest employment agency in the world a year after its founding in 1968, could provide all the temporary employment help necessary.[84] Jets quarterback legend Joe Namath was the second part of the company name.

In possibly the strangest "Yankee marketability greatness" TV commercial, Mantle appears with Willie Mays for Blue Bonnet margarine. Both wear blue bonnets while eating corn on the cob.[85] George Steinbrenner was in favor of doing the Miller commercial with Martin because "…he thought the script benefited him and the Yankees' personality … that it was fun and in good taste…. He had no problem making fun of himself."

In 1978, Miller Lite commercials were done a few weeks before Martin famously tagged Reggie Jackson and Steinbrenner with the description "One's a born liar and the other's convicted." The fallout from this was Martin's resignation as manager, followed five days later by Steinbrenner's announcement that Martin was to be re-hired to manage the Yankees in 1980.[86]

BBD&O suggested Visa use the Steinbrenner-Jeter contretemps as a commercial: "'It's perfect for what we want to communicate about leadership and acceptance.'" Visa aired the commercial in June 2003 showing Steinbrenner, in blue blazer and white turtleneck, ushering Jeter into his office and asking, "'How can you possibly afford to spend two nights dancing, two nights eating out and three nights just carousing with your friends?'" Jeter silently flashes his Visa card, rendering Steinbrenner speechless. The action cuts to a nightclub where Jeter leads a conga line with Steinbrenner as the last member of the line and a final shot of Steinbrenner's rear.[87]

Steinbrenner's performance in the Visa commercial is striking for how much he acts like the character based on him in *Seinfeld*, with an actor whose face was never seen, but whose wild gesticulating was evident, and whose voice was provided by *Seinfeld* co-creator Larry David.

In the commercial, Steinbrenner's voice is lightly inflected with David's staccato, slightly manic rhythms, and exaggerated gestures. David gave voice to an apocryphal George Steinbrenner, whom viewers embraced as a true characterization of the man known as The Boss.

Besides the Yankees' overwhelming presence in commercials and on nationally-televised baseball games, many different programs have carried Yankee story lines. The Yankee brand has been on *Saturday Night Live,* hosted by both Derek Jeter[88] and George Steinbrenner[89] on separate occasions. Before Donald Trump captured the imagination as the embodiment of business success, there was Steinbrenner, the charismatic and controversial Yankee owner who represented winning the World Series as the only worthwhile result of the baseball season. Steinbrenner goaded the Yankees to be winners at all costs and kept the Yankees in the spotlight during the 1990s, when it was a mediocre organization. Steinbrenner made the Yankees important even when the team was irrelevant to the pennant chase.

Perhaps the greatest Yankee action in the domestic area was the Kekich-Peterson trade in 1973. During spring training, Mike Kekich and Fritz Peterson announced that during the off- season, they had traded families. While this non-baseball-related occurrence was not a scandal, it did ruffle feathers in the staid world of the New York Yankees. Jake Gibbs, their former catcher, was stunned by the announcement. He remembered them as "fun-loving" guys who brought their wives and children to the family picnics that the team would have. "Fritz and Mike were good friends. Both they and their families were real close, we just didn't know how close. Of course, you can never tell about lefties!" General Manager Lee MacPhail signaled that the Yankees were accepting this news, remarking, "We may have to call off 'Family Day.'"[90]

Family-centric Yankees fans were far from happy when Meat Loaf released *Bat Out of Hell* in 1977 featuring "Paradise by the Dashboard Light," which had an extended baseball metaphor on scoring, with play-by-play from Yankee icon Phil Rizzuto. As a lifelong Yankee fan, Meat Loaf made sure to get Rizzuto to do the baseball interlude. Rizzuto didn't understand why Meat Loaf wanted him to record the interlude, especially as the play described a suicide squeeze play with two outs because getting the out at first would end the inning and negate the run.

Rizzuto supposedly asked Meat Loaf why he wanted the play-by-play sequence, and Meat Loaf supposedly told Rizzuto that he was taking artistic license with the sequence. Ultimately, Rizzuto took the money to record the interlude, later claiming he did not know it referred to sex. Later when Bill White brought up the controversy on a Yankee broadcast, Rizzuto said it wasn't until he got calls from priests and nuns and angry letters from Yankee fans about the bawdy extended metaphor that he tried to distance himself from the song. And when Meat Loaf asked Rizzuto to tour with him, Rizzuto turned him down.[91]

*The Simpsons*, currently at the pinnacle of popular culture, often referenced the Yankees. In "'Tis the Fifteenth Season,"[92] a Joe DiMaggio rookie card is Homer's Christmas bonus; nuclear power plant owner C. Montgomery Burns remarks that "they're letting ethnics into the big leagues now." "Homer at the Bat,"[93] labeled by some as "perhaps the greatest episode of *The Simpsons* ever aired,"[94] shows Homer Simpson embracing the idea of the American underdog. It is the first time that *The Simpsons* manifests its symbiotic relationship with baseball. Airing on February 20, 1992, on FOX, the episode represents a popular-culture milestone.

More viewers tuned into *The Simpsons* than *The Cosby Show* or the Winter Olympics from Albertville, France, giving FOX its first-ever prime time victory.[95] The overarching reason why Mr. Burns hired major leaguers to work at the power plant is to win the championship game and a million-dollar side bet "to make it interesting." The players include Yankee first baseman Don Mattingly, who shaved his sideburns so completely that Mattingly wound up sporting a Mohawk-like hairdo, which did not please Mr. Burns. As Mattingly is thrown off the power plant team for sideburn insubordination, he says, "I still like him more than Steinbrenner."[96]

This nostalgic look at baseball culminates with Terry Cashman's *Talkin' Softball*, which uses the same music as his nostalgia-soaked early 1980s tune *Talkin' Baseball*. The lyrics concern the people and events in the episode. When discussing the seminal song and requests for it, the chorus line mentioning Willie Mays, Mickey Mantle, and Duke Snider is often taken as the title, again invoking the Yankees' popular-culture importance. Mantle was not the only Yankee cultural icon referenced in the song—Yogi Berra, the Scooter (Phil Rizzuto), the Barber (Sal Maglie, who played for the Dodgers and Giants as well), and Reggie Jackson.

The Yankees have figured significantly in popular music. From Les Brown's 1941 hit "Joltin' Joe DiMaggio," inspired by his hitting streak, to "Haya Doin," a 2009 New York radio tribute song to Yankee history, the Yankees have been part of the aural landscape. Most people think that "New York, New York" is Frank Sinatra's ode to the Yankees, rather than Kander and Ebb's song extolling the hurdles of making it in New York. Phil Linz was famed on the Mantle-era teams for his harmonica chops and his declaration, "Play me or keep me" when it looked like Linz might lose his Yankee back-up role for full-time duty with the Washington Senators, who coveted Linz's services.[97] Joe DiMaggio is the soul of Paul Simon's Academy Award-winning and Grammy Award-winning "Mrs. Robinson," which asks about Joe DiMaggio's whereabouts for a nation in troubling times. For the "Me and Julio" music video, Simon played stickball with Mickey Mantle. He was invited to sing "Mrs. Robinson" at the unveiling of DiMaggio's statue at Yankee Stadium in 1998.[98]

Billy Joel, who played the last concert at the original Yankee Stadium (renovated in the mid–1970s), employed Yankee imagery in three songs: "Miami 2017," "Zanzibar," and "We Didn't Start the Fire." Each use was not solely a baseball related reference, but pointed to the Yankees' cultural importance. "Miami 2017" describes a dystopian New York; "Zanzibar" explains the goings-on at a bar with the same name as the song title; and "We Didn't Start the Fire" lists the historical turning points between World War II and the end of the 1980s. Joe DiMaggio and Mickey Mantle are named in "We Didn't Start the Fire." Their import is enough to make them culturally valuable without any explanation.

Youth is treasured and served especially in America. The vibrancy of youth flows through all the accomplishments of American culture. The young Yankees—Ruth, Gehrig, DiMaggio, Berra, Mantle, Ford, to name a few—began the team's youthful legacy of champions. And the Yankees were nothing if not champions, with each generation of fans venerating the champions of their youth with whom they identified and then revering and honoring the athletes for their feats when they were no longer young.

But athletes who die young give us pause, culturally. The Yankees have greatly affected the popular culture in tales about an athlete dying young. While there might be nothing more poignant than an athlete dying young, the Yankees have three overarching tales in the deaths of Ray Chapman, Lou Gehrig, and Thurman Munson. Ray Chapman was the Cleveland shortstop beaned by Yankee pitch Carl Mays in an August 17, 1920, game at the Polo Grounds, the Yankees' home at the time. Chapman was the only player to die from the events of a major- league game. That day was foggy and overcast. Yankee pitcher Carl Mays, a known headhunter, was a submarining, legal spitball pitcher regularly among the American League hit batsmen leaders. In the fifth inning on that foggy, overcast afternoon, Chapman took his usual "crowd the plate" stance, and Mays let loose with a high and tight pitch that Chapman reportedly never saw nor moved to avoid.

A loud crack, and the ball rolled to the mound where Mays tossed it to first for the inning's first out. The ball that hit Roy Chapman was tossed out of play as Mays had requested a new ball to pitch to the next batter. Chapman was still in the batter's box on one knee with his eyes shut and his mouth open. Catcher Muddy Ruel grabbed the unconscious Chapman and lowered him to the ground as the umpire called for a doctor in the house. While the doctor and players tried to revive Chapman, Mays never left the mound. Chapman did revive and took a few steps toward the clubhouse, but he again collapsed and had to be carried from the field.

Cleveland won the game. Chapman had surgery for the skull fracture caused by Mays's pitch, and he was given a prognosis for recovery as his pulse improved and he was breathing normally. Player-manager Tris Speaker and Chapman's teammates returned to their hotel on this good news, only to learn in the morning that Ray Chapman had died just before sunrise. Mays broke down when learned of Chapman's death. He voluntarily told the New York district attorney that the fastball he had thrown was high and tight, adding, "It is the most regrettable incident of my career and I would give anything to undo what has happened."[99] Mays was exonerated, but his remorse was skeptically received. American League umpires William Evans and William Dinneen observed, "No pitcher in the American League resorted to trickery more than Carl Mays in attempting to rough a ball in order to get a break on it which would make it more difficult to hit."[100] Owners had complained that "hundreds" of balls were being thrown out of play every year costing them thousands of dollars because of this act by Mays and his fellow spitballers. Umpires were urged to keep balls in play as much as possible even though the darkened baseballs were more difficult to see. After the Chapman incident, umpires were urged to take any balls that were not bright white out of play. Stricter "bean ball" rules for the next season banned new pitchers from throwing spitballs (those previously sanctioned to use the pitch were grandfathered on the issue). These results advanced the game's safety and helped in aiding the higher scoring live ball era personified by Babe Ruth.

Although his record was comparable to pitchers in the Hall of Fame, Mays was never elected. In an interview with author Bob McGarigle, who chronicled Mays's career in *Baseball's Great Tragedy*, Mays said, "Nobody, it seems, ever remembers anything about me except one thing—that a pitch I threw caused a man to die. It was an accident. Nothing else."[101]

Lou Gehrig's story is well known, and chronicled in *The Pride of the Yankees*. Gehrig's life and the details about his infirmity and his heroic stature as he fought amyotrophic lateral sclerosis (ALS), commonly known as Lou Gehrig's disease, is a well-known cultural touchstone. (As the essay on *The Pride of the Yankees* deals with Gehrig's life and career, it won't be discussed here in further detail.)

Thurman Munson's death reveals the dichotomy between the dream of a big-league career and the reality of that dream's impact on a player's desire for a home life. Munson began flying in 1976 so he could get home to Ohio to see his family on days off. "Thurman had a routine," said long-time Yankees trainer Gene Monahan. "He used to come to the ballpark, have a couple of cookies and a glass of milk."[102]

Reggie Jackson, Munson's co-star and rival, and eventual friend, recalled that Munson had become weary of the sport he played and all the time spent away from his wife and three children. Manager Billy Martin was worried about Munson flying between games: "I just kept telling him, you know, 'I don't like to see you flying during the season.'"[103] Both Martin and Jackson said that George Steinbrenner had granted Munson special permission to fly his plane from city to city during the season, separate from the team. "He had a special deal with Steinbrenner," Jackson said. "You know, Thurman was the most special Yankee when he was here. He could do anything he wanted to."[104]

Munson died in a plane crash on August 2, 1979, while practicing takeoffs and landings at the Canton airport. At the time of the accident, the Yankees were 14 games out of first place in the American League East. That was virtually the same deficit they had overcome the year before, in one of the most notable comebacks in baseball history. It would not happen again. "When Thurman got killed, you know, we just lost all—the whole season was just kind of lost," Graig Nettles said. "We just realized we couldn't do it and, you know, it demoralized a lot of us." The Yankees kept Munson's locker vacant as a low-key, classy tribute, and moved Munson's locker to the museum at the new Yankee Stadium.[105]

More than a favorite sports team, the Yankees are a way of life for their fans.

And for just as many others, the Yankees organization is the Evil Empire that scores 13 runs in the first inning and slowly pulls away. Overall, the Yankees have left and continue to leave a mark on society and culture going into its second century. What Yogi Berra said about life could apply to the Yankees place in the culture: "Love is the most important thing in the world, but baseball is pretty good, too."[106]

Thurman Munson was the American League Rookie of the Year in 1970 and the American League Most Valuable Player in 1976. His death in a 1979 plane crash devastated the Yankees and their fans. Munson was practicing landings and takeoffs in his small plane. Two passengers survived (National Baseball Hall of Fame and Museum, Cooperstown, NY).

## Notes

1. Bill Baer, "Survey Says: Yankees Still Most Hated In Baseball," *Hardball Talk,* NBC Sports, Mlb.Nbcsports.com/2017/07/20/Survey-Says-Yankees-Still-The-Most-Hated-In-Baseball/, last accessed July 20, 2017.

2. "Go Figure," Scorecard, *Sports Illustrated*, July 24–31, 2017, 13.

3. Tyler Kepner, "The True Outlook in the Bronx: Fair to Middling," *New York Times*, August 31, 2017: B13.

4. Birdie Tebbetts, "New York Yankee Quotations," *Baseball Almanac*, http://www.baseballalmanac.com/teams/yankquot.shtml, last accessed July 27, 2018.

5. Murray Chass, "Schilling Is Out to Silence Mystique, Aura and Fans," *New York Times*, October 12, 2004: D1.

6. Richard Sandomir, "Yankee Caps Pulled After Protesters See Gang Links in Symbols and Colors," *New York Times*, August 25, 2007: B3.

7. Wheaties Baseball Boxes, Baseball Almanac, www.baseball-almanac.com/legendary/wheaties_baseball_boxes.shtml, last accessed October 26, 2016.

8. Louie Lazar, "The Bloomingdale's That Ruth Built," *New York Times*, August 21, 2017: D1.

9. Brendan Kuty, "Did Yankees Really Give Fidel Castro Castro a Tryout?" *NJ Advance Media for NJ.Com*, www.nj.com/yankees/index.ssf/2016/12/did_yankees_really_give_fidel_castro_a_tryout.html, December 1, 2016, last accessed September 7, 2017.

10. Jerome Holtzman, ed. *No Cheering in the Press Box: Recollections—Personal Professional—By Eighteen Veteran American Sportswriters* (New York: Holt, Rinehart, and Winston, 1973), 17.

11. *Ibid.*, 164.

12. Fred Lieb, *Baseball as I Have Known It* (New York: Grosset & Dunlop, 1977), 165–166.

13. "Sick Boy Promised Ruth Homer Dies," Associated Press, *Los Angeles Times*, January 11, 1990: P10.

14. Robert McG. (McGill) Thomas, Jr., "Johnny Sylvester, the Inspiration for Babe Ruth Heroics, Is Dead," *New York Times*, January 11, 1990: D24.

15. Jimmy Cannon, "New York Yankee Quotations," *Baseball Almanac*, www.baseballalmanac.com/teams/yankquot.shtml, last accessed July 27, 2018.

16. Joe E. Lewis, "New York Yankee Quotations," *Baseball Almanac*, www.baseballalmanac.com/teams/yankquot.shtml, last accessed, July 27, 2018.

17. Peter Golenbock, *Dynasty: The New York Yankees* (New York: Berkley Books, 1975), 78.

18. *The Simpsons*, "Politically Inept, with Homer Simpson," Twentieth Century Fox Television, Gracie Films, FOX, January 8, 2012, John Frink.

19. Mike Royko, Mike, "New York Yankee Quotations," *Baseball Almanac*, www.baseballalmanac.com/teams/yankquot.shtml, last accessed, July 27, 2018.

20. Babe Ruth File, A. Bartlett Giamatti Research Center, National Baseball Hall of Fame and Museum, Cooperstown, NY. (Articles dating from 1911 to 1958 concerning Babe Ruth's life and career. Many are unattributed or indexed solely by publication date.)

21. "White Sox and Lawyers," *Eight Men Out*, directed by John Sayles (Los Angeles: Orion Pictures, 1988; Los Angeles: 20th Century Fox Home Entertainment, 2013, DVD). 20th Century Fox Home Entertainment distributed the film in the home video market. DVD package design copyrighted by Metro-Goldwyn-Mayer, the successor-in-interest to Orion. *Eight Men Out* stars John Cusack as Buck Weaver, Charlie Sheen as Happy Felsch, and D.B. Sweeney as Shoeless Joe Jackson.

22. Robert Smith, *Babe Ruth's America* (New York: Thomas Y. Crowell Company, 1974), 184.

23. Robert Creamer, "That Big Son of a Bitch," *Baseball*, "Fourth Inning: A National Heirloom," Written by Geoffrey C. Ward and Ken Burns, Narrated by John Chancellor, Directed by Ken Burns, Florentine Films and WETA-TV, PBS, 1994; PBS Distribution 2010, DVD.

24. Ritter, Lawrence S. and Mark Rucker, *The Babe: A Life in Pictures*, New York: Ticknor Fields, 1988), 79; 142.

25. Creamer, quoting Waite Hoyt, "That Big Son of a Bitch," *Baseball*, "Fourth Inning: A National Heirloom," See Note 23.

26. *bid.*, Chancellor, quoting Jimmy Cannon,.

27. Robert W. Creamer, *Babe: The Legend Comes to Life* (New York: Penguin Books, 1983), 236.

28. Harold Seymour. *Baseball: The Golden Age*, vol. 2 (New York: Oxford University Press, 1971), 392.

29. Daniel Okrent and Steve Wulf. *Baseball Anecdotes* (New York: Harper & Row, 1989), 91.

30. "Babe Ruth Repents; Quits Exhibitions," *New York Times*, October 22, 1921: 16.

31. Lawrence S. Ritter, "Ladies and Gentlemen, Presenting Marty McHale," in *The Armchair Book of Baseball*, ed. John Thorn (New York: Charles Scribner's Sons, 1985), 51, 87.

32. Robert Smith, *Babe Ruth's America* (New York: Thomas Y. Crowell Company, 1974), 117.

33. "Ruth Top-Liner on Keith Circuit," *New York Times*, October 28, 1921: 24.

34. Holtzman, 18.

35. "George Bernard Shaw Wants to Know 'Whose Baby Is Ruth?,'" *New York Times*, October 29, 1921: 1.

36. Smith, 117.

37. "Ruth Makes Debut as Vaudeville Star," *New York Times*, November 4, 1921: 24.

38. *Ibid.*

39. Creamer, 250.

40. "Babe Ruth Warmly Greeted in Debut on New York Stage," *New York Times*, November 15, 1921: 25.

41. *Ibid.*

42. Smith, 117.

43. Creamer, 250.

44. *Ibid.*, 257.

45. Donald Honig, *Baseball America: The Heroes of the Game and the Times of Their Glory* (New York: MacMillian Publishing Co., 1985), 139.

46. Michael Gallagher, Michael. *Day by Day in New York Yankees History* (New York: Leisure Press, 983), 63.

47. Lawrence S. Ritter, "Ladies and Gentlemen, Presenting Marty McHale," *The Armchair Book of Baseball,* ed. John Thorn (New York: Charles Scribner's Sons, 1985), 148.

48. Holtzman, 21–22.

49. "Ruth Forfeits $500 Bail," *New York Times,* January 26, 1927: 23.

50. *Babe Comes Home,* directed by Ted Wilde (Burbank, CA: First National Pictures, 1927).

51. "Babe Ruth to Try Skill on a New Lot; Yankee Star Signs to Appear in Movie," *New York Times,* January 23, 1927: S1.

52. "Babe Ruth Accused Again," *New York Times,* February 26, 1927: 32.

53. Gallagher, 64.

54. *Headin' Home,* directed by Lawrence Windom (Kessel & Baumann, 1920).

55. *Speedy,* directed by Ted Wilde (The Harold Lloyd Corporation, 1928).

56. *Manhattan Merry-Go-Round,* directed by Charles F. Reisner (Republic Pictures, 1937).

57. Lawrence Baldassaro, "Joe DiMaggio," Society for American Baseball Research Baseball Biography Project, sabr.org/bioproj/person/a48f1830, last accessed August 14, 2018.

58. *Safe at Home!,* directed by Walter Doniger (Culver City, CA: Columbia Pictures, 1962).

59. "Reggie Jackson Attempts to Assassinate Queen Elizabeth II," *The Naked Gun: From the Files of Police Squad!* directed by Jerry Zucker (Los Angeles: Paramount Pictures, 1988; Paramount Home Video, 2002). *Police Squad!* was a television series that Paramount Television produced for ABC in 1982. It lasted six episodes. David Zucker, Jim Abrahams, and Jerry Zucker created *Police Squad!,* which had similarities in tone and physical comedy to *Airplane!* (1980), the trio's spoof of Paramount's *Zero Hour* (1957). As of 2018, there are three movies in the *Naked Gun* franchise. Leslie Nielsen starred in all three, reprising his *Police Squad!* role of Frank Drebin, a police detective.

60. *The Other Guys,* directed by Adam McKay (Culver City, CA: Columbia Pictures, 2010; Culver City, CA: Sony Pictures Home Entertainment, 2010, DVD).

61. "Derek Jeter Gets Shot During the World Series," *The Other Guys.* Will Ferrell plays Wahlberg's detective-partner. The movie also starts Eva Mendes and Michael Keaton. Derek Jeter makes brief appearances as himself.

62. Robert Creamer, "Mantle and Maris in the Movies," *Sports Illustrated,* April 2, 1962, 90; www.si.com/vault/1962/04/02/593549/mantle-and-maris-in-the-movies, last accessed September 9, 2017.

63. *I Love Lucy,* CBS, 1951–1957.

64. Carl Anthony, "The Movie Mickey Mantle & Maris Made … with Fred Mertz," Carl Anthony Online, carlanthonyonline.com/2012/10/29/, October 29, 2012, last accessed August 27, 2018.

65. *The Pride of the Yankees,* directed by Sam Wood (The Samuel Goldwyn Company, 1942).

66. *The Old Man and the Sea,* directed by John Sturges (Burbank, CA: Warner Brothers, 1958).

67. Ernest Hemingway, *The Old Man and the Sea* (New York: Charles Scribner & Sons, 1952).

68. Douglass Wallop, *The Year the Yankees Lost the Pennant* (New York: W.W. Norton & Company, 1954).

69. *Damn Yankees,* directed by George Abbott, Stanley Donen (Burbank, CA: Warner Brothers, 1958).

70. Ernest Hemingway, *The Old Man and the Sea* (New York: Scribner Classics, 1996), 18. Page references are to 1996 edition.

71. "Clue Haywood at Bat," *Major League,* directed by David S. Ward (Los Angeles: Paramount Pictures, 1989; Paramount Home Video, 2007, DVD ["Wild Thing Edition"]). As of 2018, there are three movies in the *Major League* franchise. Pete Vuckovich played Yankees first baseman Clue [sic] Haywood, the slugger referenced by Uecker. Vuckovich pitched in the major leagues from 1975 to 1986: White Sox, Blue Jays, Cardinals, Brewers. His career win-loss record is 93–69. *Major League* stars Tom Berenger, Charlie Sheen, Bob Uecker, Rene Russo, Corbin Bernsen, and Wesley Snipes.

72. Andrew Mearns, "The Greatest Yankee Commercials of All Time," Pinstripe Alley, www.pinstripealley.com/2014/1/27/5349060/yankees-best-commercials-tv-cone-el-duque-jeter-martin-steinbrenner, January 27, 2014, last accessed September 9, 2017.

73. Luis Tiant, www.imdb.com/name/nm1495405/.

74. "Ballantine Beer and Baseball," Way Back and Gone, waybackandgone.wordpress.com/2009/05/27, May 27, 2009, last accessed, September 9, 2017.

75. Richard Sandomir, "For Yoo-Hoo and Yogi, It's Déjà Vu All Over Again," *New York Times,* April 20, 1993; www.nytimes.com/1993/04/20/business/for-yoo-hoo-and-yogi-it-s-deja-vu-all-over-again, last accessed, July 27, 2018.

76. *The Huckleberry Hound Show,* Hanna-Barbera Productions, Syndicated, 1958–1962.

77. *The Yogi Bear Show*, Hanna-Barbera Productions, Syndicated, 1961–62.

78. Eriq Gardner, "Yogi Berra Suing Over Yogi Bear? Take It with a Grin of Salt," *Hollywood Reporter*, September 23, 2015, www.hollywoodreporter.com/print/826820', last accessed July 27, 2018.

79. *Ibid.*

80. Terry Lefton, "Gillette's Century of Close Shaves in Baseball," *Sports Business Daily*, June 22, 2009, sportsbusinessdaily.com/Journal/2009/06/20090622/SBJ-In-Depth/Gillette-Century-of-Close-Shaves-in-Baseball, last accessed July 27, 2018.

81. Jay Maeder, "After Hours: Yankees on the Town, 1957," Big Town Replay: Sports and the Sporting Life in New York City," *Daily News* (New York): 37.

82. "Six Players on Yankees Fined Total of $5,500 in Cafe Visit," *New York Times*, June 4, 1957: 41. The article was a front-page story that continued on page 41.

83. "Holy Cow! It's Phil Rizzuto for The Money Store!" The Retroist, "Holy Cow! It's Phil Rizzuto for The Money Store!," July 29, 2014, www.retroist.com/2014/07/09/holy-cow-its-phil-rizzuto-for-the-money-store/, last accessed, July 27, 2018.

84. *Inside the Apple: A Streetwise History of New York City* (blog), by Michelle and James Nevius, "Mantle Men and Namath Girls," blog.inside the apple.net/2011/12mantle-men-and-namath-girls.html, December 1, 2011, last accessed, July 27, 2018.

85. Mearns, "The Greatest Yankee Commercials of All Time."

86. Richard Sandomir, "TV Sports; Echo of '78: Steinbrenner in an Ad," *New York Times*, May 30, 2003; www.nytimes.com/2003/05/30/sports/tv-sports-echo-of-78-steinbrenner-in-an-ad, Last accessed, July 27, 2018.

87. *Ibid.*

88. *Saturday Night Live*, NBC, Broadway Video, December 1, 2001.

89. *Saturday Night Live*, NBC, Broadway Video, October 20, 1990.

90. Bob Hurte, "The Infamous Trade of '72," Seamheads, August 4, 2012, seamheads.com/blog/2012/08/04/the-infamous-trade-of-72/, last accessed, July 27, 2018.

91. "Paradise by the Dashboard Light," www.songfacts.com/detail.php?id=1711. Last accessed, July 30, 2018. "But whether Phil had known what was going on or not, he never gave Mr. Loaf a refund on the paycheck." Bill White, *Uppity: My Untold Story About the Games People Play* (New York: Grand Central Publishing, 2011), 141.

92. *The Simpsons*, "'Tis the Fifteenth Season," Twentieth Century Fox Television, Gracie Films FOX, December 14, 2003, Michael Price.

93. *The Simpsons*, "Homer at the Bat," Twentieth Century Fox Television, Gracie Films, FOX, February 20, 1992.

94. Nathan Rubin, "The Making of 'Homer at the Bat,'" *AVClub.Com*, July 17, 2011, last accessed July 27, 2018.

95. Erik Malinowski, "The Making of 'Homer at the Bat,' The Episode That Conquered Prime Time 20 Years Ago Tonight," Deadspin, February 20, 2012, deadspin.com/5886723/the-making-of-homer-at-the-bat-the-episode-that-conquered-prime-time-20-years-ago-tonight, last accessed August 28, 2018.

96. *The Simpsons*, "Homer at the Bat."

97. Joe Guzzardi, "Phil Linz: 'Play Me or Keep Me!'" Seamheads.com, August 3, 2012, seamheads.com/blog/2012/08/03/phil-linz-play-me-or-keep-me/, last accessed, August 3, 2018.

98. Simon, Paul, "Songs Open Doors to the Inner Sanctum," *New York Times*, September 19, 2008, www.nytimes.com/2008/09/21/sports/baseball/21simon.html?mtrref=www.google.com&gwh=E29B6628 CB6418DDE611C62512B93E51&gwt=pay, last accessed August 29, 2018.

99. "Ray Chapman Dies; Mays Exonerated," *New York Times*, August 18, 1920: 12.

100. "Ray Chapman's Body Reaches Cleveland," *Brooklyn Daily Eagle*, August 18, 1920: 3.

101. Bob McGarigle, *Baseball's Great Tragedy: The Story of Carl Mays—Submarine Pitcher* (Jericho, New York: Exposition Press, 1972), 157.

102. David Waldstein, "Shedding Light on a Yankee's Death," *New York Times*, August 2, 2018: B12. The article was a front-page story for the Sports section, which began on B9. It continued on B12.

103. *Ibid.*

104. *Ibid.*

105. *Bats* (blog), "So Many Years Later, Munson's Memory Lives On," by Tyler Kepner, the web site of the *New York Times* online, bats.blogs.nytimes.com/2008/02/05/so-many-years-later-munsons-memory-lives-on/, last accessed, August 3, 2018.

106. Yogi Berra, Brainy Quote, www.brainyquote.com/quotes/quotes/y/yogiberra621244.html, last accessed July 27, 2018.

# E-61*

## MATT ROTHENBERG

We made too many wrong mistakes.—Yogi Berra[1]

This quote from Lawrence Peter (Yogi) Berra is reputed to have been said after the Yankees fell flat during a pennant race[2] or when they dropped the 1960 World Series to the Pittsburgh Pirates.[3] However, it could also easily apply itself to *61\**, a roughly two-hour motion picture that premiered on cable television network HBO on April 28, 2001.[4] Billy Crystal, the director and an executive producer, re-created the story behind the 1961 home run race between New York Yankees outfielders Mickey Mantle and Roger Maris. Each man began to hit home runs at such prodigious paces that Babe Ruth's single-season home-run record of 60, which he hit in 1927, was deemed to be in danger of falling.[5] The question was: Who would accomplish the feat first?

The movie débuted to generally positive acclaim. Robert Bianco of *USA Today*, in his three-star review, called the script "sentimental at best," but described stars Barry Pepper, who played Maris, and Thomas Jane, who played Mantle, as "a potent combination" reminiscent of "their real-life counterparts." Bianco felt "[e]verything about the look and feel of *61\** seems both first-rate and right" and, despite the sappy script, "[b]aseball fans will likely love it nonetheless."[6]

*ESPN The Magazine*'s Steve Wulf agreed that the casting of Pepper and Jane was "a master stroke," though he wrote that the "rest of the casting is hit-and-miss." Wulf intentionally ignored historical inaccuracies in his review of *61\** and instead opted to inform readers about the emotional aspects of the film, noting, "if you want to have your first guilt-free baseball movie cry since *Field of Dreams*, then you'll have to succumb to all the endless promotion for *61\**."[7]

It is easy, perhaps, to get caught up in the emotions of Maris and Mantle as they find themselves in the throes of chasing the Bambino's record, but the historical inaccuracies that Wulf ignored in his review are quite a few in number. Most average baseball fans might not notice them. Not-so-average baseball fans, for example, President George W. Bush, a former owner of the Texas Rangers, amazed Crystal with their knowledge of Major League Baseball in 1961. Hopefully, President Bush identified Pedro Ramos as the starting pitcher for the Twins on Opening Day. The film claims it is Camilo Pascual, though the uniform number (14) is correct.

"I couldn't believe (Bush's) memory of minutiae," said Crystal, who privately screened the movie for Bush and others at the White House on April 9, 2001, and claimed to be in preproduction for the movie ever since attending his first Yankees game on May 30, 1956. "He would turn to me and say the name of a guy not even mentioned in the film. He knew the pitcher on that opening day before our Mel Allen character said it."[8]

Crystal is not quoted as to whom Bush said was the Opening Day pitcher. Was it Ramos, the person the fictional Mel Allen names, or was it Pascual, the actual starting pitcher for the rechristened franchise now known as the Minnesota Twins?[9]

The casual viewer may not know—and, truly, may not even care about—the difference. It is not uncommon in television or motion-picture productions based on true events to have some kind of stretching of the truth, even to the point where the "facts" portrayed are downright false.

That theme comes up quite often in *61\**—the appearance of alternative facts and inaccuracies which, while they do not take anything away from the greater story, are no less annoying to those who wish to see the truth maintained.

One may subdivide these inaccuracies and falsehoods into several groups. They are: mistaken identities and roster imposters; missed plays; stadium snafus; fake news; and the ever-present miscellany. Some mix themselves into two or more groups.

Because the focus of this movie is on the home-run race between Mantle and Maris, it also generally ignores other storylines that permeated the Yankees' 1961 season, including the standout seasons for Elston Howard and Whitey Ford, the exceptional relief pitching of Luis Arroyo, Ralph Houk's major-league managerial début, and a World Championship secured in five games against Cincinnati. Those topics will also be explored here.

## Mistaken Identities and Roster Imposters

It has long been noted that you can't tell the players without a scorecard, and when it comes to *61\**, having rosters, photos, and backgrounds handy for each team in the American League is not just a necessity for knowing what you are watching. They are also helpful for knowing whom you are not watching.

Thankfully, a variety of resources, including Baseball-Reference.com, Retrosheet.org, team publications, and *Baseball Digest* help pick up the slack.

At the beginning of the film, the Maris family arrives in St. Louis as the Cardinals' Mark McGwire threatens to break Maris's home-run record. Not long after, the scene shifts from 1998 St. Louis to 1961 New York, where the Yankees are celebrating Opening Day at Yankee Stadium on April 11th, against the Twins, who are playing their first season in Minnesota following an off-season move from Washington, D.C. The original Washington Senators pulled up stakes after the 1960 season and relocated to the Minneapolis-St. Paul area. They were replaced in 1961 by an expansion Senators club that later became the Texas Rangers. Roger Maris is shagging fly balls in the outfield during pre-game batting practice. His teammate out there in the furthest reaches of the Yankee Stadium playing surface? None other than Bob Cerv, who is about to begin his 11th season in the majors.

That is all well and good, except for one thing: On April 11th, Cerv was patrolling left field at Baltimore's Memorial Stadium, not left field in the House that Ruth Built. He did so as a member of the expansion Los Angeles Angels, who began their inaugural season on the road against the Orioles.[10] Cerv's character is critical to the movie as he is Maris's confidant; the two had played for the Kansas City Athletics in 1958 and 1959. Separate trades brought each man—Maris in December 1959 and Cerv in May 1960—to the Yankees. Cerv was plucked by the Angels in the expansion draft; however, he did not re-join New York until a trade on May 8, 1961.[11]

Swinging in the batting cage for the Yankees is a fellow wearing a No. 12 uniform. A glance at the Yankees' scorecard for their season lid-lifter against Minnesota shows no No. 12 for New York. The only person who would wear No. 12 for the Yankees in 1961 could be found on that scorecard wearing No. 9 for the Twins—infielder Billy Gardner.[12] He did not don the pinstripes until after a June 14th trade.[13] We would see a No. 12 on the Yankees quite often when the movie's timeline made it apparent it was not yet mid–June.

Another roster question comes in the form of an individual wearing a Yankees jersey with No. 55 on the back. No one wore No. 55 for the Yankees during the regular season, and it seems there was no one on the preseason 40-man roster with that numeral.[14]

As the Twins make warm-up throws in front of their dugout, most of them generally possess the correct attributes of the real-life individuals they are portraying. No. 7, however, is a right-handed throwing Caucasian person—not the left-handed throwing African-American that Lenny Green is. No one else would have worn No. 7 for the Twins in 1961.[15]

Later in the movie, another Twins pitcher is shown wearing No. 47, a number that was not worn by anyone on Minnesota's big league club in 1961.[16]

At one point Elston Howard comes out to catch, and it appears that Yogi Berra is heading for the outfield. It turns out, in fact, that Berra caught Yankee pitching throughout the Opening Day game. Howard did not play. Perhaps Howard was warming up the Yankees' pitcher before Berra put on his catcher's equipment. It is hard to tell, but this scenario is not likely.[17]

Angels pitcher Ted Bowsfield is depicted as a right-handed pitcher when he actually was a left-handed pitcher. He also never allowed a home run to either Maris or Mantle in 1961, despite what is shown in the film.[18]

On September 2, 1961, in the Bronx, Maris connected for his 53rd home run in the eighth inning off Detroit Tigers pitcher Hank Aguirre, not Frank Lary as is depicted. Aguirre had just replaced Lary, who served up Maris's 52nd round tripper earlier in the game. Further, the catcher wears Dick Brown's No. 10 on his sleeve, but the two catchers who played in the 7–2 Detroit loss were Mike Roarke and Frank House. All three catchers played the following day, September 3rd, but it is Roarke who was behind the plate—and not Brown again—when Mantle connects off Jim Bunning for his first of two home runs on the day.[19]

When New York travels to Baltimore for a series affected by the foul weather of Hurricane Esther, Maris reluctantly agrees to play on September 20th, despite asking Houk for the day off. He responds with home run No. 59 off Milt Pappas. Berra followed Maris in the batter's box that evening, but we see Cerv on deck when Berra is up. Johnny Blanchard should have been on deck, as he hit behind Berra. Cerv was not in the lineup that evening.[20]

## Missed Plays

Again, thanks to the work of the folks at Retrosheet.org and Baseball-Reference.com, it is easy to pull up box scores and play-by-play accounts for many major-league games, including those for the 1961 season.

While there still may be slight deviances between what actually happened in those games, and the play-by-play accounts offered by those websites, the latter sources are generally reliable in nature and certainly enough to refute some of the accounts shown in *61\**.

Once more, the hits—or errors, that is—keep on coming, starting on Opening Day. In his broadcast, Mel Allen claims that the Yanks are down by four runs to Minnesota going into the bottom of the sixth inning. Reality, however, shows that there was no score between the clubs in the sixth inning. The Twins put three runs on the board in the seventh inning.[21]

Against the expansion Washington Senators, Roger Maris is shown presumably striking out against opposing pitcher Pete Burnside. This could not have happened, as Maris never struck out against Burnside in 1961—he only had three career strikeouts of Maris in 40 plate appearances over five seasons.[22]

Again we see Burnside appear, this time giving up a home run to Mickey Mantle in Yankee Stadium. However, the only time that Mantle connected for a round tripper on Burnside occurred on August 11th at Griffith Stadium in Washington, D.C.[23]

When the Yankees arrive in Detroit, probably for the June 16–18 series against the Tigers, we see an extended sequence of plays that did not happen in real life.

The movie has Yankees second baseman Bobby Richardson on second and shortstop Tony Kubek on first, as Maris steps into the box against Lary. Maris follows with a double to right field, scoring Richardson. Mantle is then intentionally walked. In the real three-game series, Maris's only double occurs on June 17th in the ninth inning against Detroit reliever Paul Foytack. Kubek had been on first base with a single, but Richardson never reached base in the inning. Mantle follows Maris's two-base hit with a home run. Lary pitched on June 18th, but Kubek did not play and Maris did not hit a double.[24]

When it is learned that Yankees legend Joe DiMaggio would return to the Bronx to throw a ceremonial first pitch prior to a game, a star struck and hung-over Mantle responded with three strikeouts. In the narrative of the film, it is likely that this took place in May or June, but the only time Mantle struck out three times in one home game in 1961 occurred on September 1st. He had three three-strikeout games on the road that season.[25]

Mantle is also depicted as having hit a home run against Baltimore at Yankee Stadium, but his home-run log shows his only blasts against the Orioles came in Charm City.[26] Bob Cerv, who strides to the plate after Mantle's round tripper, only hit behind Mantle once in a 1961 home game against Baltimore: in the first game of a doubleheader on July 30.[27]

Minnesota visits the Bronx in for a four-game set from August 4–6. Maris, in the film, beats out a bunt for a single on a squeeze play. In real life, though, Maris does not have any RBI bunt singles in any one of those four games against the Twins.[28]

In another game against the Tigers in the Bronx, Jake Wood is on first base as Al Kaline comes to bat against Whitey Ford. Kaline hits one into the gap and Wood is forced to stop at third base. This scenario never happened in any of the three games that Ford started against Detroit at Yankee Stadium in 1961, as Wood was never on first base when Kaline came to the plate.[29]

Almost a month later, the Yankees are playing Detroit again at Yankee Stadium. As we saw in the mistaken identity section, Maris is depicted hitting his 53rd home run against the Tigers' Lary, as opposed to Aguirre, who really allowed the dinger on September 2nd. Aguirre served up the home-run pitch in the eighth inning, while Maris's 52nd home run came in the sixth inning against Lary. Aguirre came in the ballgame after Lary surrendered a two-run single to Kubek, just prior to Maris's at-bat.

The film shows that Mantle hurt his forearm following Maris's 53rd home run when the injury actually occurred in the 6th inning, after the 52nd home run.[30]

The next day, September 3rd, an ailing Mantle hits his 49th and 50th home runs, practically one-armed, against the Tigers. The first round-tripper is hit off Jim Bunning in the 1st inning, but the movie has the scoreboard showing that the game is in the 9th inning. Mantle's second home run of the day, which he hits off Gerry Staley, is actually the one that happens in the final frame.[31]

A couple of weeks later, the Yanks are visiting Motor City and both Maris and Mantle remain in pursuit of the Babe's record. Bunning is once again featured in the film as being on the hill when Maris takes him deep for home run no. 58. Maris's two-run shot on September 17th actually is hit off Terry Fox.[32]

Back in Baltimore for the late-season set against the Orioles, Maris has already hit his 59th home run against Milt Pappas on September 20th. Later in the game, Dick Hall comes in to pitch for the O's. When Maris steps to the plate in the seventh inning, Mel Allen mentions Hall's striking out Maris in the sixth. In fact, it was the fourth when that happened. Maris did not have a plate appearance in the sixth inning.

Even later in the game, in the ninth inning, Maris gets his last chance to tie Ruth's record. (Ruth hit 60 home runs in an era when teams played a 154-game schedule; however, with the American League's expansion in 1961, eight more games were added to the schedule. The National League remained at 154 games until its expansion the following year.) When Maris comes to bat, leading off the inning, Orioles manager Paul Richards decides to lift Hall in favor of knuckleballer Hoyt Wilhelm. Alas, this is also removed from reality, which shows that in

Roger Maris visits with John F. Kennedy during a series against the Washington Senators in 1962 on behalf of the Multiple Sclerosis Society. Maris was the society's national campaign co-chairman. HBO's 2001 TV-movie *61\** revealed the controversies, pressures, and misperceptions faced by Mickey Mantle and Maris as they chased Babe Ruth's single-season record of 60 home runs in 1961. Maris broke it with his 61st home run on the last day of the season (courtesy of John F. Kennedy Presidential Library and Museum).

the bottom of the eighth, Richards sent Marv Throneberry to pinch-hit for Hall. Wilhelm was already in the game when Maris, who hit third in the inning, came to the plate.[33]

When the Orioles arrive at Yankee Stadium the following week, Maris is still on the verge of tying Ruth's mark. Maris would take Jack Fisher deep on September 26th to reach 60 home runs, but Mantle was not in the hospital convalescing, as the movie shows—he was in the starting lineup, playing center field. Drawing a walk in the first inning, his only plate appearance, Mantle was replaced by Hector Lopez on the bases, and Lopez took Maris's place in right field in the top of the second, with Maris replacing Mantle in center.[34] Mantle underwent surgery to lance his abscess later that day.[35]

At long last, on October 1st, the final day—and Game 162—of the regular season, Maris connects off Boston's Tracy Stallard for his 61st home run. Though reluctant, he comes out for two curtain calls. When he does, the scoreboard shows Yogi Berra at bat, but there are two outs. If Berra was still at bat when Maris came out for the curtain call, then there should only be one out in the inning. (Kubek struck out to lead off the inning, before Maris hit his home run.)[36]

## Stadium Snafus

Detroit's Tiger Stadium did double duty for *61\**, providing the backdrop for the games played at Yankee Stadium and Tiger Stadium in 1961.

The Tigers abandoned their home ballpark following the 1999 season in favor of the newly-built Comerica Park. Sitting vacant at the famed corner of Michigan and Trumbull Avenues, the venerable old stadium, opened in 1912 by Tigers owner Frank Navin, became Crystal's clear choice for a filming location in the summer of 2000.[37]

According to the *Detroit News*, new seating had been added along the baselines and in right field. The familiar blue, which was first painted as part of late-1970s renovations, turned into a more greenish hue, spray-painted to help give the feel of 1961 Yankee Stadium. It was not appreciated by all, as one Detroit-area resident felt it was "sacrilegious how they painted everything."[38]

Though the installation of seats and a paint job went a long way in helping Tiger Stadium appear to be 1961-era Yankee Stadium, computers helped recreate many of the images, turning the double-decked House that Navin Built into the triple-decked House that Ruth Built, complete with the iconic façade.[39]

"The biggest challenge was creating the environment I grew up in, and that Yankee fans remember," Crystal told (New York) *Daily News* writer Richard Huff in 2001. "The House that Ruth Built is another character in the movie.

"It was a magical moment to walk on that field in Detroit and it wasn't Detroit, it was Yankee Stadium the way I knew it."[40]

What Crystal remembered and what is shown in the movie might be two slightly different things, however.

Prominent throughout the movie were the painted section numbers on the beams throughout the stadium. Images of Yankee Stadium from the time period including 1961 show that there were, indeed, section numbers painted on the beams.[41]

A check of Yankee Stadium seating diagrams, compared to those stadium images, reveals that the section numbers painted on beams and façades in *61\** do not correspond to those that would have been in Yankee Stadium in 1961. In fact, they would not even have been in Tiger Stadium in 1961. One of the earliest instances we see occurs around the six-and-a-half minute mark of the film. There is a sign for Section 504 in left-center field. In Yankee Stadium, bleachers would likely have been present where this seating was, but in 1961 Tiger Stadium, there was no Section 504—instead, those seating areas were part of the lower-level General Admission seating. There would be no Section 504 in Tiger Stadium for another 17 years or so, following the late-1970s renovations.

The fences along the box seats near the dugout have a sign for Section 224, which corresponds to the Lower Deck reserved section in that area of 1999 Tiger Stadium. Late in the season, when Roger Maris is being taunted by the Detroit fan dressed as Babe Ruth, there is a sign for Section 434, which is the Upper Deck reserved section in right field, just to the right of the foul pole. The seating sections end there and then another section starts on the second tier, wrapping around the outfield. At the old Yankee Stadium—before and after the mid–1970s renovation—the third tier continued around the foul pole and into right field before stopping not far from right-center field.

Yankee Stadium used single- and double-digit numbers for its seating sections, both before and after the renovations. Eventually, triple-digit numbers came into play for luxury suites and club seating areas, as well as to separate box seats from reserved seats in its various levels. In any case, the section numbers do not match up.

Tiger Stadium would have also used single- and double-digit numbers for its seating sections in 1961. The section numbers were not re-numbered until the late-1970s renovations, in which all sections received new triple-digit numbers—the same ones reflected in *61*\*.[42]

Not only section numbers are mistakes. There is a scoreboard seen hanging from the façade of what is essentially the second deck of Tiger Stadium. This is also apparent when the stadium is serving as Yankee Stadium. Yet, Yankee Stadium at that time did not feature secondary scoreboards affixed to the façade of either the second or third deck of the stadium.[43]

Often, when opting for a panoramic view of Yankee Stadium, the computer-graphic model is featured on the screen. While it does look like the old Yankee Stadium, the feel is more contrived—it is obvious that Crystal and the designers are trying to get it right, but it just does not feel natural. A couple of scenes manage to up-end any doubts that this is not Yankee Stadium, however.

In a scene that is probably meant to take place in late August or early September, Yankees owner Dan Topping is seated in the Lower Deck talking with Ralph Houk about changing the lineup. When the camera comes in and shows the vast sections of empty seats, it is clear that this was not filmed at Yankee Stadium and there are no computer graphics to help. When one sees the General Admission seats of Tiger Stadium beginning to wrap around the outfield with the bleacher section in between, almost any baseball fan should realize this is not Yankee Stadium. Further, it becomes clear that the seats are not the wooden slat seats typical of the day; rather, they are the molded plastic seats that have been painted. The spray-paint residue on the concrete is plainly visible. The blue and orange plastic seats would have been blue and wooden at Tiger Stadium in 1961, and they would have been green and wooden at Yankee Stadium in 1961.[44]

As it turned out, money was a factor in the decision to undertake these projects. Eighty percent of the stadium received a fresh green coat, and it took three months to remove the paint following shooting. Rusty Smith, production designer for *61*\*, told Wired.com that "although painting [Tiger Stadium] and then removing the paint ended up costing a couple hundred thousand dollars, it was still much less than it would have cost to have done it digitally."[45]

Though digital graphics and plenty of paint were used to make 2000 Tiger Stadium look and feel like 1961 Yankee Stadium, there were just enough snafus or incorrect aspects which made it obvious that it was not the House That Ruth Built in *61\**.

## Fake News

Throughout the film *61\** and in real-life 1961, the news media hounded Roger Maris as he and Mickey Mantle provided serious challenges to Babe Ruth's hallowed single-season home-run record. In a city like New York, with several daily newspapers, it might be hard to escape for someone unaccustomed to the constant questioning. For Maris, as is depicted in the movie, a post-game respite in the trainer's room helped stave off the media horde.[46]

The primary members of the media in the film are the characters Sam Simon, Milton Kahn, and Artie Green, each of whom has a different take on the home-run race and the interpersonal relationship between Maris and Mantle. It becomes clear that the sportswriters are meant to play the villains—that they are anti–Maris and prefer to throw their support behind Mantle, the home-grown Yankee, even inducing fans to boo Maris's home runs. Simon, who resembles (New York) *Daily News* sportswriter Dick Young, and Kahn, who is supposed to represent *New York Post* sportswriter Milton Gross, were not the Maris detractors they were made out to be.

"Gross and Young supported Maris,"[47] said Phil Pepe, a longtime New York City sportswriter whose substantial authorship included co-writing a book with Mickey Mantle describing another epic year—*My Favorite Summer: 1956*.[48] Pepe chronicled the chase of Ruth's record for the *New York World-Telegram and Sun*.

Steve Jacobson of *Newsday*, a Yankees beat writer in 1961, called the portrayal of writers as villains as "inaccurate. And so was the booing." His contemporary, Jack Lang of the *Long Island Press*, noted "the beat writers who traveled with the club had a very good relationship with Roger almost the entire season."[49]

While there may be some doubts as to the role of the sportswriters in *61\**, there are several instances that make you wonder where the news is coming from.

Although it is still seemingly early in the season, an undated news headline comes up that says Mantle has hit his 40th home run as the Yankees lost to the Cleveland Indians, 3–2. The Yankees never lost to the Indians by that score during the 1961 season. Furthermore, Mantle actually hit his 40th home run against Kansas City's Art Ditmar, in the second game of an August 2nd doubleheader.[50]

Later it becomes obvious that the dates on these fake newspapers do not correspond to any particular dates in real life. The next newspaper seen is the *New York Journal-American*, dated August 14th, and the baseball headlines state that the Yankees lost their series opener to the Senators, while Pittsburgh took a doubleheader from Cincinnati. Reality shows that the Yankees split a doubleheader in Washington on August 13th, while the Pirates defeated the Philadelphia Phillies. Since the *Journal-American* was an afternoon and evening publication, if it was referring to games on August 14th, it still would not be correct.[51] Even the boxing headline is inaccurate. Emile Griffith (referred to in *61\** as "Griffin") took the welterweight title back from Kid Paret (referred to as "Perot") on

April 1, 1961. Paret recaptured the title on September 30, 1961, but once again lost it to Griffith on March 24, 1962.[52]

Another newspaper, the *Daily News* dated August 5th, talks about Mantle hitting his 44th home run, but it must have been looking into the future. That did not actually happen until August 11th against Washington's Pete Burnside.[53] The *Daily News* also mentions that rain was in the forecast all day, but there was no precipitation in the Bronx for the game on August 5th and the field conditions were dry. A *San Francisco Chronicle* dated August 19th has a photo caption that could only refer to the Yankees game played on July 2nd, when Maris hit a third-inning home run in a win against the Senators— except that the catcher in the photo may not be a Washington Senator, and the comparison of Maris's at-bats to Mantle's does not mention a home run in the third inning.

Another unknown fake newspaper claims that the Yankees beat the Red Sox 6–1 in Boston, which never happened during the 1961 season.[54]

The fake news in the July 16, 1961, *New York Daily Mirror* mentions that Commissioner Ford Frick announced the addition of a separate record for the home run total if someone surpassed Ruth in 162 games as opposed to 154 games, as Ruth had in 1927. The headline shows an asterisk next to the number 61. The date on the *Mirror,* a morning newspaper, is July 16th, inferring that the announcement was made on July 15th, but the real *New York Times* reported Frick's announcement was made on July 17th. There is no mention of an asterisk; rather, Frick is quoted as saying a "distinctive mark" would be in the record books if someone equaled or surpassed the Babe as a result of the longer schedule.[55]

A television news report in *61\** claims that President John F. Kennedy interrupted a press briefing to acknowledge Maris hitting his 47th and 48th home runs. Maris knocked those on August 16th against Chicago, but Kennedy never mentioned them to the press, nor did he have any press conferences that week.[56]

It was not uncommon for newspapers to print figures on such things as home-run chases, tracking the candidates as they went for the record. However, those figures are consistently incorrect in *61\**. The first time this happens is when the tallies are measured through Game 130. For the 1961 Yankees, this occurred on August 27th in Kansas City. For the 1927 Yankees, this happened on September 5th in Boston. The TV-movie states that Mantle had 51 home runs by that point, except in actuality, he did not hit his 51st home run until September 5th (Game 139). Maris is given 53 home runs, but he did not hit his 52nd and 53rd home runs until September 2nd (Game 135). Viewers are told Ruth had 48 home runs by Game 130, but he actually had 44.[57]

Similar scenarios happen again a couple of times later in the film.

## Miscellany

There are, of course, multiple other errors or questionable situations which appear in *61\**, all of which defy categorization, so they will appear in a miscellaneous group.

At the hospital in St. Louis, one of the Maris sons enters his mother's room with a bag containing the bat Roger Maris used to hit his 61st home run. According to another son, the National Baseball Hall of Fame and Museum—where the real bat actually resides— sent the bat to their hotel, where it was picked up. The son removes the bat from the bag with bare hands, and hands it to his mother whose hands are likewise ungloved.

Although it seemed, to this viewer, like a doubtful occurrence in 1998, some 20 years later in the present day, this would be unthinkable. Anyone handling artifacts at the Baseball Hall of Fame must wear gloves to protect the artifact from any potential damage. The likelihood of an artifact being unaccompanied by a Hall of Fame staff member—especially such a prominent one like the Maris bat—is also very slim nowadays.

As it turns out, the TV-movie's account is pure fiction. Jeff Idelson, now President of the Hall of Fame, was leading the Hall's communications department at the time and was with the bat in St. Louis. It never ventured—unaccompanied or not—to a hospital, only Idelson's hotel room and the ballpark. White gloves were also used for handling purposes.[58]

When returning to Opening Day at Yankee Stadium in 1961, there appears to be a very full crowd that afternoon in the Bronx. The reality of the matter, however, is that the attendance was only 14,607 in a ballpark with capacity of more than 67,000 at the time.[59] That figure might have been partly attributable to the chilly weather that day, which is not really reflected in the movie—there are plenty of individuals in the stands wearing short-sleeved shirts.

There might have been a nip in the air, but the crowd gave a warm reception to Maris, who was presented with his American League Most Valuable Player Award for 1960. The film depicts Mrs. Claire Ruth as presenting the award, but in actuality, it was *Daily News* sportswriter Dick Young, chairman of the New York chapter of the Baseball Writers' Association of America. The BBWAA votes for the MVP Award winners. Young's character, Sam Simon, is not even pictured on the field during the pre-game ceremony.[60]

The Yankees logo on the cap that the team wears resembles more the logo typically on the Yankees' home uniform. Photos of Yankees taken during that time period show the logo on the hat to be slightly different, generally similar to the one used today.[61]

One of the reporters, Artie Green, mentions that Maris, the 1960 AL MVP, is batting .200 in the team's first 25 games. By that point—the 25th game was on May 13th—Maris was actually hitting .217.[62]

While the Yankees are out having post-game drinks and find out about DiMaggio's expected appearance at the stadium the next day, Whitey Ford mentions how Mickey Mantle was 18 years old when he came up to the big leagues. When Mantle debuted on April 17, 1951, he was actually 19 years old.[63]

The *Sports Illustrated* cover featuring Mantle and Maris that was placed in the Maris family's scrapbook never was printed in real life. *SI* featured Maris on its cover for the October 2, 1961, issue, but never had both men on the same cover in 1961.[64] On the scrapbook page opposite the magazine cover, there is a ticket stub for the 74th home game at Yankee Stadium, with the correct date of September 9, 1961. Yet, the stub is already affixed to the scrapbook when the magazine cover—which appears to have a date of sometime in June 1961—is being put in. This leads one to wonder whether the magazine cover was added after the season, when it would make sense to have the stub already there, or more likely, was added in "real time," so to speak, which would cause one to wonder why a ticket stub for a game three months away has been placed in there. Also, in the movie, Patricia Maris does not return to New York until the Baltimore series in late September, so how would she have had a ticket stub for a game a couple weeks earlier?

With regard to the scrapbook, at the beginning of *61\**, as Patricia leafs through it at her home, there appears to be a page in between the page with the ticket stub and the page with the fake *Sports Illustrated*. Later in the movie, there is no page in between.

While at the commissioner's office, Milton Kahn explains that when Babe Ruth set "his first record in 1921, he played 14 more games" than the person whose record he broke. It is unclear which record Kahn is referring to: the single-season home run record or the career home run record. When Ruth initially broke the single-season home run record in 1919, he did have almost 30 more games on his schedule than Ned Williamson would have had in 1884. Likewise, when Ruth broke the career home run record in 1921, the season was roughly 20 games or so longer than Roger Connor would have had in 1897. Ruth only surpassed his own records after that point.[65]

Artie Green mentions to Maris that when Ruth set the record, he hit .343 that season—obviously a jab at Maris's far lower batting average, meant to show his failings compared to Ruth. Maris, despite leading the Yankees with 61 home runs, 132 runs scored, and 141 RBI, only hit .269 in 1961. Ruth, however, never hit .343 in any season in his career.[66]

It is often assumed that Maris had 162 games, instead of 154, to surpass Ruth's record, thanks to the longer schedule resulting from expansion. The Yankees actually played 163 games in 1961, as there was a seven-inning 5–5 tie game played against the Orioles in Baltimore, the second game of an April 22 day-night doubleheader. Statistics compiled in tie games count, although the game does not figure into the standings and must be replayed from the start.

Coincidentally enough, the 1998 St. Louis Cardinals also played 163 games, as they, too, had a seven-inning 5–5 tie game, though theirs was on August 24th against Pittsburgh. The 1998 Chicago Cubs also played 163 games, but their extra game was needed to determine whether they would make the playoffs. Though Maris needed all 163 games to surpass Ruth, Mark McGwire only needed 145 to surpass Maris. Chicago's Sammy Sosa, linked with McGwire in the 1998 home run chase, surpassed Maris and tied McGwire on Sept. 13, the Cubs' 150th game. McGwire finished 1998 with 70 round-trippers and Sosa had 66.[67]

Probably the biggest error in *61** might be the title itself. There was never an asterisk or any other mark to reflect that Maris' record was in any way different than the record Ruth set. Sam Simon suggests separate records with an asterisk. Commissioner Frick only indicates that the two records be listed together, noting the circumstances under which they occurred.

The chatter about the asterisk may have begun when Frick made his ruling, but the notion gained speed in the media. Frick felt determined to defend himself, telling reporters in September: "As for that star or asterisk business, I don't know how that cropped up or was attributed to me, because I never said it. I certainly never meant to belittle Maris's feat should he wind up with more than sixty. Both names will appear in the book as having set records, but under different conditions."[68]

Frick also reiterated that the same action would apply to other records set in the 162-game schedule that the American League adopted to accommodate the 1961 expansion clubs, the Los Angeles Angels and the re-incarnated Washington Senators. The National League was scheduled to adopt the longer slate when it expanded for the 1962 season. Frick expected baseball to return to a 154-game schedule.[69] As it turns out, 162 games has been the standard—for full seasons—ever since.

Obviously, many of these errors might not be readily apparent to the casual viewer or baseball fan. They do not necessarily detract from the film for those viewers who are not aware of them or who do not expect them. One might expect filmmakers to utilize some amount of artistic license, but many of these mistakes are ones that could have been researched and portrayed correctly, even in 1999 or 2000.

Executive Producer Ross Greenburg felt differently when confronted with some of the film's inaccuracies, believing that "[i]f you analyze film to see how they depicted actual events, you can hold up our film to any other and we'd get an A-plus."[70]

Perhaps that grade might be generous.

There were other storylines following the Yankees in 1961, many of which did not make the final script, much less the cutting-room floor. Maris alludes to these during one scene in the film where he wonders why the press is hounding him for quotes and focusing on the home run race when he has many teammates having great games or seasons.

"I don't think you do understand. You were there," Maris tells Milton Kahn after a game against Detroit when he failed to homer. "Moose won the game for us, Ellie's batting .340, Whitey's going to win 20 games this season. Why don't you talk to them? I'm not the only one on this team."

Some of those individuals involved in those storylines were consultants to Crystal in *61\**. Others were not for one reason or another. We will go into a few of those subplots here.

## The New "Perfessor"

When the Yankees reported to Spring Training in St. Petersburg, Florida, in February 1961, the change in leadership that had been expected for some time finally became visible to the players. Roy Hamey replaced George Weiss as General Manager, and Ralph Houk would be piloting the club, replacing Casey Stengel, who managed New York from 1949 through 1960.

Houk, a rarely used Yankees catcher for eight seasons, who also served on Stengel's coaching staff and for three seasons managed the club's Triple-A affiliate in Denver, was named to the position on October 20, 1960. Stengel had signed a two-year contract after the 1958 season, but the 70-year-old skipper would not return after dropping a seven-game World Series to the Pittsburgh Pirates.

Assured by owner Dan Topping that there would be "no interference from the front office," Houk accepted a one-year contract "because at the end of the year I want the Yankees to feel free to do what they want if they don't think I did a good job" he told reporters at his introductory press conference.[71]

Houk already had managing experience at the major-league level, if not officially so. He filled in for an ailing Stengel on May 28, 1960, and remained acting manager until Stengel returned from his illness on June 7th. In 12 games over 10 days, Houk had a record of six wins and six losses.[72]

He had been deemed the "heir apparent" to Stengel and reportedly turned down offers from several other clubs in order to have his chance one day at managing the Yankees.[73]

All Houk proceeded to do in 1961 was lead the Yankees to 109 wins in the expanded regular season, their most since the 110-win 1927 season, and then capped that off with four additional wins over Cincinnati in the World Series.

He recapped the 1961 season in the book that he wrote with Charles Dexter, *Ballplay-*

*ers Are Human, Too.* Over half the book retells the season from his point of view, with interjections from his wife Bette. Following the World Series, Houk described the season as an "incredible year" with "not one beef from a player, not one phone call from someone who says one of your players is down somewhere causing trouble. Nothing but great games, great pitching, the greatest of all hitting … and Rog's…."[74]

Forty years later, Houk was asked to reflect on that season and *61\**. While he noted some aspects of the film were accurate and others a bit off, it was nevertheless generally well done. Houk claimed that the movie made the 1961 season to be all about the home run chase, but in actuality, "it was all about winning the pennant. The home-run thing wasn't built up at all on the team. You were trying to win a game."[75]

Even in mid–July 1961, he hoped "they both break the record," as he told the Baltimore Sports Reporters Association at a luncheon. "But our job is to win pennants, not worry about setting individual records," he maintained.[76]

## Ellie's Career Season

By the start of the 1950 season, the New York Yankees were one of many major-league clubs that had not yet débuted an African-American after Jackie Robinson took his bow with the Dodgers in 1947. A small Associated Press blurb in *The New York Times* on July 20, 1950, announced the purchase of Elston Howard and Frank Barnes by the Yankees from the Kansas City Monarchs.[77]

Despite missing time to serve in the armed forces during the Korean War, Howard integrated the big league club on April 14, 1955.[78] He had been signed as an outfielder but gradually spent more time behind the plate as Yogi Berra's understudy. Though he played first base more than catcher in 1959, Howard became the Yankees' full-time receiver in 1960.[79]

The change from Stengel to Houk would benefit Howard in 1961. Arlene Howard, Elston's wife, recalled that "he found Houk to be more approachable" and that the new skipper "loved Elston's attitude, the way he handled pitchers, and his rifle-like arm."[80] Coach Wally Moses tinkered with Howard's stance, which allowed him "to hit the ball much better through the middle and to the opposite field."[81]

Howard turned in what was his career year, to that point, in 1961. Hitting .348 with 155 hits, 21 home runs, and 77 RBI, he offered production surpassed by few on the team not named Mantle and Maris. His batting average was good for third best in the majors. He was also named to his sixth and seventh (of his 12 total) All-Star Games.[82]

All those factors led to a 10th-place finish in the 1961 American League MVP voting, a ballot that ended up seeing four of his teammates ahead of him. Howard would receive his due in 1963, winning the AL MVP Award and his first of two Gold Gloves.[83]

Arlene Howard recalled her husband saying that he stopped trying to hit home runs, but he guessed, "it is true that if you meet the pitch, the homers will come." So did the reporters, as Mrs. Howard recounted her husband "would just smile as the press asked Roger (Maris) the same questions over and over again" as he sat at the next locker, as reporters were fixated on the home run race, rather than the batting championship.[84]

Seemingly enough, so, too, were the folks creating *61\**. Mrs. Howard enjoyed the film, but noted that Bobby Hosea, the actor who played her husband, did not receive many lines in the movie. Other than mentioning his batting average once, Howard's character was largely overlooked other than in a supporting role.[85]

Yankees catchers had a big season. Howard's backup, Johnny Blanchard, hit .305 to go along with 21 home runs and 54 RBI in 93 games played.

## Ford's Model Year

Despite his All-Star status, Whitey Ford did not have a great season in 1960. However, with an offense firing on all pistons, he rebounded in 1961, becoming a workhorse for the Yankees as they captured the World Series.

Typically pitching on three days of rest, Ford powered through the heart of the season, winning 14 straight decisions from June 2nd through August 10th, as his record climbed to 20 wins and two losses. In a league-high 39 starts, he finished with a league-leading 25 victories to go against four losses. Ford also achieved a career-high 209 strike-outs en route to the Cy Young Award, which he secured by only three votes over Milwaukee's Warren Spahn. He came in fifth in the American League MVP balloting, as well.[86]

The unquestioned ace of the Yankees' pitching staff, Ford pitched 14 scoreless innings in two wins to help New York beat the Cincinnati Reds, earning World Series MVP honors.

Ford became the first Yankees pitcher to win at least 20 games since teammate Bob Turley did so in 1958. His 25 victories were the most by any Yankees pitcher in 27 years.

He jokingly admitted that the notion of being a 20-game winner was slow to grow on him, calling it, tongue-in-cheek, "strictly for the birds. It was so pleasant in the old days when I was only a nineteen-game winner or an eighteen-game winner or even a twelve-game winner. I'd finish a game and have a quiet coke (sic) in front of my locker. Nobody bothered me or paid attention to me."

"At least [the reporters] don't drive me as crazy as they do Mantle and Maris," Ford noted with a sense of amusement. "The questions thrown at them get sillier and sillier. I've never been able to figure out why smart guys ask such stupid questions."[87]

The jocular Ford is often depicted in *61\** as Mantle's closest friend on the team, often bailing him out of difficult situations resulting from Mantle's penchant for a lively nightlife. The two essentially grew up together on the Yankees and were inducted into the Baseball Hall of Fame together in 1974.[88]

## Bullpen Ace

For everything that Whitey Ford was to the Yankees' rotation, Luis Arroyo was to their bullpen. The Puerto Rican lefty had a modest major-league career prior to joining the Yankees, earning an All-Star berth as a rookie with the Cardinals in 1955. But 1961 would clearly be the best year of his career.

It started slowly, as he was coming off an injury suffered in Spring Training, but as May turned into June, he quickly became the go-to pitcher in the Yanks' relief corps, earning 15 wins in 65 relief appearances. Only two pitchers had more wins in relief in the previous 40 years, and only five in the 56 years since.

During Ford's winning streak in 1961, Arroyo was often the one to come in and finish off the games that the Chairman started. The two had lockers next to each other and sportswriters often could ask both the same questions.

When Tom Meany asked Ford whether Arroyo would win 20 games before he did, Whitey responded, "That's all right. We expect to sign a joint contract next winter and split it, maybe 60–40. The only trouble with that is that Luis will get the 60."[89]

Yet Ford was quick to acknowledge Arroyo's ability to come in and preserve leads when he "was lousy but lucky" as a starter. Whitey said Lefty "Gomez had Johnny Murphy as his rescue man and I've got Luis Arroyo, not to mention The Mick."[90]

Arroyo credited his All-Star work in 1961 to the development of his screwball. It allowed him to test right-handed hitters who did not always expect the sometimes two-foot break as the ball neared home plate.

"I'm a new pitcher because I have a new pitch," Arroyo said. "I keep the hitters guessing and I can usually get my stuff over the plate. There's not much more to pitching than that."

The screwball led to many ground balls, which the Yankees infield often turned into double plays. Arroyo forced 17 double plays in 1961, the most of any major league relief pitcher that season.

"Two for one," Arroyo noted. "One pitch, two outs—that's the way to get games over fast."[91]

His abilities during his career year were gaining notice among the Yankees' rivals, as well. The Detroit Tigers were locked in a pennant race with the Yankees through much of the summer. When New York swept a three-game series from Detroit in early September, Tigers manager Bob Scheffing was quick to give credit to the reliever.

"He won two games and saved the other," noted Scheffing, though one should bear in mind that Major League Baseball did not consider saves to be an official statistic until 1969. "He's changed a mediocre pitching staff into a pretty good one."[92]

## World Series Champs

Seemingly forgotten in *61\** is the fact that the Yankees won the 1961 World Series in five games over the Cincinnati Reds.

But the storylines there were different. Other than Whitey Ford earning MVP honors with 14 shutout innings in two wins, the biggest contributions came from Yankees who were not the biggest names on the team.

Mickey Mantle was relegated to pinch-hitting duty in two games as he continued to recover from the abscess on his hip that sidelined him in September; he ended his chase at 54 home runs. The M&M boys played in all five games and combined to hit .120 (3-for-25) with one home run. Maris's home run was a crucial one, however, as it came in the top of the ninth inning at Crosley Field in Game Three, giving the Yankees a 3–2 lead which Luis Arroyo would preserve.

Johnny Blanchard, Hector Lopez, Bobby Richardson, and Moose Skowron all hit over .300 in the World Series to help lift the Yankees to the championship.[93]

Houk recalled the feeling in the Game Five as the Yankees pulled ahead of the Reds in what would be a 13–5 victory.

"There was no stopping my impossible Yanks," Houk remembered. "Mickey was out of the game but Blanchard was hitting like Mickey. Yogi was out of the game but Lopez was hitting like Yogi. And the Moose was hitting like the Moose.

"Freddy Hutchinson threw every pitcher in Ohio against us. They all looked like Spud Murray in batting practice."[94]

Following the final World Series game, Mantle, Maris, and Berra immediately returned home while Houk and the remainder of the team stayed in Cincinnati to celebrate the championship.[95]

## Epilogue

While *61\** received mostly positive remarks from a variety of critics and viewers, it does fall somewhat short in some accounts of the 1961 season. From bungled play descriptions to mistaken identities of ballplayers to some of the challenges faced in transforming one ballpark to look like another, among a bunch of other inaccuracies, there are plenty of opportunities to figure out what made the film successful as well as slightly disappointing.

Even though its primary focus is the home-run chase between Mickey Mantle and Roger Maris, there are several other storylines that go largely—and unfortunately—ignored.

The 1962 New York Yankees, though successful, could not reach the same level of the previous season. Maris and Mantle once again led the team in home runs, with 33 and 30, respectively; Lopez took over in left field for an aging Berra; Blanchard provided less pop off the bench, even though he was still a crucial part of the team; Tom Tresh replaced Kubek at shortstop; Ralph Terry outshined Ford as the Yankees' only 20-game winner; and Marshall Bridges took over for Arroyo as the team's late-inning hurler. Ninety-six wins were good enough to win the American League pennant, and Houk led the club to a seven-game win over San Francisco in the World Series. Houk became the first person in major league history to win World Series titles in his first two seasons as a manager.[96]

Yet, 1961 still holds a special place with baseball fans, Yankees fans especially. Even though *61\** is not always true to the facts, it provides viewers with a special look into the season, allowing one to feel as though you were witnessing the story as it happened. If nothing else, Billy Crystal and his crew were marvelous in that regard.

NOTES

1. Nate Scott, "The 50 Greatest Yogi Berra Quotes," *USA Today*, September 23, 2015, ftw.usatoday.com/2015/09/the-50-greatest-yogi-berra-quotes, last accessed August 15, 2015.

2. Frank Litsky, "Stupid, You Say?," *Washington Post and Times Herald*, September 18, 1960: AW4.

3. "Yogi Says It's So," *Washington Post*, March 28, 1998, E2.

4. "61\* (TV Movie 2001)—Release Info," Internet Movie Database, www.imdb.com/title/tt0250934/releaseinfo?ref_=tt_dt_dt, last accessed August 28, 2017.

5. "Progressive Leaders & Records for Home Runs," Baseball Reference, Baseball-Reference.com, www.baseball-reference.com/leaders/HR_progress.shtml, last accessed August 28, 2017.

6. Robert Bianco, "Actors Smack Home Runs in Maris vs. Mantle Battle," *Usa Today*, April 27, 2001 (photocopy of article in *61\** File, A. Bartlett Giamatti Research Center, National Baseball Hall of Fame and Museum, Cooperstown, New York).

7. Steve Wulf, "Sweet Spot," *ESPN the Magazine*, espn.go.com/magazine/wulf_20010425.html, April 25, 2001, last accessed August 15, 2018 (photocopy of article in *61\** File, A. Bartlett Giamatti Research Center, National Baseball Hall of Fame and Museum, Cooperstown, New York).

8. Jeannie Williams, "On Baseball, Bush Is Crystal Clear," *Usa Today*, April 11, 2001 (Photocopy of article

in *61** clipping file at National Baseball Hall of Fame Library in Cooperstown, New York). See also: Richard Sandomir, "When Mantle and Maris Chased Babe Ruth's Ghost," *New York Times*, April 25, 2001: D3.

9. The original Washington Senators franchise in the American League relocated to the Minneapolis-St. Paul area following the 1960 season and was renamed the Minnesota Twins. For more information, see: Charles Johnson, "Cities Hit Homer!," *Minneapolis Star*, October 27, 1960: 1A, 3A.

10. "Los Angeles Angels at Baltimore Orioles Box Score, April 11, 1961," Baseball Reference, www.baseball-reference.com/boxes/BAL/BAL196104110.shtml, last accessed August 27, 2017.

11. See transaction information in each man's Baseball Reference player profile. Bob Cerv: www.baseball-reference.com/players/c/cervbo01.shtml#all_transactions_other, last accessed August 15, 2018; Roger Maris: www.baseball-reference.com/players/m/marisro01.shtml#all_transactions_other, last accessed August 15, 2018.

12. New York Yankees, *New York Yankees 1961 Official Program and Scorecard* (New York: Harry M. Stevens, Inc., 1961). Based on information inside the program, it is evident this is for the season's opening game against Minnesota on April 11, 1961.

13. See Billy Gardner's transaction information at Baseball-Reference.com player profile: www.baseball-reference.com/players/g/gardnbi02.shtml#all_transactions_other, last accessed August 15, 2018.

14. New York Yankees, *New York Yankees 1961 Press-TV-Radio Guide* (New York, 1961), 18–20. Preseason roster lists highest number as No. 53.

15. See Lenny Green's profile Baseball Reference, www.baseball-reference.com/players/g/greenle01.shtml, last accessed August 15, 2018.

16. For further information on Minnesota Twins uniform numbers during the 1961 season (and other seasons), see Mark Stang and Linda Harkness, *Baseball by the Numbers: A Guide to the Uniform Numbers of Major League Teams* (Lanham, MD: Scarecrow Press, 1997) and "1961 Minnesota Twins Uniform Numbers," Baseball Reference, last accessed August 26, 2017.

17. "Minnesota Twins at New York Yankees Box Score, April 11, 1961," Baseball Reference, www.baseball-reference.com/boxes/NYA/NYA196104110.shtml, last accessed August 26, 2017.

18. "Ted Bowsfield Career Home Runs Allowed," Baseball Reference, www.baseball-reference.com/players/b/bowsfte01.shtml, last accessed August 27, 2017.

19. Box score and play-by-play information for Yankees-Tigers games can be found at Baseball Reference, www.baseball-reference.com/boxes/NYA/NYA196109020.shtml, September 2, 1961, last accessed August 15, 2018; www.baseball-reference.com/boxes/NYA/NYA196109030.shtml, September 3, 1961, last accessed August 15, 2018.

20. "New York Yankees at Baltimore Orioles Box Score, September 20, 1961," Baseball Reference, www.baseball-reference.com/boxes/BAL/BAL196109200.shtml, last accessed August 27, 2017.

21. "Minnesota Twins at New York Yankees Box Score, April 11, 1961," Baseball Reference, www.baseball-reference.com/boxes/NYA/NYA196104110.shtml, last accessed August 26, 2017.

22. "Roger Maris vs. Pete Burnside," Baseball Reference, www.baseball-reference.com/play-index/batter_vs_pitcher.cgi?batter=marisro01&pitcher=burnspe01, last accessed August 27, 2017.

23. "Mickey Mantle Career Home Runs," Baseball Reference, www.baseball-reference.com/players/event_hr.fcgi?id=mantlmi01&t=b, last accessed August 27, 2017.

24. Box score and play-by-play information for Yankees-Tigers games can be found at Baseball Reference for June 16, 1961, www.baseball-reference.com/boxes/DET/DET196106160.shtml, Last accessed August 15, 2018; June 17, 1961, www.baseball-reference.com/boxes/DET/DET196106170.shtml, Last accessed August 15, 2018; and June 18, 1961, www.baseball-reference.com/boxes/DET/DET196106180.shtml, last accessed August 15, 2018.

25. According to Mantle's 1961 Game Log at Baseball Reference (www.baseball-reference.com/players/gl.fcgi?id=mantlmi01&t=b&year=1961), he struck out three times in one game on May 7, August 23, August 29, and September 1. The final instance was the only time he performed the feat at home.

26. "Mickey Mantle Career Home Runs," Baseball Reference, www.baseball-reference.com/players/event_hr.fcgi?id=mantlmi01&t=b, last accessed August 27, 2017.

27. "1961 New York Yankees Batting Orders," Baseball Reference, www.baseball-reference.com/teams/NYY/1961-batting-orders.shtml, last accessed August 27, 2017.

28. See box scores and play-by-play information for those games, accessible at Baseball Reference, www.baseball-reference.com/teams/NYY/1961-schedule-scores.shtml, last accessed August 15, 2018.

29. Whitey Ford was the Yankees' starting pitcher against Detroit at Yankee Stadium on May 14, 1961 (first game of a doubleheader), Baseball Reference, www.baseball-reference.com/boxes/NYA/NYA196105141.shtml, last accessed August 15, 2018; July 4, 1961 (first game of a doubleheader), Baseball Reference, www.baseball-reference.com/boxes/NYA/NYA196107041.shtml, last accessed August 15, 2018; and September 1, 1961, Baseball Reference, www.baseball-reference.com/boxes/NYA/NYA196109010.shtml, last accessed August 15, 2018.

30. Associated Press, "Mantle Pulls Muscle in Left Arm, May Miss Tigers Game Today," *Washington Post*, September 3, 1961: C1.

31. Box score and play-by-play information for Yankees-Tigers games can be found at Baseball Reference, September 2, 1961, www.baseball-reference.com/boxes/NYA/NYA196109020.shtml, last accessed August 15,

2018; September 3, 1961, www.baseball-reference.com/boxes/NYA/NYA196109030.shtml, last accessed August 15, 2018.

32. "Roger Maris Career Home Runs," Baseball Reference, www.baseball-reference.com/players/event_hr.fcgi?id=marisro01&t=b, last accessed August 27, 2017.

33. "New York Yankees at Baltimore Orioles Box Score, September 20, 1961," Baseball Reference, www.baseball-reference.com/boxes/BAL/BAL196109200.shtml, last accessed August 27, 2017.

34. "Baltimore Orioles at New York Yankees Box Score, September 26, 1961," Baseball Reference, www.baseball-reference.com/boxes/NYA/NYA196109260.shtml, last accessed August 27, 2017.

35. John Drebinger, "Maris Hitless as Yankees Beat Red Sox; Mantle to Leave Hospital Sunday," *New York Times*, September 30, 1961: 19.

36. "Boston Red Sox at New York Yankees Box Score, October 1, 1961," Baseball Reference, www.baseball-reference.com/boxes/NYA/NYA196110010.shtml, last accessed August 26, 2017.

37. "Comerica Park Information—Past Tigers Venues," Detroit Tigers, detroit.tigers.mlb.com/det/ballpark/information/index.jsp?content=pastvenues, last accessed August 28, 2017.

38. Tim Kiska and Adam Graham, "It's 1961 All Over Again at Tiger Stadium: 2,000 Locals Help Transform Tiger Stadium into Yankees' Ballpark for HBO Film '*61*,'" *Detroit News*, August 8, 2000: 1C; detnews.com/2000/tigers/0008/08/c01–101924.htm (photocopy of detnews.com article in *61*\* File, A. Bartlett Giamatti Research Center, National Baseball Hall of Fame and Museum, Cooperstown, New York).

39. Sandomir, "When Mantle and Maris Chased."

40. Richard Huff, "Crystal's '61*' a Homer-ic Odyssey," *Daily News* (New York), January 29, 2001: 75 (photocopy of article in *61*\* File, A. Bartlett Giamatti Research Center, National Baseball Hall of Fame and Museum, Cooperstown, New York).

41. As seen in various images in a file folder of interior photographs of Yankee Stadium held by the A. Bartlett Giamatti Research Center, National Baseball Hall of Fame and Museum, Cooperstown, New York.

42. Much research was undertaken in order to determine when the section numbers were switched. The *American League Red Books*, from 1960 through 1980, were the primary sources of seating diagrams for Yankee Stadium and Tiger Stadium to determine what the section numbering would have been like in 1961 and thereafter. The Tigers' media guides from 1977 through 1979 contained a section called "Tiger Stadium Facts," which detailed the various renovation projects undertaken during that time period. More recent Yankee Media Guides show the inclusion of the triple-digit box and club seating areas present well after the mid-1970s renovation of Yankee Stadium.

43. See Note 41.

44. Comparison of Yankee Stadium and Tiger Stadium seating diagrams make it perfectly clear that, in such scenes, this stadium is not Yankee Stadium, as depicted.

45. Robin Clewley, "Re-Create It, and They Will Come," Wired, www.wired.com/2001/04/re-create-it-and-they-will-come/, April 20, 2001, last accessed August 29, 2017.

46. Louis Effrat, "Maris Sulks in Trainer's Room as Futile Night Changes Mood," *New York Times*, September 16, 1961: 13.

47. Hal Bock, "Writers Find Flaws in '61*," Associated Press, *Daily Oklahoman*, May 2, 2001: 30.

48. Mickey Mantle and Phil Pepe, *My Favorite Summer: 1956* (New York: Doubleday, 1991).

49. *Ibid.*

50. "Mickey Mantle Career Home Runs," Baseball Reference, www.baseball-reference.com/players/event_hr.fcgi?id=mantlmi01&t=b, last accessed August 26, 2017.

51. Baseball-Reference.com has scores for games on August 13, 1961 (www.baseball-reference.com/boxes/?month=8&day=13&year=1961, last accessed August 15, 2018) and August 14, 1961 (www.baseball-reference.com/boxes/?year=1961&month=8&day=14, last accessed August 15, 2018).

52. Richard Goldstein, "Emile Griffith, Boxer Who Unleashed a Fatal Barrage, Dies at 75" *New York Times*, July 23, 2013, www.nytimes.com/2013/07/24/sports/emile-griffith-boxer-who-unleashed-a-fatal-barrage-dies-at-75.html?mcubz=1.

53. "Mickey Mantle Career Home Runs," Baseball Reference, www.baseball-reference.com/players/event_hr.fcgi?id=mantlmi01&t=b, last accessed August 26, 2017.

54. "1961 New York Yankees Schedule," Baseball Reference, www.baseball-reference.com/teams/NYY/1961-schedule-scores.shtml, last accessed August 26, 2017.

55. "Ruth's Record Can Be Broken Only in 154 Games, Frick Rules," *New York Times*, July 18, 1961, 20.

56. According to the JFK Presidential Library and Museum's records, press conferences were held on August 10, 1961, and August 30, 1961. The only records featuring Roger Maris were photographs taken during Maris's April 27, 1962, visit to the White House as national campaign co-chairman of the National Multiple Sclerosis Society.

57. All home run figures checked against respective season schedules at Baseball-Reference.com.

58. Jeff Idelson, email message to author, August 30, 2017.

59. Yankee Stadium capacity figure from *American League 1961 Red Book*.

60. John Drebinger, "Minnesota Breaks into Majors with a Three-Hit Shutout Over Yanks Here," *New York Times*, April 12, 1961: 50.

61. Difference in logo seen in various images of Yankee caps on baseball cards, team publications, pho
tographs, etc.

62. "Roger Maris 1961 Batting Gamelogs," Baseball Reference, www.baseball-reference.com/players/gl.
fcgi?id=marisro01&t=b&year=1961, last accessed August 15, 2018.

63. "Mickey Mantle," Baseball Reference, Baseball-Reference.com, www.baseball-reference.com/play-
ers/m/mantlmi01.shtml, last accessed August 26, 2017.

64. "*Sports Illustrated* Vault—1960s Issues," *Sports Illustrated*, www.si.com/vault/issues/1960#y1961, last
accessed August 27, 2017.

65. According to the baseball-reference.com page in Note 5, in 1919, Babe Ruth hit 29 home runs to surpass Ned Williamson's single-season home run record of 27, which Williamson set in 1884. Ruth accumulated
162 home runs through 1921, surpassing Roger Connor's career home-run record of 138. Connor's career
ended in 1897. According to the 1884 *Spalding Guide*, National League teams had a 112-game schedule, and
according to the 1919 *Spalding Guide*, American League teams had a 140-game schedule. *1884 Spalding's Base
Ball Guide* (Chicago: A.G. Spalding & Bros.), 117; *1919 Spalding's Base Ball Guide*, John Foster ed. (New York:
American Sports Publishing Co.), 397.

66. "Babe Ruth," Baseball Reference, www.baseball-reference.com/players/r/ruthba01.shtml Last accessed
August 28, 2017.

67. Schedule information taken from each team's Baseball-Reference.com page and home run information taken from each player's respective home run log.

68. "No \* Will Mar Homer Records, Says Frick With †† for Critics," *New York Times,* September 22,
1961: 38.

69. *Ibid.*

70. Sandomir, "When Mantle and Maris Chased."

71. John Drebinger, "Houk Named Manager of Yankees with One-Year Contract at $35,000 Salary," *New
York Times*, October 21, 1960: 38.

72. Louis Effrat, "White Sox Beat Yankees After Two Errors by McDougald in Ninth Inning," *New York
Times*, June 7, 1960: 39.

73. Louis Effrat, "Yanks 5–1 Victors," *New York Times*, May 29, 1960: S1.

74. Ralph Houk, *Ballplayers Are Human, Too,* taped and ed. Charles Dexter (New York: G.P. Putnam's
Sons, 1962), 247. The book's text ends with these ellipses. Nothing else follows.

75. Dick Scanlon, "Yankees' Manager Approves of '61\*,'" *Gainesville Sun*, April 18, 2001: 1C, 8C.

76. "Houk Roots for His 2 Stars," Associated Press, *New York Times*, July 18, 1961: 20.

77. "Yanks Get 2 Negro Players," Associated Press, *New York Times*, July 20, 1950: 40.

78. When Howard integrated the Yankees, three major league clubs still had yet to début an African
American: the Phillies, the Tigers, and the Red Sox. Boston was the final team to do so, in 1959.

79. "Elston Howard," Baseball Reference, www.baseball-reference.com/players/h/howarel01.shtml, last
accessed August 28, 2017.

80. Arlene Howard and Ralph Wimbish, *Elston and Me: The Story of the First Black Yankee* (Columbia:
University of Missouri Press, 2001), 103.

81. *Ibid.*, 104.

82. From 1959 through 1962, Major League Baseball held two All-Star Games in each season.

83. "Elston Howard," Baseball-Reference.com.

84. Howard and Wimbish, 106.

85. *Ibid.*, 107.

86. "Whitey Ford," Baseball Reference, www.baseball-reference.com/players/f/fordwh01.shtml Last
accessed August 28, 2017.

87. Arthur Daley, "The Flippant Flipper," Sports of the Times, *New York Times*, August 20, 1961: S2.

88. Dave Anderson, "Mickey and Whitey, Together Again," Sports of the Times, *New York Times*, January
17, 1974: 49.

89. *Ibid.*

90. Hy Hurwitz, "'Lousy but Lucky'—Ford," *Boston Globe*, July 9, 1961: 55.

91. "Luis Arroyo Proudest of All-Star Players," United Press International, *Washington Post*, July 29,
1961: A17.

92. "Arroyo, Not M-Boys, Gives Yankees Lead," Associated Press, *Washington* Post, September 6, 1961:
D1.

93. "1961 World Series—New York Yankees Over Cincinnati Reds (4–1)," Baseball Reference, www.
baseball-reference.com/postseason/1961_WS.shtml, last accessed August 27, 2017.

94. Houk and Dexter, *Ballplayers Are Human, Too*, 245.

95. *Ibid.*, 246.

96. "1962 New York Yankees Statistics," Baseball Reference, www.baseball-reference.com/teams/NYY/
1962.shtml, last accessed August 28, 2017.

# About the Contributors

Jeanine **Basinger** is the Corwin-Fuller Professor of Film Studies and founding chair of the film studies department at Wesleyan University. She is the founder and curator of Wesleyan's Cinema Archives, where she oversees the archiving of papers donated from iconic actors, directors, and producers, including Frank Capra, Clint Eastwood, Elia Kazan, Ingrid Bergman, Martin Scorsese, John Waters, and Raoul Walsh. She is the author of twelve books and numerous articles on film.

Ron **Briley** taught history and film studies for 39 years at Sandia Prep School in Albuquerque, New Mexico, where he also served as assistant head of school and is now faculty emeritus. He has also served on numerous committees for the Organization of American Historians and American Historical Association. A Distinguished Lecturer for the Organization of American Historians, he is the author of six books and numerous scholarly articles and encyclopedia entries on the history of sport, music, and film.

Ron **Coleman** is a trademark lawyer, commercial litigator and author of the popular "Likelihood of Confusion" blog on intellectual property and free expression. He led the fight by Simon Tam and his band, The Slants, to register the band's name as a trademark after refusal by the U.S. Patent and Trademark Office. As a result, in 2017 the U.S. Supreme Court invalidated the "disparagement bar" to trademark registration in *Matal v. Tam*. The author of numerous law-related works and articles and a frequent speaker, he is a partner at Mandelbaum Salsburg in Roseland, New Jersey, and a graduate of Princeton University and Northwestern University School of Law.

Erin **DiCesare** holds a Ph.D. in Interdisciplinary Humanities from Florida State University. She currently serves as the Department Chair for the Interdisciplinary Studies, Religion, and Philosophy Department at Johnson C. Smith University in Charlotte, NC, where she is also an Assistant Professor of Interdisciplinary Studies. Her areas of research focus on popular culture, with a specific focus on reality television. She has published an article entitled "The Sexual Other and Reality Television: Representations, Repression, and Recovery" in the international journal *Trans-Humanities* as well as a pedagogical focused article in the American based journal *The Atrium* entitled "Interdisciplinary Research and Education in the Digital Age."

Duke **Goldman** is a longtime member of the Society for American Baseball Research (SABR). His research is focused primarily on the Negro Leagues and the process of baseball integration. He is a two-time winner of the McFarland–SABR Baseball Research Award, given each year for the best articles on baseball history or biography. Born in the Bronx, he is a lifelong Yankee hater but has more books on the Yankees than on any other team.

Louis **Gordon** holds a J.D. from Cardozo Law School, a Master's of Professional Writing and Ph.D. in Political Science from the University of Southern California. He teaches in the Department of Political Science at California State University at San Bernardino and is a member of the National Book Critics Circle. He is the co-author, with Ian Oxnevad, of *Middle East Politics for the New Millennium* (2016).

Paul **Hensler** is a long-time member of the Society for American Baseball Research and a frequent contributor to the Cooperstown Symposium on Baseball and American Culture. He has published numerous articles on baseball history, as well as two books, the most recent of which is *The New Boys of Summer: Baseball's Radical Transformation in the Late Sixties* (2017).

Jeffrey M. **Katz** is a born-and-raised New Yorker and a lifelong Yankees fan. He is the author of *Plié Ball! Baseball Meets Dance on Stage and Screen* (McFarland, 2016) and lives in New York City, working as a librarian and educator and still rooting for the Bronx Bombers. At the age of nine, he was a Flying A Gasoline Honorary New York Yankees Bat Boy, an achievement that marked the beginning and end of his professional baseball career.

David **Krell** is the author of *Our Bums: The Brooklyn Dodgers in History, Memory and Popular Culture* (McFarland, 2015). He often contributes to SABR publications and speaks at SABR conferences, in addition to the Cooperstown Symposium on Baseball and American Culture and the Mid-Atlantic Nostalgia Convention. His "Krell's Korner" series of articles in the New York State Bar Association's *Entertainment, Arts and Sports Law Journal* often highlight sports history. He chairs SABR's Elysian Fields Chapter (Northern New Jersey) and Spring Training Committee.

Bill **Lamb** spent more than 30 years as a state/county prosecutor in New Jersey prior to his retirement in 2007. He is the editor of *The Inside Game*, the quarterly newsletter of SABR's Deadball Era Committee, and the author of *Black Sox in the Courtroom: The Grand Jury, Criminal Trial and Civil Litigation* (McFarland, 2013). His essays have been published in *Base Ball: A Journal of the Early Game*, and *Baseball Research Journal*, and *The National Pastime*.

Martin S. **Lessner** graduated from the Wharton School of the University of Pennsylvania, where he wrote feature articles for the school newspaper and attended innumerable Phillies games, and from Villanova University School of Law. He is the chairman of the Young Conaway Stargatt & Taylor corporate litigation section in Delaware, where besides litigating mergers and acquisitions, he runs the firm's Phillies season ticket plan.

Rolando **Llanes** is a State of Florida Registered Architect with a Master of Architecture from Princeton University. He is president of CIVICA Architecture, which specializes in educational, residential, and recreational projects. He has consulted on several ballpark-related design projects including efforts to preserve Fenway Park. In 2007, he produced *White Elephant: What Is There to Save?*, a film on the history of Miami Baseball Stadium, the Spring Training home of the Baltimore Orioles from 1959 to 1990.

Dashiell **Moore** is a Ph.D. student and tutor at the University of Sydney. His dissertation proposes a rethinking of contemporary poetics through the model provided by Edouard Glissant in his work, *Poetics of Relation*. He has a wide range of scholarly interests, varying from the effect of terrorism upon literature, bilingualism, the influence a sport/pastime has on the making of cultural groups, and cultural studies more generally. He has published several articles and book reviews through the *Cordite Poetry Review*.

Richard **Pioreck** has written several plays, including *Say It Ain't So, Joe; Nicolette and Aucassin* (book and lyrics); and *#1 with a Bullet*. His baseball articles have appeared in *Racism and Discrimination in the Sporting World* (forthcoming), *Memories & Dreams* (the official magazine of the Baseball Hall of Fame) and *MLB Insider*. He was editor of the essay collection celebrating the 50th anniversary of the New York Mets, which drew papers from the 2012 conference at Hofstra University.

Matt **Rothenberg** holds a master's degree in library and information studies from Rutgers University. He spent more than four years working in the library at the National Baseball Hall of Fame and Museum, where he was involved with the Cooperstown Symposium on Baseball and American Culture. He also contributes his research, writing, editing, and fact-checking skills to various Hall of Fame publications.

# Index

Numbers in **bold italics** indicate pages with illustrations